EDITED BY
I. ALEV DEGIM
JAMES JOHNSON
& TAO FU
ONLINE COURTSHIP
INTERPERSONAL
INTERACTIONS
ACROSS
BORDERS

Theory on Demand #16

Online Courship:
Interpersonal Interactions Across Borders

Editors: I. Alev Degim, James Johnson, Tao Fu
Copy-editing: Jess van Zyl
Editorial Support: Miriam Rasch

Design: Jess van Zyl
EPUB development: Gottfried Haider and Jess van Zyl
Printer: 'Print on Demand'
Publisher: Institute of Network Cultures, Amsterdam 2015
ISBN: 978-90-822345-7-2

Contact
Institute of Network Cultures
web: http://networkcultures.org

This publication is available through various print on demand services.
EPUB and PDF editions of this publication are freely downloadable from
our website, http://networkcultures.org/publications/#tods

This publication is licensed under the Creative Commons
Attribution-NonCommercial-NoDerivatives 4.0 International (CC BY-NC-SA 4.0).

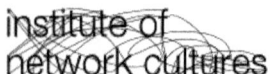

CONTENTS

Introduction I. Alev Degim and James Johnson	8
The Pre-History of Print and Online Dating, c. 1690-1990 H.G. Cocks	17
Old and New Methods for Online Research: The Case of Online Dating Murat Akser	29
Dating Maps: **Mapping Love in Online Dating Communities** Ramón Reichert	36
The Virtual Nightclub: Adolescents from Low-Income Sectors **Search for Their Couples through Facebook** Diego Basile and Joaquín Linne	47
'Dating' or 'Escaping'? Cuban Profiles **in Dating Websites** Lázaro M. Bacallao Pino	57
Self-presentation in the Portuguese Online Dating Scene: **Does Gender Matter?** Cláudia Casimiro	71
Liberalism Conquering Love: Reports and Reflections **on Mass Romantic and Sexual Consumption in the Internet Age** Pascal Lardellier	96
The Advertising and Profit Model of Leading Dating Sites in China: **A Comparison of Jianyuan, Baihe and Zhenai's Targeting and Advertising** Caiyun Wen	106
Remediating the Matchmaker: **Arranging Marriage Online in the South Asian Diaspora in America** Sheena Raja and Bryce J. Renninger	117
From Arranged to Online: **A Study of Courtship Culture in India** Amitabh Vikram Dwivedi	133

The Role of Places and Symbols:
A Cultural Interpretation of the On-line Dating Experience in Israel   148
David Levin

Stranger Stranger or Lonely Lonely? Young Chinese and Dating Apps between the Locational, the Mobile and the Social   167
Gabriele de Seta and Ge Zhang

What Are the *Shengnv* Looking for in Online Heterosexual Dating and Courtship? A Content Analysis of Shanghainese Women's Personal Profiles on Jiayuan.com   186
Tao Fu

Keeping it Unreal:
Online Dating with Chinese Characteristics   208
Yann-Ling Chin

Talking To Strangers:
Temporality, Identity and Politics in Live Webcam Sex Channels   229
Aras Ozgun

Performative Acts of Gender in Online Dating:
An Auto-ethnography Comparing Sites   242
Megan Lindsay

Media's Effect on Online Dating Practices:
Turkish TV Marriage Programs and Online Dating as a Medium   262
Enver Ozustun

INTRODUCTION

I. ALEV DEGIM AND JAMES JOHNSON

> 'Matchmaking and introductory intermediaries, particularly for the purpose of facilitating marriage, have been a component of the marriage-courtship market long before the emergence of online dating. In addition, computers have been used for romantic matching, both commercially and in university settings, for over 60 years.'[1]

This book aims to bring together articles across the world on online dating exercises as a social, economical and political phenomenon and define online dating as an important experience that should be considered as a ground for research. As the Internet's influence on social life and behaviors increase.[2,3] The virtual realm is becoming our daily reality. [4,5] So much so that dating digitally has permeated social networking territories from the very beginning stages. Looking at the changes and similarities between old and new behaviors adopted online and offline, this book aims to find commonalities and discrepancies between cultures and nations on online dating preferences, shedding light on the influences of new media on personal and interpersonal levels. This book aims to highlight the importance of online dating as a site for analysis, as well as establishing the boundaries for such research. The articles show that online dating can be studied both qualitatively and quantitatively, using existing methodologies as venues to understand and adopt this new way of social engagement.

Online dating and online courtship have been prominent parts of the daily experience of most users over the years that followed the proliferation of Internet and Web 2.0.[6] Courtship is not a new phenomenon, dating is a part of the social structure of many cultural systems. The introduction of new technologies has changed the way we interact with others, despite early negative stigmatization; forms of online dating have been integrated into the social structure of various cultural spheres fairly quickly. The anonymity aspect that had been prevalent in the early days of blogs and forums slowly lead the way to a shift from this dualistic representation model of a fake online self to an overlapping of the online and real identities. This shift can visibly be seen in the examples of online dating and courtship websites as in the recent years companies specifically created for this purpose required real information from their users. The way media in general represented online dating, especially TV shows,

---

1 E.J. Finkel, P. W. Eastwick, B.R. Karney, H.T. Reis and S. Sprecher, 'Online Dating A Critical Analysis From the Perspective of Psychological Science.' *Psychological Science in the Public Interest*, 13(1), (2012): 3-66.
2 J.A. Bargh and K.Y. McKenna, 'The Internet and social life.' *Annu. Rev. Psychol.*, 55, (2004): 573-590.
3 C.L. Hsu, and J.C.C. Lin, 'Acceptance of blog usage: The roles of technology acceptance, social influence and knowledge sharing motivation.' *Information & Management*, 45(1), (2008): 65-74.
4 S. Woolgar, (Ed.), Virtual Society?: Technology, Cyberhole, Reality. *Oxford University Press*. 2002.
5 A. Beaulieu, 'Mediating ethnography: objectivity and the making of ethnographies of the internet.' *Social Epistemology*, 18(2-3), (2004): 139-163.
6 Jessica M. Sautter, Rebecca M. Tippett and S. Philip Morgan, 'The Social Demography of Internet Dating in the United States.' *Social Science Quarterly* 91.2 (2010): 554-575.

labeled it as 'unsafe' and 'sketchy': an article on Huffington Post sheds light on the dangers of online dating especially for women[7], this stigma for online dating has slowly declined in media. This portrayal of online dating produced a stigma for the users over the years, the TV shows and other media often labeled users as 'anti-social': according to a 2013 report from the Pew Research Center, 21 percent of polled Internet users agree that "People who use online dating sites are desperate".[8] This type of atmosphere however, is changing rapidly as the Social Networking Sites (that are defined as "... web-based services that allow individuals to (1) construct a public or semi-public profile within a bounded system, (2) articulate a list of other users with whom they share a connection, and (3) view and traverse their list of connections and those made by others within the system.") [9] are becoming an eminent part of our daily lives, since they provide an online social experience that is not 'dangerous'. The increase in these and other online social experiences[10] began to change the nature of daily interpersonal interactions. This change has allowed the users to seek intimate relationships online more often. "According to a recent estimate based on ComScore Networks' analysis of Internet users' browsing behavior, 40 million Americans visited online dating sites in 2003, generating $214 million in revenues, making online dating the most important subscription-based business on the Internet."[11]

Defining Online Courtship/Dating

Courtship typically refers to the stage where two people interact with one another in an effort to get to know each other romantically; this stage typically precedes the traditional engagement and marriage stages. Digital courtship refers to the mixed-mode relationships that begin with online communication with the expectation of an offline romantic encounter. We define Online Courtship, as the romantic relationships founded on online environments - be it on Social Networking Sites (SNS) or forums or on online dating websites, blogs, mobile apps or even the comment section of a post on a Youtube video- that leads to an experience of sharing intimate or romantic thoughts, ideas and emotions via the offered features of the medium that has the potential to lead to an offline interaction.

A typical definition for online dating would only encompass the online dating sites and exclude all other online platforms.[12] This type of definition leads to a problem as it is only focusing on the websites tailored for the purpose of online dating and excluding a vast majority

---

7   Huffington Post, http://www.huffingtonpost.com/damona-hoffman/mary-kay-beckman-online-dating_b_2561380.html

8   The Gazette, http://thegazette.com/2014/03/16/online-dating-still-stigmatized-despite-popularity-sucess/

9   N.B. Ellison, 'Social network sites: Definition, history, and scholarship.' *Journal of Computer Mediated Communication*, 13(1), (2007): 210-230.

10 The Independent, http://www.independent.co.uk/life-style/gadgets-and-tech/news/daily-internet-use-has-more-than-doubled-in-past-seven-years-8752987.html.

11 G.J. Hitsch, A. Hortaçsu and D. Ariely, 'What makes you click: An empirical analysis of online dating.' 2005 Meeting Papers (Vol. 207). *Society for Economic Dynamics*. (2005).

12 It is defined functionally as 'a purposeful form of meeting new people through specifically designed Internet sites,' Barraket, Jo, and Millsom S. Henry-Waring. 'Getting it on (line) Sociological perspectives on e-dating.' *Journal of Sociology* 44.2 (2008): 149-165.

of online courtship. The previous definitions fail to acknowledge other online venues and limit the boundaries of the field for research. Hence a broader definition is needed along with identifying the boundaries of the specific study to insure a better perspective on online courtship.

As we are becoming increasingly connected to the online world, social interactions of any kind also comes into the realm with us. Online studies in general have focused thus far on a variety of different issues and subjects such as online bullying[13], self-efficacy and motivation effects in online environments[14], YouTube studies[15], video spheres[16] and alternative social media institutions.[17] The venue for studying online dating is fairly new to the field and previous studies on online dating focus on topics such as self-presentation and deception of online profiles[18],[19],[20], the match-making algorithm and process[21], homophily on online dating sites[22] and profile creation.[23] These various studies help define online courtship as a field of research and acknowledge online courtship as an important part of online studies.

The site of study then becomes the defining feature of the specific research. A good and functional definition of online dating sites is provided by Rosen et. al. as follows: "Online dating sites are all similarly structured. Participants provide a photograph and answer an array of questions including geographic location, age, weight or body type, education level, income, and other relevant demographics..."[24] The system is dependent on statistical codes running in the background that provide the 'perfect match' for the user by looking at the variables. As

---

13 Jaana Juvonen and Elisheva F. Gross, 'Extending the school grounds?—Bullying experiences in cyberspace.' *Journal of School Health* 78.9 (2008): 496-505.

14 Robert Irizarry, 'Self-efficacy and motivation effects on online psychology student retention.' *Usdla Journal* 16.12 (2002): 55-64.

15 Geert Lovink and Sabine Niederer, *Video vortex reader: Responses to YouTube*. Amsterdam: Institute of Network Cultures, 2008.

16 Andreas Treske, The inner life of video sphere. *Institute of Network Cultures*. 2013.

17 Geert Lovink and Miriam Rasch, Unlike us reader: social media monopolies and their alternatives. No. 8. *Institute of Network Cultures*, 2013.

18 Nicole Ellison, Rebecca Heino, and Jennifer Gibbs, 'Managing impressions online: Self presentation processes in the online dating environment.' *Journal of Computer Mediated Communication* 11.2 (2006): 415-441.

19 Catalina L. Toma, Jeffrey T. Hancock, and Nicole B. Ellison, 'Separating fact from fiction: An examination of deceptive self-presentation in online dating profiles.' *Personality and Social Psychology Bulletin* 34.8 (2008): 1023-1036.

20 Jeffrey T. Hancock, Catalina Toma, and Nicole Ellison, 'The truth about lying in online dating profiles.' *Proceedings of the SIGCHI conference on Human factors in computing systems*. ACM, 2007.

21 Günter J. Hitsch, Ali Hortaçsu, and Dan Ariely, 'Matching and sorting in online dating.' *The American Economic Review* (2010): 130-163.

22 Andrew T. Fiore and Judith S. Donath, 'Homophily in online dating: when do you like someone like yourself?.' *CHI'05 Extended Abstracts on Human Factors in Computing Systems*. ACM, 2005.

23 Andrew T. Fiore and Judith S. Donath, 'Homophily in online dating'.

24 L.D. Rosen, N.A. Cheever, C. Cummings and J. Felt, 'The impact of emotionality and self-disclosure on online dating versus traditional dating.' *Computers in Human Behavior*, 24(5), (2008): 2124-2157.

the sites rely on technology and the social context, the experience of one user will be rather different than the other (in a scenario where the person who uses these websites is located in a remote place that has few participants, the odds are not in their favor and hence the whole experience would be different from another user); as in the examples in this volume (see Aras, Levin, Wen, DeSeta), it can have different connotations for different cultures and contexts and hence a fixed experience is almost impossible to achieve. In more traditional societies, online courtship can take on the meaning of finding a partner in marriage (China, Turkey and India are good examples of this, see Vikram, Ozgun and Fu) whereas in other cultures it can become a place to seek one-night stands or webcam sex or to seek company to pass time. These different examples show the fluid nature of the experience of online 'courtship' or 'dating' within the globalizing world, as the local and global definitions amalgamate in virtual environments.

Digital intimacy has become a normative mode of social interaction within other mediums online, such as SNS and mobile applications. Rosen et al. gives examples of studies that have found the increase in such online environments: an early study shows that 75% of online-formed relationships became 'proper relationships'.[25] As online dating becomes a prominent part of social life, it is even more crucial for social studies to research and analyze this phenomenon.

The way we define Online Courtship helps link different parts of the phenomenon and give a clear picture of a new approach. We establish through the articles in this volume that the multifaceted structure of the online dating environment enables its study with different methodologies. However it is important to define boundaries for research; ethical concerns should be addressed before the study is conducted (which was done in all studies in this volume) and draw the limits for the specific study as the lines between websites and SNS or apps can be blurred at times.

Online dating sites may alleviate some of the spatial constraints experienced when participating in traditional face-to-face courtship, but contemporary scholarship interrogates the constraints of this socio-technological space as an environment of existing beliefs and behaviors that, at times, maintain a hetero-normative hierarchy. Identity construction in online dating environments is impacted by social norms offline. Within the digital dating realm self-presentation and self-disclosure strategies are adapted to gain the attention of potential online daters.[26] Singles utilize online dating interfaces with preset attributes, creating their online identity with identity markers provided by the site. Online personal ads are user-generated dossiers aimed to construct online daters' identity. This scholarship examines online dating sites as social sites where technology sustains and reproduces existing gender roles. Recent online dating research also highlights the limitations of gender construction and the

---

25 L.D. Rosen, N.A. Cheever, C. Cummings and J. Felt, 'The impact of emotionality and self-disclosure on online dating versus traditional dating.' p. 2124-2157.

26 J.T. Hancock and C. L. Toma, 'Putting your best face forward: The accuracy of online dating photographs.' *Journal of Communication*, 59(2), (2009): 367-386.

marginalization that occurs within hetero-normative dating spaces.[27]

Early Internet and gender identity research analyzed men and women experimenting with the gender roles of gaming avatars.[28] Online daters have substituted avatars with profile pictures and personal summaries. Internet scholars are examining gender constructions in online spaces, more specifically within online dating environments. Explorative research analyzes self-presentation and self-disclosure strategies that reproduce hetero-normative hierarchies in online spaces. Gender equality continues to be a topic of interests in many spaces across the world. Computer-mediated-communication within the Online dating context is another environment investigated to determine whether or not these are safe spaces for LGBTQ online identities. Literature on online dating has not focused on different parts of the world. Dating practices vary from one cultural context to the next, different cultures view romance through different religious, political, and gendered lenses. This volume contributes to the existing body of study that exists on online dating and expands upon the different dynamics within the World Wide Web by asking questions of different identities and nationalities. Previous research has not answered the following question adequately as of yet: If online dating sites are socio-technological spaces, what happens when the space is geared towards a particular demographic? Who is left out? What are the social implications of these online spaces of desire?

This volume includes different methodologies and approaches to examine online courtship. Murat Akser looks at the history of online dating and identifies how the research field has dealt with this phenomenon. It is through his analysis that we see the various fields of research and the ways they dealt with specific cases. He predicts the future of the research field to move forward with the introduction of social networking sites and other technology.

Gabriele de Seta and Ge Zhang's *Stranger Stranger or Lonely Lonely? Young Chinese and Dating Apps between the Locational, the Mobile and the Social* is an ethnographic study about a location-based social app – Momo, and the floating population who use it. Rather than 'a one-night stand mythical device' as portrayed in media narratives, Momo users' use of the mobile app emanates the immobility of 'strangers' in populated metropolises. Studying apps specifically on online dating is a new approach and is a crucial part of the discussion of the contemporary social context of online dating.

Unlike in the West, courtship and marriage convey more social pressures to Chinese in the dating age. Dating websites and broadcasting media reap millions in this gold mine. Caiyun Wen's case study of three leading Chinese dating websites – Baihe, Jiayuan and Zhenai – brought us to see their 'secrets' of profit making with a Chinese touch. Yann L. Chin examined how *wanglian*, or online romance, is conceptualized by Chinese Internet users based on

---

27 J.A. Hall, N. Park, H. Song and M.J. Cody, 'Strategic misrepresentation in online dating: The effects of gender, self-monitoring, and personality traits.' *Journal of Social and Personal Relationships*, 27(1), (2010): 117-135.

28 A. Vasalou and A.N. Joinson, 'Me, myself and I: The role of interactional context on self-presentation through avatars.' *Computers in Human Behavior*, 25(2), (2009): 510-520.

two key constructs: 'Platonic emotional love' and 'play'. Her categorization of online daters as pragmatist fantasists, skeptics and romantic realists is more than a fun of oxymoron's but an in-depth analysis of the dichotomous and interconnected reality and virtuality and a modern Chinese society where materialistic prosperity and spiritual emptiness co-exist. Sheena Raja and Bryce J. Renninger's in-depth interviews scrutinized the interplay of people, technology and media brought by globalization and its influence to South Asian diasporas in the New York City metro area in their pursuit of courtship. Computer-mediated communication remediates matchmaking, biodata of online daters and the subjectivity of diasporas. Amitabh Vikram Dwivedi delineated how married, divorced, unmarried, widowed, awaiting divorce, and annulled Indians seek partners at three online matrimonial sites – Shaadi, BharatMatrimony and Jeevansathi. Through this lens, the dynamics between online and offline dating activities, technology and individuals, and tradition and modernity in Indian society is presented to us.

The ubiquitous nature of technology often blurs the lines, in some cases completely rewrite, society's popular social norms. This holds true in online courtship. The emergence of online courtship has gained attention from media as well as new sociological and behavioral studies examining humans' participation and practices in mixed mode relationships (relationships that begin online with the expectation of an intimate offline encounter). This section consists of case studies examining the social and legal boundaries that helped shape the business of personal ads, dating sites as doorways, Facebook as an adolescent dating scene, and mapping dating culture within digital communities.

This volume explores digital courtship across mediums. Harry Cocks provides a historical trajectory of mediated courtship in Western Europe, exploring third party involvement in courtship, which is not a modern phenomenon. Western Europe has a history of third party involvement with courtship ranging from arranged marriages, via parents and kin, and through professional matchmakers. Web 2.0 has turned Internet consumers into producers by allowing users to generate content. The Internet has created a communication culture of mutual and permanent evaluation. Ramón Reichert discusses dating maps as a way to analyze dating cultures as digital communities consisting of user-generated content creating a feedback loop that results in media-specific forms of subjectification. Looking at virtual realms as venues, Facebook is analyzed as an Argentinian nightclub for adolescence, as Basil and Linne examine adolescent impression management strategies when romantically pursuing relationships via Facebook. The Internet has become a social tool for many Internet users. Casmiro examines the influence that gender has on self-presentation practices in Portuguese online dating profiles. This research highlights how gender roles influence self-presentation constructions within the Portuguese dating context. Dating practices reveal that dating sites serve as a door to other regions. Cuba's Internet access is one of the lowest in Latin America, inhibiting private use of the World Wide Web. Pino uses online dating profiles in conjunction with interviews, analyzing the dating practices of singles seeking singles in Cuba and Cuban singles seeking intimacy outside of Cuba. These researchers open up and extend insight on how digital dating practices utilize different mediums to alleviate spatial boundaries and cultural constraints.

This section explores courtship across mediums. Harry Cocks provides a historical trajectory of mediated courtship in Western Europe, exploring third party involvement in courtship, which is not a modern phenomenon. Western Europe has a history of third party involvement with courtship ranging from arranged marriages, via parents and kin, and through professional matchmakers. Basil and Linne examine adolescents in Buenos Aires, Argentina use of Facebook as a venue for Internet dating. Researchers examine adolescent impression management strategies when romantically pursuing relationships via Facebook. Virtual Nightclub references this social network as a venue for adolescent matchmaking. Pino's study explores the social implications of poor Internet access and online dating in Cuba. Discourse analysis is conducted on online dating profiles, in conjunction with interviews, analyzing the dating practices of singles seeking singles in Cuba and Cuban singles seeking intimacy outside of Cuba. Dating practices reveal that dating sites serve as a door spaces outside of Cuba. The corollary of this study correlates politics, technological and financial reasons to the current formation of Cuban online dating practices.

The Internet has become a social tool for many online users. This chapter examines the influence that gender has on self-presentation practices in Portuguese online dating profiles. Data is analyzed via content analysis and grounded theory. This research highlights how modern gender roles influence self-presentation constructions within the Portuguese dating context.

Web 2.0 has turned Internet consumers into producers by allowing users to generate content. The Internet has created a communication culture of mutual and permanent evaluation. This study discusses dating maps as a way to analyze dating cultures of digital communities. User generated content creates a feedback loop that results in media-specific forms of subjectification.

The tension between the global experience that the Internet provides and the physical restrictions of one's geographical location is an interesting asymmetry when forming online intimate relationships. David Levin invokes the speech theory to examine the Israeli online dating experience that he characterizes as a cultural construct that follows the traditional paths for marriage. The local-global tension becomes apparent with the analysis, as the particular vocabulary and language the users adopt on these sites reveal a diasporic mode of identity construction. Being closely tied with social norms and traditions, societies face a shift in the experiences of identities and national, ethnic selfhood descriptions. Aras Ozgun identifies an interesting example of Webcam channels, where the participants can perform erotic/sexual performances for strangers and how this relates to national identity politics. By introducing the identity formation angle, Ozgun draws unique features of the semi-secular culture of Turkish identity and the male-female gender constructs that play into these relationships. Enver Ozustun identifies a case study of the Turkish marriage programs that became a benchmark for the online dating experience. It is through these channels that the vocabulary of the online dating sites are built upon in Turkey and these programs determined what the individuals are to expect from a relationship.

Defining the self in an online environment is a crucial point in finding a potential romantic partner on the web. Analyzing the relations of users from an inside perspective (with ethical considerations) Megan Lindsay explores the online dating sites by participant observation and auto-ethnography methods. Her experiences reflect the socio-cultural environment of OkCupid and Match.com websites. Attracting an audience, building an image for a specific target audience and expectations from other parties compose the major framework of her analysis.

The industry behind the online dating phenomenon is a large one. The online dating market has become a $2 billion industry.[29] Pascal Lardellier explores the political economy of dating sites in France and analyzes the underlying structures that are at play. The commodification of love now assisted by the computerized technology also takes away from the intimate experience, monetizing the relationship. Also Reichert's analysis examines the cartographic visualizations and the underlying structures within this system. The changing role of digital intimacy within the market is affecting the way we perceive relationships, especially considering that Google, Facebook and Twitter form the largest shares in the market.

This book attempts to shed light on the online dating phenomenon through various methodologies with an eclectic approach. If we think about the data and analysis of the use of these websites and other platforms employed for online dating purposes, it is easy to see that online courtship will become an increasingly embedded social norm for communities around the world. The philosophical, socio-political and social network analysis (SNA) approaches to the discussion of online courtship will enhance existing knowledge and broaden our understanding of the subject in further studies.

References:

Barraket, Jo and Millsom S. Henry-Waring. 'Getting it on (line) Sociological perspectives on e-dating.' *Journal of Sociology* 44.2 (2008): 149-165.

Bargh, J. A. and K. Y. McKenna. 'The Internet and social life.' *Annu. Rev. Psychol.*, 55, (2004): 573-590.

Bauman, Z. 'Liquid Modernity, Cambridge (Reino Unido), Polity Press, 2000; Liquid Love: On the Frailty of Human Bonds, Cambridge (Reino Unido), Polity Press, 2003, por Jesus M. de Miguel y Jara D. Sanchez.' *Revista Espanola De Investiagiones Sociologicas – Spanish Edition*. (110), (2005): 239-256.

Beaulieu, A. 'Mediating ethnography: objectivity and the making of ethnographies of the internet.' *Social Epistemology*, 18(2-3), (2004): 139-163.

Ellison, Nicole B. 'Social network sites: Definition, history, and scholarship.' *Journal of Computer-Mediated Communication* 13.1 (2007): 210-230.

Ellison, Nicole, Rebecca Heino, and Jennifer Gibbs. 'Managing impressions online: Self presentation processes in the online dating environment.' *Journal of Computer Mediated Communication* 11.2 (2006): 415-441.

Finkel, E. J., P. W. Eastwick, B. R. Karney, H. T. Reis and S. Sprecher, 'Online Dating A Critical Analysis From the Perspective of Psychological Science.' *Psychological Science in the Public Interest*, 13(1), (2012): 3-66.

Fiore, Andrew T. and Judith S. Donath. 'Homophily in online dating: when do you like someone like yourself?.' *CHI'05 Extended Abstracts on Human Factors in Computing Systems*. ACM, 2005.

---

29 S. Yoder, How Online Dating Became a $2 Billion Industry, *Fiscal Times*, 2014. http://www.thefiscaltimes.com/Articles/2014/02/14/Valentines-Day-2014-How-Online-Dating-Became-2-Billion-Industry.

Lovink, Geert and Sabine Niederer. *Video vortex reader: Responses to YouTube*. Amsterdam: Institute of Network Cultures, 2008.

Lovink, Geert and Miriam Rasch. Unlike us reader: social media monopolies and their alternatives. No. 8. *Institute of Network Cultures*, 2013.

Hall, J. A., N. Park, H. Song and M. J. Cody. 'Strategic misrepresentation in online dating: The effects of gender, self-monitoring, and personality traits.' Journal of Social and Personal Relationships, 27(1), (2010): 117-135.J. T. Hancock and C. L. Toma, 'Putting your best face forward: The accuracy of online dating photographs.' *Journal of Communication*, 59(2), (2009): 367-386.

Hancock, Jeffrey T., Catalina Toma, and Nicole Ellison. 'The truth about lying in online dating profiles.' *Proceedings of the SIGCHI conference on Human factors in computing systems*. ACM, 2007.

Hitsch, Günter J., Ali Hortaçsu and D. Ariely. 'What makes you click: An empirical analysis of online dating.' 2005 Meeting Papers (Vol. 207). *Society for Economic Dynamics*. (2005).

Hitsch, Günter J., Ali Hortaçsu, and Dan Ariely. 'Matching and sorting in online dating.' *The American Economic Review* (2010): 130-163.

Hsu, C.L. and J.C.C. Lin. 'Acceptance of blog usage: The roles of technology acceptance, social influence and knowledge sharing motivation.' *Information & Management*, 45(1), (2008): 65-74.

Irizarry, Robert. 'Self-efficacy and motivation effects on online psychology student retention.' *Usdla Journal* 16.12 (2002): 55-64.

Juvonen, Jaana and Elisheva F. Gross. 'Extending the school grounds?—Bullying experiences in cyberspace.' *Journal of School health* 78.9 (2008): 496-505.

Rosen, L.D., N. A. Cheever, C. Cummings and J. Felt. 'The impact of emotionality and self-disclosure on online dating versus traditional dating.' *Computers in Human Behavior*, 24(5), (2008): 2124-2157.

Sautter, Jessica M., Rebecca M. Tippett and S. Philip Morgan. 'The Social Demography of Internet Dating in the United States.' *Social Science Quarterly* 91.2 (2010): 554-575.

Vasalou, A. and A. N. Joinson. 'Me, myself and I: The role of interactional context on self-presentation through avatars.' *Computers in Human Behavior*, 25(2), (2009): 510-520.

Treske, Andreas. *The inner life of video sphere*. Amsterdam: Institute of Network Cultures. 2013.

Toma, Catalina L., Jeffrey T. Hancock, and Nicole B. Ellison. 'Separating fact from fiction: An examination of deceptive self-presentation in online dating profiles.' *Personality and Social Psychology Bulletin* 34.8 (2008): 1023-1036.

Steve Woolgar, (Ed.). *Virtual Society?: Technology, Cyberbole, Reality*. Oxford: Oxford University Press. 2002.

Huffington Post. http://www.huffingtonpost.com/damona-hoffman/mary-kay-beckman-online-dating_b_2561380.html.

The Independent. http://www.independent.co.uk/life-style/gadgets-and-tech/news/daily-internet-use-has-more-than-doubled-in-past-seven-years-8752987.html.

The Fiscal Times. http://www.thefiscaltimes.com/Articles/2014/02/14/Valentines-Day-2014-How-Online-Dating-Became-2-Billion-Industry.

The Gazette. http://thegazette.com/2014/03/16/online-dating-still-stigmatized-despite-popularity-sucess/.

THE PRE-HISTORY OF PRINT AND ONLINE DATING, C. 1690-1990

H.G. COCKS

It is often argued that the rise of online dating reflects the increasing dominance of economic liberalism in western societies. This is said to extend even into the personal sphere where modern courtship is epitomised by the dating website which turns its customers into self-marketing managers of their own emotional capital. In that sense online dating is seen to represent a particular social constituency – the urban, late-marrying type, perhaps a member of the new white-collar "precariat" working in professional employment on short-term contracts, settling down much later, and as a result on the dating market for a correspondingly longer period.

Whatever the rights and wrongs of that argument, changing patterns of courtship (and the rise of print and later digital media to arrange it) do reflect changes in the organisation of marriage, employment and the relationship of self and society. Although a successful market of this kind requires a free press and thriving print culture, in historical terms advertising for love has become popular in conjunction with three things: first, a mostly urban population of insecure workers seeking to break away from established courtship patterns; secondly, the idea of marriage as a contract freely entered into by contracting parties, and thirdly, some kind of announced "crisis" in marriage or romantic intimacy. The latter is normally discovered by more conservative voices, is often part of an attack on the contractual idea, and tends to see "modern marriage" (or partnership) as an unromantic and mercenary transaction.

Arranging courtship or marriage via a third party is not especially modern. Many peasant or pre-industrial societies outside Western Europe practiced systems of arranged marriage – either via parents and close kin, or through the offices of a professional matchmaker and still do. In societies where production is based on the home, arranged or brokered marriages result from the importance of the marital couple as an economic unit, and their significance to local economic relations involving wider kin groups. The intervention of parents and community in the process of courtship reflected the effort to ensure that property would be transferred legitimately and that the new household would be able to make an effective and sustainable contribution to the economic life of the community. In the past historians have argued that the decay of this communal model and its replacement by one in which courtship was almost wholly determined by the wishes of the parties concerned reflected the emergence of free labour and capitalism. While the former model is characterised by the intervention of parents, kin and community, the latter is said to have been marked by the rise of romantic love, the personal choice of partners free from parental interference, and the establishment of a separate marital household. This transition, from the "arranged" system that belonged more to what is known as the "stem family" defined by broad kinship among a wide group of relatives, to one in which romantic love and free choice of partners is allowed has been seen as a significant moment of transition in Western history. Most famously, Lawrence Stone argued that the emphasis on the self and its wants over and above the needs of kinship, alliance, or economy, beginning in the late sixteenth century, highlighted the gradual rise of affective individualism, the decay of communality, and hence the coming of modernity.

Critics of Stone were quick to point out that even in late-medieval texts, especially legal codes, individual choice and romantic love could be found as an element of marriage among all classes, and hence had to predate Stone's chronology. Jack Goody and Alan Macfarlane see this individualistic model not as the creation of modernity, but of late-medieval Europe going back as far as the late thirteenth century. For them, the fact that canon law in medieval Europe defined marriage as an agreement of mutual consent between the parties concerned meant that the narrow conjugal family based on the couple, in which romantic love and not material interest is the prime motivation, was the norm in Western European history.[1]

In that sense, Stone's critics have discounted any evidence of intermediaries, arrangements and closely-calculated marriage settlements that might reflect communal interest in or control over the conjugal couple as the exception rather than the rule. However, more recent work on northern Europe has pointed out that freedoms asserted (or legally codified) and freedoms practised are two different things and that in reality, most couples even in the West European marriage system had to deal with parental and community pressures. Actual courtship was a much more complex affair than the desiccated calculations of rationally-choosing subjects. Moreover, community interest was often at stake, and intermediaries were employed, even if their roles were not formalised or professional. As Diana O'Hara has pointed out, sixteenth-century Britain was not unfamiliar with brokers, "utterers," "medlers" and "matrimonial bawds" who intervened in the process of courtship, not to mention the many aristocrats anxious over the destination of their estates. For instance, in 1664 it was said of the Duchess of Newcastle that "women do fee her to get them husbands, and men to get them rich wives, so as she is become the huckster, or broker of males and females...indeed she is a matrimonial bawd."[2] That the influence of these third parties on the marriage bargain was more or less informal did not make it less important.

In northern Europe at least, the older model of communally-organised marriage gradually gave way from the late sixteenth century onwards. In these areas couples were expected to establish a separate household and so in order to marry they required access to property or an artisanal trade that would support them. However, by 1600 or so it was increasingly difficult to ensure that new couples could support themselves in this way, and a new category of "masterless men" or wage-earners began to emerge. John Gillis calculates that by 1600 around one third of the population no longer had access to land or trades, and that as a result they became increasingly detached from traditional customs and institutions and more willing to indulge in "private spousals."[3] By the early eighteenth century, Gillis calculates, perhaps one-third of marriages were outside the purview of communal custom. This process

---

1   Lawrence Stone, *The Family, Sex and Marriage in England 1500-1800*, London: Weidenfeld & Nicolson, 1977; Alan Macfarlane, *Marriage and Love in England, Modes of Reproduction 1300-1840*, Oxford: Blackwell, 1986; Jack Goody, *The European Family: A Historico-Anthroplogical Essay*, Oxford, Blackwell 2000.

2   Diana O'Hara, *Courtship and Constraint: Rethinking the Making of Marriage in Tudor England*, Manchester: Manchester University Press, 2000, ch 3; quoted in Macfarlane, Marriage and Love, 259. E. A. Wrigley and R. S. Schofield, The Population 1541-1871, London: Edward Arnold, 1981, pp. 257-6

3   John Gillis, *For Better, for Worse: British Marriages, 1600 to the Present*, Oxford: Oxford University Press, 1985, p.14.

went hand in hand with the rise of Puritanism, which tended to narrow the courtship process to one that focussed primarily on the family and not the wider community. Two marriage practices reflected these changes: first, the custom of marriage by licence, in which the couple could (if they could afford it) pay the local bishop to marry them without publishing the banns and therefore attracting the interest of parents and others; and secondly, clandestine marriages conducted in mostly urban locales known as "liberties" in which ecclesiastical authority did not apply.

This is the historical background against which we should see the rise of advertising for husbands and wives. Although the involvement of third parties in courtship did not necessarily mean that families or communities were not involved in the process, in general, we might take the development of advertising to reflect the rise of "private spousals" free from familial or community pressure. Advertising of this kind emerged in the 1680s or 1690s, about forty years after the appearance of the first newspapers. Most of these early newspapers contained small announcements about events, crimes or incidents. One of the first references to matrimonial advertising was from the British weekly *The Athenian Mercury*, which in 1692 responded to a series of questions about marriage and love with a comment on the practice.[4] By the mid-eighteenth century advertising for husbands, wives, and other less conventional arrangements had a secure foothold in British print culture.

Until the early twentieth century, the matrimonial advertisement dominated the market. Stating an intent to marry was seen to provide at least some guarantee of respectability. However, other less conventional arrangements were also common in the 18th century, for instance, the gentleman who in 1768 expressed a desire to meet a "young lady dressed in a black nightgown, with a letter in her hand" whom he had followed about the City the previous Friday. Others seemed to be advertising openly for mistresses, such as the "Gentleman of independent fortune, in possession, and very considerable expectations" who in 1770 announced an intention to make a tour through France and Italy. He thought it would be "a particular happiness could he meet with an agreeable young lady, whose education and sentiments would engage his esteem and affections, to accompany him on his travels." Other men advertised for single women to board with them possibly as a way of making an informal marriage. Financial arrangements very much like prostitution were sometimes offered by women advertisers. One 1769 ad, to "any real *gentleman*, from a *lady* of character," promised that in exchange for £100, a man could have "an advantage, which cannot be named in a public newspaper." Another who was "at present so critically circumstanced as to want the immediate friendship and assistance of a gentleman of honour and benevolence," offered in return to "render essential services."[5]

While individual advertisements began to be common in a wide variety of different papers, organised matrimonial agencies were also a feature of eighteenth century society. One such

---

4   See Helen Berry, *Gender, Society and Print Culture in Late-Stuart England: The World of the Athenian Mercury*, Aldershot: Scholar Press, 2003, p.189.

5   Oxford Magazine, December 1770, in Anon., *Matrimonial Advertisements*, Private Collection, 1740-1859, British Library.

agency, which presented itself as the solution to the difficulties of modern marriage, was the Imprejudicate Nuptial Society, or the Grand Matrimonial Intercourse Institution, probably established in the mid-century. This organisation, run by a clergyman from an address in the City of London, presented itself as a philanthropic society which would enable more people to marry, thereby saving British morals and preventing the increase of "vagabond children." The Rev. Watson, the proprietor, proposed to recruit clergymen in every town who would give sermons on the benefits of marriage, thereby collecting money which would be placed in a communal fund for those who could not afford marriage expenses. There would also be list of subscribers, divided into three classes according to income and property, the estimation of which was at the heart of the enterprise. Advertisers with the agency, such as the "Gentleman, 40 yrs of age...a little corpulent, rather of a dark complexion, wears his own hair," were compelled to be honest about their status. He estimated his wealth at £200 per annum, with £750 in the public funds, and "a small Estate in Surry." This method of proceeding, Rev Watson proclaimed, avoided "the common way" which was for men to fall in love, "and then disgracefully retreat, if there is not money enough." In his scheme, as in most other matrimonial ads of this period, "the circumstances are first known, and nothing to prevent sincere love afterwards."[6]

Allegations of fraud, which were to dog the matrimonial business for the rest of its days, quickly followed the rise of formal marriage brokers. In the early 1770s, a Mr R was supposed to have made a huge fortune in London by acting as an agent for young, rich women looking to marry. Every spring, he would place a series of ads in the press, offering to arrange marriages for ladies with fortunes of £30,000. These wealthy women would be installed at his house, while he again advertised for potential suitors, who, it was said, paid him as much as £500 for the privilege of paying court to his clients. He was then supposed to have "touched several five hundreds without the candidates for matrimony being successful," and kept everybody dangling on a string while he pocketed the proceeds.[7] However, rumours like this did not dent the popularity of the medium, and by 1777, a young lady could aver that "the mode of advertising is become too general." However, she herself was not deterred from seeking "a man of fashion, honour, and sentiment, blended with good nature, and a noble spirit, such a one she would chuse for her guardian and protector."[8]

The feeling expressed by one advertiser in 1749 that "the mode of advertising... may be looked upon with disdain and contempt by some," was not mitigated by its association with some unsavoury episodes.[9] Suspicions about the type of man who might advertise were compounded by one of the most famous crimes in British history, the murder of Maria Marten by her sweetheart William Corder at the infamous Red Barn in the village of Polstead in Suffolk in 1827. Part of the sensation that surrounded the trial of Corder in 1828 was the revelation that he had been a regular user of matrimonial columns. In that sense, the case

---

6   Pamphlet of The Imprejudicate Nuptial Society, undated, in Anon., *Matrimonial Advertisements*, Private Collection, BL.

7   *Town and Country Magazine*, March 1772, in Anon., *Matrimonial Advertisements*, Private Collection, BL.

8   Unattributed cutting, 1777, in Anon., *Matrimonial Advertisements*, BL.

9   Gazetteer, 5 August 1749, in *Matrimonial Advertisements*, Private Collection, BL.

offers a rare glimpse into the style of advertising in this period. In the winter of 1827, fleeing his crime which was still undetected, Corder moved to a tavern in the City of London, from where he took out ads in the *Morning Herald* and *Sunday Times*. His announcement, headed "MATRIMONY," described him as a "A Private Gentleman, aged 25, entirely independent," seeking "any female of respectability, who would study for domestic comfort," and who was willing "to confide her future happiness in one every way qualified to render the marriage state desirable." He was, the ad said, a "sociable, tender, kind, and sympathising companion," and instructed correspondents to write to Mr Foster's stationer's shop in the City, from where he would collect the letters. More than fifty replies came in from women mostly in their late teens and early twenties, and still more women came to Foster's shop – later luridly described in the press as a "*Love Depot*" – to inquire after the advertiser's character. The means of getting to know advertisers like Corder varied widely. Some respondents offered to pair him with their sisters, others did not want to meet him but preferred to get to know him first by an extended correspondence, and some wanted to arrange an interview at their homes. One reply instructed Corder to take a walk on the south side of Northampton Square in the City of London, between the hours of 12 and 1 on the following Monday, and to carry a white pocket-handkerchief. "I shall be there and may perhaps have an interview with you," the writer promised.

Corder eventually made the acquaintance of one Mary Moore and, with his past still completely unknown, offered the promise of marriage. Ms Moore's mother was set against such a proceeding, mainly because the anonymity of the ad did not allow them to know or investigate Corder's family connections. Her brother was also suspicious of this man who had appeared apparently from nowhere, and angrily denounced the whole business. However, as Miss Moore pointed out to him, the matrimonial ad was for financially independent individuals like herself who did not have to put up with the interference of their families. Most of Corder's respondents were the same – they were young women who were distanced from parental interference, either through the death of parents or relatives, or through their own financial independence. Miss Moore, who had inherited some of her father's wealth, was one of many such women. She told her brother "that she was fully satisfied in her own mind," about Corder's connections, "and urged that as she was her own mistress, she should use her own discretion, and in defiance of anything her brother might urge to the contrary, she should marry him on the morrow."[10] She carried out her threat, and she and Corder moved to Ealing in West London to open a girls' boarding school, living in what appeared to be marital bliss right up the moment when her husband was arrested in the spring of 1828 for the murder of Maria Marten.

Most observers agreed that Corder's career after the murder showed him to be the exact epitome of a "cool, calculating, deliberate villain." One of the key lessons of the tale, played out in the countless shows, songs and plays which followed the trial and played continuously throughout the following century, was never to trust a man who advertised for a wife. Mainly, though, it was suggested that the case should act as a warning against the kind of independ-

---

10   J. Curtis, *An Authentic and Faithful History of the Mysterious Murder of Maria Marten*, London: Thomas Kelly, 1828, p. 92.

ence shown by Mary Moore.[11]

Cases like these may have put off respectable middle class readers and helped to confine the appeal of matrimonial advertisements to the working class. When a new craze for it reappeared in the new penny press of London in the 1860s, in titles like the *London Journal*, *Family Herald* or the *Halfpenny Paper*, it was certainly felt by most editors that the practice belonged almost wholly to the less educated working classes. However, although it was regarded as far from respectable, by 1900 the matrimonial press in Britain at least had developed into a particular form of journalism. This was in marked contrast to the European continent, where most mainstream newspapers like the *Frankfurter Zeitung* included extensive sections of matrimonial advertising as a means of financing their news coverage.[12] In Britain, respectable papers like the *Times* or *Morning Chronicle* refused to carry matrimonial ads, thereby encouraging the development of a specialist press devoted solely to publishing them.

As a consequence of this ban a specialised matrimonial press began to flourish in late-nineteenth century Britain. The British Library lists twenty-two matrimonial papers established between 1870 and 1914, while several other titles also contained matrimonial columns around this time. Most of the dedicated matrimonial press was allied to a related agency where advertisers could obtain the personal services of a matrimonial agent.[13] Of these titles some were more long-lived than others. Among them were the *Matrimonial News and Special Advertiser* which claimed to date from 1848 (though wound up in 1895), the *Internationale Matrimonial Gazette* of Sheffield, which in various guises ran from 1909 to 1944, and the most venerable of the British papers, the *Matrimonial Post and Fashionable Marriage Advertiser*, published in Bristol, which claimed lineage from 1860 and was run by the same man – R. Charlesworth – between 1894 and 1948. Some other titles appear to have lasted only a few months. Most of the papers were based in London, though several existed in provincial cities. The larger papers carried between 200 and 600 ads, though several of these would have been reinsertions over several issues. In addition to this dedicated press, there were many others, ranging from W. T. Stead's high class matrimonial monthly the *Round About* (1898-1903), to the comic paper *Ally Sloper's Half Holiday*, or the fiction series *My Pocket Novels* (1900-1934) that carried matrimonial ads or operated agencies by post at various times in the same period.

These papers appealed to, and were mainly used, by two main social groups: white collar workers such as clerks, and the upper working class – tradesmen and domestic servants. Advertising rates were generally kept low – in the 1890s matrimonial papers cost around 3d, while advertising costs were around 1 shilling for between 20 and 50 words, depending on the paper. Personal interviews with the editor/agent cost around 5 shillings. Further costs

---

11   Curtis, *An Authentic and Faithful History of the Mysterious Murder of Maria Marten*, 400.
12   On the German press see Karl-Christian Fuhrer, *Contradicting Nazi Propaganda: Classified Advertisements as Documents of Jewish Life in Nazi Germany, 1933-1938*, Media History 18:1 (February 2012): 65-76.
13   Twenty-two different papers are listed in the British Library catalogue but others are mentioned in different sources, so the total figure is probably higher.

could be incurred on marriage. In 1893, for instance, one advertiser was asked for £10 up front and then two and a half per cent of any marriage settlement.[14]

These practices were revealed by the trial of the Skates brothers, proprietors of the World's Great Marriage Association (and the *Matrimonial Herald*) in 1895. The case resulted from the fact that in order to keep unsuccessful (and unappealing) male suitors on their books they had sent out form letters to a few advertisers from ladies that did not exist. The agency profited mainly from its personal services, for instance, charging some clients between £2 and £17 for such assistance in the marriage market, including personal interviews, advice and introductions. The trial also revealed the social constituency of matrimonial papers and agencies at this time. Its male clients were mainly shopkeepers and skilled workers, such as tobacconists, tailors, hairdressers, decorators, printers and other "well to do artisans," while its female ones were mostly domestic servants and some widows with capital.[15]

It was widely held at the time that the matrimonial press provided a useful service to the generally impoverished white collar worker, who, uncertain of his income and status, could find respectability helpfully quantified by the requirement of most papers for the advertiser to state his or her income. Matrimonial ads were also seen as a response to the "surplus woman" problem that emerged from a gender imbalance in Britain's population from the 1860s onwards. Another factor that assisted the rise of the matrimonial press was the increasingly popular idea of marriage as a type of negotiable contract. This view had emerged in the mid-nineteenth century in Britain as part of the attempt to reform the laws governing divorce and married women's right to property. By the end of the century marriage-as-contract had a number of powerful feminist advocates including the writers Mona Caird and Cicely Hamilton, the latter the author of the 1909 protest against *Marriage as a Trade*. The contractual idea appealed to feminists as it seemed to allow women to circumvent the suffocating restrictions of class, custom and family that dictated who and how a woman should marry. It also appeared to undermine the idea of patriarchal authority within marriage by suggesting that both parties met on the basis of equality. These ideas were accompanied by a widespread feeling that modern love had degenerated into a merely pragmatic and often monetary relation.

Caird had become famous in 1888 when an article by her in the London *Daily Telegraph* entitled "Is Marriage a Failure?" caused a national sensation. In the years following, Caird promoted the idea that marriage should evolve from primitive practices towards contractual agreement. She argued that science, and especially Charles Darwin, had shown that marriage had begun in savage practices like wife-capture, and the problem was that it continued in much the same coercive form. To break away from the "barbaric" elements of marital coercion, men and women should, Caird argued, "*form their own contract,* and not be forced

---

14   See 'Matrimonial Adlets', *The Sun*, 31 July 1893, p. 4.
15   See 'The Alleged Matrimonial Frauds', *(London) Times*, 3 December 1895, p. 12; 'Police', Times, 1 January 1896, p. 14; Times,3, 18, 24 December 1895, 12; 8, 29, January; 29 February; 2 March 1896. On this case see Angus McLaren, The *Trials of Masculinity: Policing Sexual Boundaries 1870-1930* Chicago, University of Chicago Press, 1997, ch. 2. The principals were sentenced to between three and five years penal servitude for fraud.

to accept one whose terms they have had no voice in deciding."[16] The problem then was how to invent a place where such contractual ideas could be put into practice. For an answer many progressive thinkers turned to the matrimonial advertisement and agency. Advocates of eugenically-influenced "rational reproduction" adopted it as a way round the "dsygenic" courtship practices associated with the rituals of respectability that prevented healthy men and women marrying across class boundaries, while others, such as the pioneering editor W. T. Stead established their own version of a social network. Stead's idea, which ran from 1898 to 1903, was called the Round-About, and was modelled on a matrimonial agency but with the important difference that clients did not have to state a "matrimonial intention," and could therefore interact without the anxiety thereby imposed. Men and women would see their ads in the Round-About newspaper, and then write to each other via a central office of the "Controller" where profiles of themselves were also kept. If the profile took your fancy, a correspondence would follow and if so inclined, marriage might result. This, Stead argued, was a key solution to the problem of modern urban alienation that especially afflicted the young white collar or professional worker living in what he called "the City of Dreadful Solitude." Others also took up the matrimonial bureau as a philanthropic idea and rational solution to modern problems, including the founder of the Salvation Army, William Booth. He envisaged a "colony scheme" – a gigantic programme for exporting Britain's urban poor to Canada and Australia, part of which would be a matrimonial agency ensuring that healthy marriages were made.[17]

Even though all these efforts gained national attention, they were never as commercially successful as the established matrimonial industry. However, in 1913 a new form of advertising appeared on the British scene in the literary periodical *T. P.'s Weekly*, named after its founder the Irish politician Thomas Power O'Connor. In its "Friends in Council" column, *T. P.'s Weekly* allowed advertisers to solve the problem of modern solitude by searching for friends and "companions," without stating any matrimonial intent. The respectability of the column was – at first at least – protected by the fact that all those seeking such friends had to provide two letters of reference, one of which had to be provided by a clergyman. Similarly, suggestive self-descriptions such as "unconventional" or "bohemian" were banned. By 1915 Friends in Council had processed over 8,000 ads at a rate of five to six hundred a week and had started a national trend.

The origins of lonely hearts ads, as opposed to matrimonial ones, can be found here, and also in the craze for advertising that sprung up during World War One to cater for servicemen. From the outbreak of the war in 1914 it became something of a national duty to write to those serving in the armed forces and several newspapers in Britain opened schemes that organised the sending of parcels and care packages to the various theatres of the war. In France this sort of correspondence was officially sponsored, and French women could become "*marraines de guerre*" (godmothers of war) in order to exchange letters with *filleuls* (adopted sons) in need of epistolary companionship. In Britain, this form of letter-writing operated in

---

16 Mona Caird, untitled essay, in Harry Quilter, (ed.), *Is Marriage a Failure?*, London: Swan Sonnenschein 1888, pp. 41-2. Original emphasis.

17 William Booth, *In Darkest England and the Way out*, London: Salvation Army, 1890.

a less formal sense through the columns of papers like *T. P.'s Weekly* and other periodicals where "lonely soldiers" and their admirers of both sexes could advertise for pen-pals or other types of companionship. The volume of this correspondence could be readily estimated from the complaints made by the British Army's postal service about its size and potential for disrupting military logistics. In February 1915 it was pointed out that one ad, which ran for a few issues of the *Daily Chronicle*, and had been placed by a driver in the artillery, had generated three sacks of mail, one containing 3,000 letters, plus 98 parcels.[18] The lonely soldier craze reached a peak in the summer of 1916 when the newspaper *Pearson's Weekly* ran a competition for servicemen, the prize for which was a chance to woo the soldiers' pin-up and theatre star Phyllis Monkman. By that time though, the authorities had lost their patience and after a while they forced the paper to abandon the scheme.[19]

The success of the lonely soldier movement encouraged others to enter the wartime market, not least the *Link*, the first periodical in Britain wholly devoted to the publication of "companionship" ads. The *Link* (which was originally given the more enticing name *Cupid's Messenger*) was founded in 1915 by the career journalist and comic novelist Alfred Barrett (a former editor of the *Family Circle* and *Woman's World*), and its masthead firmly stated that it was a "Great Social Medium – Not Matrimonial." The *Link* cost 8d, though advertising was only 1d per word, and it sold around 5-6,000 per issue. However, along with the contemporaneous lonely soldier movement and the other papers such as the racy bachelor periodical *London Life*, which were also opening their own "friendship" columns, the *Link* seemed to represent to many commentators the leading edge of modernity, bad and good. Before long, the *Link's* announced non-matrimonial intent, not to mention its clientele of "sporty" and "unconventional" female advertisers, began to attract the attention of moral campaigners and the police, who tended to view it as morally dangerous, if not a medium for open prostitution. Stories of girls disappearing into white slavery through its columns began to circulate in the more sensational newspapers, and the police began to take a keener interest. Although they discovered very little evidence of prostitution by women, the authorities did uncover a series of ads that appeared to be arranging contacts between gay men, and which were therefore more obviously illegal. In their ads, these men commonly cited a canon of homosexual heroes, from Hercules and Iolaus to Walt Whitman and Oscar Wilde, declared themselves "theatrical," "musical," and "sincere," before announcing a willingness to meet a potential friend or chum, "own sex." In 1921, a police investigation of these ads, and a discovery of a cache of intimate letters between two men who had met through the *Link*, landed the paper, its proprietor Alfred Barrett, and three advertisers in court. They were all charged with procuring and inciting "acts of gross indecency" and all sentenced to two years imprisonment with hard labour.

That episode put an end to the wartime craze for companions and friends, and seemed to confirm once again the low reputation of such enterprises. However, the matrimonial industry, which had generally held itself aloof from the fashion for companionship, continued unperturbed through the interwar period, though it was still associated with an unfashionable lower-middle and working class clientele. The *Link* case contributed to an atmosphere of

---

18   'Lonely Soldier Correspondence', *National Archives UK*, Kew: HO 139/32.
19   'Who Will Marry Phyllis Monkman, A Chance for Single Men', *Pearson's Weekly*, 8 July 1916, p. 67.

distrust that prevented any more "lonely hearts" or companionship ads appearing in the legitimate matrimonial press. Other papers that had followed the *Link* and *T. P.'s Weekly* into the trend dropped their columns after the trial. After 1921 the requirement to state a matrimonial intent was restored to its dominance and it was not really until the 1960s that the dubious status of the lonely hearts ad ended. Correspondence clubs such as the longest-lasting one, the Universal (established in 1916 and still in existence in the 1940s) continued to exist, and others grew up at the end of World War Two to cater for a newly-perceived epidemic of solitude and a short-lived post-war boom in divorce (that peaked in 1948 and soon fell away to almost nothing in the 1950s). However, these "friendship" organisations, such as the Victory Correspondence Club or the Two-Ways Correspondence Club, remained on a small scale and most were run by an odd collection of ex-military men from their homes in provincial towns and seaside resorts.[20] Marriage bureaux also enjoyed a new vogue in this climate, some of which began to use psychological and psychoanalytical profiles in order to match people.[21] Responding to the apparent crisis in marriage that seemed to overcome British society in the 1940s, some observers even argued that such organisations should be a state-sponsored element of the new welfare state which grew up under the post-war Labour government.

Even in the 1960s, when the matrimonial industry had produced new "scientific" offshoots such as Dateline, founded in 1966 to match partners using computer analysis, the authorities still suspected the intentions of many advertisers and editors. This became obvious as part of the backlash against the counterculture at the end of the 1960s when the police repeatedly attempted to prosecute the hippy paper *International Times* (more often known as *IT*) for "corrupting public morals," one of the crimes supposedly perpetrated by the *Link* in 1921. This charge was a sort of legal catch-all usually directed against the organisation of prostitution through advertising or publicity of various kinds – it had also been used in 1960 against a list of call-girl contacts known as the *Ladies' Directory*. *IT* got into trouble for the same reason as the *Link*: publishing gay contact ads. Even though homosexuality between men was decriminalised in Britain in 1967 (as long as it remained in private and only two people over 21 were present), the police decided in 1969 that *IT* should be prosecuted and a long-drawn-out series of trials and appeals began that lasted until the paper was finally convicted in 1972. The whole process was part of a pattern of prosecutions against countercultural magazines for obscenity – the most famous being the case against *Oz* magazine in 1971, which resulted in long prison terms (overturned on appeal) for its editors.

The *IT* trial ended up making the efforts of the police look rather ridiculous however. Their attempts to clamp down on ads that sought to facilitate a wholly legal activity (gay men over 21 meeting each other) along with the lengthy process of appeal, ensured that the case (with many others like it) was widely ridiculed.[22] The revelations that followed a few years later of extensive police corruption in London's Obscene Publications Squad, the branch that

---

20 'Friendship Clubs', Mass Observation Archive, University of Sussex, TC 12 Box 16 File E.
21 'The Answer to the Marriage Muddle,' Sunday Pictorial, 18 April 1948, p. 4.
22 For instance in articles by Bernard Levin, Times, 21 and 22 June 1972. See also "International Times", NA UK, DPP 2/4338.

masterminded the whole operation, further dented the credibility of such efforts. Moreover, the small ad (in its various forms) was a key technology of the counterculture, which had popularised its use in freesheets and magazines as a method of organising political and cultural groups. Its widespread use in these forms, as well as to facilitate straight lonely hearts and the contacts of gay men, made it unlikely that any further attacks on the latter would be successful. This was especially true since following the emergence of gay liberation at the end of the 1960s, there was an explosion of gay magazines like *Jeffrey* (est. 1972) that made extensive use of "Photo Pen Pals," and "Jeffrey's Beautiful Butch Little Ads."[23] Once these forms of contact had been pioneered, and their legality tested by the gay press and the counterculture, it was far safer in the 1970s for anyone to advertise in any way they wanted, for partners, group sex, or even for old-fashioned relationships.

Advertising for love has made halting progress towards respectability in the previous three centuries. Its rise in the 18th century reflected the long gradual breakdown of early-modern courtship rituals and marital practices, and it has subsequently appealed to (among others) people experiencing the "dreadful solitude" of the modern city, those contesting traditional heterosexuality and its rituals, and those at the edges of conventional morality like gay people and the counterculture. For much of its history, advertising for love was usually done in the context of a marital intention, and most advertising was contained in papers strictly devoted to finding husbands and wives. The clientele of these papers, which mainly came from the lower-middle or upper working class, tended to ensure that matrimonial advertising remained on the other side of respectability. It was only in the early 20th century, with the dislocations of war, that a new style of "companionship" emerged, one that has since come to dominate digital technologies.

References

'Friendship Clubs', Mass Observation Archive, University of Sussex, TC 12 Box 16 File E.

'International Times', National Archives UK, DPP 2/4338.

'Lonely Soldier Correspondence', National Archives UK, Kew, HO 139/32.

Berry, Helen. Gender, Society and Print Culture in Late-Stuart England: The World of the Athenian Mercury, Aldershot, Scholar Press, 2003.

Booth, William, In Darkest England and the Way out, London, Salvation Army 1890.

Curtis, J., An Authentic and Faithful History of the Mysterious Murder of Maria Marten, London, Thomas Kelly, 1828.

Fuhrer, Karl-Christian, "Contradicting Nazi Propaganda: Classified Advertisements as Documents of Jewish Life in Nazi Germany, 1933-1938", Media History 18, 1 (February 2012): 65-76.

Gillis, John, For Better, for Worse: British Marriages, 1600 to the Present, Oxford, Oxford University Press, 1985.

Goody, Jack. The European Family: A Historico-Anthropological Essay, Oxford, Blackwell, 2000.

Jeffrey no. 1 and no. 2 (1973), p. 22.

Macfarlane, Alan. Marriage and Love in England, Modes of Reproduction 1300-1840, Oxford, Blackwell,

---

23 *Jeffrey* no. 1 and no. 2 (1973), p. 22.

1986.

(Matrimonial Adlets), *The Sun*, 31 July 1893, p. 4.

Matrimonial Advertisements, Private Collection, 1740-1859, British Library.

McLaren, Angus. The *Trials of Masculinity: Policing Sexual Boundaries 1870-1930*, Chicago, University of Chicago Press, 1997.

O'Hara, Diana, Courtship and Constraint: Rethinking the Making of Marriage in Tudor England, Manchester, Manchester University Press, 2000.

Quilter, Harry. (ed.) Is Marriage a Failure?, London, Swan Sonnenschein, 1888,

Stone, Lawrence. The Family, Sex and Marriage in England 1500-1800, London, 1977.

(The Alleged Matrimonial Frauds), *(London) Times*, 3 December 1895, p. 12; 'Police', Times, 1 January 1896, p. 14; Times,3, 18, 24 December 1895, 12; 8, 29, January; 29 February; 2 March 1896.

(The Answer to the Marriage Muddle), *Sunday Pictorial*, 18 April 1948, p. 4.

(Who Will Marry Phyllis Monkman, A Chance for Single Men), *Pearson's Weekly*, 8 July 1916, p. 67.

Wrigley, E. A., and R. S. Schofield. The Population 1541-1871, London, Edward Arnold, 1981.

OLD AND NEW METHODS FOR ONLINE RESEARCH: THE CASE OF ONLINE DATING

MURAT AKSER

The proverbial opening of the 2004 film *Closer* shows us a passionate online chat message exchange between two people. Believing to be courting a young woman Dan Woolf (Jude Law) makes advances with sexual innuendos towards a woman or so he believes. The message exchange is indeed a fake one, in fact, between two heterosexual men, one pretending to be a woman Larry Gray (Clive Owen). This very virtual, gendered and insecure nature of online intimacy makes it a complex phenomenon to analyze. The psychological need for intimacy intertwines with the corporate networked ad machine, which sells gendered images of men and women to each other. Digital Technologies and mediated personal lives overlap with the gendered nature of these digital landscapes.[1]

Today intimacy and networked individualism go hand in hand through online dating sites and social networks such as Facebook. These new spaces function as courting places for millions. Yet these spaces are also flowing sites of information that present new practices and modes of existence for couples. Today online dating is a 100 million US$ industry operating worldwide, answering both general and niche demand for singles. Match.com's own statistics estimate that about 10 percent of all paying users find a partner within a year.[2] Deborah Chambers states 'the fluidity and choice apparently offered by online dating fits in neatly with today's ethos of elective intimacy'.[3]

What is done through online dating is a reflexive and self-engaged impression management. Singles using online dating services are project-managing the outcomes of their mediated romantic encounters. Dysfunctional behavior such as stalking is also encountered in this space. Teenagers and young people are now: 'reconfiguring their notions of privacy and publicity and their concepts of personal and intimate'.[4] Chambers is surprised how conventional intimacy remains the same in new media. She states how the alienating pressures of work life are countered by online dating that allows people to relive romance in the most traditional way.[5]

A Humanities or a Social Science Issue?

The gathering and use of data related to online courtship seem to be within the domain of psychology since the inception of the World Wide Web, as the first articles and books go back to 1997. From the early articles on, the emphasis has always been to find out who uses

---

1   K. Orton-Johnson and Nick Prior (eds) *Digital Sociology: Critical Perspectives*, Basingstoke: Palgrave Macmillan, 2013, p. 4.
2   Arvidsson, Adam. ''Quality Singles': Internet Dating and the Work of Fantasy', *New Media & Society* 8.4 (2006): 686.
3   Deborah Chamber, *Social Media and Personal Relationships: Online Intimacies and Networked Friendship*, Basingstoke: Palgrave Macmillan, 2013, p. 139.
4   Deborah Chamber, *Social Media and Personal Relationships*, p. 140.
5   Deborah Chamber, *Social Media and Personal Relationships*, p. 141.

these services and on deceptive self-presentation. The users of online dating services were assumed to be shy people who could not experience face to face interaction, but instead resorted to a behind the computer approach.

The second assumption of the early researchers was that the users who misrepresented themselves through their profile photos and age-weight-height information wanted to have their romance chances higher, so they lied to get an advantage. This deception can take various forms: physical (both as data and information), discursive (false representation of self during online interaction). The personal impact of false representation on an individual can be devastating. The interest of psychologist in the area is understandable in terms of prevention of mental health problems such as depression and breakdown that could lead to suicide. Yet positive impact of online dating in terms of having a dialogue, however virtual, has been appreciated by such researchers. The online dating of widows after the death of their loved ones proves to be a cure for life long misery on the bereaving parties.[6]

Who Dates Online?

The early studies focused on who uses online dating sites. Question of what happened after the online couples met dominated the late 1990s. Qualitative research by Andrea Baker between 1997-99 is a case in point. Baker interviewed 43 couples to find out if they got along after they met online. Baker analyzed email exchange between couples and did a follow up interview with a small subsection of the people. The finding can reflect the current status of online courtship after the arrival of social networks today. The common similarities of online couples (circa 1997) were age (late thirties), marital status (were married), education (at least a bachelor's degree), offline meeting (4-7 months later), distance (lived thousands of miles away), prior online relationships (females none, males had experience). Online nicknames, modes and content of communication, timing, and presentation of the photo have had an impact on the research.[7]

Studies done a decade later to find who goes online for courting have revealed more results. The methods used changed from email analysis to online surveys. A study done on Dutch Internet users aged between 18-60 through online questionnaire reveals that online dating was unrelated to income and educational level. The high activity age of the users shifted. Respondents between 30 and 50 years old were the most active online daters. People low in dating anxiety were found to be more active online daters than people high in dating anxiety.[8] The measures for the study were age, education, income, dating anxiety and frequency of visit of dating sites. The study wanted to debunk the myth that only the shy use online dating; in fact the less shy had more frequency in attending these sites. The average age of

---

6 Dannagal Goldthwaite Young and Scott E. Caplan, 'Online Dating and Conjugal Bereavement', *Death Studies* 34.7 (2010): 575.

7 Andrea Baker, 'Two by Two in Cyberspace: Getting Together and Connecting online', *CyberPsychology and Behavior*, 3.2 (2000): 239-242.

8 Patti M. Valkenburg and Jochen Peter, 'Who Visits Online Dating Sites? Exploring Some Characteristics of Online Daters', *CyberPsychology & Behavior* 10.6 (2007): 849.

the users was twenty-nine as opposed to the Baker study's 35 and over.[9]

By 2010, the social demographic of Internet dating had changed. Sautter, Tippett and Morgan used a larger sample with quantitative methods. Multivariate logistic regression was used to analyze 3,215 respondents a nationally representative U.S. survey of Internet dating. The results yielded that sociodemographic factors have strong effects on Internet access and single status but weak effects on the use of Internet dating services. The presence of computer literate users in social networks increase the chances of Internet dating. The researchers found that Internet dating is a 'common mate selection strategy among the highly selective subpopulation of single Internet users and may continue to grow through social networks. Material and virtual elements of the digital divide have direct and indirect effects on Internet dating'.[10]

Case studies and qualitative analyses revealed that filtering process is developed by online users when it comes to online dating. Danielle Couch and Pranee Liamputtong used a qualitative approach with 15 people who use online dating took part in in-depth, online chat interviews. The results showed that nearly all participants used more than one dating site to seek partners. They also made use of email, chat and webcam to qualify their potential partners. They utilized a variety of filters and filtering processes before progressing to a face-to-face meeting. 'Participants filtered using the text, photographs, chat, and webcam opportunities available online, and followed progressive personalized steps in communication and engagement in the lead-up to meeting other online daters in person'.[11]

Recent research reveals that online courtship has shifted to social networks such as Facebook among youth. Craig and Wright found that 'attitude similarity and social attraction may be important perceptions that influence self-disclosure, and may eventually lead to predictability and interdependence, both important outcomes in terms of developing=maintaining relationships'.[12] Perceptions of similarity and attraction are found to be influencing two relational maintenance strategies (positivity and openness). They also found out that many Facebook users supplement their Facebook communications with face-to-face interactions. Through these encounters, the online couples take care of any potential misunderstandings.

Deceptive Self-Presentation: A Psychological or A Security Issue?

Misrepresentation has been, and it still is the most studied phenomenon in online dating. Ellison et al explore how users conceptualize misrepresentation (their own and others') in a specific genre of online self-presentation: the online dating profile. Using qualitative data

---

9   Patti M. Valkenburg and Jochen Peter, *Who Visits Online Dating Sites?*, p. 850.
10 Jessica M. Sautter, Rebecca M. Tippett, and S. Philip Morgan. 'The Social Demography of Internet Dating in the United States', *Social Science Quarterly* 91.2 (2010): 554.
11 Danielle Couch and Pranee Liamputtong, 'Online Dating and Mating: The Use of the Internet to Meet Sexual Partners', *Qualitative Health Research* 18.2 (2008): 268.
12 Elizabeth Craig and Kevin B. Wright, 'Computer-mediated Relational Development and Maintenance on Facebook®', *Communication Research Reports* 29.2 (2012): 119.

collected from 37 online dating participants, the researchers tried to understand self-presentational practices 'specifically how discrepancies between one's online profile and offline presentation are constructed, assessed, and justified'.[13] New York City was chosen as the location having access to a variety of online dating site users. Participants were invited through the *Village Voice* and Craigslist.com advertisements. Users of the most popular online dating sites (Yahoo! Personals, Match.com/MSN Match.com, American Singles, and Webdate) were included in the study. Overall eighty participants took part in the study. The first thirty-seven were interviewed (12 men and 25 women) ranging in age from 18 to 47. The near ethnographic field work yielded interesting results:

> First, participants were presented with a printed copy of their online dating profile and asked to rate the accuracy of each profile element, as well as the general acceptability of lying on that topic. Profile elements included age, height, occupation, and religion. Participants then completed a survey and were interviewed by the third author. Finally, participants were asked to engage in measurement procedures and were thanked, debriefed, and given a $30 incentive.[14]

The end result showed that online daters used their profile as a promise when it came to creating their own online representation: The participants gave themselves 'a flexible sense of identity that drew upon past, present, and future selves. The profile as promise framework enables us to better understand these dynamics and to consider when a misrepresentation is a lie and when it is merely a promise that may soon be fulfilled'.[15]

Toma and Hancock (2010) examined the role of online daters' deception in physical attractiveness in their profiles. Sixty-nine online daters identified the deceptions in their online dating profiles and had their photograph taken in the lab. Independent judges rated the online daters' physical attractiveness. Results showed that the online daters were to change their profile photographs and lie about their physical description (height, weight, age) when they had low self esteem. The relationship between attractiveness and deception did not extend to profile parts unrelated to their physical appearance such as income, occupation, suggesting that their deceptions were limited and strategic.[16]

Uncertainty plays a role in building trust in intimacy. Toma and Hancock's further study investigated whether deceptions in online dating profiles match what daters write about themselves in the text part of the profile. Computerized analyses found that deceptions showed themselves through linguistic cues pertaining to liars' emotions and liars' strategic efforts to manage their self-presentations. The findings add to the research base on deception, media, and self-pres-

---

13   Nicole B. Ellison, Jeffrey T. Hancock, and Catalina L. Toma. 'Profile as Promise: A Framework for Conceptualizing Veracity in Online Dating Self-presentations', *New Media & Society* 14.1 (2012): 45.
14   Nicole B. Ellison, Jeffrey T. Hancock, and Catalina L. Toma. 'Profile as Promise', p. 60.
15   Nicole B. Ellison, Jeffrey T. Hancock, and Catalina L. Toma. 'Profile as Promise', p. 60.
16   Catalina L.Toma and Jeffrey T. Hancock. 'Looks and lies: The role of Physical Attractiveness in Online Dating Self-presentation and Deception', *Communication Research* 37.3 (2010): 335.

entation, and also show how writing style influences perceived trustworthiness.[17]

Toma, Hancock and Ellison (2008: 1023) examined self-presentation in online dating profiles using a novel cross-validation technique for establishing accuracy. Eighty online daters rated the accuracy of their online self-presentation. Information about participants' physical attributes was then collected (height, weight, and age) and compared with their online profile, revealing that deviations tended to be ubiquitous but small in magnitude. Men lied more about their height, and women lied more about their weight, with participants farther from the mean lying more. Participants' self-ratings of accuracy were significantly correlated with observed accuracy, suggesting that inaccuracies were intentional rather than self-deceptive. Overall, participants reported being the least accurate about their photographs and the most accurate about their relationship information. This study conflicts with previous studies that

On the other hand, Deandrea et al confirmed that online daters lied about their weight and height not to create social desirability. The study found that 'height/weight misstatements are self-serving but do not serve a social influence strategy to affect others' impressions'. The self-deception literature shows that distorted self-presentations can represent simple ignorance about oneself, a strategic message to deceive others, or a self-directed response to self-affirmation or the avoidance of threats to self-esteem.[18]

Kraeger et al questioned the tendency for spouses to resemble each other across a variety of valued social characteristics, such as income, education, and health. The idea was to check if homogamy played an important role in the creation of intergroup social distance, inequality among families, and the intergenerational transmission of (dis)advantage.[19] Hall et al examined factors found that seven categories of misrepresentation exist: 'personal assets, relationship goals, personal interests, personal attributes, past relationships, weight, and age'. The study found that men are more likely to misrepresent personal assets, relationship goals, personal interests, and personal attributes, whereas women are more likely to misrepresent weight.[20]

Conclusion

The research literature on online dating has mostly concentrated on two strands of research: on who uses these services and why-how misrepresentation of self happens. The early assumptions of who were the shy people used online dating to their advantage. Yet further studies revealed that more aggressive, and less shy people overly use these services. As

---

17   Catalina L. Toma and Jeffrey T. Hancock. 'What Lies Beneath: The Linguistic Traces of Deception in Online Dating Profiles'.*Journal of Communication* 62.1 (2012): 78.
18   David C. DeAndrea et al. 'When Do People Misrepresent Themselves to Others? The Effects of Social Desirability, Ground Truth, and Accountability on Deceptive Self-Presentations', *Journal of Communication* 62.3 (2012): 415.
19   Derek A. Kreager et al. '"Where Have All the Good Men Gone?" Gendered Interactions in Online Dating', *Journal of Marriage and Family* 76.2 (2014): 387.
20   Jeffrey A. Hall et al. 'Strategic Misrepresentation in Online Dating: The Effects of Gender, Self-monitoring, and Personality Traits', *Journal of Social and Personal Relationships* 27.1 (2010): 117-118.

for the misrepresentation each study conflicted with another. The physical qualities were thought to be determining misrepresentation. Yet money and status were mist lied about by men. The variety of research methods used such as questionnaire and online surveys seem to be more reliable that computerized aggregate analyses. The future of online dating studies is yet to be determined by a new factor, the use of social networks. Such networks can change the assumptions and the actual uses of these sites in unpredictable ways. The online dating services are big, and the services they provide are on demand. The next decade of online dating research will questions today's assumptions and give way to a better understanding of online romance.

References

Arvidsson, Adam. ''Quality singles': Internet Dating and the Work of Fantasy', *New Media & Society* 8.4 (2006): 671-690.

Baker, Andrea. 'Two by Two in Cyberspace: Getting Together and Connecting Online', *CyberPsychology and Behavior*, 3.2 (2000): 237-242.

Chambers, Deborah. *Social Media and Personal Relationships: Online Intimacies and Networked Friendship*, Basingstoke: Palgrave Macmillan, 2013.

Closer. Mike Nichols. 2004. Film.

Couch, Danielle, and Liamputtong, Pranee. 'Online Dating and Mating: The Use of the Internet to Meet Sexual Partners', *Qualitative Health Research* 18.2 (2008): 268-279.

Craig, Elizabeth, and Wright, Kevin B. 'Computer-mediated Relational Development and Maintenance on Facebook®', *Communication Research Reports* 29.2 (2012): 119-129.

DeAndrea, David C., et al. 'When Do People Misrepresent Themselves to Others? The Effects of Social Desirability, Ground Truth, and Accountability on Deceptive Self-Presentations', *Journal of Communication* 62.3 (2012): 400-417.

Ellison, Nicole B., Hancock, Jeffrey T., and Toma, Catalina L. 'Profile as Promise: A Framework for Conceptualizing Veracity in Online Dating Self-presentations', *New Media & Society* 14.1 (2012): 45-62.

Ellison, Nicole, Heino, Rebecca and Gibbs, Jennifer. 'Managing Impressions Online: Self-presentation Processes in the Online Dating Environment', *Journal of Computer-Mediated Communication* 11.2 (2006): 415-441.

Guadagno, Rosanna E., Okdie, Bradley M., and Kruse, Sara A. 'Dating Deception: Gender, Online Dating, and Exaggerated Self-presentation', *Computers in Human Behavior* 28.2 (2012): 642-647.

Hall, Jeffrey A., et al. 'Strategic Misrepresentation in Online Dating: The Effects of Gender, Self-monitoring, and Personality Traits', *Journal of Social and Personal Relationships* 27.1 (2010): 117-135.

Hitsch, Günter J., Hortaçsu, Ali and Ariely, Dan. 'What Makes you Click? Mate Preferences in Online Dating', *Quantitative Marketing and Economics* 8.4 (2010): 393-427.

Kreager, Derek A., et al. '"Where Have All the Good Men Gone?" Gendered Interactions in Online Dating', *Journal of Marriage and Family* 76.2 (2014): 387-410.

Orton-Johnson, K. and Prior, Nick. (eds). *Digital Sociology: Critical Perspectives*, Basingstoke: Palgrave Macmillan, 2013.

Sautter, Jessica M., Rebecca M. Tippett, and S. Philip Morgan. 'The Social Demography of Internet Dating in the United States', *Social Science Quarterly* 91.2 (2010): 554-575.

Toma, Catalina L., Hancock, Jeffrey T. and Ellison, Nicole B. 'Separating Fact from Fiction: An Examination of Deceptive Self-presentation in Online Dating Profiles', *Personality and Social Psychology*

Bulletin 34.8 (2008): 1023-1036.

Toma, Catalina L., and Hancock, Jeffrey T. 'Looks and Lies: The Role of Physical Attractiveness in Online Dating Self-presentation and Deception', *Communication Research* 37.3 (2010): 335-351.

_____. 'What Lies Beneath: The Linguistic Traces of Deception in Online Dating Profiles', *Journal of Communication* 62.1 (2012): 78-97.

Valkenburg, Patti M., and Peter, Jochen. 'Who Visits Online Dating Sites? Exploring Some Characteristics of Online Daters', *CyberPsychology & Behavior* 10.6 (2007): 849-852.

Whitty, Monica, and Gavin, Jeff. 'Age/sex/location: Uncovering the Social Cues in the Development of Online Relationships', *CyberPsychology & Behavior* 4.5 (2001): 623-630.

Whitty, Monica T., & Carr, Adrian N. Cyberspace *Romance: The Psychology of Online Relationships*, Basingstoke: Palgrave Macmillan, 2010.

Young, Dannagal Goldthwaite, and Caplan, Scott E. 'Online Dating and Conjugal Bereavement', *Death Studies* 34.7 (2010): 575-605.

DATING MAPS:
MAPPING LOVE IN ONLINE DATING COMMUNITIES

RAMÓN REICHERT

Introduction

The development of the web into a living web, where a multitude of users create their own content, led to consumers becoming the producers. With this role reversal, the perception of network processes changed, creating an altered need to view and systematically research one's own network environment and certain areas from an overview perspective. Before this background, visualization and mapping rose to become key technologies of Web 2.0. This stands for the spatial data collection for the creation of maps with computer-aided surveillance systems. One kind of the quickest growing online communities in Web 2.0 is dating communities. They not only considerably advanced the research and the development, but also the possibilities and the empowerment of the individual with their cognitive and visual remixes. Therefore, location determination with satellite-aided orientation technologies is no longer the monopoly of the most technologically advanced military equipment. Interactive mapping technologies of social relationships in computer-aided data banks can be placed at the interface between the *individual mapping and the collaborative mapping*. From there, new dimensions of a technology-aided orientation of social visibility can be created.

The spatial mapping technologies for data recording of network workers operate less as the access to uninteresting knowledge, but primarily as device in the competition for economic advantages and power as part of effective dating management. From a historical standpoint, the dating maps of the social media in Web 2.0 also actively influenced the manner in which cartography of the digital knowledge spaces of the Internet generates the collective memory of date cultures and love organizations. In that respect, they visually organize space pursuant to varying criteria, in which the time and culture association of the perception are tied to the discussions on: 1. Information (i.e. the availability of finding, assessing, and managing information), 2. Identity (i.e. the availability of presenting aspects of oneself on the Internet), and 3. Relationships (i.e. the availability of establishing contact, nurture contact, and form new combinations). Thus, dating maps can be understood as Internet-based applications, supporting the management of information, identity, and relations in specific public domains of hyper- textual and social networks. When comprehended as historicizable cultural techniques, the technologies, discussions, and practices of dating maps also communicate certain spatial concepts, realization and media cultures, iconic qualities, and political theories of the representation. On one hand, cartographic visualizations by the dating communities attempts to meet the growing needs of the computer-aided representation of social networks on the Internet. On the other hand, their navigation tools are advancing to a decisive tool in the medial formatting of the dating cultures of digital communities.

Love Organizations on Web 2.0

The new digital dating cultures are part of the E-commerce business. Flirting and dating exchanges on Web 2.0 are popular entertainment, connected to the commercial use of the net. This commercial framework can be found in all areas of the love organization on the net. Initially, mapping of the dating culture takes place in the bit-mapping sector, at a level constitutively inaccessible to the female and male users. Bit mapping principally differs from the cartographic mapping of the interface architecture, and, according to Wolfgang Ernst, can be understood as a technological and mathematical process, "topological instead of geographical, non-narrative (data-based) instead of narrative, connective instead of spatial in nature (... and) deals with the code (software) instead of images, numbers instead of sensual realization."[1] The spy technologies used in online dating exchanges are learning programs, which study the habits of the users, create user profiles, and offers by suitable partners. With the help of the cookies on the user's hard drive, the spy programs of commercial dating services providers own an archive of the love customs of their users. They store the preferences and options of its users, constantly learn their habits, and attempt to increase the effectiveness and efficiency of the search for partners. In that sense, the spy technologies and their cookies superpose the dating and consumer culture.

The distinct difference between the "free" contact ads portals and the Internet partner agencies "for a fee" is that singles of the "fee-charging" dating agencies do not need to go search themselves. The singles of the largest provider of online dating services, that is the US competitor match.com, receive suggestions for possible partners with the help of evaluations, expert assessments, and matching processes. "Matching" is the English and new German term for the finding of partner suggestions, based on search algorithms, comparing the profiles of singles of an online dating site, releasing the hits with the mutual largest concordance (match point score).

In 1987, the first-ever a computer-based dating agency offered its services in Austin (Texas). The company operated under the name Matchmaker, and developed a personality questionnaire with 50 questions, including questions concerning one's own person and the desired partner, aside from the usual social-statistical data such as sex, age, height, and weight. The order "Make me a match" had to conclude the data inquiry. Through changing the desired characteristics based on the respective supply situation on the relationship market, the number of suggestions could either be increased or reduced. This basic structure of the search still is used today in data banks as a selection criterion. As a whole, the matching procedures suggest codifiable and self-programming social relationships.

Differing from contact exchanges, the so-called "serious" platforms like *match.com, eharmony.com, or parship.com*, operate with a software program based on the mathematical search algorithms of key matching. This procedure determines within limited time, whether a respective search value is in concordance with a key value within a limited search area. Contrary to pattern recognition (the finding of patterns in signals), the search procedure for the best matching units depends on words entered.

Like the Assessment Center, the online dating agencies use psychological tests, in particular personality tests, for documenting the self-image of the candidates in search and evaluation

---

1   Wolfgang Ernst, Jenseits des Archivs: Bit Mapping, 2007. http://www.medienkunstnetz.de/themen/medienkunst_im_ueberblick/

procedures.² Like the Assessment Center, partner agencies consist of complex processes of self and second-party evaluation, combining self-techniques in the form of self-evaluation and feedback with disciplinary techniques.³ Diverse versions of the feedback software offer all members on the community sites the opportunity of mutual evaluation and assessment. Feedback records provide extensive and flexible information on the persons, and create comparisons between supply and demand by statistical evaluation of the respective preferences and capabilities, and offering couples' psychological coaching on that basis.

The monitoring and control knowledge collected then is listed in various manners in graphic overview maps, lists, or quantitatively assessed diagrams. In order of successfully placing in dating communities, the users must develop certain *mapping and monitoring* capacities in the area of everyday and relationship management. The mapping technologies of most dating forums promise to render social relationships and social behavior storable in spatial orders and knowledge recording technologies, manageable, and assessable, that is basically controllable and directable.

The software architecture and the screen design of the flirt and love culture on Web 2.0 not only represents the technological processes for the mapping of social networks, but can also be placed generally with *social monitoring*, based on its discourses. Monitoring is a collective term for all types of systematic recording, observing and monitoring of a process with the aid of technical devices or other monitoring systems. Social control, understood as monitoring, comprises a multitude of knowledge technologies, which combine the safety, risk, care, and monitoring discourses to the mapping of life conduct discourses.

Geomapping I: Street Maps and Satellite Images

Social software-based networks like contact exchanges, dating agencies, real-time chat services utilize geographical information services (GIS), and the distance research by satellite photography, in order to visualize their online databanks on clearly arranged world maps.⁴ One differentiating field of digital technologies among the field of web mapping and web GIS comprises far spread offers of zoomable street, land, and satellite maps with hyperlinks, plug-ins, viewers, micro maps, cartographic animation technologies, and visually responsive terrain overflights.

The cartographies of the online dating communities transform flirting and dating into spatial information. Their visualization processes are superposed with knowledge technologies, concerned with aspects of topography, infrastructure, settlement geography, economic geography, territory, social geography, politics, history, biology, geology, tectonics, and others.

For visualizing the *exploration* of the digital space, the community sites have used *street*

---

2   Ramón Reichert, *Amateure im Netz. Selbstmanagement und Wissenstechnik im Web 2.0*, Bielefeld: transcript, 2008, pp. 124-129.
3   Marilyn Strathern, *Audit Cultures: Anthropological Studies in Accountability, Ethics and the Academy*, London: Routledge, 2000, p. 15f.
4   Martin Dodge and Rob Kitchin, *Mapping Cyberspace*, London: Routledge, 2000, p. 22.

maps and *satellite image* for some time. With the adaptation of these two image traditions, they attempted to transfer cartographic characteristics of the *oriented* space to the knowledge representation of the love organization. In a further step, the dating sites localize their players on the selected cartographic blueprint. With the respective geographical coordinates determinable for certain, the individuals can be entered as dots, nicknames, or profile photos into a landscape, city, or building. Thus, geomapping concerns translating the online dates into the physical action and living space to enable a spatial orientation. The proximity to neighborhoods here is determined by *proximity,* and participates in the logic of strong ties. This suggests intensive relationships in the social space in particular through *geographical proximity* or *neighboring* of players in the physical space. This presentation superposes social and spatial proximity without rendering them significant. Thus, the interpretation of this spatial arrangement remains with the female and male users.

As a rule, at the map design level a selection can be made between various map models and visualization processes - frequently, a choice between schematic street map and photographic satellite image is given. With the adaptation of the *street map*, attempts are made to display social networks, contacts, and relationships as route planning and geographical route-target orientation. Based on the model of geographical maps, borders, traffic routes, main roads, centers, and outlying zones simulate the dating topographies of potential partners. Flirting and dating maps provide a visual abstraction, and record distances and the relative position of the members to each other on two-dimensional maps.

The street and city maps used in dating processes represent a spatialized level of classificatory knowledge, and address the observer as a subject, with an overview of all potential partners, adopting the respective profiles as spatial-navigating. With simple geometrical figures, decisive connotations are marked, presenting a clear, uncomplicated world of order, targeting primarily quick understanding. Dating maps synthesize from the original material (email addresses, online status etc.) the respective actors and transform them into items that can be clicked on, or clicked away. Interactive media technologies are connected with aspects of older media types, but form tools for structural, constructed identities. The possible interactions between the members take place in a determined action space, provided by the mapping software as so-called tech-tree.

In the era of Google Maps, *satellite images* represent a dominant topographical model of knowledge. Satellite photography not only offers realistic visual graphic quality, but also a kinesthetic sensation of movement through the shown virtual spaces (zooming). Different from the graphic schematizing of street maps, satellite images intensify the impression of reality: on one hand, they give evidence and plausibility to the social reality; on the other hand, they blur the social-hegemonial conditions of the knowledge technologies of visualization in their assumed creation of evidence. The satellite images of the surface of the earth are medial products of the military-technological knowledge complex, and always also represent the demand for visual empowerment and the "complete" discovery of military relevant knowledge objects.[5]

---

5   Georg Gartner, 'Internet Cartography and Web Mapping', *International Handbook Military Geography* 41.7

Most frequently, the community maps are based on a geographical pattern of national belonging and identity. Their external appearance frequently shows common characteristics with the route maps of online route planners, and city map services. They offer on one hand a *selective image* of what the respective services would like to emphasize, and, for example, mark potential flirting partners with signal colors, arrows, inserts, speech bubbles, or icons. On the other hand, they create *imaginary pictures* of global availability and omnipresent world dominance. They simulate a deistic view of the globe. As *image of power*, maps always had been used for military strategic planning, social monitoring, economic control, theoretical analysis and structuring, the conquest of new territories, and the judicial legalization of property. Therefore, it is not surprising that the commercial providers on the net present their own community as knowledge object, capable of testing, recording for planning purposes, and mutually checking themselves. With the interactive maps, the relationship networks themselves turn into location questions. Even in the so-called real life, cities more and more turn into competing enterprises, rivals for the investments from the high tech sector. Online mapping passes on this aspect, assembling profiles as "critical mass" in often-frequented places, thus garnering the respective attention.

Geomapping II: World Map and Globe

The knowledge representations of the street map and the satellite images orients at the cartographic overview presentations, and operates with the map design of the *world map* or the *globe*. Even though cartography presents the attempt to reduce the meaning surplus of its images to the essential as far as possible, it connects to a multitude of imaginary relations between individual actions, and social meanings. The *world maps* represent the life of the individual as a tangible and presentable phenomenon, and provide the individual with the impression that his own life is of social, political, and "world historic" significance.

The knowledge representation of the *world atlas* familiar to most people is easily created with GIS software, and is frequently used for the mapping of member profiles. There, one-dimensional data are projected onto nation-state contours before a geographical background. For example, the sites *flickrvision.com* and *twittermap.com*, visualize the real-time public chats of their communities onto a political world map. The maps show at what location in the world an online blog is being written. With the help of an operating menu, the users can adapt their personal needs, for example restrict them to a certain region. With a selection menu, the most varied map layers can be hidden or shown and personal dot coordinates stored. A RSS feed subscribing to the entries of a *certain geographical region* can be created by entering location and radius. Interactive mapping technologies such as the zoom function and geographical regionalization via RSS feed serve the above referenced visual needs of complexity reduction. Unlike the panorama map, they provide less of a comprehensive overview, but depict limited sections of the social world as *framed surfaces*. Their fragmentation corresponds to the changed architecture of the world map as part of globalization: margins move more and more into the center and the former power center as defining locations lose more and more significance. However, this assessment may not be generalized.

(2006): 416-432.

Paul Butler, who completed an internship with Facebook, created a graphic representation of friendship relations on Facebook. He visualized millions of friendships in relation to the respective city. He used all the friendship relationships of more than 500 million Facebook users as the basis. The continents are still well recognizable on the social maps, sometimes even the political borders. This statement, however, does not include the entire world. The map is as dark in Russia as in China. This has different reasons. While Facebook is blocked in China, Russia has its own social network with VContacts.

With the interactive use of the map, the views disperse, and the static dots and lines dissolve into heterogenic and discontinued moments. The numerous options for selection, generalization, and classification of data, as well as the numerous selection criteria in the usage area of map design integrate subjective decision processes in the creation of maps. The multitude of complex interactive maps simulates the divine ability of navigating on a virtual information globe. However, the simulation of theological view constellations cannot disguise that the interface channels the manipulation of the map by the actor, thereby constitutively hiding the complexity of the sociotechnological order of protocols, addresses, and hardware components.

Global navigation maps target the increase in physical immersion experiences, the creation of movement illusion, and the interconnection of subject and device. On the other hand, they enable an additional semiotization of other members, who can be consumed as part of a map storyline running in the background. The comprehensive narrative of the overview map creates a mega-story of the world, and claims to comprise the entity of what is happening in the world, and to connect it - from the macro level to the micro level.

Who just made love around the world? A new website titled "I Just Made Love!" by 26-year-old programmer Cyprian Cie kiewicz from Warsaw uses GPS and Google Map for integrating sexuality into a global tale. Users around the globe may anonymously mark the locations where they are sexually active right now. Nearly 80,000 respective experiences already were listed on that Internet site. The site does not sink to the level of pornography, but uses humor and playfulness to attract as many users as possible: little bunnies serve as comic symbols for encoding the details of sexual activities.

The world map developed by *Twittervision* shows a twofold inscription of meaning. On one hand, the statement aspect of the world map supports political-territorial hegemony with straight-line borders. On the other hand, the map emphasizes a relational orientation through personalizing inserts depicting the dynamic appropriation raster of the cartographic space. The linear borderlines stabilize the canon of geopolitical maps and the power relations. The micro blogs do not question the postulate of the borderlines, and remain true to the idea of the national state as associated territory. However, the reproduction of nation-state order functions of borders and traffic networks discharges the technical utopia of non-personifed and fleeting discussion groups - an idea once significantly carrying the hype of the "spirit" of the cyberspace.

In the spatial distance of maps, the hectic world of social relations appears as a unit withdrawn from temporality: what appears on the level of the world map happens at the threshold of the visible. Since distances are difficult to estimate in the depth of maps, distance transforms into an aerial presentation. The panorama view of the social always also refers to a panoptical projection attempting to overcome the contradictions resulting from the confusion of the search questions and search results. At the same time, digital mapping technologies are a panoptical projection relying on the power of overview, and operating with a fictive overview.

Mapping can be understood as a visualization process, able to summarize and represent data and information on the operational state of complex knowledge areas into a single visual image. The community maps drafted approximately in 2005 reproduce the cartographic standards of *planimetric map views*. The two-dimensional maps show a direct view, and utilize a uniform reduction of the scale. The spatialization process started where a map-like structure is applied to data collections is intended to visualize extensive databanks of abstract information in generalized and simplified images that reduce the research time and show relations otherwise going unnoted. Today, these continuations of the geographical-empirical space gradually are replaced by the information visualization of the social network maps marking the recent changes in the visualization culture of the social.

Ego Networks

In the area of visualization of social networks, only a few prototypical developments are still found today, such as the analysis software Vizster,[6] Social Landscape[7] or Matrix Explorer.[8] Here, social networks are represented in their formal relationship structures between formal actors in an abstract "social space." This abstraction allows disassociation from all other relations and only shows the position of the actors in a network of social connections and characteristics. The design study *Vizster* by Danah Boyd and Jeffrey Heer visualizes the friendship relations of the dating platform "Friendster" (www.friendster.com) along the following order criteria:

> Friendster was designed to be an online dating site, complete with profiles, demographic and interest driven search, and a private messaging system. What made Friendster unique was its articulated social networking component and testimonial feature. Users were asked to declare "friends" on the system whose pictures would also appear on the profile when the friends confirmed the relationship. [...] Yet, when the early adopters began to use the service, they did not view it as a dating service, but a site where they could gather and communicate with their friends, surf for entertaining profiles and explore

---

6   Jeffrey Heer and danah boyd, 'Vizster: Visualizing Online Social Networks.' IEEE Symposium on Information Visualization. Minneapolis, Minnesota, October 23-25, 2005.

7   Yuya Nomata and Junichi Hoshino. 'Social Landscapes: Visual Interface to Improve Awareness in Human Relationships on Social Networking Sites'. ICEC, Volume 4161, Lecture Notes in Computer Science. Ed. Richard Harper, Matthias Rauterberg, Marco Combetto, New York, Springer, 2006, pp. 350-353.

8   Nathalie Henry and Jean-Daniel Fekete, 'Visualization and Computer Graphics', IEEE Transactions 12.5 (2006): 677-684.

public displays of identity and relationships.[9]

With the mapping tool *Vizster*, Friendster users can explore their social environment. With the mouse pointer, they can activate a focus that displays profile data such as name, gender, number of friends, interests, favorite movies, and other. In addition, by selecting certain characteristics, certain players in the network with these characteristics can be highlighted. Under that aspect, mutual friends and communication carriers can be identified relevant for the connection of specific (sub-) groups. Finally, partial networks can be filtered which include a higher density of relations between the actors. For easier recognition, these partial networks can have a colored background. Vizster is designed as an analysis tool intended to encourage laypeople to discover friendship relations and similarities between networks. With its high-grade usability for network analysis, Vizster provided the development direction for a number of additional projects. Today, several versions are available for all important social networking sites like MySpace, Facebook, and its German language clone StudiVZ.

We want to introduce one of these network visualization tools as an example, since it demonstrates in detail the interactive-explorative network analysis. *Touchgraph,* the visualization software of search hits developed in 2001 for the search engine Google, is among the most favorite social mapping tools of today. The mapping tool *Touchgraph* visualizes the following questions: with whom am I in direct contact, and what is the connection between my contacts? Is there a definite group formation, and if yes, what is it like? To whom else are the contacts connected I have among the search results? Touchgraph is an independent Java application, requiring an installed Java environment that can be opened in the browser. The operation is interactive and easy to understand. Individual relations can be hidden or expanded. Relationship groups can be color-coded, thus rendering them more distinguishable. The left side also displays a list of the relationships including ranking. *Touchgraph* organizes the central relationships pursuant to the model of ego networks. Friends are placed concentrically around the ego point. The application *Touchgraph* is allowed as plug-in software without installation on Facebook, and automatically shows all Facebook contacts as animated cluster. This structure of presentation helps to view the structures in hundreds of contacts in one image, and helps to detect who knows whom via which person. Another mode of presentation of this actor mapping hides the profile photo on Facebook, and concentrates on the relational relationships. This spatial embedding of the individual actors, however, exposes the classical information deficit of social network analysis. As in most social networks, the actors are shown as uniform dots that do not allow conclusions concerning individual characteristics, except for the relational position. This visualization does not communicate any information relating to demographical or biographical differences, or individual forms of knowledge, responsibility, or diverse competences.

Vizster and the *Touchgraph Facebook browser* are so-called ego networks. These exclusively show network members directly connected to the central actor ("ego"), or at least in close relationship. More distant network members are hidden. However, spatial order in

---

9   Jeffrey Heer and danah boyd, 'Vizster: Visualizing Online Social Networks.' IEEE Symposium on Information Visualization. Minneapolis, Minnesota, October 23-25, 2005, p.2.

ego networks must first be interpreted. Other than the presentation form of the social circle where all actors are placed on a circle, focusing, for example, on those actors, whose mails receive a particularly large quantity of responses, Vizster focuses on a certain actor around who clusters form, where friends show particularly many connections amongst them. Since the social network is determined based on the ego, the central focus in such presentations appears over proportionately well connected - which does not need to correspond to the actual conditions. In order to remove this distortion, the *Touchgraph Facebook browser* offers the opportunity to hide the ego function, with a new order of the graph ensuing, forming a socio-centered network.

This free-floating item of the relationship cloud shows that the ego floats in the center of connections, but no longer is able to stabilize the social order. Thus, the ego primarily appears as secondary observer of social networks letting the structural position of the ego seem permanently changeable and fluid. The computer-aided medialization of a permanent fluid and volatile social presence radically breaks away from the classical forms of social legitimization conditions, for example the ancestry tree or the family portrait. In that sense, the ego no longer acts as the statistic nucleus itself, but is subject to the aggregate state of the network structure. Concomitant, the ego loses the aura of the confirmed, universal, and important. The graphic design of the social relationship cloud suggests that the social localization of the ego is a collaborative process, and that the ego cannot escape the aggregate-like state of the entire system.

Conclusion

In liberal democratic societies, inspection procedures constitute a dominant form and practice of knowledge.[10] Inspection procedures are widely recognised and usually referred to by the collective term 'evaluation'. Evaluation is believed to be the predominant vehicle to measure the impact of emancipation, democratisation and social equity. Vast areas of everyday and popular culture are surrounded by a variety of evaluation practices. In this context, not only has a new control instrument emerged, but new forms of managing oneself and others have arisen as well. The term 'evaluation' is on everyone's lips because it is aptly malleable and expansible and colloquially used in a meaning somewhere along the way between 'assessing' and 'grading'. The social media of web 2.0 play an important role in the current boom of evaluation.[11] In other words, the Internet has born a communication culture of mutual and permanent evaluation, which takes hold of the entire social and cultural space and often adopts the form of entrepreneurial practices.

Everyday and popular culture is flooded to a large extent by a multitude of performance determination methods, verification procedures, diagnostic methods and personality tests.[12] Evaluations, testing procedures, questionnaires and statistics have become the norm on the

---

10   Giorgio Agamben, *The Coming Community*, Minneapolis: University of Minnesota Press, 1993.
11   Mark Andrejevic. 'Surveillance and alienation in the online economy', *Surveillance & Society* 8/3 (2011): 278-287.
12   Christian Christensen 'Discourses of Technology and Liberation: State Aid to Net Activists in an Era of 'Twitter Revolutions', *The Communication Review* 14 (2011): 233-253.

Internet as well, where they influence how we think, perceive, work, remember and communicate. Feedback systems, performance comparisons, quality rankings, monitoring, matching, benchmarking, statistical controls, flexible process control, self-awareness catalysts, satisfaction surveys – all of these systemic-cybernetic control functions and observatory connections of mutual assessment and judgement are functional elements of media technology in web 2.0. Applications of post-disciplinary web 2.0 technologies are based on a cybernetic model which presupposes the individual as a system that processes information and adapts as flexibly as possible to existing standards set by its environment as long as it continues to be 'informed' by responses (feedback).[13] The 'informational control' of vast parts of society by means of search and analysis engines is a power mode of its own, which is based on the logic of self-organisation, interconnectedness and feedback, and results in media-specific forms of subjectification: Instead of regulating individuals directly, which would bring about vast amounts of overhead, feedback loops are installed to signal to the individual when aberrations of the norm occur. In the field of online media, the "conduct of conduct" as identified by Michel Foucault[14] as the key formula for the exercise of power takes the shape of control via feedback-driven self-control.

When an individual observes themselves or others, continuous feedback creates a cycle of mutual observation, on the basis of which adaptations are possible and interventions can be planned.[15] In this context, the individual is supposed to be able to perceive specific effects and, at the same time, the causes of these effects. This indicates a characteristic understanding of causality, i.e. a systemic-cybernetic observatory connection constituted by creating control cycles in the form of feedback loops, which can be used to regulate either oneself or others, depending on the direction the observation takes. Expanding systemic-cybernetic control functions in web 2.0 raises issues concerning systems and models, regulation, circular causality, feedback, equilibrium, adaptation and control. The required adaptations do not suggest to those controlled to achieve a certain ideal value. The control technology of 'gentle adaptation' attempts to set an interminable dynamic of self-optimisation in motion, which is supposed to be produced by the subject him- or herself within the boundaries of his or her own individual initiative and self-responsibility.

Accordingly, a new kind of dynamic of informatisation of self-practices begins to emerge against the backdrop of global distribution of web-based applications and of administrative institutions strategically opening up towards systems of open knowledge. Not unlike scientific evaluation, everyday evaluation presupposes the option of changing and controlling the behaviour of the subjects involved. Response systems and feedback loops suggest that the subjects be shaped to a certain extent in order to become socially effective. Their technological scheme aims to assert knowledge on the level of everyday practices. Response systems will turn 'general everyday perception' into 'structural monitoring' used to systematically ob-

---

13   Ramón Reichert, 'Social Media Storytelling'. Expanded Narration. Ed. Bernd Kracke, Marc Ries, Bielefeld: transcript, 2013, pp. 341-358.
14   Michel Foucault,*Dits et écrits IV*, Paris: Gallimard, 1994, p. 237.
15   Matthew Causey, *Theatre and Performance in Digital Culture: From Simulation to Embeddedness*, London/New York: Routledge, 2006.

serve, score, judge and successfully change a certain kind of behaviour. Feedback systems can substantially help activate practices of evaluative self-observation. However, manifold codes of observatory knowledge based on 'objectifying' and 'neutralising' knowledge technologies cannot belie the fact that every kind of knowledge has inherent social and normative concepts and is fundamentally dependent on political and economic contexts.

References

Agamben, Giorgio. *The Coming Community*. Minneapolis: University of Minnesota Press, 1993.

Andrejevic, Mark. 'Surveillance and Alienation in the Online Economy', *Surveillance & Society*, 8/3 (2011): 278-287.

Causey, Matthew. *Theatre and Performance in Digital Culture: From Simulation to Embeddedness*, London/New York: Routledge, 2006.

Christensen, Christian. 'Discourses of Technology and Liberation: State Aid to Net Activists in an Era of 'Twitter Revolutions', *The Communication Review* 14 (2011): 233-253.

Dodge, Martin and Kitchin, Rob. *Mapping Cyberspace*, London: Routledge, 2000.

Foucault, Michel. *Dits et écrits IV*, Paris: Gallimard, 1994.

Gartner, Georg. 'Internet Cartography and Web Mapping'. *International Handbook Military Geography* 41.7 (2006): 416-432.

Heer, Jeffrey and boyd, danah. 'Vizster: Visualizing Online Social Networks', IEEE Symposium on Information Visualization. Minneapolis, Minnesota, October 23-25, 2005.

Henry, Nathalie and Fekete, Jean-Daniel. 'Visualization and Computer Graphics', IEEE Transactions 12.5 (2006): 677-684.

Nomata, Yuya and Hoshino, Junichi. 'Social Landscapes: Visual Interface to Improve Awareness in Human Relationships on Social Networking Sites'. ICEC, Volume 4161, Lecture Notes in Computer Science. Ed. Richard Harper, Matthias Rauterberg, Marco Combetto, New York, Springer, 2006.

Reichert, Ramón. *Amateure im Netz. Selbstmanagement und Wissenstechnik im Web 2.0*, Bielefeld: transcript, 2008.

Reichert, Ramón. 'Social Media Storytelling', in: Bernd Kracke, Marc Ries (eds.): *Expanded Narration*, Bielefeld: transcript, 2013.

Strathern, Marilyn. *Audit Cultures: Anthropological Studies in Accountability, Ethics and the Academy*, London: Routledge, 2000.

Wolfgang, Ernst. Jenseits des Archivs: Bit Mapping. 2007. Web 15 April 2014. http://www.medienkunstnetz.de/themen/mapping_und_text/jenseits-des-archivs/.

THE VIRTUAL NIGHTCLUB: ADOLESCENTS FROM LOW-INCOME SECTORS SEARCH FOR THEIR COUPLES THROUGH FACEBOOK

DIEGO BASILE AND JOAQUÍN LINNE

Introduction

Along with the popularization of Internet produced in the first decade of the century, the ways of obtaining knowledge and youth socialization has changed. As Manuel Castells argued, this social-computer revolution has also changed the way we think about love and sexuality and has contributed in the transformation expressed in the ways we relate with others and the imaginaries believed regarding dating. This is why we understand the multiple strategies that adolescents carry on to appear attractive compared to others, trying to seduce, conquer and establish emotional, romantic and sexual relationships. That is why in this qualitative study we explore the online matchmaking practices performed by adolescents from low-income sectors (from here on LIS) of the City of Buenos Aires. We have investigated these practices and their representations about love and sexuality following these questions: what seduction strategies are deployed through the Internet? What relationship exists between images and texts of self-presentation with the construction of gender? What data is provided in virtual social networks? What are the advantages and disadvantages of meeting a partner through Internet? What are the expectations while searching for a couple through Internet?

Among the more than one hundred million active users that Facebook (FB) has, Argentines are in twelfth place with over twenty-two million users.[1] In this multi-platform, adolescents are more numerous and active regarding the publication of personal photos. This can be explained to some extent by their elevated free time, their digital native condition[2] and, also, because they are living a stage of experimentation and identity construction in which they find this platform especially useful and satisfactory. Unlike the "Kodak culture",[3] mobile digital technologies allow photographic exploration and visual-identity configuration to be recorded and tested by the community.

On the other hand, we find that one of the justifications for this research is that the pioneering concepts used to describe adolescents have begun to lose sense. A more complex analysis from a sociological perspective is necessary to analyze the ways in which society makes use of ICT. With this intention, our work focuses on the LIS, and their gender differences. While we use these categories in a general way, we note that the uses of the Internet in the LIS have specific differences that the concepts of digital natives and digital immigrants (Prensky, 2001) cannot distinguish them satisfactorily.

We also find it necessary to contribute in the research of LIS adolescents because they are one of the populations with more difficulties: the economic, social, educational and housing difficulties are often shared with other problems such as social stigma, gender violence, ad-

---

1   Internet World Stats, http://www.internetworldstats.com.
2   Marc Prensky, 'Digital Natives, Digital Inmigrants', *On the Horizon* 9.5 (2001): 1-6.
3   Richard Chalfen, *Snapshots Versions of Life*, Ohio: University Popular Press, 1987.

dictions and early pregnancy. Apart from the difficulties often faced, their daily lives include various activities: going to school, having jobs in poor labor conditions (temporally, not registered), taking care of the children of the family, and, in some cases, work and participate in art, sports, crafts and computers workshops. In their free time they get together with friends, chat on Whatsapp and send text messages over the cell phone, entertain themselves with the "Play",[4] they watch audiovisual content online, display, take and edit photos, and use social network sites. In this context, FB appears as their main entertainment and communication media.

Methodology

Fieldwork consisted of observations and twenty in-depth interviews to adolescents of LIS in schools, commercial *spots* with Internet and community centers, as well as virtual observations through FB. We define LIS adolescents as adolescents who are between 12 and 18 years old, whose parents have not finish high school and lack in their homes of at least one basic social service (such as water or gas).

A significant part of the fieldwork was possible due to our performance as volunteer teachers in the computer workshop *Conviven*, located in the streets *Murgiondo* and *Avenida Eva Perón* (neighborhood called *Lugano*, South Zone of the City). During 2011 and 2012 we went to this workshop where we made participant observations and interviews to adolescents from LIS. By doing so we were able to approach in their daily communication and self-presentation practices through their technological environments.

Finally, using the "snowball" method implemented by our key informants of the community center, we created an ad hoc profile on FB that currently has more than 2,500 contacts (mostly adolescents of the LIS of City of Buenos Aires). These virtual observations that we develop during two years (2012-2013), allowed us to investigate the practices of sociability and the strategies that adolescents display while searching for a couple and seducing others by publishing text and personal images on the network.

Adolescents, digital natives and multitasking

Studies about new technologies and the Internet have elaborated categories that contributed in fighting against conservative positions in various areas –such as academic, educational and intellectual– that opposed strong resistance to such innovations and did not allow them to display their potentials. Following this line of thought, the category "natives and digital immigrants" was useful to start talking about this new way of communication.

The simplicity, easiness and 'naturalness' that adolescents have in managing Internet clearly define them as digital natives. They were born after 1990, being raised along with multimedia tools, but especially "breathing the Internet atmosphere"[5]. This new generation is considered a "native" speaker of the language of computers, video games and the Internet. The "digital

---

4   Meaning Playstation, a well-known brand of videogames.
5   Manuel Castells, *Communication Power*, Oxford: Oxford University Press, 2009.

natives" are also defined as "Generation @"[6] or "multi-media generation".[7]

Multitasking category, definition shared by most adolescents, refers to the ability to perform multiple tasks at the same time on different screens or interfaces within a single screen. This concept serves to exemplify the use of dichotomous categories, since it is an actual practice of digital natives, which is absent in immigrants.

> The computer has over passed television in its capacity as totem, but with the difference that the "digital natives" project on this device a lot of expectations, tied to entertainment such as games, experimentation, learning and sociality, to the point that they consider the computer as part of their identity.[8]

These categories of digital natives are starting to lose their explanatory potential, but we still find them useful to frame some characteristics shared by the contemporary generation of adolescents. Let's focus now on our specific topic for this research, practices and representations of adolescents of LIS of the City of Buenos Aires while searching for a date online.

Results
Searching for a couple on Facebook

In a way FB has helped to create millions of couples but has also contributed to the dissolution of many others. Since the platform keeps track of all actions that create users (and this record is often available to the public), users can, easily, monitor the actions of others. This ability to monitor or control, as well as the simplicity in tracking down ex lovers, affairs or potential couples, becomes a sort of multilateral surveillance, at least in part, it is symptomatic to what Bauman[9] calls " liquid relationships ", in the sense that adolescents tend to have relationships with high levels of mobility and instability. However, this does not imply that future generations live in a spirality of sex and extreme experiences. In this respect, Lipovetsky states:

In mass culture eroticism is widespread and all the love "positions" are legitimate, but actual sexual practices are usually not risky, nor diversified: multiple sex, exchange, sodomy, homosexuality, sexual intercourse with someone you just met are still minority experiences.[10]

We have observed in our fieldwork that while there is greater visibility of new practices and new ways of presenting the bodies through images, as well as increased exhibitionism stories and visual esthetics, attitudes prevalent in most adolescents through FB usually show that they take care of themselves by controlling what is visible and the selection of significant

---

6   Alejandro Piscitelli, *Nativos digitales*, Buenos Aires: Santillana, 2009.
7   Roxana Morduchowicz, *La generación multimedia. Significados, consumos y prácticas culturales de los jóvenes*, Buenos Aires: Paidós, 2008.
8   Francisco Albarello, *Leer y navegar en Internet*, Buenos Aires: La Crujía, 2011.
9   Zigmunt Bauman, *Liquid Modernity*, Cambridge: Polity, 2000.
10 Gilles Lipovetsky, *El crepúsculo del deber*, Barcelona: Anagrama, 1994.

contacts.

Adolescent interactions are conducted in a daily life continually related to social networks, where the practices are multitasking: while performing simultaneous tasks around screens, also in many cases –both male and women– activate searches for couples in parallel or explore different emotional erotic relationships. In this new practice, while men tend to be popular and successful in and out of FB, women tend to be more challenged by their gender, who accuses them of "easy girls " or " boyfriend stealers."

> In the computer workshop, a girl of Bolivian nationality watches videos of hip hop that her boyfriend made for her. Her other colleagues are envious and tell her to never leave him, another adolescent is chatting on FB in a passionate way with her boyfriend (because the mother discovered the relationship and forbade her to see him, so now they only communicate by chat and text messages), another girl adds digital effects like stars and glitter to her photo album on FB, a teenage male sees photos and profiles of girls and sends them friend requests, another one watches goals from Messi on Youtube.[11]

Adolescents perform all these activities as they check all the time their profile on the social network. This combined use of networks, sociability and everyday life, for example in an educational environment, is often more "natural" for teens than for adults. They are who prefer FB as a platform for convergence of communication and entertainment, while adults prefer –even when they use Internet– to separate their places of recreation and erotic-emotional sociality. While adults over forty tend to search for a couple through dating sites and contacts (where they feel it is easier to refine the search for the other), youth and adolescents have FB as their main matchmaker.

Strategies
In a context where social networks, communication, and entertainment with friends and classmates are part of daily activity, adolescents use FB when searching for a couple. To do so, they develop presentation strategies towards others. In the presentation they display of themselves in FB, both central elements that can be viewed first in their profile are the cover photo and the profile picture. In most cases, they are personal pictures, of themselves, either alone, with intimate friends or with their family members.

Pictures posted about their bodies – usually 'selfies' – are central in the configuration of their online ID. With these pictures they show themselves to others exposing photos they consider the most attractive, in hope for feedback from their peers' community. Through comments that they write and receive from others, the daily sociability is displayed. In certain cases, this dynamic is explicit, for example in pictures of esthetic duels between two friends. These sets of personal pictures specifically search for the approval of adolescents as desired bodies and

---

11 Joaquín Linne, Adolescentes y redes sociales. Usos y apropiaciones de Facebook en sectores populares de la Ciudad de Buenos Aires (Adolescents & social networking. *Uses and appropiations of Facebook in low-income sectors of the City of Buenos Aires)*, Master thesis unpublished, Faculty of Social Sciences, University of Buenos Aires, Buenos Aires, 2013.

'legitimate bodies'[12]. A ludic strategy regarding this issue is holding an esthetic duel between intimate friends. A few hours after the post, feedback of their peers' community will give their verdict expressing them in how many 'likes' and quality and quantity of comments. Both images and personal texts can be commented. Through 'like', and 'signatures' of timelines and emoticons, they give sense to personal posts, assigning them as attractive or desired, or indifferent and ignored inside their community. For example, a girl asks her audience (the network), as if she was in a beauty contest, to qualify her: "From 1 to 10, what's my rating?"

Regarding the written discourse, information is provided related to the place of residence, age, where you study or work and relationship status, which complement the ID configuration of adolescents in their respective profiles. FB defines certain characteristics to describe a relationship status (in this order: single, in a relationship, engaged, married, it's complicated, in an open relationship). When the relationship status is modified by the user, it is posted as a novelty in the wall of their contacts. These status updates work as a public manifestation of the starting point or dissolution of a relationship, and being or not available for seduction and dating. Posting these relationship status' helps multilateral surveillance and horizontal monitoring between themselves. When someone posts that a friend has started or ended a relationship, it usually brings out many comments which express the sociability inside their friendship groups.

What is new regarding the ways adolescents present themselves? Unlike previous generations, they display, through textual and audiovisual fragments of their daily life, a 'visual autobiography'[13] in their FB profile. From the daily practice of personal pictures, posting and commentating on them, they choose what to show and monitor their profiles and their group of peers in search of creating their best presentation possible. This skill is not spontaneous since it is the result of the experience in the use of a social network and what they learn with other adolescents. By having much more control over the impressions they choose to expose in front of others,[14] the sites of social networks like FB allow them to present a very selective version of themselves. Therefore, they often expose positive aspects of their intimacy on the network. In LIS, personal photos of adolescents with their son or daughter are frequent. At the same time that they expose their condition of parents, they take care of their image and are still active in the game of seduction. For example, they put make up on, comb themselves with dedication and pick out carefully their wardrobe and the angle of the camera, and at the same time present their baby 'in society' (in the net).

There are certain differences in the forms of presentation of women and men in this daily practice. Women adolescents concentrate, on one side, in the search of a boy that satisfies with the expectancies of commitment, activities, projects and attraction, and on the other hand, in becoming *femme fatales* with a high grade of autonomy regarding the exclusivity

---

12 Judith Butler, *Bodies that Matter: On the Discursive Limits of "Sex"*, Psychology Press: Cambridge, 1993.
13 Andrew Mendelson and Zizi Papacharissi, 'Look at Us: Collective Narcissism in College Student Facebook PhotoGalleries', in Papacharissi, Z. (ed.), *The Networked Self: Identity, Community and Culture on Social Network Sites*. Illinois: Routledge, 2010.
14 Erving Goffman, *The Presentation of Self in Everyday Life*, New York: Anchor Books, 1959.

that a monogamous couple demands. While this poses a high rhetorical component, because it's a performance that both boys and girls want to represent, and at the same time celebrate in posts of others, this ambivalent posture regarding traditional representations of gender is usually a constant in most profiles and walls of adolescents.

At the same time, boys concentrate in the search and seduction of feminine contacts with whom to explore their sexuality, but also aspire in having a stable couple, a girl that is "faithful, loving, romantic and a family person". Even though this also forms part of a personal marketing, it also has an honest message and an expression of desire. These messages are inserted inside an environment where their main idea is to seduce others by showing what they consider is their best image. By multimedia, chat, private messages and posts of others and their own ones, they generate ingenious or romantic messages under the format of texts, pictures, memes, video clips and animations.

Advantages

From the adolescent's point of view, the search of a couple in FB has both advantages and disadvantages. When we asked the adolescents we interviewed about what they consider are the advantages of meeting a couple on FB, they responded in diverse ways. On one side, adolescents value the possibility of knowing aspects of the other person before deciding to meet ("you can get to know him-her and see him-her before meeting in person"; "you know all about them"; "FB shows everything you like and you get to know each other better"). On the other side, they are aware that the Net helps them build their own image ("you can show yourself different to others").

Nevertheless, they point out that it is 'easier' meeting people this way; that it generates a lower grade of inhibition to communicate and establish bonds ("maybe you get to meet him/her better"; "while you're getting to know him-her you can have a better communication"; "perhaps you can say things that if he/she were in front of you, you wouldn't dare say"); that they can meet people from different neighborhoods and cities ("the possibility to meet people from a remote location"); for them to learn communicating and observing the communication of others ("they teach you strategies and give you tips to speak to others"). As a result, the social network operates as a location and an instance of socialization, since adolescents socialise with their peers meanwhile they learn from observing the most popular posts which are the code lines and models to follow in search of a couple.

Disadvantages

When asked about the disadvantages of meeting a couple on FB, women responses present more concern than men. In social networks, the 'other' —primarily the other unknown— can lie about some important aspects of his/her identity. In regard of the place of residence, there are two attitudes towards this. On one hand, the concealment, because this information is a strong reference that may be seen as an obstacle regarding the possibilities of building a relationship; stigmatized neighborhoods with low resources, those who port a negative sense, usually are not present in adolescents 'profiles', which provokes a great deal of confusion in the expectancies of others. But this concealment of their place of residence is not an exclusive characteristic in the use of networks, since is also a generalized practice in which LIS evaluate the costs and benefits that carry on the presentation of such stigmatised information.

On the other hand, it is necessary to qualify the stigma of being 'villero' or living in a humble neighborhood, because the same adolescents, in different cases, defend the culture of the ghetto, or their neighborhood. Both boys as girls add "ghetto', 'villera' or another neighborhood identity reference next to their names or nicknames in FB. They also add a reference to their neighborhood with their name (for example, 'Mtd' is a contraction for the neighborhood *Mataderos*, or 'Lgn' contraction of the neighborhood *Lugano*). This territorial reference that they include in their profile name operates in a way that anchors their identity and sociability inside the website. Even though any user can interact with anyone and there are inter-neighborhoods and inter-classist contacts, most of the contacts are between users of close, if not the same territory and the same or similar social class-sector.

For adolescents from LIS the neighborhood is a strong identity mark from which they build their online profile. In a way of territorial and culture claim, they redeem their place of belonging and the values that they associate to it, as for example 'bravery', 'loyalty', 'perseverance', 'resistance' and 'history'. Sociability in Internet is not generated in an ubiquitous way, since it is produced, in most cases, between equals that live in the same territory, and claim the same neighborhood and share similar social conditions.[15]

On the other hand, meanwhile teenage girls of LIS have fears related to their psychical integrity ("he can be a rapist"; "he can rob you"), boys have fears related to the loss of autonomy ("if you have a girlfriend she controls everything you do in FB"; "you lose your liberty because they're controlling all your posts"). This fear has started to appear also in a recurring way in the timelines of teenage LIS girls.

Both boys as girls of our research agree on the inconvenient of meeting people through FB: in first place, they point out that you're always going to have a superficial and selective knowledge of the other person; in second place, the person can fail you on the date, or being someone very different from the identity built in the social network. The testimonies show that, even though the platform is an essential tool to search for a couple, it also possess its risks and disadvantages, because a performance is built up that not always meets the identity in person. These gaps between virtual and physical performance generate diverse daily problems in adolescents: from a couple that finds very difficult to trespass the fluidity of their virtual communication to the physical terrain, to the jealousy because one acts like he/she is single on FB, or the sensation of not being valued or acknowledged by the other person in any level. For example, an adolescent of 15 years old from *Lugano* told us about her relationship: "when we were online everything was fine and on weekends too, but later in the week he didn't pay attention to me, never calls, he is an idiot."

---

15   Joaquín Linne, Adolescentes y redes sociales. Usos y apropiaciones de Facebook en sectores populares de la Ciudad de Buenos Aires.

The Virtual Nightclub

Considering all these aspects, we can think of the social network as a virtual nightclub. There is a difference between the traditional modes of searching for a couple, and the new forms develop from the interactions in the net. In this sense, we shall emphasize some of the characteristics of the virtual nightclub:

• It is open 24 hours: the platform works in a never ending way, without interruptions, it is a space where you can leave messages to a specific user or to a set of contacts. Since communication is mostly delayed, it is not necessary that both emissary and receptor be active. This way, whoever wants to start a conversation, makes a comment or sends a private message or 'like' during any part of the day.

• Access is free: Anyone who has Internet and is willing to give certain personal information can interact with another sending and accepting 'friend requests'. The access is free because nobody controls the admission to the Internet; no one is 'kicked out' of a place due to his-her appearance, manner of dressing or footwear. In this sense, adolescents prefer the security and the free-of-charge net communication from those in a private club or store where there is usually an entrance fee, a dressing way is required and sometimes disputes between peer groups are displayed.

• The presentation in front of others: it doesn't require the ability that demands the face to face protocol, neither the management of gestures or body-language on scene. For example, knowing or not knowing how to dance will not affect the possibilities of the candidates. Or being nervous in front of the presence of others will not affect the performance of the virtual seduction that every user displays. On the contrary, practice of showing oneself to others counts with the possibility of making a slow, meditated and selective work in the elaboration and sharing of pictures as well as in the comments. In this way, the ability that the user has to express himself in FB, is exercised and consolidated with the use of the net.

• The approaching of strangers: is one of the newest aspects, because by sharing the contacts of 'friends of friends' (concept in FB) it's much easier to approach others that rapidly can contact themselves. Once the friend request is accepted, it is possible to elaborate an idea of the tastes and preferences of that person, see their group of friends and their families. The chat works as an intermediate instance between delayed communication and face-to-face encounters. Within the chat there is a sense of uncertainty expressed in spontaneous communication. Rapidly, a user can obtain a general scope of the tastes and preferences of a stranger from a distance.

Especially for shy people, the possibility of previous communication is an advantage. The sociability in the social network eases the trial and error without the pressure of a face-to-face situation. Said in another way, it generates less inhibition because of the 'semi-anonymity' (acquaintances of acquaintances that haven't met in person) or because interactions are not 'one to one'. At the same time, a great advantage for adolescents, which usually are less experimented in interpersonal erotic-affective relationships, is the possibility of learning through the observation of others attitudes, posts and comments. In this way, FB operates as an instance of loving socialization, since it provides contacts to interact and learn from: they are the profiles, walls and posts of their most exhibitionist, effective, popular and self-confident peers whom operate as 'style manual' and provide a guide of instructions for seduction, presentation and affective expressions, of what is liked and disliked, pictures or images and words that 'fall in love' or those that produce indifference.

To be an outstanding person in the 'virtual nightclub' one must have a high level of visibility. Adolescents know how to accomplish this: 'signing' dozens, hundreds and even thousands of timelines/walls, but above all having a lot of 'signatures' (comments), likes, subscriptions and mentions of others. This is why there is a permanent search in accomplishing this visibility, and for that they gather their peers to leave their signatures in their own timeline. This usually occurs as an interchange: you sign my wall and I'll sign yours, as observed in the following example:

The step towards a face-to-face encounter: this step usually implicates a high risk. When they meet face to face, it's much more difficult to conceal nerves, anxiety, desires and fear of rejection. Besides the fear of deception through false identities and the possibility of concrete danger by thefts and physical assaults, adolescents also fear that the person won't fulfill their expectancy generated online. In this sense, a great performance capacity is possible thanks to the network, ability that adolescents value and exploit to the maximum, comes with an important setback: the possibility of deception when they meet face to face. In other words, FB facilitates enormously the 'first approach' but, at the same time, makes it much more difficult the rupture of the tension in a face to face encounter, which adolescents declare when they express their fear of "not knowing who the other really is".

Conclusions

Just like before the massification of Internet, girls try to decode what message – and which candidates – are most suitable for dating, and the boys do their best to show them that they are the best choice. But what has changed with the popular use of 2.0 technologies and in particular with the existence of different online communities regarding neighborhood, age-based and cultural affinities? One change we observe about Internet is linked to the proliferation of desire and the variety of images of possible partners. Like a virtual nightclub (without a define body or territory), adolescents start out chatting trying to lead the relationship to a higher stage of intimacy. Therefore, social spaces such as school, parks, bars and nightclub spaces are overlap with a virtual sociability regarding FB, chat channels and instant messaging services.

We have made an exploratory journey about the seduction and matchmaking strategies carried out by LIS adolescents of the City of Buenos Aires regarding FB. We point out here the importance of digital photography used for their presentation, as well as for the sociability expressed through the comments of the pictures. We also note that the statements of 'relationship status' are central regarding relationships. We focused on the importance that adolescents give to their profiles trying to make them have high visibility and the ways they carry out this objective.

Finally, we have described the main advantages and disadvantages mentioned by LIS adolescents about meeting a couple in FB. We note here the importance of knowledge of their tastes and preferences as well as how to anticipate a first approach. We also identify the fear of meeting face to face and the lack of trust regarding what is presented as 'true' in the profiles. In conclusion, we define the social network as a 'virtual nightclub', to highlight the changes that have occurred in the ways of social interaction between adolescents regarding matchmaking.

References

Albarello, Francisco. *Leer y navegar en Internet*, Buenos Aires: La Crujía, 2011.

Bauman, Zigmunt. *Liquid Modernity*, Cambridge: Polity, 2000.

Beck, Ulrich. *Risk Society: Towards a New Modernity*, London: Sage, 1992.

Bouille, Julieta. 'Cibercafés o la nueva esquina. Usos y apropiaciones de Internet en jóvenes de sectores populares', in Urresti, M. (ed.), *Ciberculturas juveniles*, Buenos Aires: La Crujía, 2008, pp. 105-120.

Butler, Judith. *Bodies that Matter: On the Discursive Limits of "Sex"*, Cambridge: Psychology Press, 1993.

Castells, Manuel. *Communication Power*, Oxford: Oxford University Press, 2009.

Chalfen, Richard. *Snapshots Versions of Life*, Ohio: University Popular Press, 1987.

Goffman, Erving. *The Presentation of Self in Everyday Life*, New York: Anchor Books, 1959.

Igarza, Roberto. *Burbujas de Ocio*, Buenos Aires: La Crujía, 2009.

Internet World Stats, http://www.Internetworldstats.com

Linne, Joaquín. Adolescentes y redes sociales. Usos y apropiaciones de Facebook en sectores populares de la Ciudad de Buenos Aires (Adolescents & social networking. *Uses and appropiations of Facebook in low-income sectors of the City of Buenos Aires)*, Master thesis unpublished, Faculty of Social Sciences, University of Buenos Aires, Buenos Aires, 2013.

Lipovetsky, Gilles. *El crepúsculo del deber*, trans. Juana Bignozzi, Barcelona: Anagrama, 1994.

Mendelson, Andrew & Papacharissi, Zizi. 'Look at us: Collective Narcissism in College Student Facebook PhotoGalleries', in Papacharissi, Z. (ed.), *The Networked Self: Identity, Community and Culture on Social Network Sites*. Illinois: Routledge, 2010.

Morduchowicz, Roxana. *La generación multimedia. Significados, consumos y prácticas culturales de los jóvenes*, Buenos Aires: Paidós, 2008.

Piscitelli, Alejandro. *Nativos Digitales*, Buenos Aires: Santillana, 2009.

Prensky, Marc, 'Digital Natives, Digital Inmigrants', *On the Horizon*, 9.5 (2001): 1-6.

Social Bakers, socialbakers.com

Urresti, Marcelo. 'Ciberculturas juveniles: vida cotidiana, subjetividad y pertenencia entre los jóvenes ante el impacto de las nuevas tecnologías de la comunicación y la información', in Urresti, Marcelo (ed.), *Ciberculturas juveniles* (pp. 18-49). Buenos Aires: La Crujía, 2008.

'DATING' OR 'ESCAPING'? CUBAN PROFILES IN DATING WEBSITES

LÁZARO M. BACALLAO PINO

Introduction

Cuba has one of the lowest Internet access rates in Latin America. Despite the uncertainty in the available statistics of Internet access,[1] most sources agree in placing the island among the countries with the lowest rate of access in the Western Hemisphere.

For instance, according to the World Bank, 14.3 of every 100 Cubans were users of the Internet in 1999. This figure rose to 15.9 in 2010, reaching 23.2 per 100 inhabitants in 2011 and 25.6 in 2012.[2] The International Telecommunication Union (ITU), based on 2010 data, showed that there were 40,097 fixed Internet subscriptions in Cuba; it means, 0.36 fixed Internet subscriptions per 100 inhabitants.[3] Meanwhile, according United Nations (UN), based on July 2013 data, there were 9.76 Cuban users of Internet per 100 inhabitants in 2005, 11.16 in 2006, 11.69 in 2007, 12.94 in 2008, 14.33 in 2009, 15.9 in 2010, 23.23 in 2011 and 25.64 in 2012, but the UN clarifies that, for example, in 2010, only 2.9 % of the 1,702, 206 users had Internet access.[4] Officially, according to the Cuban government, there were 724,000 personal computers in Cuba in 2011, and the 65% of them were connected to networks of data with Internet access.[5]

Besides this, the prices of Internet access are extraordinarily high. For example, in June 2013, the government opened 118 public centers for Internet access that offers three kind of services at three different prices: 4.50 USD per hour of full Internet access; 1.50 USD per hour of access to the national intranet network, plus international email access; and 0.60 USD per hour of access to the national intranet network. As a Cuban blogger explained to the Spanish newspaper El País, the price of an hour of Internet access "is roughly equivalent to what I spend in a week on eating".[6]

In such a scenario, where Internet access is not only a real privilege but almost an impossible action for most people, does it make sense to have a profile on a dating website? Moreover, what would be the purpose of a profile of this type and how does the context of accessibility

---

1   Michel D. Suárez Sian, 'Cuba: Internet, acceso y sociedad del conocimiento', *Razón y Palabra* 81 (December 2013, January 2013),http://www.razonypalabra.org.mx/N/N81/M81/07_Suarez_M81.pdf.

2   The World Bank, Internet users (per 100 people), http://data.worldbank.org/indicator/IT.NET.USER.P2..

3   International Telecommunication Union, 'Fixed Internet subscriptions', Geneva 2011, http://www.itu.int/en/ITU-D/Statistics/Documents/statistics/2014/Fixed_broadband_2000-2013.xls.

4   United Nations, Indicators of the Millennium Development Goals, 2013, http://unstats.un.org/unsd/mdg/Data.aspx.

5   Pedro Oliva, *'International Internet Connectivity (IIC) - Individual Country and Organization Experiences'*, Geneva, January 23-24, 2012, http://www.itu.int/ITU-D/finance/work-cost-tariffs/events/tariff-seminars/Geneva-IIC/pdf/Session4_P3_Oliva-sp.pdf.

6   Maye Primera, 'Internet cubano a precios del "imperio"', *El País*, June 5, 2013, http://internacional.elpais.com/internacional/2013/06/05/actualidad/1370398720_289648.html.

influence their characteristics and dynamics? But, besides that specific digital context, there is a particular Cuban socio-political environment regarding the Internet access, characterized by the official emphasis on a "social use" of the World Wide Web, providing Internet access mainly from universities, official media and other governmental institutions, it is, from institutions and activities related to education, research, governmental politics and media. Then, another relevant question would be: does such an over politicization of the use of Internet and that "social" perspective of it mediate its private uses in the case of Cuban profiles in online dating sites? If yes, how does it mediate the discourses and practices of the users?

These issues are added to the existing debates on dating websites, particularly those related to the user behaviour, the presentation of the self on Internet dating sites, the narratives and attractiveness of the profiles, the veracity in online dating self-representations and the interrelationships between truth and lie on it, or the comparisons between online dating and conventional offline dating. For instance, whether online dating dynamics are fundamentally different from offline ones, or if it promotes better romantic outcomes. All those issues are, in the Cuban case, mediated by the above mentioned specificities of the context. We aim to analyze that mediation: how does it influence the configuration of the profiles, to what extend that mediation plays a central role in the dynamics of online courtship, or its presence in the narratives and representations mobilized on the profiles.

Methods and Techniques of Research

The analysis of online dating websites sets a number of methodological challenges. The complexity of the issue recommends a qualitative approach, mainly based on the discourse analysis of the profiles and, when possible, email interviews with the users.[7] A qualitative perspective is appropriate for the proposed analysis, since it offers an insider's view of the subject of research and descriptions that suggest possible interrelationships, explain causes and effects and describe dynamic processes.[8] The importance of the context for qualitative research and its holistic perspective[9] -seeing the experience as a whole-, and its interpretative approach[10] are also significant for the theme to be examined, due to the singularities of the scenario of research, both digital and sociopolitical ones. At the same time, the flexibility and contextualized way in which should be conducted qualitative research, as well as its critical enquiry approach,[11] will permit to deal with the inherent complexity of the topic of research.

Since there are no specifically Cuban websites for online dating, we will analyze Cuban profiles at two international dating websites: Connectingsingles.com and Datehookup.com. We will also include the only Cuban classified ads site, called Revolico.com.[12] As we will see,

---

7   There was a really low response rate (20%). Only two users replied to messages from the author.
8   Robert B. Burns, *Introduction to Research Methods*, London: Sage, 2000.
9   Margaret Ely, Margot Anzul, Teri Friedman, Diane Garner and Ann Mccormack-Steinmetz, *Doing Qualitative Research: Circles within Circles*, London: Falmer, 1991.
10 Norman K. Denzin and Yvonna S. Lincoln, *Handbook of Qualitative Research*, Thousand Oaks, CA: Sage, 1994.
11 Jennifer Mason, *Qualitative Researching*, London: Sage, 1996.
12 In Cuba, the word *revolico* means "confusion", "hubbub" or "disorder". It is often used to refer to a group of

although it is not a dating website, and it does not have a particular section of dating or contacts, we can find a few announcements of that kind. Its inclusion will allow us to have a case to compare Cuban profiles in dating websites with listings of contact with a more explicit sexual purpose, which is relevant for the analysis of the first.

Mediation of 'the Cuban Condition' in Profiles from Cuba in Dating Websites

Relationships between real and virtual worlds -or, better, between the social, cultural, economic and political context of individuals and their behaviours in digital scenarios- have been a critical topic of research in the field of the appropriations of information and communication technologies (ICTs). From the distinction among "virtual reality" and "real virtuality on its complex interrelationships and the proposal of "real virtuality" as the specificity of ICTs,[13] to the exam of the implications of mapping the social onto the digital and vice versa, or the study of the efficacy of digital connectivity on some specific social practices and its articulation with other social networks,[14] there is a really extensive and multidimensional field of research on these relationships.

In this study, the analysis of the context is a relevant dimension, given the scenario from which Cuban profiles in dating websites are generated. This Cuban condition has both a specific technological dimension – previously described on its general aspects-, and a socio-economic and political one.

Since the 90s, Cuban society is experiencing a deep crisis whose origin is in the fall of socialism in the Soviet Union and the important consequences it had on special for the Cuban economy, beginning what was named the "Special Period", characterized by serious real-life economic problems, especially a significant scarcity of products, increasing prices and a loss of the real value of the national currency. In macro-economic terms,

> the end of economic aid and drastic reduction in commerce with the vanished socialist camp, preceded by errors and frequent changes in domestic economic policies, caused a 35% drop in GDP between 1989 and 1993, a 78% decrease in real social expenditures per capita, an increase in unemployment to 8%, and a deterioration in social indicators.[15]

Although according to some economic analyses there was a period of economic upturn between 2011 and 2008, internal factors and the global economic crisis have hit Cuban economy, affecting macro-economic indicators, such as a severe slowdown in growth and the contraction of external financing. As a result, Cuba's social assistance programme has

---

things that are put together, but without an explicit or obvious order.
13   Manuel Castells, *The Rise of the Network Society*, Cambridge, MA, USA: Blackwell Publishers Inc., 1996.
14   Haidy Geismar and William Mohns, 'Social Relationships and Digital Relationships: Rethinking the Database at the Vanuatu Cultural Centre', *Journal of the Royal Anthropological Institute* 17, Issue Supplement s1 (May, 2011):133–155.
15   Carmelo Mesa-Lago and Pavel Vidal-Alejandro, 'The Impact of the Global Crisis on Cuba's Economy and Social Welfare', *Journal of Latin American Studies* 42 (2010), p. 692.

deteriorated, in a process reinforced by the key weaknesses in the provision of social services. The new scenario has had the adverse social effects and there is a consensus on the governmental incapacity to sustain the growing cost of social services in the future.[16]

That economic climate generates a number of social phenomena, such as the low labour motivation in those jobs with no access to incomes in Cuban Convertible Peso (CUC),[17] an important activity in the underground economy, a significant migration of skilled and university professionals who also shifted their state occupations to low skill jobs in enterprises with foreign capital or in tourism that provide formal or informal access to CUC, a decrease interest of the younger generation in higher education, or the increase of tourist-based dollar prostitution, practised even by university educated women and men.[18]

Besides that economic context and its social consequences, the Cuban scenario is also characterized by a singular political climate -just one legal party system, the governing Communist Cuban Party, the lack of legal recognition to the political opposition, or the state ownership of the media-, and, what is more relevant to the analysis, an extensive and permanent state intervention and impediment on social practices. Even the Cuban highest rulers have recognized that "the State does not have to get into anything that is attempting to regulate the relationships between individuals".[19]

However, in Cuba there were a number of prohibitions as the buying and selling of homes or private cars, or the need of an official permission to travel abroad, which are being gradually eliminated and which are clear examples of the excessive state intervention in the private lives of individuals. But, instead of a total regime of social control, some authors have argued that the system's effectiveness is based on formal and informal social control mechanisms that "simultaneously emphasize openness and rigidity",[20] combining both freedom and restraint.

In this technological, economic and sociopolitical context, it is not surprising that there are really few Cuban profiles on dating websites. Difficulties on access to Internet -due to the low level of Internet penetration, as well as the high prices- become, at first instance, a barrier that impedes the regular Internet access of individuals. But, precisely because of this circumstance, the presence of those few profiles is a significant symptom of the resistance to those obstacles and the great interest of the users to access this type of websites. In a context signed by the (ghost of a) permanent and ubiquitous social surveillance -and,

---

16 Mesa-Lago and Vidal-Alejandro, 'The Impact of the Global Crisis on Cuba's Economy and Social Welfare'.
17 In Cuba, there are two local currencies: the Cuban Peso (CUP) and the Cuban Convertible Peso (CUC). There is an official exchange rate of 25 CUP for 1 CUC, which has parity with the U.S. dollar.
18 Susan Eckstein, 'Dollarization and Its Discontents: Remittances and the Remaking of Cuba in the Post-Soviet', *Comparative Politics* 36(3) (April, 2004): 313-330.
19 Raúl Castro Ruz, 'Speech at the Sixth Ordinary Session of the Seventh Legislature of the National Assembly of People's Power', 18 December 2010, http://bvs.sld.cu/revistas/infd/n1311/infd1213.htm.
20 Benigno E. Aguirre, 'Social Control in Cuba', *Latin American Politics and Society* 44(2) (Summer, 2002): 67-98.

consequently, also a digital one-, the act of having a profile in a dating website becomes an explicit defiance to any control. But, unlike the public and more explicitly political defiance set for instance by the blogs created by independent journalists-, this is a defiance from the individual and private dimension. There are no direct references to political issues in Cuban profiles in online dating websites.

A total of 135 Cuban profiles were found in the online dating websites analysed. Of this total, 59.26% are profiles of men (looking for a woman or another man) and 40.74% are women (looking for a man). These low figures and the low frequency of connecting users confirm the difficulties in accessing the Internet. In the case of women, only 9.09% were active within the last 24 hours, 29.09% were active within four weeks and the rest (61.82%) were active over one month ago. Meanwhile, in the case of men's profiles, 6.25% were active within the last 24 hours, 28.75% of them were active within four weeks and the rest (65%) were active over one month ago.

To this low frequency of access, another fact is added: the Cuban profiles are found only in those dating websites that offer a completely free service. Here the economic dimension has an explicit influence on that trend, coherently with the before described economic scenario and the high prices of Internet access. The economic dimension has then a direct effect on one of the most important aspects linked to the uses of ICTs: the immediacy and even the permanent connectivity, increased worldwide by the Internet access from smartphones.[21] Aware of the necessity of that continuity, Cuban users with profiles in online dating sites include in some cases other contact information –such as email addresses or even telephone numbers-, maybe foreseeing the possibility of losing temporarily -or even permanently- their Internet access.

Privacy has been one of the most important concerns of Internet users from the first moments of the World Wide Web to current social networks.[22] Then, it is particularly relevant that some users provide private data such as email or telephone, especially because the open and free nature of the websites they select. This allows anyone, even without being a member of the site, to access that information. Here, the Cuban condition becomes, at the same, the cause of the need to provide private data publicly, but also, according to the subjects, a certain source of protection against this situation. Asked about it, a Cuban woman with a profile in one of those sites considers that since "almost no one in Cuba has access to the Internet, it is difficult for me to be bothered by Cubans. Besides, nobody will call to Cuba from abroad if he has no real interest, because phone calls are very expensive".[23]

---

21 From Mach 8th, 2014, Cuban users can access to their email accounts (only to those at the domain nauta.cu) from their mobile phones. There is no access to the Internet from mobile phones. See *El País*, http://economia.elpais.com/economia/2014/03/08/agencias/1394298476_945195.html.

22 Joshua Fogela and Elham Nehmad, 'Internet social network communities: Risk taking, trust, and privacy concerns', *Computers in Human Behavior* 25 (January, 2009): 153-160, 10.1016/j.chb.2008.08.006

23 Interview by email with Cuban woman with a profile in http://www.connectingsingles.com. Translation by the author.

The Cuban condition – mainly its technological dimension and the difficult Internet access-becomes this way a source of safety, at least in the opinion of the subjects. But, while some individuals make public their private data, other ones even prefer not to publish his/her pictures. Among woman, 21.82% of them does not include a picture on their profiles, while 23.75% of men's profiles does not have photos. None of the users without picture answered the question about why they not include it in their profiles, however, it could be deduced that this decision is related to the preservation of privacy and personal identity.

Profiles photographs are "a central component of online self-presentation, and one that is critical for relational success".[24] As previous studies have demonstrated, users prefer to look at a profile that contains a picture, that also are contacted about seven times more often than those that do not have it.[25] Cubans profiles in the analysed dating websites confirm this importance, since none of the profiles without photos have friends and either comments, that are possible only if associated to pictures in the case of Connectingsingles.com.

While the absence of pictures in some profiles could be understood as a strategy against social control "inside" Cuba, the fact that the majority of Cuban profiles are in English -only five of them are in Spanish-, confirms there is an explicit "outside" projection and it proves that they are mainly looking for a relationship with a foreigner. In some cases, there is an explicit call for "some person" who can be "interested in come to Cuba"[26] to meet singles; in other cases, it says that there is a particular special interest in a certain country so the person have interest in meeting people from that country: "I am searching for friendship and something else, I love Finland and I want to meet people there".[27] Here the inside/outside divide does not have (only) a technological nature but a socio-economic and even geographical one. In fact, that orientation towards daters located outside Cuba shows the strength of that divide, bringing to our minds the -poetically speaking-, "damned circumstance of water everywhere".[28]

But beyond that poetic image, the relationship of Cuban people with the "outside" has been complex since 1959. The triumph of the Cuban Revolution marks a different and rich pattern for studying external migration processes and their relationships with political and social conflicts. The main destination of Cuban emigration after 1959 has been the United States and the phenomenon has been characterized by different migration crisis (1959-60, 1980, 1994). Some authors have argued that Cuban emigration, usually interpreted as a political exile, has moved towards a process of economic nature and associate to family reunification.[29] An

---

24 Jeffrey T. Hancock and Catalina L. Toma, 'Putting Your Best Face Forward: The Accuracy of Online Dating Photographs', *Journal of Communication* 59 (2009), p. 368

25 Lee Humphreys, 'Photographs and the Presentation of Self through Online Dating Services', Paper presented at the National Communication Association, Chicago, IL, 2004.

26 Cuban woman profile from http://www.connectingsingles.com.

27 Cuban woman profile from http://www.connectingsingles.com.

28 Virgilio Piñera, 'La Isla en peso', in Antón Arrufat (comp.) Virgilio Piñera. *Poesía y crítica, México, Cien del Mundo, Consejo Nacional para la Cultura y las Artes*, 1980, p. 45.

29 Lourdes de Urrutia Barroso, 'Aproximación a un análisis del proceso migratorio cubano', *Papers* 52

analysis of the socio-demographic characteristics of Cuban migrant shows that, in the case of legal migration, there is a balanced ratio between males and females (53% and 47% respectively), while in the case of illegal departures, about 80 % are men. Other important tendencies are the predominance of young people between illegal Cuban migrants as well as the increasing educational level of migrating people.[30]

Besides the geographical condition -an island, isolated, that naturally marks the difference between inside and outside spaces- and the peculiar relevance of the migratory process after 1959, there are other circumstances that reinforce that inside/outside differentiation. For instance, the restrictions on travel abroad for Cuban citizens, slightly flexibilized by the reform of immigration policy in January 2013. Cubans are located -at least in the official discourse- outside capitalism. In such a context, the inside/outside divide becomes a matter of real and practical sense, expressed -in the case of profiles in dating websites- in the clear and even explicit orientation towards foreigners as potential partners.

Given the difficulties of access to the Internet, it does not seem to make sense that Cuban people use these kind of websites for dating between them. As a woman confesses, "it makes no sense to seek Cuban partner through these sites. Very few of us have access to Internet. […] I will not spend money on Internet access to find a Cuban man".[31] In conclusion, both the economic dimension and the technological one play a central role in the perspective from which the Cubans become members of dating websites. Internet access limitations and economic difficulties restrict the possibilities of having a profile in that kind of sites, focusing -when it is possible to access it- in foreigners as main target group. Having a profile in dating websites could be seen, then, as a certain kind of investment.

That outside or foreigner-oriented tendency is confirmed or reinforced by the presence of a number of profiles of women or men who declare to work at the sector of tourism. That is, they are people who are in regular contact with foreigners, as part of their daily work. This circumstance explains, on one hand, that these people have income levels that would allow them to access the Internet and, in the other hand, that they have perhaps more real chances to aspire to find a foreign partner. A person who works in that sector would have, probably, a more foreigner-oriented attitude, so having a profile in a dating website would be a complementary way for meeting people from abroad.

At some point, the interrelationships between personal and commercial interests even become absolute. We can find a profile that belongs not to a person, but to an enterprise: a private tourist agency called Club Friendship Cuba. The profile includes a full physical description (age, height, body type, ethnicity, religious or marital status), since these data are required to create a profile, but in fact the profile is used for advertising the services offered by a private company, in a context where there is no access to that resources for this kind

---

(1997): 49-56.
30 Urrutia Barroso, 'Aproximación a un análisis del proceso migratorio cubano'.
31 Interview by email with Cuban woman with a profile in http://www.connectingsingles.com. Translation by the author.

of enterprises, given the state monopoly in the sector. Something unimaginable in another context -the creation of a profile on a dating site by a company to advertise it-, it shows, in an extreme way, the uniqueness of the appropriation that Cubans do of this kind of websites and its clearly external orientation, as part of an inside/outside divide.

Self-representation of Cuban Profiles in Dating Websites

Self-representation is a critical issue for profiles in online dating, as previous studies have demonstrated.[32] That authors have noted, for instance, the complex interrelationships between the individuals' concerns with a favourable self-representation as well as a good impression, and a less honest behaviour in configuring their profiles, controlling their self-disclosure by presenting themselves in a more positive way and being less inclined to reveal what could be considered a negative aspect. With this being said, there is an intentional process of construction of a profile based on a more deliberate, controlled, and perhaps idealized self-presentation, taking advantage of the reduced cues and asynchronous nature of computer-mediated communication (CMC).[33]

This intentional construction of the self is associated to a tendency towards having more strategic success, benefiting those users whose profiles are more attractive, desirable, and even idealized as a result of their process of configuration. This behaviour leads us to a particularly relevant issue: the relationships between truth and falsehood in building profiles on dating websites or, in other terms, the deception of the process, defining it from a broad point of view, as "the intentional misrepresentation of information", that "can take a variety of forms, from outright lying to exaggeration".[34] In fact, as the study conducted by those authors points out, deception is a frequent trend in users of dating websites, since about 81% of them lied on at least one of the assessed variables (height, weight and age). However, with few exceptions, most of the subjects altered the information in a very slight way, as if it were acceptable to do so only to a certain point.

Certainly, the aforementioned characteristics of the CMC facilitate, to some point, the deception, since individuals are aware of it and, at the same time, they want to create attractive self-presentations since they are trying to manage the impressions they create in the other users through the profiles they construct.[35] But, in reality, certain level of deception crosses all social interactions, as a practice of package and edition of the self in order to favourably impress the others.[36] It becomes, this way, an everyday praxis and, therefore, the other individuals are prevented about it (since, probably, they follow the same scheme of quotidian action).

---

32 Jennifer L. Gibbs, Nicole B. Ellison and Rebecca D. Heino, 'Self-Presentation in Online Personals: The Role of Anticipated Future Interaction, Self-Disclosure, and Perceived Success in Internet Dating', *Communication Research* 33 (2006):152-177 DOI: 10.1177/0093650205285368.

33 Joseph B. Walther, 'Computer-mediated communication: Impersonal, interpersonal, and hyperpersonal interaction', *Communication Research* 23 (1996): 3-44.

34 Jeffrey T. Hancock, Catalina Toma and Nicole Ellison, 'The Truth about Lying in Online Dating Profiles', *CHI 2007 Proceedings Online Representation of Self*, San Jose, CA, USA April 28-May 3, 2007, p. 452.

35 Jeffrey T. Hancock, Catalina Toma and Nicole Ellison, 'The Truth about Lying in Online Dating Profiles'.

36 Erving Goffman, *The Presentation of Self in Everyday Life*, New York: Anchor, 1959.

Given that general (theoretical) scenario, it is relevant to examine the narratives mobilized by -and the specificities of- Cuban profiles in dating websites: descriptions presented, topics underlined, values declared, dimensions highlighted, or issues not revealed. The foreigners-oriented nature of the Cuban profiles in dating websites would become a core mediation in the narratives used for the construction of profiles and, consequently, in the self-presentation they do.

It seems that users are aware of the possible image that people from abroad can have about intentions linked to prostitution or, at least, to certain economic interest in those Cubans who create profiles in dating websites. Given the articulation between economic scarcity, the raise of tourism as activity during the 90s, and the increase of prostitution, one of the most important issues faced by the subjects would be to create a profile that moves away from any suspicion of prostitution or economic interest, especially since they are profiles created with a clear orientation towards foreigners as possible partners to meet.

While this is the tendency in sites such as Connectingsingles.com, in the case of the announcements of contacts published in Revolico.com, there are more direct and explicit references to be looking for some kind of sexual service by tourists or foreign residents in Cuba, or to be offering the service by Cubans. Also in the case of this website there are very few ads of this type but a higher percentage of them makes reference to that purpose. Between January 1st and February 28, 2014, a total of 2,786 ads were published in the section "others",[37] at Revolico.com, and only 14 of them were related to searching for contacts or dating. Seven of those ads were published by foreigners -tourists or residents in Cuba- who were looking either for some "temporal companion" or escort during their travel to Cuba. The other 50% of those announcements were published by Cuban people looking for sexual encounters or offering their service as escorts; any of them was looking for a formal relationship.

Since here the economic interest is explicit, then the self-presentation of both the "costumers" and the "provider" of the services are direct in those announcements: there is no need of hiding the existence of an interest. Foreigners looking for escorts or a temporary companion then emphasize aspects such as the age and physical characteristics of the persons they are looking for, ask for the possibility of sending pictures and underline their economic solvency. In turn, those who offer themselves as escorts, not only highlight their attractiveness but also they present themselves as nice, funny, serious people.

Contrary to this explicit statement of economic interest present in announcements published at Revolico.com, in the case of profiles on dating websites such as Connectingsingles.com, users try precisely to avoid being seen as "interested" persons who are trying to use some foreigner for "escaping" from Cuba by the way of marriage. In that sense, they develop some narrative strategies and underline certain aspects on their self-presentations that could be considered as common scripts for creating an adequate image of the self.

Most of the Cuban profiles frequently highlight on their description a number of personal hu-

---

37   There is no specific contact section on this website.

man values, such as honesty, sincerity, generosity, optimism, loyalty, happiness, modesty, seriousness and sensibility. This long inventory of values also includes being studious, romantic, loving and passionate. But, similarly to the self-presentation, those characteristics are used also to describe the person they are looking for: an affectionate one, a wonderful, genuine, working, true-hearted, responsible, sweet, graceful, hopeful and good person. Definition of the self can also be stated in terms of a confrontation between those things that one loves -"altruism, comprehension, truth, smile to everybody, to work and to be (in the future) good father and husband"- and the ones hated -"injustice, hypocrisy, lies, treason, inequality, egoism, dishonesty, vanity, lack of understanding and all kind of vices".[38] The image of perfection, in the case of men, reaches even to the point of trying to avoid seeming a male chauvinist, saying that he is "able to make any woman happy, [since] especially I like to cook and help my partner".[39]

There is a certain continuity between the description of the self and the description of the person wanted to de found: "I am an honest man and I am looking for an special woman like me".[40] Consistently, an almost perfect person -according to her/his self-presentation- then will desire to meet the perfect man/woman, "a person who also wants to find the perfect match".[41] Here the self and the otherness go together as part of that narrative strategy in the construction of profiles.

Coherently with those descriptions, there are a number of themes that recurs in the Cuban profiles. One theme is romanticism: most profiles state their desire of finding the true love: "I am here waiting to find my love, I know that is so difficult but not impossible, in somewhere there is this special love".[42] Usually, profiles include some romantic scenes on their characterisation, such as the commonplace of "to watch the sunset" or "to see the Moon together", or "to take nice walks together",[43] "the stars shining, the birds flying, the sea, the mountains, a blue sky, fresh air […] we must take advantage from these pleasant things everyday as a last time".[44]

At the same time, they usually underline the seriousness of their purpose, highlighting that they are looking for "a serious relationship". There are explicit mentions of the possibility of marriage and future plans, including to have a family, as well as references to not being on the dating website "to play bad games or help scammers to do their work".[45] "I am looking for a man to build a stable relationship and give him all of me. Please I would like to receive messages only from people who are interested in looking for a serious relationship in a

---

38 Cuban man profile from http://www.connectingsingles.com.
39 Cuban man profile from http://www.connectingsingles.com.
40 Cuban man profile from Connectingsingles.com.
41 Cuban woman profile from Connectingsingles.com.
42 Cuban man profile from Connectingsingles.com.
43 Cuban woman profile from Connectingsingles.com.
44 Cuban man profile from Connectingsingles.com.
45 Cuban woman profile from Connectingsingles.com.

long term",[46] states a profile, while other says that his plans is "to be a good father a a good husband in the future".[47] In that sense, someone confesses -underlining his intention to find a longterm relationship as well as the importance of feelings-, that currently he has no girlfriend because is "tired of meaningless, just physical, short relationships".[48]

Another frequent issue included in self-presentations is the incorporation of elements for making the profiles more "human". This way, some profiles include personal details such as the sons and daughters the person has, or mention that his/her parents have passed away and s/he is "alone in my country".[49] In other cases, when explaining the reasons for creating a profile, there are references to certain personal situation involving precisely a previous painful relationship: "I am in this site because I am going through a very difficult step of my relationship, the broke-up".[50] This way, self-presentations include touching stories that not only would humanize profiles, but could also generate compassion and a desire to help in those people reading it. In that sense, a woman describe the person she is looking for as "someone that enjoys a good joke as well as sharing the problems in life",[51] in a clear reference to the well-known phrase of the marriage ceremony: "in good times, in bad, for richer, for poorer, in sickness and in health".

Communicational dimension is another question included in some profiles, both in self-presentation and in the description of the person looking to meet. Thus, individuals are described as talkative persons, wanting to "meet people that love to have a conversation, by email, phone or whatever",[52] "someone friendly that enjoys communication"[53] or "a sincere person, easy to talk to, [who] takes as well as gives from a relation".[54] Also men include that dimension on their description, considering that one of the most important thing in a couple "must be communication for all agreement, plans, preferences, and ways to go, all in all...to be as a same person".[55] This is not surprising, since those websites are, precisely, a space of communicative nature where, in the first instance, a communicative relationship will be established between subjects. Then, that dimension would be central for the relations by these ICTs-based resources.

All those aspects -romanticism, serious purposes, future plans, and so on- are elements of a narrative strategy for avoiding any possible association to prostitution, a likely trend since Cubans profiles focus specifically towards foreigners as potential partners. As part of that

---

46   Cuban man profile from Connectingsingles.com.
47   Cuban man profile from Connectingsingles.com.
48   Cuban man profile from Connectingsingles.com.
49   Cuban woman profile from Connectingsingles.com.
50   Cuban woman profile from Connectingsingles.com.
51   Cuban woman profile from Connectingsingles.com.
52   Cuban woman profile from Connectingsingles.com.
53   Cuban woman profile from Connectingsingles.com.
54   Cuban woman profile from Connectingsingles.com.
55   Cuban man profile from Connectingsingles.com.

effort, it is also relevant that only two profiles answer the question about incomes, included in the data to be completed as part of the profile, and just one profile refers to the well-established position of the person on her career and her position of financial security, "with a job I enjoy".[56] On the other side, in some case, there is an explicit reference to the economic dimension, but denying any interest: "I don't have money and I am not here looking for money".[57] Although some authors have suggested that those persons involved in prostitution in Cuba -called *jineteras* and *jineteros*- do not identify themselves as prostitutes but "as being *en la lucha* (being in the struggle of daily survival to procure essential food and goods) or simply *resolviendo* (taking care of daily basic needs due to the scarcity of consumer goods in the island)", there is a consistent strategy and a narrative effort in Cuban profiles at dating websites for avoiding any association with prostitution or economic interest.

Besides the mediation of that dimension in the self-presentation of Cuba profiles, the other aspect that is explicit mentioned by a number of users is the technological one. It is also used as an argument for reinforcing the seriousness of the profile's purposes. For instance, the difficulties for accessing Internet are mentioned, explaining that "we have not time on-line for a game",[58] telling this way that s/he is looking for something "real" and serios. Another profile explains that "I also have troubles in the Internet connection. I am not all the time online, and it's difficult for me to chat online, due to the limited economic resources of my country as well. For Cubans it's forbidden Skype or webcam chat".[59] This way, the technological aspect is included as part of the self-presentation, both for underlining the limitations of the CMC in the case of Cubans profiles -an important issue, since average users expect to pass from the exchange of messages by those websites to some more multimedia communication, such as chat or Skype, before definitely passing to a face-to-face scenario-, and for insisting in the seriousness of the individual's purposes.

Conclusions

Self-presentation in Cuban profiles on dating websites are mediated by the Cuban condition, particularly its technological and socio-economical and political dimensions. Given the difficulties for Internet access and the economic situation, the are few Cuban profiles in those kind of websites and they are present mainly in those ones that offer a complete free service. This circumstance sets a particularly challenge to them, since all the information is available even for those persons who do not have a profile on these websites, creating a dilemma regarding privacy. This dilemma, however, is only explicit in a few profiles that prevent to post pictures, while most of them even include information such as mobile numbers, in order to facilitate communication in a context where losing the Internet connection is a permanent possibility.

There is a clear and significant difference between those announcements offering or demanding sexual services that recognize it, and those profiles in dating websites that, to the

---

56 Cuban woman profile from Connectingsingles.com.
57 Cuban woman profile from Datehookup.com.
58 Cuban woman profile from Connectingsingles.com.
59 Cuban woman profile from Connectingsingles.com.

contrary, try to avoid any suspicion of economic interest or link with prostitution, as well as avoid any possible perception that their intention is to use a foreign persons to "escape" from the island. Given that the majority of Cuban profiles in dating websites have a clear orientation towards foreigners as potential partners; this outside-direction can easily be associated to some economic interest or association with prostitution practices. That is why the economic dimension is carefully avoided or explicitly denied by some profiles.

All narrative strategies in self-presentation aim to avoid that association, building an ideal, almost perfect image of both the self and the other that is being sought. Precisely, one of the arguments used to underline the serious purposes of the person behind the profile, is the difficulty for accessing the Internet; it is, the technological dimension. It also limits the possibilities of passing from the exchange of messages by the dating website to other ICTs-based channels of multimedia communication, such as Skype. That limitation could probably be associated also to the effort made for building a more convincing self-presentation.

Human values included in the description, the emphasis on feelings or the recurring romantic images, all of it are elements of the narrative strategy developed for an ideal presentation of the self in Cuban profiles, to the point that sometimes there could be a certain suspicion about some exaggerations or even lies in the image of the self presented. It is relevant that such a private use of Internet does not include any reference to the context of social control and hegemonic perspective of a social use of Internet. Here the overpoliticization of Internet, a permanent issue in other communicative spaces from Cuba such as independent blogs, is silenced.

Instead of references to political issues in the presentation of self, it is preferred to present a description that explains why Cubans do not consider dating websites as resources for looking for a relationship with other inhabitants of the island and they focus their profiles towards foreigners as potential partners. In that sense, as we have seen, the technological dimension -articulated with the economic issue- becomes the core mediation in the presentation of the self by Cubans in dating websites, both on its content and its dynamics.

References

Aguirre, Benigno E. 'Social Control in Cuba', *Latin American Politics and Society* 44(2) (Summer, 2002): 67-98.

Burns, Robert B. *Introduction to Research Methods*, London: Sage, 2000.

Castells, Manuel. *The Rise of the Network Society*, Cambridge, MA, USA: Blackwell Publishers, Inc., 1996.

Castro Ruz, Raúl. 'Speech at the Sixth Ordinary Session of the Seventh Legislature of the National Assembly of People's Power', December 18, 2010, http://bvs.sld.cu/revistas/infd/n1311/infd1213.htm.

Eckstein, Susan. 'Dollarization and Its Discontents: Remittances and the Remaking of Cuba in the Post-Soviet', *Comparative Politics* 36(3) (April, 2004): 313-330.

Ely, Margaret, Anzul, Margot, Friedman, Teri, Garner, Diane and Mccormack-Steinmetz, Ann. *Doing Qualitative Research: Circles within Circles*, London: Falmer, 1991.

Fogela, Joshua and Nehmad, Elham. 'Internet social network communities: Risk taking, trust, and privacy concerns', *Computers in Human Behavior* 25 (January, 2009): 153-160.

Geismar, Haidy and Mohns, William. 'Social Relationships and Digital Relationships: Rethinking the Database at the Vanuatu Cultural Centre', *Journal of the Royal Anthropological Institute* 17, Issue Supplement s1 (May, 2011):133–155. DOI: 10.1111/j.1467-9655.2011.01693.x.

Gibbs, Jennifer L., Ellison, Nicole B. and Heino, Rebecca D. 'Self-Presentation in Online Personals: The Role of Anticipated Future Interaction, Self-Disclosure, and Perceived Success in Internet Dating', *Communication Research* 33 (2006):152-177 DOI: 10.1177/0093650205285368.

Goffman, Erving. *The Presentation of Self in Everyday Life*, New York: Anchor, 1959.

Hancock, Jeffrey T. and Toma, Catalina L. 'Putting Your Best Face Forward: The Accuracy of Online Dating Photographs', *Journal of Communication* 59 (2009): 367–386.

Hancock, Jeffrey T., Toma, Catalina and Ellison, Nicole. 'The Truth about Lying in Online Dating Profiles', *CHI 2007 Proceedings Online Representation of Self*, San Jose, CA, USA April 28-May 3, 2007: 449-452.

Humphreys, Lee. 'Photographs and the Presentation of Self through Online Dating Services', Paper presented at the National Communication Association, Chicago, IL, 2004.

International Telecommunication Union, 'Fixed Internet subscriptions', Geneva 2011, http://www.itu.int/ITU-D/ict/statistics/material/excel/2010/FixedInternetSubscriptions_00-10.xls.

Mason, Jennifer. *Qualitative Researching*, London: Sage, 1996.

Mesa-Lago, Carmelo and Vidal-Alejandro, Pavel. 'The Impact of the Global Crisis on Cuba's Economy and Social Welfare', *Journal of Latin American Studies* 42 (2010): 689-717. doi:10.1017/S0022216X10001331

Norman K. Denzin and Yvonna S. Lincoln, *Handbook of Qualitative Research*, Thousand Oaks, CA: Sage, 1994.

Oliva, Pedro. 'International Internet Connectivity (IIC) - Individual Country and Organization Experiences', Geneva, January 23-24, 2012, http://www.itu.int/ITU-D/finance/work-cost-tariffs/events/tariff-seminars/Geneva-IIC/pdf/Session4_P3_Oliva-sp.pdf

Piñera, Virgilio. 'La Isla en peso', in Antón Arrufat (comp.) Virgilio Piñera. *Poesía y crítica, México, Cien del Mundo, Consejo Nacional para la Cultura y las Artes*, 1980, pp. 45-57.

Primera, Maye. 'Internet cubano a precios del "imperio"', *El País*, June 5, 2013, http://internacional.elpais.com/internacional/2013/06/05/actualidad/1370398720_289648.html

Suárez Sian, Michel D. 'Cuba: Internet, acceso y sociedad del conocimiento', *Razón y Palabra* 81 (December 2013, January 2013), http://www.razonypalabra.org.mx/N/N81/M81/07_Suarez_M81.pdf.

The World Bank, Internet users (per 100 people), data.worldbank.org

United Nations, Indicators of the Millennium Development Goals, 2013, http://unstats.un.org/unsd/mdg/Data.aspx.

Urrutia Barroso, Lourdes de. 'Aproximación a un análisis del proceso migratorio cubano', *Papers* 52 (1997): 49-56.

Walther, Joseph B. 'Computer-mediated communication: Impersonal, interpersonal, and hyperpersonal interaction', *Communication Research* 23 (1996): 3-44.

SELF-PRESENTATION IN THE PORTUGUESE ONLINE DATING SCENE: DOES GENDER MATTER?

CLÁUDIA CASIMIRO

Man is least himself when he talks in his own person. Give him a mask, and he will tell you the truth. — Oscar Wilde

Introduction

Two decades ago, *Time* magazine, in an issue entitled 'The strange new world of the Internet', pointed out why the Internet would never go mainstream: "It was not designed for doing commerce, and it does not gracefully accommodate new arrivals."[1] The prediction could not have been more wrong. As argued by numerous authors, the reality shows that not only the Internet became very popular but it also represents a tremendous change in society. It could be argued that the Internet has brought about societal implications to the magnitude of the industrial revolution or the printing press.[2] Not only does the Internet pursue organizational and commercial purposes, but its sociability and communication features - "the *relational* Internet": practices in which people engage to interact and share information and meaning[3] - are high and will likely increase.[4]

Computer-mediated communication (CMC) through email, audio and video, has become a commonplace tool in the industrialized countries, allowing for the contact between more people, more often and through increasingly diversified channels, giving rise to a new form of social organization: the *network society*.[5] "A network of relationships, weak ties or intimate that occurs in [different] environments (...) the constant interaction between online and offline spaces".[6] Among these, online dating sites claim a prominent role in the social and love life of millions of individuals in many different countries.

Over the past few years, networking sites and particularly cyberdating, "the process of getting to know someone online via the Internet before transferring the relationship to offline or face-to-face interaction",[7] have been a growing area of research. Scholars from a variety of academic disciplines such as communication studies, psychology and sociology, making

---

1   Kevin Kelly, 'We Are the Web', *Wired*, August 2005, http://archive.wired.com/wired/archive/13.08/tech.html.
2   Gustavo Cardoso et al. (eds) *World Wide Internet: Changing Societies, Economies and Culture*. China: University of Macau, 2009, p. 4.
3   Leah A. Lievrouw, 'The Next Decade in Internet Time', *Information, Communication & Society* (2012): 616.
4   Millsom S. Henry-Waring and Jo Barraket, 'Dating & Intimacy in the 21st Century: The Use of Online Dating Sites in Australia', *International Journal of Emerging Technologies and Society* 6 (1): 14-33.
5   Manuel Castells, *The Network Society: A Cross-Cultural Perspective*, Cheltenham, UK: Edward Elgar Pub, 2004.
6   Gustavo Cardoso, 'Feel Like Going Online?' Internet Mediated Communication in Portugal', *Information, Communication & Society* 5.4 (2002): 529.
7   Andrea J. Baker, 'Cyberdating', in Karen Christensen and David Levinson (eds) *Encyclopedia of Community: From the Village to the Virtual World*, Thousand Oaks, CA: Sage Publications, 2003, p. 372.

use of distinct approaches, models and theories, have shown interest for the analysis of a myriad of issues linked with: self-presentation strategies and mate preferences; online communication and attraction; sincerity and deception; trust and privacy; self-disclosure; identity; sexuality; infidelity; and gender differences in online dating.[8] Previous studies have mainly dealt with the textual parts of online dating Profiles and only recently researchers started to use images and photographs as a data source.[9]

This paper opens with a general account of the role of the Internet as a matchmaker, discussing primarily the strategies employed by users when constructing their online dating Profiles. It then focuses on social representations of gender, sex roles stereotypes, and in the differences between male and female dating advertisements. The goal of the paper is to explain the gender dynamics characterizing the process of online dating self-presentation, particularly in the cultural context of Portugal. The main research question which guided the study was: to what extent do Portuguese men and women adhere to established traditional gender roles in the composition of their online dating Profiles? To gain new knowledge about the subject, sub-questions emerged: to what extent do users self-disclose and what kind of information do they show in their presentation messages? Which options do male and female daters choose for self-characterization regarding physical appearance, personality traits and socioeconomic status and social capital? What do portraits and images uploaded reveal? The paper concludes with the idea of the persistence versus change of gender stereotypes and lastly presents considerations for a future research agenda.

Cupid Lurking Online

Millions of people across the globe know, by personal experience, something that the literature confirms: the Internet is a valid mean of initiating intimate, romantic and personally fulfilling relationships.[10] In fact, online dating, more particularly in the US but in the future, possibly, in the rest of the Western world as well, is becoming one of the most common ways of meeting potential love partners. The Internet has been gaining ground on more traditional forms of meeting romantic partners such as friends, family, school or neighborhood. Rosenfeld and Thomas, have found that "for heterosexual couples who met in 2009, the Internet was the third most likely way of meeting."[11] Also in the US context, the study of Cacioppo et al.,[12] using a representative sample of 19,131 respondents, married between the years 2005

---

8 For a selection of bibliography about these topics, see: Barrie Gunter, 'The Study of Online Relationships and Dating', in William H. Dutton (ed.) *The Oxford Handbook of Internet Studies*, Oxford: Oxford University Press, 2013, pp. 173-193 and Monica Whitty and Adam Joinson, Truth, *Lies and Trust on the Internet*, London: Routledge, 2008.

9 Lee Humphreys, 'Photographs and the Presentation of Self through Online Dating Services', in Paul Messaris and Lee Humphreys (eds) *Digital Media: Transformations in Human Communication*, New York: Peter Lang, 2006, pp. 39-49.

10 William H. Dutton et al., 'The Role of the Internet in Reconfiguring Marriages: A Cross-national Study', *Interpersona* 3.2 (2009): 3-18.

11 Michael J. Rosenfeld and Reuben J. Thomas, 'Searching for a Mate: The Rise of the Internet as a Social Intermediary', American Sociological Review 77.4 (2012): 531.

12 John T. Cacioppo et al., 'Marital Satisfaction and Break-ups differ across On-line and Off-line Meeting Venues', Proceedings of the National Academy of the United States of America, Published online before

and 2012, concluded that more than one third of North American marriages start now online.

Virtual spaces where individuals can meet include, but are not limited to, online dating sites; internet classifieds; chat rooms; instant messaging; online games; and social networking websites. Forms of finding romantic or sexual partners, beyond the traditional ways, namely, the use of matrimonial advertisements, date back to the end of the 17th century. "By the early eighteen century, matrimonial advertising was booming, along with the expansion of print and the proliferation of newspapers, pamphlets and periodicals."[13] And around the 19th century there are records of the phenomenon of mail-order brides and matchmaker services among certain religious groups in the Northwest of the US[14]

It may be said that love has no price. However, it can - and it was - transformed and developed into a highly profitable business: dating sites are a million dollar industry. The number of unmarried people has been increasing for the last decades in the Western society, but the social pressure for a conjugal life persists. Thus, although differently from the way partners met through matrimonial ads posted in newspapers and magazines in old times, the internet became from the outset a way for people to browse hundreds of databases with millions of users, filtering them by age, location, physical attractiveness, income, etc. They did it in the search for "Mr. or Ms. Right".[15] Then, in the beginning of the 21st century, with the advent of more sophisticated computer software, began the age of the algorithm, allowing partners to find more compatible matches. The popularity of online dating sites seems to represent an unexpected and truly magical instrument to open up new venues in the world of date and romance. Nowadays, according to a recent article from Forbes Magazine:

> The pool has deepened such that around half of all single people use online dating services at some point, and the algorithms that power them have gotten about as smart as they're going to get for the time being. What users want isn't more or better matches on the screen (…). What they want is an easier and faster way to meet them IRL - in real life. "The big thing now is offline"[16]

Possible selves: managing online presentations

Over the years, personal presentations on the Internet have been changing significantly. In its early days, the Internet was seen as a space where, thanks to anonymity, individuals were able to create and recreate their identities, composing fictional characters and playing roles of people different from their own self. Gender switching practices were common in chat rooms, online games, forums and other virtual spaces.

---

print, (June 3 2013).
13 Harry G. Cocks, Classified: The Secret History of the Personal Column. UK: Random House, 2009, p. viii-ix.
14 Elizabeth Jagger, 'Marketing Molly and Melville: Dating in a Postmodern, Consumer Society', Sociology 35.1 (2001): 39.
15 Stanley B. Woll and Peter Young, 'Looking for Mr. or Ms. Right: Self-Presentation in Videodating', Journal of Marriage and the Family 51.2 (1989): 483-488.
16 Jeff Bercovici, 'Love On The Run: The Next Revolution In Online Dating', http://www.Forbes.com.

Currently, the Internet evolved in the creation of personalized environments where users build realistic presentations of themselves.[17] The aim is to achieve inter-personal objectives: bond with the family and real friends, establish new friendships, create virtual communities of mutual interests, find sexual and romantic partners or set (future) professional contacts. On the contrary of their predecessors, nowadays, self-presentations tend to be carefully constructed in order to allow personal agendas in the offline environment. Thus, self-presentation on dating sites, according to literature, follows rational choices about what to write on Profiles and what images to show.[18] Self-presentation strategies, and the way individuals (re)create their online identities, are important in relationship initiation and self-disclosure plays an important role. For this reason, as it occurs in circumstances others than online dating,[19] daters feel the need to please and attract others. They seek to create a good impression on others by stressing and bringing out the attributes and personal characteristics deemed most valuable.

Occasionally, in order to attract others, daters lie about themselves. Those lies, usually, are not perceived as factual lies. More than having to do with intrinsic personal features, they have to do with external ones (e.g. age, height – normally men lie more about this item then women, weight – women tend to lie more about this characteristic, smoking habits, or number of children). Hence, deviations tend "to be ubiquitous but small in magnitude".[20] As Ellison et al. argue "the notion that people frequently, explicitly, and intentionally 'lie' online is simplistic and inaccurate".[21] Self-presentation and the construction of an online Profile can be a complex process mixing different domains: "Real-I", "Social-I" and "Ideal-I".[22] That is not necessarily bad, since "possible selves"[23] may act as an important element of one's self-knowledge.

> Giddens (1990) argues that one important aspect of identity in modernity is the ability to self-narrate… Those who actively engage in the 'reflexive project of the self' (…) that is, rewriting the personal narrative as identity construction, can presumably function well in the modern world, and as a corollary through online spheres that cater for these narrative constructions of self.[24]

---

17   From the famous cartoon of Steiner published on The New Yorker, in 1993: 'On the Internet nobody knows you're a dog' http://www.unc.edu/depts/jomc/academics/dri/idog.html, times have changed to: "Damn webcam! Know everyone knows I'm a dog!" http://www.andertoons.com/dog/cartoon/6205/damn-webcam-now-everyone-knows-im-dog.

18   Joseph B. Walther et al. 'Is a Picture Worth a Thousand Words? Photographic Images in Long-Term and Short-Term Computer-Mediated Communication', Communication Research 28.1 (2001): 105-134.

19   Erving Goffman, The Presentation of Self in Everyday Life, New York: Anchor, 1959.

20   Catalina L. Toma et al. 'Separating Fact From Fiction: An Examination of Deceptive Self-Presentation in Online Dating Profiles', Personality and Social Psychology Bulletin 34.8 (2008): 1023.

21   Nicole Ellison et al., 'Managing Impressions Online: Self-Presentation Processes in the Online Dating Environment', Journal of Computer-Mediated Communication 11.2 (2006): 431.

22   I. Alev Degim, 'Identity Construction in Facebook: A Lacanian Analysis of Profiles and Facebook Generated Games', in Andreas Treske et al. (eds) Image, Time and Motion: New Media Critique from Turkey, Institute of Network Cultures, n.7, 2011, p. 112.

23   Hazel Markus and Paula Nurius, 'Possible Selves', American Psychologist 41.9 (1986): 954-969.

24   I. Alev Degim, 'Identity Construction in Facebook: A Lacanian Analysis of Profiles and Facebook Gener-

Social Representations of Gender and Stereotypes

Social representations can be understood as a way of interpreting and thinking about everyday reality, a form of social knowledge that, in opposition to the scientific knowledge, is entitled as common sense. Bearing in mind the central purpose of this paper and to the extent that sexual belonging is related to specific ways in which one learns to be, feel, think, act and see the world, gender is a conceptual category that deserves to be explored. The same for gender stereotypes that are socially constructed around it - that is, broadly accepted judgments about men and women regarding personality traits, physical appearance, behaviors, occupations, and so on.

To understand the processes involved in the construction of gender, it is worth noting that being a man or a woman is to act accordingly to what people in society evaluate as masculine and feminine. This has little or nothing to do with the biological nature and physiology of each body. Nonetheless, it is on that body, with a biologically defined sex, that gender attributes are fixed. Attributes or traits are socially constructed and internalized, and may vary greatly in time and from one culture to the next. They are often perceived as part of the nature of the individuals. Gender roles and stereotypes are not natural, yet they are naturalized.

In recent decades, in most Western countries and Portugal is no exception, profound changes occurred in the ways men and women construct their gender identity and maintain interpersonal relationships. At this level we found a gradual abandonment of the traditional gender roles, considered complementary and asymmetric: women taking the expressive, emotionally supportive role of maintaining a balanced family structure and devoted to the household management, and men occupied with the work outside the home, carrying the instrumental and practical role of family subsistence, authority and leadership.[25]

> We have been witnessing a growing sentimentalisation, privatisation, secularisation and individualisation of families that transformed people's family lives into more plural and diverse combinations, particularly when compared with much more homogeneous models from the past. Nowadays, in family context, there's a greater importance given to gender equality but also to the sentimental aspect of relationships, in so far it carries the sense of greater accomplishment and personal well-being.[26]

Multiple Portuguese sociological studies, mainly in the field of family research, show that these gradual changes stimulated and incremented new normative guidance on forms of experiencing dating, romance, and partnership, intimacy and family life. The Carnation Revolution, in 1974, liberalized the Portuguese nation, and changed it into a democratic, fairer, and egalitarian society. This political and social transformation led and contributed to changes,

---

ated Games', in Andreas Treske et al. (eds) Image, Time and Motion: New media Critique from Turkey, Institute of Network Cultures, n.7, 2011, p. 114.

25   Talcott Parsons and Robert F. Bales, Family, Socialization and the Interaction Process, New York: MacMillan, 1955.

26   Anália Torres et al. 'Gender, Work and Family: Balancing Central Dimensions in Individuals' Lives', Sociologia Online - Revista da Associação Portuguesa de Sociologia 2 (April, 2011): 12.

also, in moral values and privacy practices supported, in their turn, by adjustments and innovations in the law occurring in terms of rights then conquered. Gender inequalities gradually fade; the perspective of an active woman, equal to man in rights and duties was progressively implemented; male domination loses legal legitimacy and the traditional and patriarchal order that ruled family life and intimate relationships shifts. Regarding the romantic, emotional and intimate biographies of Portuguese recent generations it is possible to detect an evolution in the gender based double standard, which suggests a gradual harmonization between the experiences of women and men. They seem to adhere to more egalitarian discourses showing a less distinctive pattern of female and male standards.

However, as Kimmel[27] argues, gender still remains an organizing principle around which individuals build their identities and social representations of gender role relationships. That is, partly, what explains why the accelerated transition to the dominant model of the dual earner, in which both spouses pursue careers, did not erase the traces of inequality between men and women in most Western societies, and especially in the Portuguese one. At the turn of the century, Portugal, a nation still with a conservative dimension, was regarded as one of the countries where gender stereotypes were more accentuated.[28] Traditionalist patterns of male dominance over women, especially regarding the division of housework and child care, are still felt in Portugal. Those patterns influence men's and women's behavior. Women, in particular, activate "dispositions they have been inculcated with" and continue to respond to the "traditionalist expectations for the performance of roles in our society."[29]

It is, thus, noticeable the maintenance of gender representations that lead to the (re)production of stereotypes and gender roles. Gender stereotypes transmitted by the family, at the school and in the media, continue to follow traditional clichés. Men are perceived as strong, courageous, assertive, domineering, aggressive and depicted as uninhibited, rational, independent, resistant, ambitious, confident and geared for action; while female occur more frequently in the conciliatory role – the peacemaker that does not foster conflict – and they are also portrayed as good-looking; soft, delicate, calm, dependent, caring, loving, emotional, affable and sensitive.[30]

---

27   Michael Kimmel, The Gendered Society, Oxford: Oxford University Press, 2004.
28   Furnham Apud Francisco Costa Pereira and Jorge Veríssimo, 'A Mulher na Publicidade e os Estereótipos de Género', Observatorio 5 (2008): 281-296.
29   Anália Torres et al., Homens e Mulheres entre Família e Trabalho, Lisboa: CITE, Comissão para a Igualdade no Trabalho e no Emprego, Ministério do Trabalho e da Segurança Social, 2004, p. 132.
30   Lígia Amâncio, Masculino e Feminino. A Construção Social da Diferença, Porto: Edições Afrontamento, 1994: p. 63; Adrian Furnham and Mak Twiggy, 'Sex-Role Stereotyping in Television Commercials: A Review and Comparison of Fourteen Studies Done on Five Continents Over 25 Years', Sex Roles 41.5 (1999): 524-525; Liliana Lopes, 'Diagnóstico e Implementação da Igualdade de Género na Escola Superior de Educação: Apontamentos pelos Trilhos da igualdade...', Projeto Diagnóstico e Implementação da Igualdade de Género na Escola Superior de Educação (2013): 1-2; Patrícia Miranda, 'A Construção Social das Identidades de Género nas Crianças: um Estudo Intensivo em Viseu', VI Congresso Português de Sociologia: 'Mundos Sociais: Saberes e Práticas', Universidade Nova de Lisboa, Faculdade de Ciências Sociais e Humanas, 25 a 28 de Junho, (2008): 9; Francisco Costa Pereira and Jorge Veríssimo, 'A Mulher na Publicidade e os Estereótipos de Género', Observatorio 5 (2008): 293; Simone Freitas, 'A Bela e a Fera', II Congreso Internacional Comunicación 3.0 - Libro Nuevos Medios, Nueva Comunicación,

Notwithstanding the transformations in Portuguese society that have occurred, there are two main social indicators that point to a stability in, at least, two dimensions of the feminine stereotype, namely: the sexualization and the role played in the family. In the first case it is notorious that images of sexualized women are still common in advertising and marketing material[31], in the second case, numerous studies show the persistence of a very traditional division of labor in the Portuguese families, compared with other countries.[32]

As Bourdieu suggests, the fact that male domination is no longer imposed in all contexts is far from meaning, with obvious evidence, its eradication. For the author, the principles of the dominant view - those of male domination - remain active even if they are embedded "in the form of schemes of perception and appreciation hardly accessible to consciousness."[33] Still, along with the reproduction of gender stereotypes the issue of the equalization of gender also emerges. Tradition and modernity coexist. To state it in a simplified way, in this matter of gender, change does not occur as it is expected, change, as Bourdieu explains, occurs in the permanence.

Gender Differences in Dating Advertisements

Online or offline, it is important to remember that all subjects construct their identity and try to convey a certain image of themselves. Literature concerning personal advertisements, primarily in newspapers and magazines, and more recently also on the Internet, namely in dating sites, indicates that gender stereotypes influence the way men and women describe the ideal partner and also the way they define themselves in order to attract potential partners. Gender does influence self-presentation characteristics: men's personal Profiles are more likely to offer instrumental traits (education, career, financial status, socioeconomic position), and to request expressive qualities in women; whereas women offer physical attractiveness, personality characteristics, and expressive features more often while seeking status in the form of occupation and requesting for instrumental traits in males.[34]

Though a vast majority of the literature indicates that men and women ads complement each other, there are studies challenging this assumption with some puzzling results. Men may also be looking for financially independent, successful and ambitious women[35]; and women, on their hand, relative to the opposite sex, are starting to emphasize commitment, commu-

---

Universidad de Salamanca, 4 y 5 de Octobre, (2010): 7; Anália Torres, 'Casamento e Gênero: Mudanças nas Famílias Contemporâneas a partir do Caso Português', Interseções 3.2 (2001): 58.

31 Francisco Costa Pereira and Jorge Veríssimo, 'A Mulher na Publicidade e os Estereótipos de Género', Observatorio 5: (2008): 281-296.

32 Karin Wall and Lígia Amâncio, Família e Género em Portugal e na Europa, Lisboa: Imprensa de Ciências Sociais, 2007.

33 Pierre Bourdieu, La Domination Masculine, Paris: Éditions du Seuil, 1998: 102.

34 Peter Michael Bak, 'Sex Differences in the Attractiveness Halo Effect in the Online Dating Environment', Journal of Business and Media Psychology 1 (2010): 1-7; Morgan, Elizabeth et al. 'Comparing Narratives of Personal and Preferred Partner Characteristics in Online Dating Advertisements', Computers in Human Behavior, 26.5 (2010): 883-888.

35 Donald S. Strassberg and Stephen Holty, 'An Experimental Study of Women's Internet Personal Ads', Archives of Sexual Behavior 32.3 (2003): 253-260.

nication and the ability to express feelings. Also they appear to be looking in male Profiles for "characteristics like warmth and kindness, and attractiveness".[36] In sum, research may be pointing to a "gender-specific decline in mate value".[37]

The construction of online dating Profiles tries to fit with what is considered socially acceptable in the dominant culture. Therefore, it is plausible to assume that Portuguese online self-presentations may generate significant and important materials that contribute to address concerns with the theoretical interpretation of continuity and social and cultural change (innovation and tradition) in what gender roles are concerned in the Portuguese context.

Self-presentation on the Internet: the Portuguese Case

In Portugal, printed dating ads have been studied, namely from a major daily Portuguese newspaper,[38] but online dating is severely lacking academic research. In 2002, Cardoso showed that, in the context of Portuguese Internet mediated communication (IMC) users, it was possible to see "the formation of stable environments of intimate ties, prolonging themselves outside the environment of IMC towards the offline spaces".[39] These intimate ties, concerned, among others, friendship (30,2%) and friendship and love (2,3%), and in a recent report that explores the relation of Portuguese people with the internet, the same author mentions that 78,7% of internet users adhere to social networking in order to meet new people.[40] Who are these users, what motivates them to meet new people, who do they meet and what kind of relationships are established, that is still unknown.

Digital literacy in Portugal grew exponentially from the late 1990's to the end of the last decade and the Internet gradually emerged as a "community of chronic communicators."[41] By the end of the 1990's the use of the Internet as a 'social technology' for communication among individuals was still the object of some apprehension[42] but in 2009, Portugal was already the European country with the third highest number of users accessing social networking sites – after the UK and Spain.[43]

---

36 Andrew T. Fiore et al. 'Assessing Attractiveness in Online Dating Profiles', Proceeding of the Twenty-sixth Annual SIGCHI Conference on Human Factors in Computing Systems. ACM Press, (2008): 804.

37 Skopek, Jan, et al. 'The Gendered Dynamics of Age Preferences – Empirical Evidence from Online Dating', Journal of Family Research 23.3 (2011): 267.

38 Félix Neto, 'Sex differences in Portuguese Lonely Hearts Advertisements', Perceptual and Motor Skills 101.2 (2005): 393-400.

39 Gustavo Cardoso, ''Feel Like Going Online?' Internet Mediated Communication in Portugal', Information, Communication & Society 5.4 (2002): 548.

40 Gustavo Cardoso et al. 'A Sociedade em Rede. A Internet em Portugal, 2012', OberCom - Observatório da Comunicação (2012): 29.

41 Michael Strangelove, 'The Internet, Electric Gaia and the Rise of the Uncensored Self', Computer-Mediated Communication Magazine (1994): 13.

42 Gustavo Cardoso, 'Contributos para uma Sociologia do Ciberespaço', Biblioteca on-line de Ciências da Comunicação (1998).

43 comScore, Inc. Social Networking Has Banner Year in France, Growing 45 Percent 2009. <http://www.comscore.com/por/Insights/Press_Releases/2009/2/Social_Networking_France>.

Scattered studies, in Portugal, have looked at the construction of identities through CMC;[44] at the dichotomy of online/offline environments contributing to the debate on the connections between these two worlds;[45] at the subject of cybersex;[46] and at the presentation of self in Facebook.[47] However, apart from this very few studies, the review of the literature reveals no research so far on the potential of the Internet, particularly of dating sites, to foster romantic relationships.

Falling in Line with Traditional Gender Representations?

Prior international studies have documented that dating sites are important venues to find romantic partners, and that female and male users pursue distinct self-presentation strategies to attract others online. In recent years, there has been a tremendous increase in the number of Internet users in Portugal but, as previously mentioned, there is a gap in the scientific literature on how the Portuguese use cyberspace, and specifically dating sites, to initiate romantic relationships.

In this research, the main goal was to understand if Portuguese men and women adhere to established traditional gender roles in the composition of their online dating Profiles. To gain new insight on the subject, sub-questions emerged: what does the content of the presentation messages reveal? Which options do male and female daters choose for self-characterization regarding physical appearance, personality traits and socioeconomic status and social capital? What do portraits and images uploaded reveal?

The final sample for this study included 200 Profiles - 100 men and 100 women - and 1006 photographs - 485 of men and 521 of women -, all gathered from one particular Internet dating site (Meetic.pt), during 2011. Meetic was chosen for three reasons: firstly, it is the top dating site in Europe; secondly, it was the first dating site to appear in Portugal (in 2005); and, thirdly, it is relatively widespread, recording the most registered users.

The user's Profiles were selected according to 5 criteria: firstly, there was a photograph and a self-presentation ad; secondly, they were between 25 and 60 years old; thirdly, they lived in Portugal; fourth, they lived in Lisbon; and finally, they lived within a 30km radius of Lisbon.[48] For the rest (e.g. education, income, profession physical appearance, marital status, etc.) the

---

44 Susana Nascimento, 'Para uma compreensão sociológica das identidades na CMC', Biblioteca online de Ciências da Comunicação (2001) 1-13; José Machado Pais, Nos Rastos da Solidão, Deambulações Sociológicas, Porto: Âmbar, 2006.

45 Gustavo Cardoso and Susana Nascimento, 'Online/Offline: Can You Tell the Difference? Portuguese Views on Internet Mediated Communication', Comunicazioni Sociali - Rivista di Media, Spettacolo e Studi Culturali. XXIV.1 (2002): 41-50.

46 Ana Alexandra Carvalheira Santos. Relaciones Interpersonales y Comportamientos Sexuales Através de Internet. Tesis Doctoral, Facultad de Psicologia, Universidad de Salamanca, 2005.

47 Filipa Jorge, A Apresentação do Eu em Plataformas de Comunicação On-line, Tese de Mestrado, Departamento de Comunicação e Arte, Universidade de Aveiro, 2011.

48 This criterion was chosen to include the 18 municipalities that constitute the Metropolitan Area of Lisbon. Here, remains the largest population concentration of the country and, according to the dating site Meetic, the higher number of users registered.

random effect was maintained. The sample was limited to heterosexuals (women seeking men and men seeking women). The 200 Profiles were proportionally selected among these age groups with most registered users in the site, according to the above- mentioned criteria (men: 17 aged 25–30 years; 39 aged 31–40 years; 30 aged 41–50 years; 14 aged 51–60 / women: 13 aged 25–30 years; 30 aged 31–40 years; 36 aged 41–50 years; 21 aged 51–60).

The Profiles in the dating site Meetic.pt include several items: a space to upload images; a space where users are encouraged to write a self-presentation message; a closed-ended questionnaire about personal data, traits and tastes; habits, religion, income, eye-color; type of preferred food; partner-preferences, and a set of other characteristics (to be answered with a drop-down menu); and also a questionnaire with pre-defined yes/no questions to be selected by the users, who can choose to post it in their Profiles so that visitors may respond.

The first step in this study was to select and save the Profiles to individual files in the computer and then analyze all the items with the exception of the fourth - the questionnaire with pre-defined yes/no questions. Regarding the third item, only some specific elements of the self-questionnaire with pre-defined questions were studied: physical attributes ("aspect", "silhouette" and "the most attractive in me"); socioeconomic traits ("qualifications", "profession" and "income"); and personality/psychological characteristics.

Self-presentation messages and the selected items of the self-questionnaire with pre-defined questions were analyzed using a thematic and summative content analysis methodology[49] and employing techniques of the grounded theory that Larossa defines as a "valuable set of procedures for thinking about theoretically textual materials".[50] A semi-inductive approach, qualitative and interpretative, was followed in the search for unexpected data that would contribute substantially to the construction of hypotheses in a dialectical relationship between theoretical reflection and reality.[51] From an analysis of the 200 presentation messages of both males and females, "thematic files" or "category files"[52] were created for both sexes. In each of these files, excerpts of the user's most significant descriptions were labeled and the words most often used counted. The content analysis of the messages was guided by the main research question and required an observation grid containing some possible male and female stereotypes. The grid was built based on a set of studies mainly centered in the Portuguese culture that in recent years have been discussing the topic of stereotypes and presenting lists of traits and attributes commonly considered typically masculine or feminine.

---

49 Laurence Bardin, L'analyse de Contenu, Paris: Presses Universitaires de France, 2007; Hsiu-Fang Hsieh and Sarah E. Shannon, 'Three Approaches to Qualitative Content Analysis', Qualitative Health Research 15. 9 (2005): 1277-1288.

50 Ralph Larossa, 'Grounded theory methods and qualitative family research', Journal of Marriage and Family 67.4 (2005): 838.

51 Anselm C. Strauss and Juliet Corbin, Basics of Qualitative Research: Techniques and Procedures for Developing Grounded Theory, London: Sage Publications, 1990.

52 Gery Ryan et al., 'Techniques to identify themes', Field Methods 15.1 (2003): 85-109.

For the study of Profile photographs Bell's methodology - content analysis of visual images - was followed: "an empirical (observational) and objective procedure for quantifying recorded 'audio-visual' (...) representation using reliable, explicitly defined categories".[53] Bearing in mind the research questions, the first goal was to discover the categories, common themes and subthemes emerging across the male and female Profile photos, and also to note the different or unique pictures appearing in the Profiles. In the content analysis of visual images "the researcher is usually interested in whether, say, women are depicted more or less frequently than men in relation to some variable or quality".[54] Thus, each Profile was coded for the number of photos uploaded, number of photos with face shots, and number of photos showing things other than the user (for instance, animals, places, cities, and objects) and the circumstances in which they appear. The number of photos where users exhibited parts of their body (what parts, in which positions), and the clothing they were wearing (clothing, for example, was coded on the dimensions of color and kind of clothing – sportswear, formal wear, casual wear, etc.) were also taken into account. A close reading of the images, in-depth scrutiny and "treating the visual as problematic"[55] was the next step.

Are Men from Mars and Women from Venus?

The idea that men and women belong to "distinct planets" and that the differences between them are a consequence of inner psychological differences between the genders has long been widespread. There is a belief that each gender can be understood in terms of distinct ways of being, feeling, and thinking, as if there were gender specific worldviews. In fact, there are gender differences, but what sociological research, and this study in particular, show is that gender specific frameworks are largely, if not entirely, social constructions reproduced over time.

> Discourses are conceptualized as instances of continuous production of gender. This means that it is recognized that individual discourses are structured largely by relatively stable symbolic systems that give (asymmetric) meanings to the categories of femininity and masculinity ... Discourses on gender do not merely reflect a pre-existing differentiation, they actively contribute to the construction of this differentiation and, thus, they "do gender".[56]

In this context, what does the analysis of the Profile ads reveal? Focus will be placed firstly on the presentation messages and the self-characterization online daters create. Secondly, the analysis will focus on the photographs uploaded by the female and male users. Taking

---

53 Philip Bell, 'Content Analysis of Visual Images' in Theo Van Leeuwen and Carey Jewitt (eds) Handbook of Visual Analysis, Thousand Oaks, CA: Sage, 2001, p. 13.
54 Philip Bell, 'Content Analysis of Visual Images', p. 14.
55 Jon Prosser, 'Researching With Visual Images: Some Guidance Notes and a Glossary for Beginners', ESRC National Centre for Research Methods, Working Paper Series 6/06, 2006.
56 West and Zimmerman, apud, Maria do Mar Pereira, 'Os Discursos de Género: Mudança e Continuidade nas Narrativas sobre Diferenças, Semelhanças e (Des)igualdade entre Mulheres e Homens', in Karin Wall et al. (eds) Vida Familiar no Masculino: Negociando Velhas e Novas Masculinidades, Lisboa: CITE, Comissão para a Igualdade no Trabalho e no Emprego, 2010, pp. 226-227.

into consideration the amount of data gathered and analyzed, only the aspects considered most relevant to answer the research questions will be highlighted.

Data obtained in previous studies indicates that online daters follow rational choices when presenting themselves to potential romantic partners.[57] Although more research should be carried to broadly and firmly sustain this claim, in this study it was possible to confirm that this seems true, also, for Portuguese online daters. Men and women try to present themselves as acceptable people to others. Both want to please and attract, and they underline and show up the attributes or characteristics considered most valuable for themselves and/or possibly for others. From the analysis of the presentation messages and the items previously mentioned, five aspects of the users Profiles stand out: physical attributes; socioeconomic capital; life styles and preferred activities; psychological, relational and behavioral traits; and, finally, age preferences of the potencial partner.

Physical Attributes

Comparing to men, women fill out more the physical traits of the closed-ended questionnaire that characterizes users. By physical traits, it is meant: "aspect", "silhouette" and what is considered "the most attractive in me". But the difference is not astonishing: 69% of the 100 men fill out these items against a little bit more of women: 74%. What is more notable is that 47% of women, when filling the item "aspect", by choosing options like "not bad", "attractive", "very attractive" and "an authentic model" stress much more than men (only 26% choosing these elements), their presumable beautiful and charming look. The least filled in of all items of the questionnaire, included in this major item of the "Physical attributes", is "the most attractive in me" - perhaps because it is the third on the list of all the items to be filled in by the users when completing their online profile. It is curious, though, that regarding the "silhouette" item, the second one, there are 18% of women choosing the option "with graceful curves" and only two percent of men choosing this option.

Women have managed to free themselves from the stereotype of woman and wife. However, despite all the battle, what these results may indicate is that Portuguese women still have internalized the stereotypes from 50 years ago, but now also carrying the "heightened sexuality, one of the burdens of the post sexual revolution society that freed the chains that bound the women's desires, but brought to the spotlight the female body in advertising and on the media in general"[58], thus contributing for the reproduction of the female stereotype as a sex symbol.

Socioeconomic Capital

The most salient result that emerges when analyzing the data relating the socioeconomic capital of the individuals that compose the sample of this research is that neither men nor women seem to feel very comfortable with the filling of these aspects. The percentage of

---

57 Monica Whitty, 'Revealing the 'Real' Me, Searching for the 'Actual' You: Presentations of Self on an Internet Dating Site'. Computers in Human Behavior 24.4 (2008): 1707–1723.

58 Simone Freitas, 'A Bela e a Fera', II Congreso Internacional Comunicación 3.0 - Libro Nuevos Medios, Nueva Comunicación, Universidad de Salamanca, 4 y 5 de Octobre, (2010): 16.

users that do not fill in the items of "qualifications", "profession" and "income" are high, particularly when compared to other elements of the closed-ended questionnaire. Nonetheless, there are a few more men (67%) than women (51%) doing it. Furthermore, it can be stressed that, although the numbers are not high, still, 19% of men disclose information about their "income" whereas only six percent of women fill in this element.

Although the recent literature on the European family lives, notably, the gender order within the family context, suggests that the old breadwinner model, at least concerning attitudes, is outdated[59], such detail may suggest a certain persistence of the notion of this man breadwinner model in the Portuguese society. If not in attitudes, at least, as an ideal model, particularly if we take into account that the distribution of male users that indicate this bit of information goes from men with 26 years old to men with 56 years old.

Life Styles and Preferred Activities

This is perhaps the aspect, of all those who are referred by users, in which gender does not seem to influence the responses. It is relatively accepted and widespread that both women and men appreciate traveling; going for a walk; going to the cinema; listening to music; going to concerts; enjoying the beach; watching the sea; appreciating the sunset, the moon, the stars, the countryside, or the nature; being with the family; reading; writing; laughing; having a drink; cooking; being with friends; practicing sports; dancing; shopping and breaking out of routines. Yet, the analysis of the relational and behavioral traits reveals that gender stereotypes have not been vanished. On the contrary, they are part of the scenario of how male and female online daters present themselves to others on the context of finding romantic partners in the Internet. We shall see it in the next point to be discussed.

Psychological, Relational and Behavioral Traits

The personality traits of male and female users, gathered from their written self-presentation messages and from the personality/psychological characteristics selected by them in the closed-ended questionnaire, were analyzed accordingly to the grid of male and female stereotypes previously mentioned. The main results demonstrate that women gender role stereotypes are the ones extensively more (re)produced by female online daters (see Figure 1.).

---

59   Anália Torres et al. 'A Mysterious European Threesome: Workcare Regimes, Policies and Gender', International and Multidisciplinary Journal of Social Sciences 1.1 (2012): 46.

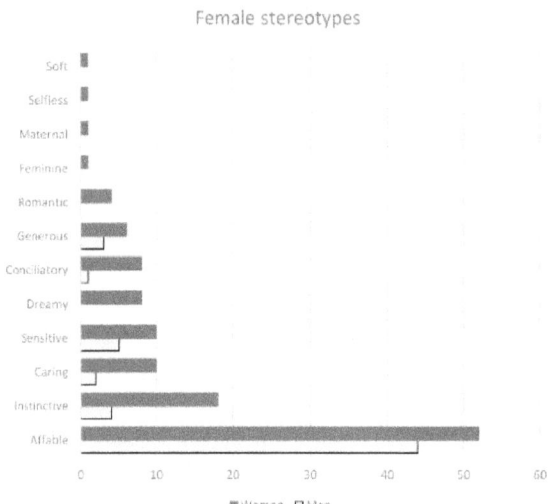

Figure 1. Female stereotypes

As Figure 1 show, it is quite significant the number of women choosing words such as: affable, instinctive, caring, sensitive, dreamy, conciliatory, and generous for their self-presentations. Also, it can be underlined that some words are exclusively used by women: feminine, maternal, selfless and soft. As for the male stereotypes they do not appear so markedly, but still, it is interesting to note that in contrast to women, there are more men emphasizing traits such as: adventurous, active, hard-worker, independent, self-confident and, above all, courteous (see Figure 2).

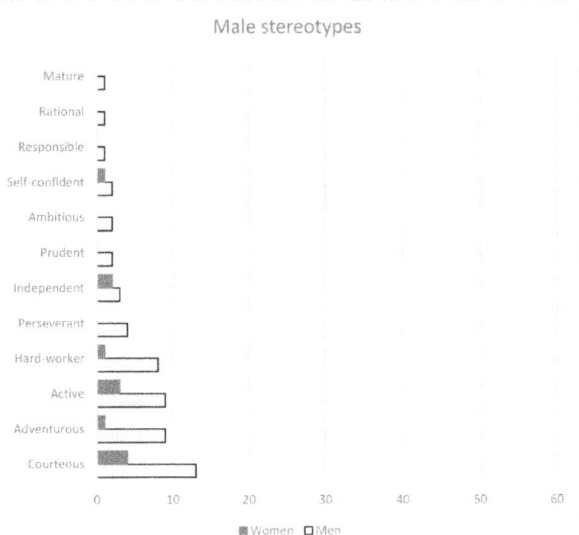

Figure 2. Male stereotypes

The traditional courtesies that have served to differentiate gentlemen from ladies, such as men opening doors for women (…), may also serve to communicate and perpetuate the expectation that men are stronger than, dominant over, and more powerful than women (…). Thus, an act of common courtesy may be viewed by some as a political statement designed to perpetuate traditional views of masculinity and femininity (…) and may sometimes serve as 'a way of preserving the inequities between the sexes' (…).[60]

Also, it is possible to detect words solely employed by men, such as: perseverant, prudent, responsible, ambitious, rational and mature.

Four basic aspects can, thusly, be highlighted. Firstly, Portuguese online daters tend to choose personal attributes and psychological characteristics that fit the still prevailing and traditionally feminine and masculine stereotypes in the Portuguese cultural context. Women give much more weight to emotional, affective, and romantic attributes, whereas, on their turn, men bring out characteristics related to work, self-determination, rationality, and the practical side of life.

Secondly, despite a relatively marked division among men and women options for, correspondingly, masculine and feminine stereotypes, there are also some men stressing their sensitive, caring, instinctive, and especially, their affable side, and a few women mentioning their active, independent and self-confident facets.

---

60   Mary B. Harris, 'When Courtesy Fails: Gender Roles and Polite Behaviors', Journal of Applied Social Psychology 22.18 (1992): 1399-1400.

Thirdly, there is a rather broad set of users that although reproducing gender stereotypes, simultaneously use gender-neutral attributes in their self-presentations like: honest, genuine, simple, cheerful and optimistic.

Finally, and to avoid too simplistic and linear explanations about the (re)production of gender role stereotypes, by Portuguese men and women, it must be taken into consideration the context where these stereotypes are being (re)produced: the online dating scene. Men and women are describing themselves accordingly to what they imagine to be the attributes and features others might be looking in a potential romantic partner. In the scenario of dating sites, when individuals use certain traits and categories they might be trying to meet what they consider to be the most desired, respected or advantageous position in that given context. Self-presentations can, thus, be interpreted as male and female performances of certain masculinities and femininities.

For example, in the context of financial business or management and administration, namely in Portugal, it is known that women employ specific strategies that enable them to be accepted as leaders and integrate teams.[61] It is highly probable that if they had to fill out a profile for an application to integrate a big company they would rather opt to use self-descriptive words like "active", "perseverant", "independent", "responsible" and "mature". Similarly, in the particular situation of online dating, recent American literature has shown that in the beginning of the 21st century, contrary to prior researches, there are women already describing themselves as financially independent, successful and ambitious. Curiously, these female online advertisements produce higher response rates comparing to those where women describe themselves as lovely, very attractive and slim.[62]

Age Preferences of the Potential Partner

Love without social constraint is a myth. The Sociology of the family, have shown, for decades, that couples tend to be homogamous, "that is, individuals are attracted to persons who are similar on one or more characteristics".[63] Homogamy is a social proximity that may be based on culture, class, religion, economic status or age: the so-called age homogamy. On the Internet the possibilities of meeting someone that otherwise would never be met are high. This means that the chances of getting to know someone from a geographically distinct zone, with different socioeconomic and cultural capitals, religion or age are immense. This is why some literature suggests that on the Internet partners are chosen with greatest differences in age or level of education though, apparently, with more similar interests and values.[64]

---

61 Paulo Loureiro and Carlos Cabral Cardoso, 'O Género e os Estereótipos na Gestão', Tékhne - Revista de Estudos Politécnicos VI. 10 (2008): 221-238.

62 Donald S. Strassberg and Stephen Holty, 'An Experimental Study of Women's Internet Personal Ads', Archives of Sexual Behavior 32.3 (2003): 253-260.

63 Jennifer Hahn and Thomas Blass, 'Dating Partner Preferences: A Function of Similarity of Love Styles', Journal of Social Behavior & Personality 12.3 (1997): 595.

64 William H. Dutton et al. 'The Role of the Internet in Reconfiguring Marriages: A Cross-national Study', Interpersona 3.2 (2009): 3-18.

In this research, results point in the direction that the age preferences of the potential partner go along the tendency that occurs between Portuguese couples who met, and got married, in the offline world. The criteria used for marital choice concerning the age of the partner in the offline world is also visible in the choices male and female online daters make when they indicate, in their profiles, the preferred age of the partner they are looking for. Hence, what this study reveals is that there is an age hypergamy (see Figures 3. and 4.). In Portugal, six in ten marital unions imply an age difference favoring men and, in most cases, the man is two to five years older than the woman.[65]

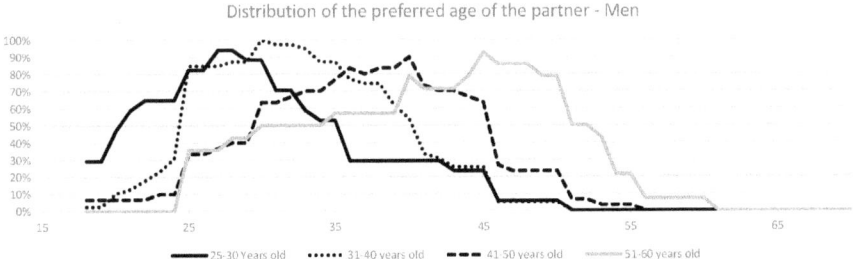

Figure 3. Distribution of the preferred age of the partner - Men

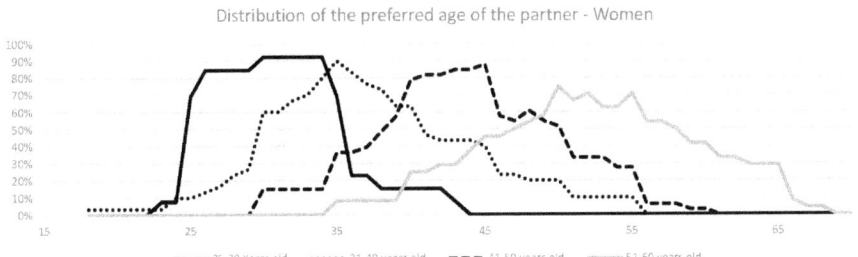

Figure 4. Distribution of the preferred age of the partner - Women

Over the decades, in Western countries, including Portugal, the age difference between marriage partners has been decreasing. Among older age groups, however, and depending of the marital status of individuals, hypergamy persists and works differently depending on the gender (men marry much younger women, and women marry not only much older man but also much younger men). In this sense, it is important to note that yes, gender does matter - not only in the strategies followed by men and women in their self-presentations, but also in the choices they make about the preferred age of the partner.

The results of this research indicate that age preferences, likewise in the offline environment, shift with age (and presumably – like in the Portuguese context happens - with the marital

---

65 Rodrigo Rosa, Escolha do Cônjuge e Modos de Construção Social no Casal. Tese de Doutoramento, Instituto Superior de Ciências do Trabalho e da Empresa, 2008, p. 156.

status). But these preferences are not random: gender does in fact matter. As they age, men prefer younger women, whereas women's partners' preferred age becomes more diverse.

And What about the Portraits?

The literature on online dating reveals that posting pictures increases several times more the chances of matching. Meetic.pt encourages users to do so. Of those who comply, many explicitly mention the importance of a photograph in the Profile:

"*Profiles with no photographs are like books without a cover*" [woman, single, 39 years]

"*Profiles without photos, no thanks: if you go fishing you've got to get wet*" [man, separated, 41 years]

"*Please, those of you that don't show their image do not contact me. Although 'what is essential is invisible to the eye' I'm not interested in those who haven't got the courage to show up! I will respect them but I will not answer. Thank you.*" [woman, divorced, 39 years]

Although the sample in this study was composed of Profiles with ads and pictures (100 men from the 2,686 found in the dating site, and 100 women, gathered from the 959 that had an advertisement and photographs), it should be mentioned that according to the criteria previously mentioned there are much more users just with self-presentation messages and without photos than users with both (8,793 men and 3,736 women without photo). Among those who upload photographs, there are only 6% of women doing it, comparing with 17% of men. However, in the sample used (N=200), the number of photographs uploaded by women (521) surpassed the number uploaded by men (485). Moreover, more women than men uploaded between just 1 and 5 photos (19 men uploaded just one photo, whereas 34 women did so). On the other hand, there are a few more women than men uploading more than 15 photos (the maximum number uploaded by a man was 23, whereas, by a woman, it was 25 – the maximum allowed). This suggests that, although there are more female Profiles without photos, when women decide to post them, they seem to upload more than men.

Three categories emerged from the content analysis of the uploaded users photographs. They focus on different aspects: the physical - photos relating to the body (body fit, body look, body presentation); the symbolic - images that suggest or represent ideas, qualities, tastes, emotions and states of mind or spirit; and the material - photos showing or pointing to physical objects, money or possessions (the material world). In these distinct categories, it is possible to find similarities and differences in the photos uploaded by the two genders.

Regarding similarities, almost one third of the total sample of photographs is composed of face shots, a number equally distributed over both genders. Regarding the physical category, men and women portray themselves in various poses and behaviors, showing physically fit bodies or parts of them - strong arms, pectoral muscles, flat bellies - on the beach, in the pool or at home, and in glamour photographs taken at marriages, baptisms or other special/party events. These photos show them from flattering angles wearing fancy, sometimes expensive clothes, accessories, and make up. Both the men and the women post symbolic photographs, or photos of non-personal identity nature trying to represent something or express intentions or feeling: sunsets, beautiful landscapes, restaurants, pets, or fine art photography.

The most notable gender effect found in the photographs in the physical category relates to the fact that women not only appear in 96.5% of the photographs, contrasting with the 85% of photographs where men portray themselves, but also reveal far more physical details than men do. Women show particular parts of their body: lips, legs, tongue and navel piercings, feet, and tattoos – on the shoulder, wrist, and nape of the neck, chest, lower back, hip, and ankles. It is interesting to consider this result in the light of the studies being made about how the media produces gender stereotypes that, on their turn, are then internalized by social actors and, again, thus, continuously reproduced. Tuna and Freitas, in a research that undertook the analysis of perfume magazine ads concluded that:

> There seems to be an emphasis on themes such as sports and business/professions in men's perfume ads, whereas women's fragrances tend to be advertised through motifs such as love, eroticism, glamour and fashion. (…) The depiction of women models is still more frequent, and that nudity and the erotic depiction of women participants prevail, when compared to similar proportion of men depicted in more business-like poses.[66]

In relation to the symbolic category of photos, it is very interesting to observe that there is not even one photograph posted by a woman representing her workplace or some scenario that could indicate her professional occupation. By contrast, eleven photos of men, though a residual number in the 485 uploaded by them, were nonetheless classified as "workplace" in the thematic files created when analyzing photographs. Those pictures show men working as architects at a drawing table, as civil engineers inspecting works, with a helmet on, as aircraft pilots, policemen or firemen, in uniform, or at the office, sitting at the computer, amid papers and files. This result is consistent with what Neto and Pinto found when analyzing gender stereotypes in Portuguese television advertisements a few years ago: "significant differences, with proportionally more females (35%) being portrayed in the home than males (12.7%) and more males being portrayed in occupational settings (37.7%) than females (22.0%)."[67]

Still, one of the more significant and explicit gender difference, if not the most, was found in the material category. In this case, men upload far more photographs (23) than women (5). They post photos of their cars (e.g. convertibles), motorbikes, and boats, and images showing indoor spaces (e.g., presumably, their houses or parts of them – the pool, the fireplace, the library, old furniture, china). Images of capital cities visited, paradisiacal beaches, desert landscapes, and ski resorts – an indirect way of showing a certain economic or financial status – are also much more commonly uploaded by men (28) than women (9). These results show that the users are pursuing strategies in their self-presentations online not only when they write their self-presentation messages, but also when they select the photographs that are

---

66   Sandra Tuna and Elsa Freitas, 'Gendered adverts: an analysis of female and male images in contemporary perfume ads', Comunicação & Sociedade 21 (2012): 104-105.

67   Félix Neto and Isabel Pinto, 'Gender Stereotypes in Portuguese Television Advertisements', Sex Roles 39.1-2 (1998): 158.

going to portray them and potentially attract dating partners.

Conclusion

Daters do not present themselves randomly or carelessly. On the contrary, there is a notable attempt to please potential partners. These findings extend those of other researches confirming that by a "selective self-presentation"[68], Portuguese men and women registered in the dating site Meetic.pt try to manage impressions and promote the relationships desired.

Women and men pursue distinct self-presentation strategies to attract others online. There are important gender differences in the self-presentation procedure and gender role stereotypes tend to be (re)produced. Men seem more inclined to underline their rational and practical attributes as well as their socioeconomic status, whereas women activating ancient dispositions that have been inculcated with, value their emotional, and affective facets, and their inclination to dream. Women also emphasize their physical attributes more than men. The findings of the current study are consistent with others who found that "when selling the self, men market their financial and occupational resources, whereas women offer physical attractiveness and appealing body shape".[69]

On one hand, it is possible to detect certain clues pointing toward modern gender roles. Men describe their emotional and relationship skills, their generosity and sensitivity, which reveals their "orientation towards a sense of belonging and intimacy"[70]. Some women refer to their active and independent facets allied to some traits of self-confidence mentioning, for instances, the importance of the hard work. On the other hand, men and women tend to offer complementary gender-based characteristics. Gender stereotypes perdure when male daters reinforce the instrumental role and female daters accentuate the expressive role. It seems, thus, that "rather than *being* modern, the Portuguese like the *idea* of being modern."[71]

It also possible to conclude that the positive attributes men and women project fall into social norms around what is considered feminine and masculine and are consistent with the contemporary gender roles in the Portuguese society. Online self-presentations reflect shared cultural values about gender and they contribute to the predominance of online stereotypical gender identities. The association of women to the world of reproduction and of men to the world of production has not been completely fractured, and important traits of conventional gender relations still persist today.[72] Or, at least, "traditionalist expectations for the perfor-

---

68 Joseph B. Walther, 'Selective Self-Presentation in Computer-Mediated Communication: Hyperpersonal Dimensions of Technology, Language, and Cognition', Computers in Human Behavior 23.5 (2007): 2538–2557.

69 Elizabeth Jagger, 'Marketing Molly and Melville: Dating in a Postmodern, Consumer Society', Sociology 35.1 (2001): 39.

70 Anália Torres et al., 'Gender, Work and Family: Balancing Central Dimensions in Individuals' Lives', Sociologia Online - Revista da Associação Portuguesa de Sociologia 2 (April, 2011): 16.

71 Anália Torres, 'Casamento e Gênero: Mudanças nas Famílias Contemporâneas a partir do Caso Português', Interseções 3.2 (2001): 62.

72 Sofia Aboim, 'Género, família e mudança em Portugal', in Karin Wall et al. (eds) A Vida Familiar no Mas-

mance of roles in our society"[73] seem to be still present.

It is clear that gender stereotypes persist along with social changes in the relationships among men and women and the way they conceive masculinity and femininity. Stereotypes may be internalized in individuals, however, that does not mean that men are from Mars and women from Venus. Sociological research reveals that differences between countries with regard to values and issues of family, work and gender roles are higher than the differences characterizing males and females from those countries. There also studies about online self-presentations that show that differences may be higher between countries than between genders.[74] Kisilevich and Last,[75] for instance, demonstrated that cultural and national differences impact the characteristics of user Profiles even for people of the same gender across countries.

Finally, one more point needs to be made. The conclusions of this research seem to be valid though they must be viewed not as definitive answers but as research proposals that deserve further investigation.

Online spaces where people can create their self-presentations, producing, or not, different profiles, differ. Therefore, as some authors have stressed, people may act differently when paying a fee for an inscription on a dating site or for, example, to be included in a discussion forum about ecological and environmental problems affecting their community. Taking into consideration the exponential and quick expansion of dating sites, there can also be significant differences between them: specific sites for speed dating, for people who just want to find a sexual partner (one night stand), for individuals who look for their future husband or wife, people looking for homosexual relationships, and so on. Therefore, when studying online dating self-presentation, researches should take into account the specificity of the site being studied since that apparently simple fact may have important implications on the results obtained. It would be interesting to study the self-descriptions impact on dating success. Also, a better understanding of how these self-presentations reflect social and cultural continuities and changes in gender roles over the recent past is needed. Additionally, more qualitative research should be carried out to give a voice to online daters, with the aim of gathering empirical knowledge about online dating practices and the process of finding love online. The influence of demographic variables such as age, educational level, socio-economic status, and marital status, on the construction of online dating Profiles, should also be studied in depth. Finally, more attention must be given to photographs and to the role of visual impression management, since it is known that Profile owners do not self-expose themselves arbitrarily. Research on images and photographs, namely self-portraits, is equally

---

culino. Negociando Velhas e Novas Masculinidades, Lisboa: Comissão para a Igualdade no Trabalho e no Emprego, 2010, pp. 39-66.

73   Anália Torres, Vida Conjugal e Trabalho, Oeiras: Celta Editora, 2004, p. 132.

74   Lauren Reichart Smith and Skye C. Cooley, 'Presenting Me! An Examination of Self-Presentation in US and Russian Online Social Networks', Russian Journal of Communication 5.5 (2013): 176-190.

75   Slava Kisilevich and Mark Last, 'Exploring Gender Differences in Member Profiles of an Online Dating Site Across 35 Countries', Lecture Notes in Computer Science 6904 (2011): 57-78.

important since as Walker explains:

> The computer screen represents the connection between the self and society (...). At the same time as we connect with society, we do the reflective work we used to do only in mirrors, in private. (...) Perhaps our fascination with self-portraits in mirrors is an expression of our collective coming into being as digital subjects. We are subjects. I am a self. This is the first step in learning how to express ourselves with digital technology, and the first step in choosing to express *ourselves* rather than simply allowing ourselves to be described by others.[76]

Acknowledgments
This paper presents research results of a postdoctoral investigation funded by a grant from the Foundation for Science and Technology - FCT (SFRH/BPD/64644/2009).

References

Aboim, Sofia. 'Género, família e mudança em Portugal', in Karin Wall et al. (eds) *A Vida Familiar no Masculino. Negociando Velhas e Novas Masculinidades*, Lisboa: Comissão para a Igualdade no Trabalho e no Emprego, 2010, pp. 39-66.

Amâncio, Lígia. *Masculino e Feminino. A Construção Social da Diferença*, Porto: Edições Afrontamento, 1994.

Bak, Peter Michael. 'Sex Differences in the Attractiveness Halo Effect in the Online Dating Environment', *Journal of Business and Media Psychology* 1 (2010): 1-7.

Baker, Andrea J. 'Cyberdating', in Karen Christensen and David Levinson (eds) *Encyclopedia of Community: From the Village to the Virtual World*, Thousand Oaks, CA: Sage Publications, 2003, pp. 372-373.

Bardin, Laurence. *L'analyse de Contenu*, Paris: Presses Universitaires de France, 2007.

Bell, Philip. 'Content Analysis of Visual Images'. In Theo Van Leeuwen and Carey Jewitt (eds) *Handbook of Visual Analysis*, Thousand Oaks, CA: Sage, 2001, pp. 10-34.

Bercovici, Jeff. 'Love On The Run: The Next Revolution in Online Dating', Forbes.com http://www.forbes.com/sites/jeffbercovici/2014/02/14/love-on-the-run-the-next-revolution-in-online-dating/.

Bourdieu, Pierre. *La Domination Masculine*, Paris: Éditions du Seuil, 1998.

Cacioppo, John T. et al. 'Marital Satisfaction and Break-ups differ Across On-line and Off-line Meeting Venues', Proceedings of the National Academy of the United States of America, Published online before print, June 3 (2013), http://www.pnas.org/content/early/2013/05/31/1222447110.full.pdf.

Cardoso, Gustavo. 'Contributos Para uma Sociologia do Ciberespaço'. Biblioteca on-line de Ciências da Comunicação (1998), http://www.bocc.ubi.pt/pag/_texto.php?html2012=cardoso-gustavo-sociologia-ciberespaco.html.

Cardoso, Gustavo. 'Feel Like Going Online?' Internet Mediated Communication in Portugal', Information, *Communication & Society* 5.4 (2002): 529-550.

Cardoso, Gustavo and Nascimento, Susana. 'Online/Offline: Can You Tell the difference? Portuguese Views on Internet Mediated Communication', Comunicazioni Sociali - Rivista di Media, *Spettacolo e Studi Culturali* XXIV.1 (2002): 41-50.

---

76 Jill Walker, 'Mirrors and Shadows: The Digital Aestheticisation of Oneself', Digital Arts & Culture Conference Proceedings, Copenhagen (December, 2005): 6-7.

Cardoso, Gustavo et al. *World Wide Internet: Changing Societies, Economies and Cultures*, China: University of Macau, 2009.

Cardoso, Gustavo et al. 'A Sociedade em Rede. A Internet em Portugal, 2012', OberCom - Observatório da Comunicação (2012): 1-35, http://www.obercom.pt/client/?newsId=548&fileName=sociedadeRede2012.pdf.

Castells, Manuel. *The Network Society: A Cross-cultural Perspective*, Cheltenham, UK: Edward Elgar, 2004.

Cocks, Harry G. *Classified: The Secret History of the Personal Column*, UK: Random House, 2009.

Degim, I. Alev. 'Identity Construction in Facebook: A Lacanian Analysis of Profiles and Facebook Generated Games', in U. Onen. Andreas Treske, Bestem Büyüm and I. Alev Degim (eds) Image, Time and Motion: New media Critique from Turkey, *Institute of Network Cultures*, n.7, 2011, pp. 111-124, http://networkcultures.org/wpmu/portal/publication/no-07-image-time-and-motion-new-media-critique-from-turkey/.

Dutton, William H. et al. 'The Role of the Internet in Reconfiguring Marriages: A Cross-national Study', *Interpersona* 3.2 (2009): 3-18.

Ellison, Nicole. 'Managing Impressions Online: Self-Presentation Processes in the Online Dating Environment', *Journal of Computer-Mediated Communication* 11.2 (2006): 415-441.

Furnham, Adrian and Twiggy, Mak. 'Sex-Role Stereotyping in Television Commercials: A Review and Comparison of Fourteen Studies Done on Five Continents Over 25 Years', *Sex Roles* 41.5 (1999): 513-537.

Fiore, Andrew T. et al. 'Assessing Attractiveness in Online Dating Profiles', *Proceeding of the twenty-sixth annual SIGCHI conference on Human factors in computing systems*, ACM Press, (2008): 797-806.

Freitas, Simone. 'A Bela e a Fera', II Congresso Internacional Comunicación 3.0 - Libro Nuevos Medios, Nueva Comunicación, Universidad de Salamanca, 4 y 5 de Octobre, (2010): 1-18.

Goffman, Erving. *The Presentation of Self in Everyday Life*, New York: Anchor, 1959.

Gunter, Barrie. "The Study of Online Relationships and Dating", in William H. Dutton (ed.) *The Oxford Handbook of Internet Studies*, Oxford: Oxford University Press, 2013, pp. 173-193.

Hahn, Jennifer and Blass, Thomas. 'Dating Partner Preferences: A Function of Similarity of Love Styles', *Journal of Social Behavior & Personality* 12.3 (1997): 595-610.

Harris, Mary B. 'When Courtesy Fails: Gender Roles and Polite Behaviors', *Journal of Applied Social Psychology* 22.18 (1992): 1399-1416.

Henry-Waring, Millsom and Barraket, Jo. 'Dating & Intimacy in the 21st Century: The Use of Online Dating Sites in Australia', International *Journal of Emerging Technologies and Society* 6.1 (2008): 14-33.

Hsieh, Hsiu-Fang and Shannon, Sarah E. 'Three Approaches to Qualitative Content Analysis', *Qualitative Health Research* 15. 9 (2005): 1277-1288.

Humphreys, Lee. 'Photographs and the Presentation of Self through Online Dating Services', in Paul Messaris and Lee Humphreys (eds) *Digital Media: Transformations in Human Communication*, New York: Peter Lang. 2006, pp. 39-49.

Jagger, Elizabeth. 'Marketing Molly and Melville: Dating in a Postmodern, Consumer Society', *Sociology* 35.1 (2001): 39-57.

Jorge, Filipa. A Apresentação do Eu em Plataformas de Comunicação On-line, Tese de Mestrado, Departamento de Comunicação e Arte, Universidade de Aveiro, 2011.

Kimmel, Michael. *The Gendered Society*, Oxford: Oxford University Press, 2004.

Kisilevich, Slava and Last Mark. 'Exploring Gender Differences in Member Profiles of an Online Dating

Site Across 35 Countries', Lecture Notes in Computer Science 6904 (2011): 57-78, http://bib.dbvis.de/uploadedFiles/359.pdf.

Kelly, Kevin. "We Are the Web", *Wired*, August 2005, http://www.wired.com/wired/archive/13.08/tech.html.

Larossa, Ralph. 'Grounded theory methods and qualitative family research', *Journal of Marriage and Family* 67.4 (2005): 837–857.

Lievrouw, Leah A. 'The Next Decade in Internet Time', Information, *Communication & Society* 15.5 (2012): 616-638.

Lopes, Liliana. 'Diagnóstico e Implementação da Igualdade de Género na Escola Superior de Educação: Apontamentos pelos Trilhos da Igualdade…', Projeto Diagnóstico e Implementação da Igualdade de Género na Escola Superior de Educação (2013): 1-3.

Loureiro, Paulo and Cardoso, Carlos Cabral. 'O Género e os Estereótipos na Gestão', Tékhne - Revista de Estudos Politécnicos VI. 10 (2008): 221-238.

Morgan, Elizabeth et al. 'Comparing Narratives of Personal and Preferred Partner Characteristics in Online Dating Advertisements', *Computers in Human Behavior*, 26.5 (2010): 883-888.

Markus, Hazel and Nurius, Paula. 'Possible Selves', *American Psychologist* 41.9 (1986): 954-969.

Miranda, Patrícia. 'A Construção Social das Identidades de Género nas Crianças: um Estudo Intensivo em Viseu', VI Congresso Português de Sociologia: "Mundos Sociais: Saberes e Práticas", Universidade Nova de Lisboa, Faculdade de Ciências Sociais e Humanas, 25 a 28 de Junho, (2008): 1-12.

Nascimento, Susana. 'Para uma compreensão sociológica das identidades na CMC', Biblioteca online de Ciências da Comunicação (2001): 1-13, http://www.bocc.ubi.pt/pag/nascimento-susana-identidades-cmc.pdf.

Neto, Félix. 'Sex differences in Portuguese Lonely Hearts Advertisements', *Perceptual and Motor Skills* 101.2 (2005): 393-400.

Neto, Félix and Pinto, Isabel. 'Gender Stereotypes in Portuguese Television Advertisements', *Sex Roles* 39.1-2 (1998): 153-164.

Pais, José Machado. *Nos Rastos da Solidão. Deambulações Sociológicas*, Porto: Âmbar, 2006.

Parsons, Talcott and Bales, Robert F. Family, *Socialization and the Interaction Process*, New York: MacMillan, 1955.

Pereira, Francisco Costa and Veríssimo, Jorge. 'A Mulher na Publicidade e os Estereótipos de Género', *Observatorio* 5 (2008): 281-296, http://obs.obercom.pt/index.php/obs/article/view/120.

Pereira, Maria do Mar. 'Os discursos de Género: Mudança e Continuidade nas Narrativas sobre Diferenças, Semelhanças e (Des)igualdade entre Mulheres e Momens', in Karin Wall, Sofia Aboim and Vanessa Cunha (eds) *Vida Familiar no Masculino: Negociando Velhas e Novas Masculinidades*, Lisboa: CITE, Comissão para a Igualdade no Trabalho e no Emprego, (2010), pp. 225-261.

Prosser, Jon. 'Researching with visual images: Some guidance notes and a glossary for beginners', ESRC National Centre for Research Methods, Working Paper Series 6/06, 2006, http://eprints.ncrm.ac.uk/481/1/0606_researching_visual_images.pdf.

Rosa, Rodrigo. Escolha do Cônjuge e Modos de Construção Social no Casal. Tese de Doutoramento, Instituto Superior de Ciências do Trabalho e da Empresa, 2008.

Rosenfeld, Michael J. and Thomas, Reuben J. 'Searching for a Mate: The Rise of the Internet as a Social Intermediary', *American Sociological Review* 77.4 (2012): 523-547.

Ryan, Gery W. et al. 'Techniques to identify themes', *Field Methods* 15.1 (2003): 85-109.

Santos, Ana Alexandra Carvalheira. *Relaciones Interpersonales y Comportamientos Sexuales Através de Internet*, Tesis Doctoral, Facultad de Psicologia, Universidad de Salamanca, 2005.

Skopek, Jan, et al. 'The Gendered Dynamics of Age Preferences – Empirical Evidence from Online Dating', *Journal of Family Research* 23.3 (2011): 267-290.

Smith, Lauren Reichart and Cooley, Skye C. 'Presenting Me! An Examination of Self-Presentation in US and Russian Online Social Networks', *Russian Journal of Communication* 5.5 (2013): 176-190.

Strangelove, Michael. 'The Internet, Electric Gaia and the Rise of the Uncensored Self', Computer-Mediated Communication Magazine (1994): 11-14, http://www.ibiblio.org/cmc/mag/1994/sep/self.html.

Strassberg, Donald S. and Holty, Stephen. 'An Experimental Study of Women's Internet Personal Ads', *Archives of Sexual Behavior* 32.3 (2003): 253–260.

Strauss, Anselm C. and Corbin, Juliet. *Basics of Qualitative Research: Techniques and Procedures for Developing Grounded Theory*, London: Sage Publications, 1990.

Toma, Catalina L. et al. 'Separating Fact From Fiction: An Examination of Deceptive Self-Presentation in Online Dating Profiles', *Personality and Social Psychology Bulletin* 34.8 (2008): 1023-1036.

Torres, Anália. 'Casamento e Gênero: Mudanças nas Famílias Contemporâneas a partir do Caso Português', Interseções 3.2 (2001): 53-70, http://analiatorres.com/pdf/Casamento_e_%20genero_mudancas_%20nas_%20famlias.pdf.

Torres, Anália. *Vida Conjugal e Trabalho*, Oeiras: Celta Editora, 2004.

Torres, Anália et al. *Homens e Mulheres entre Família e Trabalho*, Lisboa: CITE, Comissão para a Igualdade no Trabalho e no Emprego, 2004.

Torres, Anália et al. 'Gender, work and family: balancing central dimensions in individuals' lives', Sociologia Online - Revista da Associação Portuguesa de Sociologia 2 (April 2011): 11-37, http://revista.aps.pt/cms/files/artigos_pdf/ART4dc283b2a4084.pdf.

Torres, Anália et al. 'A Mysterious European Threesome: Workcare Regimes, Policies and Gender', *International and Multidisciplinary Journal of Social Sciences* 1.1 (2012): 31-61. <http://www.analiatorres.com/pdf/AMysteriousEuropeanThreesome.pdf>.

Tuna, Sandra and Freitas, Elsa. 'Gendered adverts: an analysis of female and male images in contemporary perfume ads', *Comunicação & Sociedade* 21 (2012): 95-107.

Walker, Jill. 'Mirrors and Shadows: The Digital Aestheticisation of Oneself', Digital Arts & Culture Conference Proceedings, Copenhagen, December (2005): 1-7, https://bora.uib.no/bitstream/handle/1956/1136/mirrorsandshadows-final.pdf?sequence=1.

Wall, Karin and Amâncio, Lígia. *Família e Género em Portugal e na Europa*, Lisboa: Imprensa de Ciências Sociais, 2007.

Walther, Joseph B. (2007). 'Selective Self-Presentation in Computer-Mediated Communication: Hyperpersonal Dimensions of Technology, Language, and Cognition', *Computers in Human Behavior* 23.5 (2007): 2538–2557.

Walther, Joseph B. et al. 'Is a Picture Worth a Thousand words? Photographic Images in Long-Term and Short-Term Computer-Mediated Communication', *Communication Research* 28.1 (2001): 105-134.

Whitty, Monica. 'Revealing the 'Real' Me, Searching for the 'Actual' You: Presentations of Self on an Internet Dating Site', *Computers in Human Behavior* 24.4 (2008): 1707–1723.

Whitty, Monica and Joinson, Adam. *Truth, Lies and Trust on the Internet*, London: Routledge, 2008.

Woll, Stanley B. and Young, Peter. 'Looking for Mr. or Ms. Right: Self-Presentation in Videodating', *Journal of Marriage and the Family* 51.2 (1989): 483-488.

LIBERALISM CONQUERING LOVE: REPORTS AND REFLECTIONS ON MASS ROMANTIC AND SEXUAL CONSUMPTION IN THE INTERNET AGE

PASCAL LARDELLIER

Introduction

The internet and dating websites have had a strong impact on the nature of seductive relationships over a short period of time. This statement, which is not strictly deterministic, is based on a series of observations. Over the last 15 years or so, new means of meeting, flirting and falling in love have appeared -- all behind multiple screens. The traditional methods and timescale of seduction have been turned upside down. On the internet you become acquainted with others from the inside out and many fall in love with these 'strangers.' In 1998, the movie *You've Got Mail* very explicitly put a story and images to this new phenomenon.

In 2012, the American actor-director John Malkovich pitched a contemporary production of the famous novel of Choderlos de Laclos, *Liaisons dangereuses*, in Paris. Malkovich, who in 1989 played the Vicomte de Valmont for producer Stephan Frears, has adapted this classic piece to the internet generation. In this production, social networks (Facebook, Twitter), smartphones, and texting all play important roles. It is always interesting to observe the impact of different technical interfaces on the way we fall in love. Each historical period brings its own combination of its values and approaches to love. Malkovich's Parisian adaptation shows that the role of the written word in seduction and relationships is reinforced through the use of the internet. Of course, as in the 'classic' age of love, we still find cynicism, hypocrisy, lies, and manipulation. But now, they are all technologically assisted.

It is a new state of mind and an unprecedented ideology that now presides over computer-assisted romantic-sexual relationships. Single people online commodify themselves in what we can call "romance marketing".

This chapter will begin by analyzing the manner in which liberalism has established itself as the dominant new ideology of postmodern romantic/seductive relationships. Liberalism is implicitly present in the discourse of those on the internet as much as it is in their online habits. This observation is based on surveys conducted on the subject by the author, in the French-speaking world, over the past ten years. The chapter will then discuss this phenomenon in the light of more general sociological reflections and philosophical considerations about love and the digital-network-era couple.

Methodology and Surveys

This chapter is based on two surveys carried out between 2003 and 2012, then published in 2004 and 2012.[1] In order to conduct these surveys, we partnered with four heterosexual dating websites, gathering data from both French nationals and other French-speaking people. 260 (130 from each group) questionnaires were gathered and processed along with 30 interviews. The title of this chapter, "Liberalism Conquering Love," was a theme mentioned

---

1   *cf.* bibliography, Lardellier

by the majority of those surveyed, despite some differences in wording. The analyses taken from these surveys were developed by the author, who has experience working in this field.

The Victory of Liberalism in Romantic Relationships

First of all, it should be remembered that romantic/seductive relationships on the internet have notable differences from those in real life. Online, you do not see who you are speaking to, and you do not know him or her because he or she is hidden behind a pseudonym and a screen. Likewise, things often move faster than in real life, where the temporality of seduction is often rather slow. In recent years, many authors have noted that digitized relationships are becoming subject to liberalism[2] considered both as an economic doctrine and as a collection of values and ideology. They see relationships in the internet age as commodities, governed by the principles of utilitarianism. To say that this economic theory is gaining the domain of human relationships is more than just a metaphor. If we take certain expressions literally, they can be incidentally revealing. On the subject of dating websites, the internet users interviewed spontaneously alluded to: a "shopping for love," a "supermarket," "business and commerce," "unrestrained sexual consumption," and a "store front window for singles." There are many who said that they choose a partner "like you would pick a yogurt, or any product, shopping cart in hand." In short, "people have the impression of becoming merchandise" once they sign up for a dating website. Some, disappointed by these sites, even mention prostitution, "since you pay to have relationships with a stranger"... These lexical clichés from the users themselves are all inspired by their experiences on existing dating websites.

Romantic encounters have thus become a market selling singles the possibility of quick sexual relationships, as much as the hopes of a life together. Online service providers, helped by marketing specialists, were quick to seize this opportunity, appealing to the dreams and wishes of individuals and evolving social norms.

On digital networks and dating sites, you label others using social intuition before your first encounter. This leads to homophilia (being attracted to people similar to us) and endogamy (couples forming on the basis of existing social groups, values, and similar religions). In fact, we see strong evidence of sociocultural kinship, an important organizing principle in the matrimonial market and thus in the make-up of couples. This makes it seem all the more shocking that online, we always begin talking to others anonymously. Is love not as blind as we all thought?

Several phases can be seen to have characterized the French market of romantic encounters. After the first era of general dating websites, the market appeared to have split. It began to offer websites based on certain criteria such as ethnicity, religion, sociocultural status, and socioeconomic background.

Likewise, on the internet, relationships are liberalized. We see all major principles of economic markets: an abundance of offers, rationalization of the search for love, selective targeting, the ability to choose from many offers, and the standardization of 'products.' Indeed, we faith-

---

2   *cf.* Illouz, 1997 2007, bibliography.

fully fill out anthropometric forms while strictly conforming to the sections given: a process of generalized objectification or commoditization. The immensity of the offer – hundreds of thousands of profiles[3] – underlines this commoditization, with the personal information of those registered being analyzed like products for which we would read a factsheet. We can 'test' and change whatever we find to be unsatisfactory or flawed.

Through all of the texts and images exchanged amongst strangers on dating websites, we see that liberalism has invaded the sphere of human relations. You must be efficient, attractive, and noteworthy to rise above the crowd. You must always 'perform' well, with pictures that broadcast the message that you want to be received. Romantic relationships must yield productivity, efficiency, and cost-effectiveness. The personal information pages put online must be sales-worthy and impactful in order to be noticed. These adjectives are a matter of marketing and coaching, which influence each type of intimate relationship. On dating sites, everyone conforms to the principles of romance marketing, considering themselves as exclusive products to promote, or one product in competition with thousands of others. In fact, on dating sites (like on social networks), many also indulge in personal branding, both consciously and subconsciously. In other words, they become their own brand. Once again, this is a notion and concept which takes us into the commercial domain.

There is a famous French play by Pierre Marivaux, 1688-1768, entitled "The Game of Love and Chance."[4] Today, on dating sites, we can speak of "the game of love and the market." As automated romantic relationships imply output and profitability, each member of a site becomes his or her own matrimonial cyber agent. In the era of the triumph of marketing and liberalism, we are under the impression that feelings can be reduced to consumer advantages, emotional capital, and successful interviews. In a similar vein, this is symbolized by speed-dating: a trend in which the first contact strangely resembles a job interview.

Then there is the recent appearance of love coaching. Love coaches are in charge of singles as if they were relegated beings who must be motivated in order to even think of landing a good catch. The goal of these relationship coaches is to increase the value of your capital, display your qualities, and make good use of your potential. These principles and practices are a part of managerial ideology and fall within this current liberal framing of romantic/seductive relationships.

Even though these digital networks are filled with cynicism, there is some romanticism and sincerity. But the majority of people registered on dating sites are after quick consumption, rather than searching for long-term relationships, According to the statements of members, men tend to be more pressing, eager to receive a number, an instant messenger name, or a

---

3   It is difficult to get the exact number of profiles from the sites themselves, in so far as those numbers are a strategic and jealously kept secret. However, the french market of online dating gather 5 or 6 million singles, registred on 10 main sites. Meetic, the most famous french site (that principally belongs to the American Match.com) has over than a million members for instance.

4   "The Game of Love and Chance", "Les jeux de l'amour et du hazard" in French, is a romantic comedy written by the French author Marivaux, first played in 1730.

Skype screen name, then a real-life meeting, as early as possible, to build up the relationship. That is to say, to move to a sexual relationship.

Many works, whether novels or essays, written in recent years by men who frequent dating sites confirm the idea that picking up partners is like an industrialized process. In 2005, the Frenchman Lewis Wingrove explained in his work on *Of Mice and Men* how much rationalization,[5] assisted by IT tools, can favor optimal output in the seduction process. But there are not only winners in this game of love and the market. In his novel, *Extension du domaine de la lutte* (*Broadening the Field of Struggle*), the famous French novelist Michel Houellbecq, from 1994 to the present, predicted the entrance of sexuality into the era of liberal competition, with winners and, of course, losers. In this work, he puts forth frustrated, unlikeable, pathetic anti-heroes who are tortured by insatiable urges that make them suffer. The handsome ones and those full of themselves easily obtain sexual fulfillment. As for the losers, they are left with pictures, fantasies, and masturbation as their solace.

Dating Websites: a Triple Principle of Economics

Romantic/seductive online relationships are governed by a triple principle of economics: the economics of time, money, and emotions. This concept assures their success. Once registered, which only takes a few minutes, you have access to a vast pool of singles -- thousands of people who virtually interest you and who can potentially be interested in your new profile.

The economics of money, likewise, puts you in contact with all of these people which would have been much more onerous (offering dates, etc.) in 'real life.' Accepting an offer from a letter that was copied and pasted and sent to dozens of people is a common practice that alludes to Taylorism -- since it is a question of rationalizing a task.

Lastly, we see economics of emotion on these sites, because losing face and its cost are opportunely ousted by the absence of the other. Making a digital exit does not cost anything in terms of face. However, there is fierceness in competition that is not specific to the virtual world and that can cause what psychoanalysts call a narcissistic injury: the feeling you are left with after an emotionally-invested relationship is terminated. But the internet allows you to "move on to the next one."

It is the overall system of dating sites which causes this consumption trend. You make the most rational and judicious choice, generate traffic around your page to become the focal product, and gather contact information. That is the logic behind mass sexual and emotional consumption. Certain members of dating sites even boast about their sexual adventures as if they had collected exotic items or butterflies. For them, thanks to dating sites, picking up partners has truly moved from a small-scale hobby to an industry. Dating sites sanction marriage, sexual and emotional consumption as well as marketing techniques. Clearly, our

---

5 Financial Times http://www.ft.com/intl/cms/s/288dadd2-073b-11db-9067-0000779e2340,Authorised=false.html?_i_location=http%3A%2F%2Fwww.ft.com%2Fcms%2Fs%2F0%2F288dadd2-073b-11db-9067-0000779e2340.html%3Fsiteedition%3Dintl&siteedition=intl&_i_referer=\#axzz3CJV8tuvf.

era rationalizes emotional economics. We may still talk about the heart, but it is often hard to distinguish the heart (*coeur*) and the heart of our target (*coeur de cible*), which is of course a marketing term.

One site that symbolizes this commoditization of online romantic/seductive encounters is the French site *AdopteUnMec.com* [adopt a guy]. With its overt and tongue-in-cheek feminist stance, this site allows women to walk around with a shopping cart, browsing the aisles of a virtual man-market. It is as if these men are special products that you cannot miss, the deal of the day! In this realm, men have few rights; they must obey – and only obey. The site is livened up by a commercial metaphor in which the all-powerful female user does her 'shopping' with an online list that she drew up based on her criteria. This site demands a good sense of humor, but it has had a lot of success with its young clientele, who master the relationship codes on social networks. So even if the title may seem exaggerated, we are most certainly living in the realm of love won over by liberalism.

The Internet, Romance, and Being Internationally Single

Liberalism is expressed in an even more tangible manner when you think of online romantic/seductive encounters. The global expansion of dating sites allows us to detect, more largely, the rise of a new international singles market. Thus, tens of thousands of women living in developing countries or zones of political unrest are trying to emigrate to 'rich' countries, thanks to the dating website network. This matrimonial cyber-migration has opened a new type of migratory trend, lining the pockets of cyber-café owners. In a documentary titled "Nord-Sud.com" (North-South.com), the Frenchmen François Ducat explains that in 1997, there were four cyber cafés in Yaoundé, Cameroon, and 450 in 2007. [6]

There are only two logistical demands for cyber-cafés: computers must be in individual booths and above all, equipped with webcams, since the Western men chatting with these women and want to judge them on their appearance. The competition is fierce and only the most attractive will be noticed. These women must simultaneously be pretty, docile, sensual, sweet, and offer hope for a meeting in Europe or North America. This international single life sees hordes of women from Africa, Asia, and ex-communist countries attempt to (and occasionally manage to) create a 'cyber-union.' Of course, one consequence is being uprooted from family and cultural lifestyle. These women will attempt to live a new life, far from home, (usually) with a white stranger who is wealthy and older then themselves. These men buy the 'youth' of these women in exchange for goods and a 'better life.' The success of these relationships varies. Some adapt to Western ways, while others are depressed, yet make sacrifices to stay. Then there are those who return to their country after seeing that it would be impossible to become integrated. Finally, many return after being disappointed or disillusioned by their Western 'Prince Charming'.

There is economical asymmetry in these relationships that stretches beyond the explanations of the protagonists. The men exhibit the 'privileged values' that these women look for in their

---

6   For a recent study of this phenomenon see: "La cybermigration maritale des femmes camerounaises. La quête de conjoints blancs, Brice Arsène Mankou, L'Harmattan, Paris, 2014.

future husband – a level of income and lifestyle unavailable in their countries of origin. Yet, these marital exiles also see native families torn apart for the reward of others living in the European/American Eldorado.'

If this phenomenon makes searching for love an international affair, a part of the intercultural melting pot, tearing apart destinies but also bringing happiness to the lucky few, if it is amplified it could also cause legitimate instability in the domestic marriage markets, and heighten cultural and economic differences. "In the long term, globalization of the dating market could have notable results. Western women already have a difficult time finding men who fulfill their expectations. As for Western men, even though they are seduced by dynamic women, some may prefer a woman who is not too demanding to ensure calm on the home front and thus (…) turn towards the international market to buy submission, youth, and beauty, ignoring the independent, degree-bearing women in their country. (…) However, the poor men in the West are still having a difficult time finding spouses."[7] The global singles market was created by dating sites and founded on economic principles. Feelings are not completely absent, but if they develop, it is much later on. 'Playing the love market' looks set to remain a global game.

Love on the Internet

This part of the chapter will expand the frame of analysis so as to offer more general sociological and philosophical considerations about the new types of couples found in the internet era.

Singles Enduring Paradoxical Tensions

First of all, it seems that the effects of solitude felt in our society throughout history are still just as present in the era of commoditized online relationships that made communication a social virtue. Users of dating sites come across digital heartthrobs and virtual kisses. Hundreds of people visit their personal page without meeting them offline, an act, which can lead to lasting relationships -- sometimes, of course, but not always.

Oftentimes, many of these singles feel high levels of stress on a daily basis: exposing themselves to rejection, hoping for success, symbolically risking everything, while at the same time giving themselves the means to make a couple, in obedience to the constant implicit social pressure from their entourage. If our era values those who communicate well and know how to assert themselves in relationships, then it has never been more difficult to meet others. If proof were needed, we need simply to look at the millions who have already registered for dating sites.

The Traditional Couple Transformed by Information and Communication Technologies

In all cases, internet suitors conform to a procedure which, for the first time ever, reverses the chronology of events: they become acquainted with one another before meeting, thus discovering each other from the inside out. When they meet, they sleep together very quickly if the 'feeling' is there. After that, love comes (or not). We understand that this Copernican

---

7   J.- C. Kaufmann, *Sex@mour*, Albin Michel, 2010, Paris, p. 192.

change in courting takes people away from their traditional points of reference. They have to invent a new relationship code, an unprecedented feat in the history of humanity as well as that of romantic relationships.

The internet offers a solution for finding your soulmate, but on condition that you can escape being caught in the fringe. You frequently move to the other side of the screen. Remember that in Ovid's *Metamorphosis,* Pygmalion commits himself to a virtual relationship (even then!), with his beautiful statue, Galatea. From one illusion to another, Narcissus prefers himself over even the tender love of the muse Echo, until his self-admiration becomes his own death. And how many are there on the internet who put on this performance and who gaze at the raving comments and gratification of others? "A relationship put in the public eye via the internet can allow someone to be satisfied with more or less success than the profound human need of having relationships and simultaneously promoting, in his or her own mind, a paranoid withdrawal, thus avoiding all forms of intersubjective commitment."[8] This is true because the web is all-powerful and allows you to fight against anxieties and frustrations. An internet connection can be compared to an umbilical cord; it nourishes, calms, and relies on reassurance. New technologies, in a broad sense, have become the preferred source of pleasure for people from 25-49, even before sex.[9]

We still love 'for real' in 2014, even if there is the temptation to be all powerful – or, hide behind a screen. We still continue to meet people in real life, experience physical attraction, and develop love affairs in real life. More and more, however, we use information and communication technologies and their resources in the courting process. Significantly over half of romantic encounters among thirty-year-olds are arranged by websites.

The model of the traditional couple is called into question by information and communication technologies. Clearly, the internet 'produces' a good amount of couples. But, as a consequence, it also produces 'defeats,' as digital suitors reconnect for digital adultery, polygamy and 'sexfriending.' These sites have given birth to a type of recreational sexuality. In a parallel manner, the sentimentality produced by these digital networks is fun and disengaged, but also cynical – and occasionally hurtful in this regard. Our current era is one of mass sexual and romantic consumption. We take, we make the most of things, we enjoy those things, and we throw those things away. Of course, we must not forget the numerous beautiful love stories which also have their origin the internet. However, those involved in these stories often encountered disappointment and suffering before finally finding a soulmate. This is due to the prevailing cynicism and the unpleasant impression of being referred to like a supermarket product, as others flip through a thick catalog full of people to be 'consumed.'

We do not look at it all in a moral sense: there is not only frustration or disgust in romantic and sexual consumption being industrialized by the internet. There are many who take great pleasure in the internet and use it for adventures and sexual experimentation. They live in

---

8   Michael Civin, Psychanalyse du Net, *op. cit.* pp. 46-47.

9   According to an Ipsos Survey, quoted by *Télérama* n° 3072, November 2008, the main source of pleasure for 39% of respondents is use of technology, compared to a 36% for whom it is sex.

'sensual parentheses,' filled with pleasure in order to break away from the monotony of life. Since you can seduce or be seduced online, and almost nobody shows it, casualness and immediate pleasure are the driving forces of the system. But just because something exists for a short amount of time, it does not mean that it will exist forever. After experimenting with the first option of dating sites, sex, many users set their hearts on the second promise: to find 'true love.'

But even in this case, it becomes complicated, since the internet creates stress but also reassures. Matchmaking technology has effectively opened an era of interchangeable options for romance. Not one, not ten, but hundreds or even thousands have found their significant others, virtually, thanks to digital networks. How many are there, additionally, who brag and count their dozens of simultaneous affairs and hundreds of 'one night stands'? "If the abundance of possibilities can be reassuring, it can also take on the form of an indefinite, never-ending quest. You are compulsively drawn back to the internet, in a kind of stressful addiction. That is to say that you embark upon a quest which is not only continuous, but one in which what you do not always know what you are searching for."[10]

Romantic Relationships – Fragile but Interchangeable

Nowadays, love is a fixed-term contract. But couples who have signed a permanent contract can also fall apart due to the arrival of information and communication technologies. These technologies could, at any moment, bring about unsettling news, requests, or make you want to discretely have a look around the internet. We have never previously had to see our exes and teen romances again as much as now, in an era where we can find them three clicks and a few seconds later.

The internet has introduced a sovereign restlessness to couples, most notably in couples who met online. A little flaw in your partner? A bug, an argument? Hit a rough spot? Well, there is now the enormous temptation to reconnect so as to restart the search for virtual candidates who will be less of a nuisance. But it is an illusion that brings the imaginary into contact with reality. We can call it "Bovaryism," after Emma Bovary, heroine of 19th century French novelist Gustave Flaubert, who created a utopian life based on the power of imagination.

However, we must not expect old examples to apply today. The famous Marcel Proust, in his novel *Albertine disparue*, exemplifies this idea: "this unique woman, we know that she would not have been for us if we had been in another city when we met, if we had walked in another neighborhood, if we had gone to another salon. Do we really think that she is unique? She is just one of countless many"…and how many are there on the internet, sending notifications to others about going out for a coffee, a drink, or going on a date, and never seeing this person again? On the internet, many romances end every day before even starting. Singles who try to pick up others online know this after having come across many people with whom a nice love story would have been possible. Multiply this by millions, and this sensation contributes to making the generation of internet lovers nostalgic, yet disillusioned in facing the brutality of technologically advanced and liberalized relationships. They face so many failures,

---

10   Marc Parmentier, Hermès, CNRS édition, Paris, p. 174.

and do this all while confronting the fragility of connections and the difficulty of creating a strong couple in this society of 'connected individualism.'

Computer-Assisted Romance

It is always interesting to come back to the wisdom of ancient authors in a period of change. From Ovid's *The Art of Love*, a straightforward manual on how to pick up others, to Plato's *Symposium* and its origin in tight-bonded relationships and hesitant love -- choosing one shortly after the other, even if they were not necessarily accepted in their eras. The internet and dating sites have allowed us to opt for the sentimental-sexual model of interchangeability and 'getting around,' but only for a certain time. Despite the cynics and those who've been disappointed, a lot of singles on the internet are convinced that a special person is hidden just behind a screen and that they will finally be in contact, like the androgynous couples of Plato. We finally see that the liberal ideology that we find on dating sites is counter-balanced by a romantic ideology that has always exerted its influence.

In 2014, those searching for love try to catch Venus or Cupid, the mythical gods of desire and love, thanks to technology. And indeed, they occasionally offer love to those who are constantly looking for it. Then, it is left to the internet lovers to learn how to work together until they become a real couple. Thus, the most difficult part begins. The internet, which allows us to quickly create a bond with others, can even more abruptly break this same bond. And so we see the history of romantic relationships: never ending, always reinvented, continuing to write itself.

References

Bauman, Zygmunt. *Liquid Love: On the Frailty of Human Bonds*, Cambridge: Polity Press, 2003.

Baqué, Dominique. *E-Love. Petit marketing de la rencontre*, Paris: Anabet, 2008.

Bergström, Marie. 'La loi du Supermarché? Sites de Rencontres et Représentations de L'amour ', P.U.F. *Ethnologie Française*, 3. 43, (2013:)433- 442.

Bernstein, Elisabeth. *Temporarily Yours. Intimacy, Authenticity and the Commerce of Sex*, Chicago: University of Chicago Press, 2007.

Bhattacharyya, Gargi. *Sexuality and Society. An Introduction*, London/New York: Routledge, 2002.

Chaumier, Serge. *La Déliaison Amoureuse. De la Fusion Romantique au Désir D'indépendance*, Paris: Armand Colin, 1999.

Combessie, Philippe and Sibylla Mayer, 'Une Nouvelle économie des Relations Sexuelles?' Ethnologie Française, Sexualités Négociées, *Presses Universitaires de France*, 2013.

Gagnon, John and William Simon, *Sexual Conduct. The Social Sources of Human Sexuality*, Chicago: Aldine, 1973.

Giddens, Anthony. *The Transformation of Intimacy : Sexuality, Love and Eroticism in Modern Societies*, Stanford, CA: Stanford University Press, 1992, 2004.

Granovetter, Mark. 'The Strength of Weak Ties :A Network Theory Revisited', *Sociological Theory* 1. (1983): 201-233.

Illouz, Eva. *Consuming the Romantic Utopia: Love and the Cultural Contradictions of Capitalism*, Berkeley: University of California Press, 1997.

Illouz, Eva. *Why Love Hurts : A Sociological Explanation*, Cambridge: Polity Press, 2011.

Illouz, Eva. 'Réseaux Amoureux sur Internet', *Réseaux* 138. 2006: 269-272.

Illouz, Eva. *Cold Intimacies : The Making of Emotional Capitalism*, Cambridge: Polity Press, 2007.

Kaufmann, Jean-Claude. *Sex@mour*, Paris: Armand Colin, 2010.

Kessous, Emmanuel. 'L'amour en Projet. Internet et les Conventions de la Rencontre Amoureuse', *Réseaux* 166. (2011) : 191-223.

Lardellier, Pascal. 'De la Consommation Sentimentale et Sexuelle de Masse à l'ère d'Internet ', dans Marquet J., Janssen C (dir.), @mours virtuelles. Conjugalité et Internet, Louvain-la-Neuve, Academia-Bruylandt, (2009): 17-41.

Lardellier, Pascal. Le coeur Net. Célibat et @mours sur le Web, Paris, Belin, 2004.

Lardellier, Pascal. Les Réseaux du Cœur. Sexe, Amour et Séduction sur Internet, Paris, François Bourin, 2012.

Luhmann, Niklas. *Love as Passion. The Codification of Intimacy*, Cambridge: Polity Press, 1986.

Parmentier, Marc. 'Philosophie des sites de rencontres', Hermès. 59.(2011) : 173-178, 2011.

King, Martin. *White, Dating, Mating, and Marriage*, New York: Aldine de Gruyter, 1990.

THE ADVERTISING AND PROFIT MODEL OF LEADING DATING SITES IN CHINA: A COMPARISON OF JIANYUAN, BAIHE AND ZHENAI'S TARGETING AND ADVERTISING

CAIYUN WEN

The Prosperity and Bottlenecks of the Online Dating Market in China

In China, matchmaking is an ancient occupation, which plays a key role to the marriage mode in the traditional society. With the development of the Internet in China, matchmaking is switching to the Internet model. Chinese single users aged 18 and older are expected to reach 195 million by 2015, according to iResearch.com.[1] The online dating market will reach 1.9 billion yuan (about 304 million dollars),[2] with an average annual compound growth rate at 31.3 percent. Because of new single users and the changes from traditional media to the Internet, the dating sites have a prosperous market. Founded in 2003, Jiayuan.com was listed in the NASDAQ. On January 14, 2014, Jiayuan.com announced that the Internet registers had reached 100 million.[3] In China, Jiayuan.com, Baihe.com and Zhenai.com account for about 70 percent of all the dating site business in terms of market share. By case studying these three sites, this article silhouettes the development pattern of dating sites in China.

Chinese dating sites began in the 1990s. In the first few years, because the Internet was accessible to limited users and the cost was high, the number of Internet users was only 8.9 million in 1998.[4] Dating sites were developing slowly due to small scale and unsatisfying service advantage. The short period from 2003 to 2005 saw the increased penetration of the Internet among Chinese users and the burgeoning of online dating sites, some being the copycat of foreign websites such as Match.com. In the following years till 2012, Chinese online dating sites changed from free to paid and explored new profit models. Since 2012, online dating sites have been struggling with their bottlenecks.

Although the dating sites have sufficient potential customers, the leading dating sites' growth suddenly deteriorated for nearly two years. The overall ceiling has begun in the dating sites. On December 24, 2012, Haiyan Gong, founder of Jiayuan.com announced her resignation out of operating pressure and occupation bottleneck. Fanjiang Tian, the CEO of Baihe.com, said, the single users, accumulated over the past 10 years, created a fast growth of members, but this growth would slow down with the development of dating sites to a certain extent,

---

1   As cited in Zexin Ma. 'Personal Image Construction and Communication Effect in Dating Sites', News World, 9 (2012): 124.

2   As cited in Yifan Mu. 'The Jiayuan Went to IPO Profit Model Was into a Bottleneck', China Business News, 25 April 2011: B03.

3   Sino Tech, '*Shiji Jiayuan Xuanbu Wangzhan Zhuce Yonghu Shuliang Chao 1 Yi* (Jiayuan.com Announces Registered User Accounts Surpass 100 Million)', 14 January 2014, http://tech.sina.com.cn/i/2014-01-14/19309096326.shtml

4   Xiaoying Wu. 'The Dating Sites: "Sweet" Industrial Predicament and Outlet', Sichuan Provincial Academy of Social Sciences, (2009) 38.

and online charging mode of 199-499 yuan,[5] per person per year was near to the maximum which one could accept.[6]

At the same time, the competitive threats from the social networking sites (SNSs)[7] also affected the stability of the dating sites' user group. For example, as a "real" social website like Facebook, Renren provides a search function to find friends. If "single" is entered as the filter, all the single users' information will show up. This is a great threat to the dating sites. More importantly, these SNSs have greater users and the users are more fixed than dating websites. The listing prospectus of Sina Weibo showed that the monthly active users are 129 million.[8] Many people begin to use Renren from high school or college, and will continue because this platform helps maintain the network and offers functions such as games to make users adhesive.

In this case, to attract new users is the most effective means to the dating sites. At present advertising produces the main income for several Chinese leading dating sites. They increased advertising efforts, expanded the advertising media (from the Internet to TV, outdoor and printed media). According to statistics of Market Research Center of CCTV, only from 2011 to June 2013, at the China Central Television (CCTV), the advertising time of dating sites was 53,530 seconds, up to 3,573 pieces. The total cost was 146,588,100 yuan (about 23.46 million U.S. dollars).

At present, Jiayuan.com spends most money on online search advertising, in which Baidu.com leads with tens of millions yuan,[9] in addition to the portal websites,[10] the vertical websites[11] and navigation websites.[12] The Spring Festival, or the Chinese New Year, is as important to Chinese as Christmas to Christians. It is a time for family reunion, togetherness, and leisure activities, and the best timing for advertisers. Baihe.com spent 30 million yuan (about 4.8 million U.S. dollars) only during the Spring Festival on buses, subway trains, television and the Internet in 2011.[13] Zhenai.com also put a lot of advertisement on television and outdoor

---

5   The fee of 499 yuan is equivalent to the monthly food cost for one person living in a medium-sized city in China.
6   Fengtao Li and Xujie Wang, 'The Traditional Mode Met Bottleneck, Three Dating Site Run into the Deep Era', Chinese Economic Weekly Z1 (2013) 76.
7   For example, the free dating platform of Renren, Sina Weibo and other social networking sites. In China, Renren is a real social website like Facebook. Sina Weibo is another social network service like Twitter.
8   iResearch, '129 Million Active Users Monthly: How to Estimate the Value of Sina Weibo', 15 March 2014, http://web2.iresearch.cn/weibo/20140315/228594.shtml.
9   Lei Li, 'Dating Sites Started the New User Battle', China Business Journal, 12 March 2012: E02.
10 Portal web refers to comprehensive Internet information resources and provides relevant information service of the application system.
11 Vertical website refers to a certain industry professional website, refers to the profound development trend of industry-specific site.
12 Navigation website refers to a collection of many web sites, to classify the websites according to certain conditions.
13 Lei Li, 'Dating Sites Started the New User Battle'.

billboards in recent years.

Although the leading dating sites all spend money on advertising, their advertising aims, advertising media and the campaigns are different. Baihe.com used television advertising to enhance brand awareness. Jiayuan.com, the first advertiser on CCTV among dating sites, steered to new media in 2011. In contrast Zhenai.com and Baihe.com frequently advertise on CCTV.

Jiayuan.com: the Multi-dimensional Strategy

In the construction of the advertising model, Jiayuan.com adopted a multi-dimensional strategy. These include, but are not limited to, Internet marketing, topics marketing, and entertainment marketing.

The Internet Media Marketing - Micro Film for the Single Youth*

In China, many young urban professionals are from the rural areas or small cities. Because of their limited circle of communication and tight work schedules, they have few chances to find their prospective partners. But according to traditional Chinese beliefs, if a woman remains single at 30, she is odd. Her parents will be very anxious about this because parents take children's marriage as their responsibility. They will lose face in front of friends and relatives, especially during the Spring Festival, a time for visiting each other. Although the single group is under the psychological pressure from the family and the people around, and they yearn for affection themselves, they still pursue their own love, and don't want to lower mate-selection criteria. They are young, faddish and patient. They desire for the real love instead of the marriage form or sex.

This group is Jiayuan's target audience. The Internet marketing strategies are as follows.

The micro film (*Wei Dianying*) is a small film, produced by professional person, with movie narrative methods, played through the Internet or other new media platform.[14] The micro film is no longer than 30 minutes commonly. Now, the micro film is a popular form among young people. It has the entertainment features of films and the commercial essence of advertising, which weave the corporate brand goals and business activities into a small story so that the advertising is more acceptable than ordinary commercials. Jiayuan's target audience is aged 20 to 35, and they work alone in a strange city. These young people are the major audience of the micro film. Therefore, the micro film was the proper media in Jiayuan's advertising strategy. Jiayuan.com launched a series of micro films such as "*Waiting (2013)*","*Fear (2013)*", "*Busy (2013)*" and "*Dilemma (2013)*". "*Waiting*" is about a city girl. She was waiting for an elevator, a bus, a dinner, a green light, a reply, a courier, and her friends' visits. She waited a lot, but most importantly, for love. "*Fear*" features the same girl but more determined. She insisted living independently in a strange city. In the end, she knew although she could face the pressure from work, actually, she had fear of loneliness in all forms. This film disclosed her vulnerability under a strong appearance. The theme is no matter how strong

---

14   Xiaobo Chen, 'The Micro Film: A Visual Culture Transmutation of Concept First', Contemporary Cinema, 10(2013): 199.

a girl is, she needs a partner. It shows a girl's longing for a family as affected by traditional Chinese values. *"Busy"* is about *"no matter how busy one is, she has to stop and hunt for a personal companionship". "Dilemma"* features *"love is not what you possess, but what you regard it as."*[15]

Ranging from the life details to the psychological concepts, this series of micro film highlight the same theme of obstacles to love and marriage. The advertisement is an inspiration from concept of living to the idea of love for the urban wandering group *(Dushi Piaobozu)*. The urban wandering group is very common in big cities in China.

They were born in rural areas, and settled down in the city after college. They live in the city alone, far away from their families and relatives. In China, a person working far away from hometown often indicates that she has few friends and no house, both important to marriage. As one of the most basic conditions for survival, the house is usually ancestral property. When the children get married, the parents will provide the house for them. Even now, few young people are willing to live in a rented place after marriage.

By telling the stories in the advertisement, Jiayuan.com discovered the love predicament of the urban wandering group, broke their vulnerable psychological defense and moved them by love.

With the speed of the dissemination of information and the development of recording equipment, many young people like taking pictures to record and share their lives with others. In 2012, Jiayuan.com, cooperating with Kugou.com,[16] launched "*My Time*" themed activities on the Internet, encouraging users to create a postcard about the wonderful moments in life and post it to the most beloved person. Users created, downloaded and printed postcards, with a Jiayuan's stamp, then sent them to relatives and friends. This activity combined the Internet and the traditional media, from online to offline, and received about 4.58 million hits. These activities added about 45,681 new users to Jiayuan.

Topics Marketing - Hot Topics from TV Dramas
Hot topics are of human interest. If these hot topics are capitalized on in marketing, a very good marketing effect will be achieved.

In 2009, a TV drama "*A Beautiful Daughter-in-law Era*" (*Xifu De Meihao Shidai*) was a hit. The hero, an ordinary guy, impressed many women with his understanding, tolerance, diligence and honesty. The TV drama returned to traditional values, which emphasize that understanding, tolerance and mutual support are more important than a solemn pledge of love in marriage. To love, one needs to express and take action. Thus, Jiayuan.com launched a big discussion on mate-selection criteria about *A Beautiful Daughter-in-law Era*. Although it took the conventional way of advertising, such as music videos (MV), banners, clients, product placement, many young people responded. Nearly 300,000 people participated in

---

15 A line in the ad.
16 Kugou.com is a popular website for music and entertainment in China.

21 days, promoting registration and the awareness of Jiayuan's brand. This activity facilitated the exploration of the significance of marriage in modern China where people feel baffled at the great social change. Jiayuan.com achieved good advertising effects by making use of hot issues.

Entertainment Marketing - Joining Dating Reality Shows

The fast-paced lifestyle and pressure force people to turn to entertainment for relaxation. Entertainment marketing emerges as the time requires. Many advertisers combine the brand image with different entertainments so that effects can be achieved in an invisible but effective way.

In China, male bachelors are generally referred to as *guanggun*, literally "bare branches". Originally pejorative only to men, now it has become a neutral word for both men and women, sometimes in a helpless and joking tone. In China, the technology to identify the sex of a fetus made the sex ratio unbalanced. "The sex ratio for children up through age 4 is over 120:100 (120 boys for every 100 girls), according to the 2000 census. By comparison, a normal sex ratio for this age group is 105 or less."[17] According to the 1 percent population sample survey data in 2005, birth sex ratio even reached 128:100 in Hubei, a populous province.[18] These partly result in more bare branches. November 11th (11/11) of every year is celebrated as Singles Day in China because the figure "1" looks like a lonely person ("bare branches"). And the day is for people without partners.

Now Singles Day is used as one of the commodity promotion opportunity by many businesses. It even turned into an online shopping day. On November 11, 2013, Taobao.com's[19] sales amount reached 35 billion yuan (about 5.6 billion U.S. dollars). On November 11, 2011, Jiayuan.com launched the "Bare Branches Revolution"[20] (*Guanggun Da Geming*) campaign, in which they called for single men and women to try to find their significant other, and make self-made marriage certificate in online games. This activity was again in cooperation with Kugou.com and had the significant effect: 2.49 billion users displayed the information on the Kugou.com platform with 32.61 million hits, users made 1.76 million marriage certificates and 323,246 new users registered at Jiayuan.com.[21]

In addition, with the increasing popularity of dating reality show in China, Jiayuan.com used product placement in the hottest television dating program *"Romance in Car" (Langman Manche)*. It is imported and adapted from the British online dating reality show *"Date My Car"*.

---

17   Valerie M. Hudson and Andrea M. Den Boer, '"Bare Branches" and Danger in Asia', The Washington Post, 4 July, 2004, http://www.washingtonpost.com/wp-dyn/articles/A24761-2004Jul2.html

18   National Bureau of Statistics of the People's Republic of China, 'Hubei Population Development Characteristics and Future Prospects in the 10th Five-Year Plan', 24 May 2006, http://www.stats.gov.cn/ztjc/ztfx/dfxx/200605/t20060522_32504.html

19   Taobao.com started in 2003. It is the biggest auction website and online transaction platform in China.

20   Translated by the author.

21   iResearch, 'Jiayuan.com: "Bare Branch Revolution" Viral Marketing', 28 February 2012, http://www.cnadtop.com/brand/superBrands/2012/2/28/ab6afb02-ef91-4c34-a17d-8bae677182c6.htm

The program combines cars with human personalities by integrating global success into local culture. In the program, the guests guess the master's character through his or her automobile brand, appearance and the interior of the car. In the program four male guests compete with each other, until only one is left. The competition gained high popularity in the audience. Later, the program changed to four female guests and one male, but also achieved good results. In the program, Jiayuan's brand occupied the main position all the time. Because Jiayuan's theme was accordant with the dating program, so brand implanting achieved good results. The search about Jiayuan.com was as high as 12,000 on Baidu.com one quarter, grew by about 137 times than the previous quarter.[22]

Compared with Jiayuan's diversified marketing strategies, several other dating sites were unwilling to lag behind.

Baihe.com: the Model of Chinese Culture

Baihe.com stands out with its unique name and advertising model. "Baihe" is the homonym of a flower, lily, symbolizing nobility and purity in Chinese culture, and *bai nian hao he,* a wish for a hundred-year-long harmonious marriage. This name of the website shows the characteristics of Chinese culture - marriage connotating more responsibilities and obligations than love. In addition, because Chinese tend to constrain their emotions rather than speaking out, many Chinese couples never say "I love you" to their significant other until death. Chinese pay more attention to the length and continuity of marriage. *Bai nian hao he* conveys the best wishes.

The series of Baihe's campaigns also featured such consistent thoughts. In *"Father and Daughter ",* an old father was worried about the daughter's marriage, but he lacked Internet literacy. So he asked neighbors to register on Baihe.com for his daughter. This advertisement reflects the traditional culture in which parents are one of the main driving forces of marriage. Because the theme is full of tender feelings, the advertisement tends to be more acceptable than the mandatory. In addition, highlighting advantages of a real-name registration system gives customers a sense of security. In another advertisement themed *"House",* a young man made a serious proposal in front of the girl's parents because he had purchased a house for their wedding. In *"Pay Card",* a young man sent his pay card to a girl and the girl was touched. This series of advertisements reflect the courtship with Chinese characteristics, marriage in the life of the parents, housing guarantee and the financial power of women. Another long advertisement was full of interviews of ordinary people about the different understanding of love, the heartbeat-scene description, the expectations to marriage partner, and the interpretation of marriage. These remarks were appealing to the people who had no more illusions about love, but only want to live steadfastly.

Baihe's advertisements are more traditional and populist, lack of fashion and fantasy. This is consistent with the traditional belief of love in the Chinese culture: love does not need a solemn pledge of affection and romance, but shared duties and mutual understanding of the

---

22 Golden Mouse, Jiayuan.com implanted *Romance in Car* 9 April 2013, http://huaban.com/pins/57147465/\#zoom/?&_suid=140999770429606156231237150 92

couple. The husband and the wife live together through life. In the same vein, the male in the advertising is neither sleek nor romantic. He is pragmatic and down-to-earth, only preparing the money and the house for the marriage. On the other hand, the advertisements also reflect that the consumerism culture has a profound influence to modern Chinese marriage. Many single women lay emphasis on the materials men can provide rather than emotional elements. In addition, parents showed up in these ads, common in Chinese culture. Because Chinese pay more attention to the interpersonal relationship network, so the marriage is not only for two individuals, but two families. Family members, especially parents, have a big impact on marriage.

Even in the micro film advertising "*One Day of an IT Grassroot Man*"[23] (*IT Diaosinan De Yitian*), a young man who was a typical ordinary single IT male lived his life like this: traditional, black-frame glasses, backpack, headset always in the ears, never changing shirts, mobile phone always in hand, getting up in the dream hastily, having breakfast on the way, subway... IT men are considered as social elites according to the income in China. But due to their heavy work schedules, they account for a large percentage of bachelors in large cities. Mu Yan, founder and vice president of Baihe, said, "I am a pure IT man. IT man is a special group."[24] Of course, the stereotype of young men who work in the information technology industry is dangerous, not all IT men are in accordance with this image. Although the man in the ad resonates with some IT peers, it may impose a wrong impression of IT man on the audience.

Consistent with the above style, the advertising features numbers for the reasons why IT men were single:

- 50.1% of IT man think "The IT circle is too small"

- There are 41. 8% of IT man think "the other half's requirements is too high"

- 21.3% of IT man think that "IT is busy"

- According to the survey: IT man lives as follows

- The average sleep time is 5.6 hours every day

- The average working time is 12.8 hours every day

- The annual average time of "blind date" is only 3.5 times[25]

This disciplined mindset and down-to-earth style may make the target audiences of Baihe.

---

23 Translated by the author.
24 Donews, 'Baihe's Micro Film: IT Male Need the Counteroffensive Courage in Love and Marriage', 24 October 2012, http://www.donews.com/net/201210/1683363.shtm
25 Lines in the advertisement, translated by the author.

com more focused. To help resonate with such an audience, Baihe.com chose Honglei Sun, an ordinary-looking actor who gained popularity by playing brilliant, honest, and responsible characters, as its spokesman. Sun has played tough guys and reliable husbands in films and television dramas. To the single young people who want to find a partner to go through ups and downs, the image is very suitable. In general, Baihe's slogan – Love Seriously, advertising style and the target groups are more consistent.

However, not all of Baihe's commercials are successful. In another campaign, "*Through the Night*"[26] *(Zou Yelu)*, a single female college student walked alone in a dark corridor. Then a ghost who covered her face with long hairs is here and there behind her back with horror music on. When the girl went to the washroom, the ghost came. When the ghost traced the hair covering the face, the audience saw that the ghost was a girl without a comb. This advertisement is neither appealing nor meaningful. It kicks up a cloud of dust. Obviously, it ruined the consistency and the cultural connotation of Baihe.com. In a word, it is a meaningless advertisement.

Zhenai.com: From Romance to Consumerism

Founded in 1998, Zhenai.com is another leader offering online dating services, which was named "*Best Chinese Dating Website 2010*" by China Internet Weekly.[27] Zhenai's target audience is white-collars between 25 to 45 years old. To be received by target groups, Zhenai.com collaborates with nationally well-known television dating shows, such as "*You Are the One (Fei Cheng Wu Rao)*", "*Only One in a Hundred Is Chosen (Bai Li Tiao Yi)*",[28] "*Try Connecting Love (Ai Qing Lian Lian Kan)*".[29] Because some users use false information to cheat online, single young users are doubtful to online information. Zhenai.com used the matchmaker offline as a countermeasure. In the mean time, the registers' information needs to be verified by the Ministry of Public Security. In this way, Zhenai.com gained the fame of seriousness and discretion.

In the first several years, Zhenai's advertisements featured romance and warmth, offering attractiveness to the single white-collar. It ran its advertisements on TV and outdoor media such as subway stations and trains. However, in recent years, shifts were seen in the theme of Zhenai's advertisements such as "*Gold Digger*" *(Bai Jin Nu Pian)*, "*For Only Love*" *(Zhi Ai Lang Man Nu Pian)*, "*Appearance Association*" *(Wai Mao Xie Hui Pian)*,[30] which caused controversy. Zhenai.com changed its target audience from company white-collars to looks ordinary earners. The advertisements are the modern use of ridicule, from a few extremes to one common theme: no matter what values the registered user is looking for, she can find a suitable partner at Zhenai.com.

---

26 Translated by the author.
27 *China Internet Weekly* was founded in Beijing in 1998, accompanied by China Internet industry. It is one of the China Internet and IT industry's most successful leading business magazines at present.
28 Translated by the author.
29 Translated by the author.
30 These three ad names are translated by the author.

In the "*Gold Digger* ", an ordinary-looking girl with a Northeastern accent found her spouse. She said, "You are ugly and knock gritty. Never mind. You are twenty or thirty years old, even you are in your seventies or eighties. Never mind. As long as you have money, I will marry you." Then she mentioned the large house and the luxury car are also important. In "*For Only Love* ", a girl put forward, "Do not care about height or weight. Do not care about his looking. Do not care about his figure. Forget the family and schooling. Only if you are romantic, that will do." In the "*Appearance Association*", a girl presented another view, "A suitable man should be tall and slim with a handsome face. He'd better be as good-looking as an actor. Even if you are autistic, womanish, or promiscuous in sex relations, I love you as long as you have a pretty face."

Mate-selection criteria were externalized and materialized so the advertisements were criticized. Although the advertisements ridicule some people and exactly reflect their criteria, these criteria are external which do not comply with the traditional Chinese values and violated the basic human values focusing on inherent qualities. Both Baihe and Zhenai's advertisements were about the external qualities of love and marriage, but Baihe.com highlighted responsibility and sincerity in marriage, while Zhenai.com emanated superficiality and irresponsibility for love. For thousands of years, Chinese always attach more importance to inner beauty than the external. Chinese men are supposed to be responsible and diligent, Chinese women warm-hearted and down-to-earth. If one focuses on appearance, he or she will be considered wanton. Self-cultivation is the main way to enhance oneself.

In this series of campaigns, the unabashed money worship, advocating of one's physical appearance and the so-called romance contribute to a Zhenai that only values materialism, at least to some users. Although consumerism is prevalent in China, the lack of cultural connotation and a standard of value accepted by Chinese consumers does not bring good reputation to the site. Zhenai's transformation is not successful.

Problems and Suggestions

Although the above leading dating sites of China used different advertising models to build their brand image and increase the number of registered members, their advertising models have common problems and affected their development.

One of the most important problems is that the advertising model lacks in-depth cultural values. The current marriage websites make externalized marriage matching criteria, such as Jiayuan's "dream lover" that was overly materialistic and superficial. Zhenai.com also highlighted the pursuit of money and appearance in their advertisement. In the advertisements, romance was not the form of love but the standard for the young to select their partners.

The materialistic and external standard above is against the traditional marriage concept in China, traditional values and common human values. On the other hand, it is also the consumerism society's material extrusion on people. With the development of economy, a materialistic consumerism trend sweeps Chinese. The consumerism consciousness is strong. Marriage is no exception. Lisa Rofel argues that the "desiring subjects" is at the core of

China's contingent.[31] With the spread of public culture, materialism has insinuated into every field. Materialism has encroached upon and eroded people's spiritual life, including the pursuit of love and romance. Affected by consumerism, mate-selection criteria have changed from focusing on the internal to external, from the spirit to substance.

Of course, Baihe.com tried to change the external standards. It used a personality assessment system, which matched the register users' character with psychological characteristics and personality. Although there are some improvements, it needs highly specialized personnel for testing and evaluating results because the psychological test is professional. Current employees of the dating sites in China don't meet such standards. So the match can produce limited effects.

The harmonious marriage is the fit of intrinsic values, and the involvement of emotional experiences. How to evaluate the deep values and make the customers feel the emotional experience is the most important challenge the dating sites are facing. The author believes that emotional experience is the main demand of dating website advertising. To do this, in-depth mining of the Eastern marriage values in advertising can be further explored. China is known for its high-context culture. Chinese are family-oriented and committed to a lifelong and continuous marriage and tolerance. Such values would be the guidelines for advertising. This way, the inner psychological experience of users and the information campaigns convey will resonate.

In addition, the profit model of dating sites not only relies on the advertising model, but strengthens the function of dating websites. At present, the main problem of Chinese dating sites is that the user viscosity is not enough and the users are not willing to pay for services on the website.[32] The key to these problems lies in the dating sites' service mode. If users can get high-quality services on the dating website, they will want to stay on the site and be willing to pay.

Although Jiayuan.com invested 20 million yuan (about 3.24 million U.S. dollars) on establishing the Magpies site, which provides one-stop service of marriage for just successful partners, a good start, on the whole it was incomplete. The author thinks the dating sites should offer a series of long-term service besides dating. They can provide the real information and advice services according to the different courtship stages, such as wedding planning, marriage program, parental advisory services and children's education. When customers have various emotional problems in love, want to get married, on the way to the altar, or have child-rearing problems, they will get professional advice and consulting services. So, won't he want to revisit the website? Won't he like to pay for the valuable customized service? If the dating sites do not have these services, they can cooperate with corresponding portal websites and traditional media to capitalize on each other's resources.

---

31 Lisa Rofel, *Desiring China: Experiments in Neoliberalism, Sexuality, and Public Culture*, Duke Univeristy Press, 2007.
32 Ruoxi Lin, 'The Dating Sites, Confused of the Fiancee', China Internet Weekly, 5 April 2012, 30.

At present, 6 to 12 months is the longest retention time for the customers of dating sites. Once customers find the prospective partner, they will immediately leave the dating site.[33] Therefore, the advertisers on the banner ads on a dating website will consider the long-term effects of advertising and may not want to advertise. Once the customer viscosity increases and membership information needs are met through the fee, profitability of website will also be greatly improved. Website banner ads also will increase profits. This would be a virtuous cycle.

References

Chen, Xiaobo. 'The Micro Film: A Visual Culture Transmutation of Concept First', Contemporary Cinema, 10(2013): p.199.

Donews. 'Baihe's Micro Film: IT Male Need the Counteroffensive Courage in Love and Marriage', 24 October 2012, http://www.donews.com/net/201210/1683363.shtm

Golden Mouse. 'Jiayuan.com Implanted "Romance in Car"', 9 April 2013, http://huaban.com/pins/57147465/\#zoom/?&_suid=14099977042960615623123715092

Hudson, Valerie M. and Boer, Andrea M. Den. '"Bare Branches" and Danger in Asia', 4 July 4 2004, http://www.washingtonpost.com/wp-dyn/articles/A24761-2004Jul2.html

iResearch. 'Jiayuan.com: "Bare Branch Revolution" Viral Marketing', 28 February 2012, http://www.cnadtop.com/brand/superBrands/2012/2/28/ab6afb02-ef91-4c34-a17d-8bae677182c6.htm

Li, Fengtao and Wang, Xujie. 'The Traditional Mode Met Bottleneck, Three Dating Site Run into the Deep Era', Chinese Economic Weekly Z1 (2013): p. 76.

Li, Lei. 'Dating Sites Started the New User Battle', China Business Journal, 12 March 2012: E02.

Lin, Ruoxi. 'The Dating Sites, Confused of the Fiancee', China Internet Weekly, 5 April 2012.

Ma, Zexin. 'Personal Image Construction and Communication Effect in Dating Sites', News World, 9 (2012): p.124.

Mu, Yifan. 'The Jiayuan Went to IPO Profit Model Was into a Bottleneck', China Business News, 25 April 2011: B03.

National Bureau of Statistics of the People's Republic of China, 'Hubei Population Development Characteristics and Future Prospects in the 10th Five-Year Plan', 24 May 2006, http://www.stats.gov.cn/ztjc/ztfx/dfxx/200605/t20060522_32504.html

Rofel, Lisa. Desiring China: Experiments in Neoliberalism, Sexuality, and Public Culture. https://www.dukeupress.edu/Desiring-China

Wu, Xiaoying. 'The Dating Sites: "Sweet" Industrial Predicament and Outlet', Sichuan Provincial Academy of Social Sciences, 2009: p. 38.

Fanyi Baidu. http://fanyi.baidu.com/translate######

Fanyi Baidu. http://fanyi.baidu.com/translate######http://fanyi.baidu.com/translate######

---

33 Lin, 'The Dating Sites, Confused of the Fiancee'.

REMEDIATING THE MATCHMAKER: ARRANGING MARRIAGE ONLINE IN THE SOUTH ASIAN DIASPORA IN AMERICA

SHEENA RAJA AND BRYCE J. RENNINGER

The topic of marriage is a major focus of conversations about the "modernization" of South Asian culture in the face of social processes that fall under the vague and multivalent concept of globalization.[1] This chapter seeks to destabilize various assumptions about the contemporary status of marriage in a globalized world by focusing on the role of matrimonial websites in the lives of diasporic South Asians in New Jersey and New York. In what follows, we acknowledge how "tradition" and "modernity" coexist and coincide in the South Asian diaspora in the United States with regards to the use of information and communication technologies (ICTs) to pursue intimacy, love, and marriage.

Globalization is often thought of in terms of global flows of capital. But when one takes note of the forms of capital that flow in a globalized world – money, products, labor, specialized knowledge, it is hard to ignore the role of humans in these transnational flows. As subjects migrate and reimagine space, ICTs impact the maintenance of family and other social ties, cultural production and consumption, and pursuit of intimacy, love, and marriage for members of the South Asian diaspora. In addition to using ICTs to maintain local and national ties, South Asians on the Indian subcontinent and in the diaspora also use ICTs to seek out information and communication on a transnational scale, creating transnational ethnoscapes, technoscapes, and mediascapes, a dynamic interplay between people, technology, and audio/visual media.[2]

This chapter distinguishes itself among other studies of contemporary arranged marriage amongst South Asians by focusing on the practices of U.S. diasporic South Asians and by acknowledging the many actors – human and non-human – that factor into the arranged marriage process amongst this social group. In what follows, we use the term "South Asian diaspora," even though the subjects in the study are of Indian descent. Though there are small regional differences in marriage practices between villages, cities, nations, regions, and religious and ethnic groups, the coeval existence of arranged and love marriages, matchmakers and Internet sites is standard for many across the region and its diaspora.

Marriage in the South Asian Diaspora: Arrangements, Assisting, and Love

Within South Asia and the South Asian diaspora, marriages are popularly conceived in one of two genres: the arranged marriage or the love marriage. In this formulation, love marriages are tied to modernity, or, alternatively, to "Western culture." This kind of analysis may or may not acknowledge that in the West, love became a priority in the pursuit of marriages

---

1   Arjun Appudarai, *Modernity at Large: Cultural Dimensions of Globalization*, Minneapolis: University of Minnesota, 1996.
2   Arjun Appudarai, *Modernity at Large: Cultural Dimensions of Globalization*.

only in the eighteenth century.³ In the West, tying love marriages to modernity has led to representations of arranged marriages as old-fashioned or outdated. These perspectives ignored reasons why arranged marriages existed. Speaking of the cultural conditions that shape arranged marriage in the Indian context, Seth and Patnayakuni commented,

> From a very young age, children are socialized to identify with the family as a whole and discouraged from developing an autonomous self. They are conditioned to place the interests of the family ahead of their own. Alienating and confronting parents and family is still an anathema to most young people, especially in important decisions such as career selection and marriage. Furthermore, cultural mores frown upon the socialization among men and women in the form of dating and relationships. As a result, arranged marriage is still the dominant way for families and individuals to find partners for marriage.⁴

This formulation did not account for the many ways that transnational migration and diasporic subjectivity impact marriage configurations. Seth and Patnayakuni later acknowledged,

> over the past several decades, social and geographical mobility have weakened the extended family structure and increasingly replaced it with a more nuclear family structure. As a consequence, social networks provided by the extended family structure are no longer available to parents for finding suitable partners for their marriageable offspring. ⁵

Here, Seth and Patnayakuni have argued that these factors had made online matrimonial sites ever more popular from within the educated (diasporic) middle class. Although love and arranged marriages have been popular classifications from within the South Asian context, this dichotomy simplified the processes that lead to each of these marriages. Especially in families with transnational networks or the possibility of transnational networks, assisted marriages are popular. In assisted marriages,

> the parents/kin arrange for a set of prospective spouses based on criteria around religion, caste, education, occupation, age, and geography, among others. They find socially acceptable ways to introduce their children. These may be through large family get togethers, weddings, and other social or cultural events.⁶

As is implied in this quote, assisted marriages are sometimes based on transnational networks of sociality that have pre-existed, but sometimes trusted consultants like matchmak-

---

3   Stephanie Coontz, *Marriage, a History: How Love Conquered Marriage*, New York: Viking, 2005.
4   Nainika Seth and Ravi Patnayakuni, 'Online Matrimonial Sites and the Transformation of Arranged Marriage in India', in Celia Romm Livermo (ed) *Gender and Social Computing: Interactions, Differences and Relationships*, Hershey, PA: IGI Global, 2011, p. 276.
5   Nainika Seth and Ravi Patnayakuni, 'Online Matrimonial Sites and the Transformation of Arranged Marriage in India'.
6   Narayan Gopalkrishnan and Hurriyet Babacan, 'Ties That Bind: Marriage and Partner Choice in the Indian Community in Australia in a Transnational Context', *Identities: Global Studies in Culture and Power* 14.4 (2007), p. 519.

ers or astrologers are consulted[7] or matrimonial sites are used[8] to start or expand the search. Parents who participate in assisted marriages "allow[ ] their sons and daughters choice among nominees screened for caste, lineage, and geography, among other measures – and giv[e] the children veto power."[9]

There are many contexts where dating and love marriages, arranged marriages, and assisted marriages all coexist as potentials and possibilities for members of the South Asian diaspora. These coeval possibilities and potentialities have the ability to be configured in different ways by members of the same community, caste, or regional ancestry or even within the same person. The diverse courtship practices can also play a role in marking nationality, as noted by Marian Aguiar:

> The meaning of [India] is not a given, nor is it identical across different historical-geographical locations. Arranged marriage might become a way to 'be Indian' for a highly educated, professional man in New Jersey, and it might become a way to 'be Bangladeshi' for a woman from East London working in a garment factory, but these forms of imagining the nation are mediated by the structures of gender, class, and religion.[10]

What is left unsaid in this quote is that in certain situations, pursuing configurations other than arranged marriages may also be tied up in national or diasporic identity, how one's real possibilities for both arranged and love marriages may indicate a way of being diasporic.

This paper considers the ways that the model of the arranged marriage as a model or an option coexists, coincides, and informs various other pursuits of relationships for members of the South Asian diaspora. While "dating violates the traditional Indian understanding of sexuality as something to be encountered only in marriage,"[11] various Indian nationals and members of the diaspora, against tradition, see dating as a possibility. It is indisputable, for instance, that contemporary youth on the subcontinent have more exposure to the possibility of dating,[12] but other configurations of these possibilities exist amongst many members of the South Asian diaspora. While transnational migration is certainly facilitated by these

---

7 Sheena Raja, 'A Match Made in Heaven: A Study of Changing Hindu Marriage Practices amongst Gujarati Eligibles' in Sharmina Mawani and Anjoom Mukadam (eds.) *Gujarati Communities across the Globe: Memory, Identity, and Continuity*, London, UK: Trentham Books, 2012.

8 Nainika Seth and Ravi Patnayakuni, *'Online Matrimonial Sites and the Transformation of Arranged Marriage in India'*, University of Alabama in Huntsville, USA, 2009.

9 Ginia Bellafante, 'Courtship Ideas of South Asians Get a U.S. Touch', *The New York Times*. (23 August, 2005). Which page? A1, A13…quotes are from A13

10 Marian Aguiar, 'Arranged Marriage: Cultural Regeneration in Transnational South Asian Popular Culture.' *Cultural Critique* 84 (Spring, 2013), 193.

11 Paul C. Adams and Rina Ghose, 'India.com: The construction of a Space Between', *Progress in Human Geography* 27.4 (2003), p. 431.

12 Kabita Chakraborty, 'Virtual Mate-seeking in the Urban Slums of Kolkata, India', *South Asian Popular Culture* 10.2 (July, 2012).

sites[13] (and, in fact, sites like Shaadi.com have developed strategic business partners that help with issues around immigration), the subjects interviewed for this chapter are citizens of the United States who, for the most part, focused on finding other Americans for reasons explored in the analysis of our interviews.

In a study of use of the Internet that related specifically to South Asian diasporic identity, Adams and Ghose have found that South Asian matrimonial sites, rather than focusing on photographs of the eligible subject, include more information related to "caste, religion, ethnicity, education and employment, which are considered by families to be of greater relevance to marital happiness than physical appearance."[14] Various studies have pointed out that the desirability of light-skinned mates has led to pursuits of romance that emphasized skin color and caste and either misreported[15] or omitted data[16] that would be unattractive.

Methods

The aim of this study was to understand the motivations and practices of diasporic South Asians when it came to the use of computer-mediated platforms for courtship. The subjects for this study were recruited by one of the researchers from within the New Jersey/New York South Asian community of which she is a part.[17] The total South Asian diaspora in the U.S. is overwhelmingly comprised of individuals with reported ancestry from India (80%), and the rest from Pakistan, Bangladesh, Nepal, Sri Lanka, Bhutan, and the Maldives.[18] According to the 2010 US Census, the New York Metro area[19] has the largest number of residents identifying as Asian Indians, with over 500,000 counted.[20] Starting from a sample of two previously known contacts, the sample expanded using snowball sampling to total ten overall subjects.

Participants were selected if they were a diasporic South Asian living in New York or New Jersey and had any first hand experience creating a profile on any dating website or matrimonial website. Dating websites allow users to search and contact individuals through filters,

---

13 Dana Diminescu and Matthieu Renault, 'The Matrimonial Web of Migrants: The Economics of Profiling as a New Form of Ethnic Business', *Social Science Information* 50 (2011).

14 Paul C. Adams and Rina Ghose, 'India.com: The construction of a Space Between.'

15 Sonora Jha and Mara Adelman, 'Looking for Love in All the White Places: A Study of Skin Color Preferences on Indian Matrimonial and Mate-Seeking Websites', *Studies in South Asian Film and Media* 1.1 (2009).

16 Dana Diminescu and Matthieu Renault, 'The Matrimonial Web of Migrants: The Economics of Profiling as a New Form of Ethnic Business', *Social Science Information* 50 (2011), p. 687.

17 While both authors have studied sociality within the Indian (diasporic) context, for this study only Raja conducted interviews with the subjects. The interview protocol, designed collaboratively by both authors, has been used for other research projects with other research designs not about the South Asian diaspora.

18 SAALT, 'A Demographic Snapshot of South Asians in the United States', July 2012. Retrieved from http://saalt.org/wp-content/uploads/2012/09/Demographic-Snapshot-Asian-American-Foundation-2012.pdf

19 The NY Metropolitan statistical area spans across 3 states and is comprised of 10 counties in New York; 12 counties in northern New Jersey; and 1 county in Pennsylvania.

20 US Census Bureau, 'The Asian Population: 2010', March 2012. Retrieved from http://www.census.gov/prod/cen2010/briefs/c2010br-11.pdf

and offer suggestions potential communication often with the intention to set up a physical meeting. Matrimonial websites offer a similar functionality, however, they do so with the clear intention that all communication is in the service of pursuing marriage. All of the participants in the study have either used or witnessed the first hand experience of the South Asian-specific matrimonial site Shaadi.com[21] or one of its subsidiaries for specific South Asian ethnicities (e.g. GujaratMatrimony.com, where all users are from or have family from the state of Gujarat). The popular dating sites Match.com and eHarmony.com used by our participants are mass-marketed to American users as sites without any ethnic identification (though eHarmony.com was started by a Christian psychologist and theologian). All sites allow browsing to be based on geographic proximity.

Interviews followed a guide that was developed to learn the tactics users employed and purposes they had when creating profiles on both dating and matrimonial sites. The guide also allowed users to talk about the many different sites they used (if applicable). During interviews, special attention was made to understand the types of interaction and communication pursued and enacted on each website that they used.

After interviews, subjects were asked if they knew any South Asians in the area who used matrimonial or dating sites. All interviews were done in person or over Skype in early 2014. From the ten subjects, who ranged from 26 to 35 years old, three were male, and seven were female. Most conversations were about heterosexual courtship, although one subject self-identified as bisexual. Of the men, two were born in the US and one was born in India; of the women, five were born in the US and two were born in India. All seven subjects born in the US are first-generation Americans. Their religious affiliations, which included Hindu, Buddhist, and Jain, were revealed over the course of interviews as it became important for their courtship practices. All subjects have ethnic ties to North India; they sometimes brought up their regional ethnicities when those ethnicities played a factor in the pursuit of mates. Our subjects' steady access to high-speed Internet at home and on their mobile phones were trappings of their presumed membership within the American middle class. We coded each interview subject with a number, which was used throughout to identify different subjects. A list of subjects with age, gender, birth country, and religion, when provided, is provided in the Appendix. Interviews were transcribed and coded based on themes that emerged, some of which are explored below.

In the analysis that follows, we hope to reveal our findings that the various actors that have existed in the South Asian matchmaking process before the Internet – young people, their parents and other relatives, matchmakers, astrologers, biodata – have been remediated by various digital tools. Here, we borrow the term "remediation" from critics of digital aesthetic forms Bolter and Grusin to note the ways that, new media forms, in this case matrimonial sites and dating websites, transmute previous forms into something somehow experienced in a both more immediate and more hypermediated way.[22] In other words, with the digital

---

21   Shaadi is the Urdu word for marriage.
22   Jay David Bolter and Richard Grusin, *Remediation: Understanding New Media*, Cambridge, MA: MIT Press, 2000.

remediation of matchmaking processes, users are more aware of both the process and structure of the mediated practice.

Before we provide our analyses of the interviews at the center of the chapter, we first take a detour to a hotel and conference center in Edison, New Jersey.

Spectacular Matchmaking in Edison, New Jersey

Traditionally, arranged marriages in India are brokered by matchmakers, or *nayans*, who serve as community scouts and neutral liaisons organizing communications between families, with little or no input from the eligible individuals themselves.[23] Though matchmakers may be friends or extended family members, professional matchmakers have played a historical role in Indian society aligning families according to wealth, property, caste, religion, and social status. Today, newspaper advertisements, informal biodata (demographic information) profile circulation, matrimonial websites and matchmaking cultural events have also entered this space as the South Asian diaspora reimagines courtship practices. The various methods of matchmaking each allows for various configurations of individual autonomy and cultural expectations.

In 1995, a non-profit organization called Matri was founded by Yashvant Patel to assist Gujarati eligibles in New Jersey in their quest to find "life partners" that spoke Gujarati and shared common cultural values. At its inception, Matri focused on organizing annual conventions where hundreds of prospective brides, grooms and their parents across the U.S. gathered in business casual attire for a weekend of food, music, and dance as well as other social events that allowed people looking for marriage partners to meet each other. Before arriving at the annual convention, registered participants were asked to select the names of five prospects they would like to meet from a booklet of colored photographs and biodata profiles. At the event, participants were asked to walk on stage, share their name, registration number, and a brief introduction in 40 seconds or less. Afterwards, parents moved to a separate area for a parents meeting guided by adult volunteers, and young participants are broken up into groups for individual interviews.

Since then, attendance at Matri has expanded and the organization itself has grown to include local chapters in areas across the country with a high density of Gujarati Americans. Matri has also forged a partnership with GujaratiMatrimony.com, a subsidiary of Bharatmatrimony.com, the profitable Indian matrimonial website and self-proclaimed "trusted partner in marriage." As Patel boasts in a video interview embedded on GujaratiMatrimony.com, users of the website have been able to "connect to millions of Gujaratis worldwide."[24] Not only has this organization drawn a sponsor facilitating entrance into the digital space, but the annual events have also been revamped to include a "speed dating" session. Here we find that matrimonial sites such as Matri are remediations of older forms of arrangement practices that now coexist in complex systems of matchmaking.

---

23 V.V. Prakasa Rao and V. Nandini Rao, *Marriage, the Family, and Women in India*, Delhi: Heritage, 1982.

24 Yashvant Patel, founder Matri, Inc. USA on Gujarati Matrimony.com, https://www.youtube.com/watch?v=d-JrZBMzpRBE

Remediating the Matchmaker

Following the lead of actor-network theory,[25] in addition to noting the cultural forces of diaspora, immigration, and the transnational, we should be attuned to the various human and non-human actors involved in matchmaking. We have identified the eligible young people, their parents and family, matchmakers, astrologists, dating and matrimonial sites, online profiles, and social matching algorithms as key actors within the system of South Asian diasporiccourtship. All of these actors have the capability to be considered matchmakers. If hybrid forms like assisted marriages are becoming popular for diasporic subjects, then what roles do these actors in arrangement play in various forms of courtship pursuit in the South Asian diasporic context? In answering this question, it is important to note that all ten subjects saw themselves as the primary agents in their pursuit of partners or dates.

Speaking about the interface of the site Indiandating.com, not a matrimonial site but an ethnic dating site, Participant 1 noted that the site and its database of users seemed more "traditional."

> RAJA: So what do you mean by more traditional?
>
> PARTICIPANT 1: The questions they ask, they ask about caste. It was all voluntary. They were asking about things that I didn't even know what it was like um...I mean...subcaste and..."manglik"[26] or something like that. Is that something?
>
> R: Is that astrology?
>
> P1: Yeah. So they ask about that. It was kind of funny because there's a feature like a special feature where you had to pay more to see it. It seemed like they put a lot of weight on that. But like I don't really care about that stuff [chuckle]...But yeah, it has like a piece of paper that is covered and there is a little piece that is turned up. So it is like hidden, but if you pay more then you can see what is underneath. Maybe that's what they do at matchmakers [sic] in India...I don't know.

Though this is a direct example of remediation, in which the role of the astrologer has been digitized onto a matrimonial site. The role of the astrologer was one that was seen as irrelevant for the kinds of pursuits our subjects were engaged in.

People dedicating themselves to matchmaking were rarely mentioned as specific actors in the courtship practices of those interviewed. When asked about how sites could better meet their own specific needs, Participant 10 wished that the role of a human matchmaker was more a part of the websites he used,

> I think someone from the website should interview new members and take notes to get to

---

25 Bruno Latour, *Reassembling the Social: An Introduction to Actor-Network-Theory*, Oxford: Oxford University Press, 2007.

26 Manglik is an astrological designation based on the position of Mars.

know a person...almost like a coverage person for them. I envision it being someone who doesn't keep in touch with you but someone that covers your profile. They would have a brief conversation with you when you join the site or at the period of time you request just to get a sense of who you are. Maybe they could even record a Q&A and then put it on the profile with the customer's approval. And that person through other conversations could match up people rather than just relying on an algorithm. I know there are people in real life that do this. I like the big audience of Match, they would have to have someone to do it for a specialized group which is a high cost but also a smaller pool. Like in the traditional sense like an Indian matchmaker. I know this would cost more but augmenting the site with humans would result in more matches. Websites should be merely for introduction and they shouldn't position themselves as a wedding connector basically. [emphasis added]

Later on, this subject said that he did not fill out the horoscope portions of the site because "he didn't place weight on [it]." Though his courtship pursuits have been mediated by matrimonial sites and dating sites such as Match.com, OkCupid.com, and eHarmony.com, Participant 10 sees value in the role of the human matchmaker, especially when compared to the social recommendation algorithms that push certain profiles to users on dating and matrimonial sites. To compensate for the ways that the sites did not completely correspond with the ways he wanted to find eligibles, Participant 10 noted a number of ways that he could become attractive to other users: he would write more when responding to questions, be more active on sites that allow one to write more, fill out as much as he found relevant in profiles, and used keywords that could help users and algorithms find him amongst the other profiles. So while he was submitting to the dating and matrimonial sites, he was more excited about the possibilities of human-mediated matchmaking. To make up for this incongruence, he tried to anticipate the structures of the matching algorithms and "game" the system so that his profile would be shown to as many other eligibles as possible.

The matchmaking algorithm and the mediated nature of dating and matrimonial sites were carefully considered by our subjects. Participant 8 also spoke about her discomfort with matchmaking algorithms, though in her case, she was more resistant to the idea of recommending in general.

> I didn't find it helpful to be on eHarmony because it didn't let you search yourself. They give you options. I guess it's like computerized. You fill out a huge profile and depending on what score you get they will match you with guys that would be compatible with you. So you can't necessarily go through and filter. I don't think. I didn't give myself too much time on there. I found it irritating because they select guys for you. I didn't let my mom do that. A majority of the times it didn't even make sense...like how did they come up with this? Why would they think I would be compatible with this guy? [Emphasis added.]

In her case, Participant 8 did not welcome recommendations from eHarmony, but also mentioned that she would feel uncomfortable if her mother did that for her. So Participant 8 was uncomfortable with the whole matchmaking apparatus, no matter how it was carried out. She was aware of the various actors availing themselves to her, but she resisted – or wished to resist — their offers because they did not give her the agency to do the searching herself.

Participant 6 also saw their use of matrimonial sites in relationship to the ability of their parents to match them. But she joined Shaadi.com and Bharatmatrimony.com when she decided she should "settle down." She noted,

> Since I was young, it has been instilled in me that I am to, to marry a Sindhi [a regional ethnicity] man one day. I was actively involved in the Sindhi community back in 2007, but completely lost touch after I graduated college and got a job. My parents aren't as involved in the community, either. So I figured joining matrimonial websites which has Sindhi men would make my search easier.

Participant 6 was eager to fulfill her culturally mandated role to find a man of her regional ethnicity, but her parents were not involved enough in the cultural networks to help serve the role as a matchmaker. Recognizing this fact, she has become a part of the networks on two sites in order to fulfill the desire to find a Sindhi partner despite the fact that it would be difficult for her parents to find someone with whom to arrange her.

Though all subjects talked about the sites from the perspective of managing the sites for themselves, one subject, Participant 1, did admit that his friends set up most of his profiles for him and then relinquished control to him. The use of matrimonial sites by family members became a factor in our subjects' use of matrimonial sites. Several subjects mentioned stories of encountering the parents and family members of other users who contacted them for the eligible. These contacts with parents were usually framed as undesirable interactions with eligibles on the subcontinent. Participant 2, in explaining her preference for a site that had more diasporic South Asians as opposed to Indian nationals, noted about one South Asian site, "I felt that Shaadi.com was not about people speaking about their personality and what makes them happy. It was more like people's parents looking to marry off their kids."

Several subjects who are members of Shaadi.com, which uses phone numbers to verify accounts and makes those numbers public at first by default, explained that they received calls from India. Not only were they not interested in pursuing relationships with Indian nationals, but they were extra turned off by the idea of dealing with someone other than the eligible him or herself. Take, for instance, the experience of Participant 1:

> I even put my phone number on there and there was like a bad awkward experience. Some girl's dad called me 6 times and left messages saying call back...blah blah. It was weird. Maybe I shouldn't have put my phone number. Going from not talking to anybody to straight up giving you calls and leaving you messages. I had never spoken to her or anything. But a lot of the profiles on Shaadi.com are created by siblings, parents, friends. That's the other part about Shaadi. There are a lot of parents that put up profiles for their kids and it clearly says, "profile created by." So you know if it was created by the parent or the person themselves, or a sibling, or something like that.

Participant 10 expressed a discomfort with not knowing who was behind the profile. He says,

"The South Asian one, Shaadi, I've tried off and on over the last couple years. You really don't know who is on the other side. It could be a sibling, a parent, friends…"

While users knew that the South Asian sites were often used by family member actors and that was not particularly attractive, the use of these sites was still attractive for some reasons.

Finally, those subjects who were less serious about the pursuit of a spouse came to dating sties and, somewhat awkwardly or reluctantly, to matrimonial sites with a particular perspective on these sites as actors. Participant 5 explained her preference for dating sites by saying, "Shaadi's name says it all. It's about marriage. If you talk to someone on there, you are only talking to them because you want to get married. That feels desperate. At least on sites like OkCupid.com, it's not as serious. It's about dating…"

Participant 1 felt that there was a spectrum, and he was looking for something just right. He starts by echoing Participant 5,

> Shaadi.com is very hard core serious. The name says it... you know. It's the seriousness of it about finding a life partner. Indiandating seemed less hardcore so I thought I would check that out. Indiandating was a bit too much though. I wasn't on there for very long but from what I heard from other folks it was just a hook up site. It wasn't serious at all. And so the quality of people on there wasn't so great.

Our subjects, who all knew well their options and the traditions associated with arranged, assisted, and love marriages as well as dating, see their use of sites in relation to their pursuit of one of these options or a hybrid of them. No one found that any one site was the perfect structure to pursue the courtship they were seeking, but many were aware of how certain attributes of certain sites did or did not correspond to their desires.

In this section, we have noted the ways in which the remediation of certain social and non-social actors that could be seen as providing a matchmaking function played a role in our subjects' preference for or thoughts on various sites. In the next section, we will look at the remediation of a tool – the biodata – in the pursuit of courtship.

Remediating Biodata

For those who are specifically designated as a matchmaker, one crucial tool to maintain a repository of eligibles is the biodata. Biodata allow matchmakers to keep track of the people who they are working with to find matches. Biodata fill the matchmakers' database. These one-page entries, when used by professional matchmakers, are tools for mediating the process of arrangement. Whereas some arranged and assisted marriage connections are made by family or social ties that are made solely with the agency of the eligibles and/or their parents or other family members, biodata are a medium that are necessitated only by the presence of a separate matchmaker. They are a technology of the matchmaker.

> Biodata vary in format, layout and style. Still, the characteristics most commonly mentioned are date of birth, caste, religion, education, occupation, income, height, weight,

complexion, accomplishments, family status, personal interests, conditions of marriage, and partner expectations. Most profiles are accompanied by a photograph either in the body of the biodata or as a separate attachment.[27]

The awareness of our subjects with these forms of courtship and this technology came up implicitly and explicitly throughout our interviews.

Because the biodata form is tied to traditional modes of courtship or arrangement, diasporic South Asians, unlike members of some other ethnicities in the American context, have long faced the model of tying the act of representing oneself in terms of numbers, categories, and words, to courtship. It was surprising to find out, then, that many of the subjects in this study expressed discomfort at filling out the forms on various dating and matrimonial sites. While subjects like Participant 10 (above) found it important to use many of the fields on dating and matrimonial sites strategically, many of the users were using other modes of matchmaking to get away from the strictures of a technology like the biodata and a process like traditional matchmaking.

Participant 7, who was not only interested in South Asian eligibles[28] spoke about her preference for online platforms that created opportunities to pursue dates based on mutual interest expressed quickly, such as Tinder, or through a group date, facilitated by Grouper. After speaking about these models, she said,

> I would feel better about meeting someone like that rather than on Shaadi.com where it feels like a business deal. I feel like other sites provide other areas you can explore rather than the traditional Indian criteria of finding someone. If I wanted that I would create a biodata and have my parents pass it around and maybe not even need to go on Shaadi. But I want more than that.

The models of matching that Participant 7 expressed interest in were not incredibly tied to presenting intense amounts of data. Both examples she presented as positive options require very little to be provided, and she specifically resisted the idea of biodata as appropriate ways of presenting oneself to potential suitors. In this case, though she is mostly interested in a South Asian-American, she is most interested in models of courtship that are not remediations of "traditional" South Asian modes.

When asked how she felt about the various sites she used, Participant 2 noted,

> Well, obviously, any software package is going to try and make a digital representation of the real world. And it's only going to do it so accurately…I feel like eHarmony was the best because it brought the personality dimension into it rather than just the biodata…I think

---

27 Sheena Raja, 'A Match Made in Heaven: A Study of Changing Hindu Marriage Practices amongst Gujarati Eligibles' in Sharmina Mawani and Anjoom Mukadam (eds.) *Gujarati Communities across the Globe: Memory, Identity, and Continuity*, London, UK: Trentham Books, 2012, page 126.

28 Participant 7 said that she would "like someone South Asian, but [is] open-minded to anything."

people are busy so there may be a better match for you out there, but...people can get inundated. A part of it is a little dehumanizing. You are taking something that is inherently emotional and channeling it through a machine. These are real human beings. You may connect with somebody, and it could be a spark, but it could be a one sided spark, but to the machine it doesn't take into an account that somebody is damaged in the process.

Here Participant 2 puts the biodata in its context, as a tool of matchmaking, and notes that the software that each site runs uses different protocols for using the biodata-like profile. Though she doesn't mention the roles of human matchmakers, she implies that certain algorithms and software can be more humane.

Finally, Participant 1 brought up the ways that Shaadi.com's profiles mirrored the kinds of information that went into biodata. This was seen as unattractive to him as a user. When asked why Shaadi.com's structure was not attractive to him, "too traditional," he said,

> It was more bio-data-ish. Stuff that you would put on a biodata. Like some of the standard stuff is like you know, height, weight and skin tone...That's all standard and not that detailed. Well I thought that the skin tone thing, in particular, was very traditional. Like they are very fair or wheatish. They are dark or whatever. They had like 7 different kinds of skin tone like that you can pick from. [Chuckle]

Here, the structure of the online sites' structures were seen as comparable but favorable to biodata. This last comment brings up directly the idea of different uses of the site for diasporic subjects as compared to the use of sites by Indian nationals. No matter how much skin tone might become a part of mate selection in the American context, articulating this is seen to go against the social practices of a post-racial American culture. In the next section, we will discuss the remediation of diasporic identity with regards to the sites that our subjects used.

Remediating Diasporic Subjectivity

The concepts of ethnoscapes, technoscapes, and mediascapes remind us that in the contemporary era, the nation-state becomes a less compelling way to organize culture. By characterizing the contemporary shape of culture as *-scapes*, Appadurai brings attention to the ways that the relationships between people, nation-states, and cultures of tradition are inconsistent but shaped by a series of forces that constitute the transnational flows of people, technology, and media, for instance. [29] The diasporic subjects in this study have all made a home for themselves in the United States, specifically in the New York City area in New York and New Jersey. Though it was not necessarily a surprise that the subjects considered sites that both do and do not market themselves specifically to the South Asian diasporic communities, we were surprised by the various ways that our subjects justified the sites that they used, especially as those justifications pertained to one's pursuit of a suitor that fitted within a specific set of constraints.

---

29   Arjun Appudarai, *Modernity at Large: Cultural Dimensions of Globalization.*

While all respondents considered both South Asian diasporic and multiethnic sites, most of them used some of both. For the most part, the subjects expressed a desire to browse or search South Asian-American eligibles. Many of our subjects mentioned their tactics for finding appropriate eligibles on a number of sites. On multiethnic sites targeted towards Americans, they spoke specifically about tactics to find other South Asians. To do this, users often used sites where they could sort through profiles by ethnicity. Ethnicity is also often listed on profiles on dating and matrimonial sites. The category South Asian, it turns out, isn't particularly universally legible as a standard. On some sites, "South Asian" was a category. On sites where "Asian" was a category, but not "South Asian," those looking for Hindu eligibles were able to narrow down their search results by using both the ethnicity and religion fields. On still other sites, "East Indian" was the particular designation that users needed to use.

Another theme that arose throughout our interviews was the ways in which sites for South Asian users did not meet the needs of the diasporic subjects, and rather were too targeted towards users on the subcontinent. Without prompting, several of the subjects we interviewed specifically stated that they were not interested in the prospects of meeting someone living in India. Participant 1 noted, "They ask if you wanted to put your income or if you wanted to put HIV status, or your citizenship status. I don't know. It felt like it was very much geared towards folks overseas." Here, Participant 1 noted that the citizenship status felt out of place considering his own priorities, because he wanted to find eligibles who lived nearby and implied that a field for HIV status was unexpected and felt out-of-place. [30]

Many participants who were looking for South Asian-American mates were interested specifically in people with specific regional ethnic or religious identities, like Participant 6 above. For these subjects, membership in a site designed specifically for intra-group marriage was a part of the user's repertoire of sites used. Often this was a spin-off of BharatMatrimony.com for specific ethnic groups, but sometimes it was a specific matrimonial site for a religious group. In one case, a subject used a small, elite secret site for members with a specific regional, ethnic and caste intersection. These examples show how affiliations specific to culture on the subcontinent are still important for the diasporic subjects.

The pursuit of diasporic South Asians specifically was strategized in a number of ways. Participant 7 articulated a common desire to pursue courtship with South Asian-Americans by talking about her justifications for not using Shaadi.com seriously.

> Because I'm under the impression that most of the people on Shaadi.com are from India and I'm not sure if...I guess I'm under the impression that most of the people live in India and I'm not open to doing anything long distance. I'm not really interested in...anything that complicated. And different samajes[31] and associations have their own private sites, I think. I'm more interested in something close by... Somebody that was brought up in a similar Indian and American culture here would be a nice starting point...

---

30 It, indeed, is rarely asked on American-targeted sites that facilitate heterosexual coupling. It is sometimes a field on sites for men seeking men.

31 Samajes are ethnic caste communities.

Further contextualizing her earlier desire to avoid the transactional nature of Shaadi.com (above), she continued,

> But I'm also not going to just limit myself to Indians and that's what Shaadi.com does. If you're Indian and are serious to get married...like right away, and only want another Indian, then you go to that site. I'm not into just meeting someone to talk about "shaadi" so I don't think I'm the right person to be on Shaadi.

Here, Participant 7 noted the specific reasons for preferring the American-targeted multi-ethnic sites and emphasized her diasporic subjectivity as something that is best addressed by these sites.

Like Participant 7's observation that encountering others who are Indian-American would be a "nice starting point," others expressed a desire to pursue relationships with other Indian-Americans exclusively. Participant 8 also discussed her desire for a specific mix of Indian and Indian-American:

> [I'm not so into Shaadi, because] there are a lot of men on there that are not citizens and not [my] type. I *dunno*. It's just guys I would never be interested in. And citizenship is definitely a big thing. That's why I rely on Match.com more. It's more Americanized guys that do have that Indian culture, too. That's what I'm looking for - someone like me. But with Shaadi.com it could get a little more...I don't know how to say the right word, but... *desi* I guess.

In this regard, Participant 8 echoed a sentiment expressed or assumed by many of our subjects: for a number of reasons, another South Asian-American was what they were using matchmaking technologies to find. These desires were articulated through the various technological and human actors surrounding these subjects.

Conclusion

In this chapter, we have explored the use of dating and matrimonial sites by South Asian-Americans in the New York City metro area. In so doing, we have noted the ways that the various human and non-human actors in "traditional" matchmaking processes have been remediated, as have the tools involved in mediated matchmaking, and the users' own diasporic identities and subjectivities. Understanding South Asian marriage as all about matchmaking and courtship and American/Western marriage as solely invested in the pursuit of love, dating, and/or sex, one simplifies the ways that modernity is actually experienced, and the many possibilities that modern or contemporary subjects engage in.

While modernity affords "the pure relationship," an equitable one that is based on the affinity for two people for each other or the loss of interest in each other, which leads Giddens to advocate for the no-fault divorce, human beings blind ourselves to other systems of relating other than "love."[32] Or, alternatively, we limit our definition of "love." Instances of mediated

---

32 Anthony Giddens, *The Transformation of Intimacy, Sexuality, Love, and Eroticism in Modern Societies*,

matchmaking lay bare the technologized and mediated pursuit of courtship and its complicity in models of arrangement, assisted marriages, and, in fact, love. Diasporic subjectivity, as described in this essay, is a particularly interesting boundary object that points out the ways that various modes of relating are coeval in a contemporary globalized world. In considering the experiences of diasporic South Asians' use of dating and matrimonial sites to pursue relationships, we are reminded of the various courses and pathways enabled by transnational ethno-, techno-, and mediascapes. As courts, legislatures, social scientists, and culture at large attempt to codify certain modes of marriage and courtship within the United States and other nations, it is helpful to be reminded of the many coexisting and varied models for these modes of relating.

Appendix

Participant 1: Male/34/U.S.-born/Raised Hindu Participant
2: Male/35/Indian-born Participant
3: Female/35/Indian-born/Raised Hindu Participant
4: Female/29/U.S.-born/Raised Hindu Participant
5: Female/33/U.S.-born/Raised Buddhist Participant
6: Female/26/Indian-born Participant
7: Female/30/U.S.-born/Raised Hindu Participant
8: Female/32/U.S.-born/Raised Hindu Participant
9: Female/29/U.S.-born/Raised Jain Participant
10: Male/33/U.S.-born/Raised Hindu

References

Adams, Paul C. and Ghose, Rina. 'India.com: The construction of a Space Between', *Progress in Human Geography* 27.4 (2003) 414-37.

Aguiar, Marian. 'Arranged Marriage: Cultural Regeneration in Transnational South Asian Popular Culture', *Cultural Critique* 84 (Spring, 2013) 181-213.

Appudarai, Arjun. *Modernity at Large: Cultural Dimensions of Globalization*, Minneapolis: University of Minnesota, 1996.

Bellafante, Ginia, 'Courtship Ideas of South Asians Get a U.S. Touch', *The New York Times*. (23 August, 2005).

Bolter, Jay David and Grusin, Richard. *Remediation: Understanding New Media*, Cambridge, MA: MIT Press, 2000.

Chakraborty, Kabita. 'Virtual Mate-seeking in the Urban Slums of Kolkata, India.' *South Asian Popular Culture* 10.2 (July, 2012) 197-216.

Coontz, Stephanie. *Marriage, a History*, New York: Viking, 2005.

Diminescu, Dana and Renault, Matthieu. 'The Matrimonial Web of Migrants: The Economics of Profiling as a New Form of Ethnic Business', *Social Science Information* 50 (2011) 678-704.

Giddens, Anthony. *The Transformation of Intimacy, Sexuality, Love, and Eroticism in Modern Societies*, Stanford, CA: Stanford University Press, 1993.

Gopalkrishnan, Narayan and Babacan, Hurriyet. 'Ties That Bind: Marriage and Partner Choice in the In-

Stanford, CA: Stanford University Press, 1993.

dian Community in Australia in a Transnational Context', *Identities: Global Studies in Culture and Power* 14.4 (2007) 507-26.

Eva Illouz, *Consuming the Romantic Utopia: Love and the Cultural Contradictions of Capitalism*, Berkeley: University of California Press, 1997.

Jha, Sonora and Adelman, Mara. 'Looking for Love in All the White Places: A Study of Skin Color Preferences on Indian Matrimonial and Mate-Seeking Websites.' *Studies in South Asian Film and Media* 1.1 (2009) 65-83.

Latour, Bruno. *Reassembling the Social: An Introduction to Actor-Network-Theory*, Oxford: Oxford University Press, 2007.

Raja, Sheena, 'A Match Made in Heaven: A Study of Changing Hindu Marriage Practices amongst Gujarati Eligibles' in Sharmina Mawani and Anjoom Mukadam (eds.) *Gujarati Communities across the Globe: Memory, Identity, and Continuity*, London, UK: Trentham Books, 2012.

Rao, V.V. Prakasa and Rao, V. Nandini. *Marriage, the Family, and Women in India*, Delhi: Heritage, 1982.

SAALT, 'A Demographic Snapshot of South Asians in the United States', July 2012. Retrieved from http://saalt.org/wp-content/uploads/2012/09/Demographic-Snapshot-Asian-American-Foundation-2012.pdf.

Seth, Nainika and Patnayakuni, Ravi. 'Online Matrimonial Sites and the Transformation of Arranged Marriage in India', in Celia Romm Livermo (ed) *Gender and Social Computing: Interactions, Differences, and Relationships*, Hershey, PA: IGI Global, 2011, pp. 272-93.

US Census Bureau, 'The Asian Population: 2010', March 2012. Retrieved from http://www.census.gov/prod/cen2010/briefs/c2010br-11.pdf.

FROM ARRANGED TO ONLINE: A STUDY OF COURTSHIP CULTURE IN INDIA

AMITABH VIKRAM DWIVEDI

Introduction

This chapter is a result of an ethnographic study conducted between January and March 2014 for three online matrimonial sites. It studied the factors responsible for the online culture prevalent in Indian marriages. Nothing much has been changed in marriages and promises across cultures in India. Earlier they were arranged now they are arranged online, too. Traditionally, Indian families had a great deal of involvement in the marriage processes. Those marriages were popularly known as *'arranged marriages'*. Now this culture has been supported by an online courtship culture where two online searchers initiate on commercial matrimonial sites. Table 2 compares the offline generation to the online generation in partner search. The goal of this study, began in 2013, was to provide reliable and sound information with which to identify how modern technology corresponds to societal traditions. This research studies three sites, namely *shadi.com, jeevansahti.com* and *bharatmatrimony.com* in India, and seeks to examine how these matrimonial sites in the process of arranging marriages interact with the partner seekers. Since the marriage processes and traditions are closely associated with each other, there would be an exploration of how modern technologies confront and consequently change societal traditions. The study is informed by the ethnographic approach, and the information is analyzed by feedback and content analysis. This study does not promote or reject online or offline ways of selecting a prospective partner but it gives an insight where technology is changing complex social process.

Matrimonial sites that assist in arranging marriages were founded by the young Indian entrepreneurs a couple of decades ago. In 1996, Anupam Mittal pioneered online matrimonial by founding *Shaadi.com* and he claims that this website has affected the lives of 20 million people and 3.2 million people found their life partners on this site.[1] *Bharat Matrimony*, founded in 1997, holds the *Limca Book of World Record* for the highest number of online documented marriages and also set a *Guinness World Record* for creating the Largest Wedding Photo Album on April 14, 2012.[2] *Jeevansahti.com*, a recent establishment, has 850,000 members, and it finds a match primarily on the basis of community, religion, caste, and profession.[3]

In India every state has its own type of wedding ceremonies with mostly diverse customs and traditions. Some typical Indian weddings include the Punjabi wedding, Hindu wedding, Indian Muslim wedding and Christian wedding. The ways marriages are organized keep changing in India. Earlier there were only arranged marriages in the same caste and religion. Now there is love, love-arranged, arranged-love, inter-caste, inter-religion, court-marriage and live-in relationship. Moreover, most of these marriages are arranged online.

This chapter addressed the following research questions:

---

1   Shaadi.com, 2014, www.shaddi.com.
2   BharatMatrimony.com, 2014, www.bharatmatrimony.com.
3   Jeevansathi.com, 2014, www.jeevansathi.com.

1. What is the magnitude of modern technology against the societal traditions in India? Especially, on these three online matrimonial sites, how do they penetrate in the complex social practices confrontational or supplementary to old traditional searching practices?

2. How do family and individual differ in their opinions for searching a partner?

3. What technological, individual, and family factors are associated with the online searching practices?

This study has three components: a. Assessing trends and patterns of online marriages by studying three matrimonial sites and analyzing existing data sets; b. Conducting interview-based surveys to increase the understanding of changing behaviors of the users of the matrimonial sites; and c. Distilling findings from an analysis of participant-observation and telephone interviews.

This chapter actively admits that though online searching environment complements the traditional offline markets, it seeks to explore how the change and difference related to the online activities in the marriages is carried out, and recounts how the knowledge of the technology and social action go together. The remainder of the chapter is organized under the following headings: "Arranged Marriages" describes the historical background of marriages in India, "Online Searchers" specifies participants of this study, under the "Theoretical Foundation" a brief account of previous studies conducted is presented and the impact of technology on searching partners is discussed, the next section "How Matrimonial Sites Work" provides an overview of the matrimonial sites, "Facilities on Matrimonial Sites" enumerates the technical reasons for the success of these sites in India, "Methodology" discusses various methods used for the study, the heading "Analysis" indicates the behavior of the users and abusers on these sites, and the heading "Conclusion" concludes the paper, finally the "Limitations" enumerates a few limitations of this research.

Arranged Marriages

Ancient Indian text *Manusmriti*, or *The Writings of Manu*, identifies the marriage ceremony as a rite of initiation for women, by which they became the members of Hindu society.[4] Manu says that "the nuptial ceremony is considered as the complete institution of women, ordained for them in the Veda, together with the reference to their husbands."[5] No traditional Indian text prescribes requisite to be in love first before marriage as it is against the constitution of the marriage institution in ancient India[6]. However, there were instances when marriages followed love, or at times a child was born out of the wedlock in love.[7]

---

4   Mary McGee, 'Samskåra', in Sushil Mittal and Gene Thursby (eds) The Hindu World, New York: Routledge, 2005, pp. 332-356.
5   Rev. J. E. Padfield, The Hindu at Home. Delhi: B. R. Publishing Company, ([1895] 2007).
6   Hinduism recognizes eight types of marriages. *Gandharva vivah* (love marriages) and *Bhrama vivah* (arranged marriages) are presently found in Indian society. See *Atharvavedh* for more detail.
7   The ancient story of "Dushyant and Shakuntala" in Shakuntalam written by Sanskrit poet Kalidas.

The compound lexeme 'arranged marriages' gives a vague picture of obedient sons and daughters who cannot select a partner for themselves and therefore their parents generally arrange their marriages. But fairly this can be seen as men and women seek each other and their parents endorse the wedding, and in some cases the "groom's family may ask for a dowry of cash and other items."[8] The stamp provided by the parents also approves only such arranged marriages where traditional ideologies pertaining to female chastity, prohibition of inter-caste and inter-religion marriages are maintained, and issues of elopements, conversions and remarriages are properly taken care of.[9]

Arranging marriages are a socio-economic decision for the parents of the brides and grooms. Both the parties who participate in this transactional institution try to secure their profits in this social investment. With or without dowry after *Kanyadan*,[10] where the father of the bride gives the hand of her daughter to the groom, the woman becomes the life-partner and responsibility of the man. This important decision of marriage is made after matching the social, economic, cultural, and educational equality. The major critique of love marriages crops up from the fact that it promotes inter-caste marriages and consequently weakens the society. The caste system restores its equilibrium even in the arranged online marriages where matrimonial sites are classified under the headings of castes and sub-castes.

Generally, love follows marriage in arranged marriages.[11] The pragmatic considerations for such marriages are that it will outlast the quickly fading infatuation and romantic love.[12] In the colonial period, the radical supporters of English culture, language and ideology who were disgusted by the evil practices of Indian society, for example, *Sati*, or self-immolation of a widow, child marriages, the prohibition of widow remarriage, and questioning female chastity supported and promoted the idea to be in love first and then to go for a marriage. The Constitution of India provides various acts to regulate marriages in this country with many religions. Muslim Personal Law Application Act XXVI of 1937 and Indian Christian Marriage Act XV of 1872 regulate Muslim and Christian marriages in modern India respectively. Post-independence India witnessed Marriage Act of 1955 to curb child marriages and dowry system, and Hindus, Jains, Sikhs, and Buddhists come under this law.[13]

Online Searchers

The online searchers largely consist of relatively computer-literate, working middle class men and women who believe in finding their own life-partners. They approve of the idea that

---

8   Robin Rinehart, 'Hearing and Remembering: Oral and Written Texts in Hinduism', in Robin Rinehart (ed) Contemporary Hinduism: Ritual, Culture, and Practice, Which city, California: ABC-CLIO, Inc., 2004, p. 92.

9   Economic and Political Weekly, 'Search', 2014, http://www.epw.in/search/apachesolr_search/matchmakers%20and%20intermediation.

10 Translated by the author. Donating daughter, a ritual popular in Hindu marriages.

11 While acquaintances and friendship between prospective partners develop after marriage, this generalization is based on the replies given by many online users when interviewed telephonically.

12 Economic and Political Weekly, 'Search'.

13 Jiban K. Pal, 'Social Networks Enabling Matrimonial Information Services in India', International Journal of Library and Information Science May (2010): 55-64.

though marriages are made in heaven, they can be arranged online. Most of the eligible partner seekers are single and some of them are migrated from their country, states, cities, and towns in the search of jobs and better livelihood. Their days are busy and nights are lonely, and they are quite assured that they can find a better partner than their parents' traditional methods. The information age has impacted their psyche as much as they want to be informed about everything related to their prospective partners before they tie a knot. They want a confidential environment to maximize their searches for the competent partner. Wagner says that "people choose to use online dating services because they create opportunities to meet people they would not have otherwise met."[14]

Online partner searchers on matrimonial sites are of six types: married, divorced, single, widowed, awaiting divorce, and annulled.

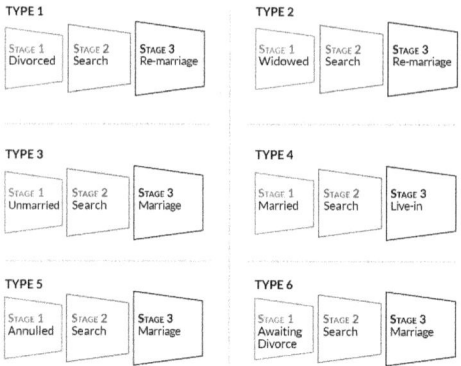

Figure 1 Online partner searchers

The online matrimonial sites work as a bridge in their search to place them from a stage without a partner to where they have a partner. The term divorced in Type 1, widowed in Type 2, annulled in Type 5, and awaiting divorce in Type 6 are people who have experienced failure in their previous marriages which was either love or arranged, offline or online. The single in Type 3, generally refers to individuals who are never married in their lives, and married in Type 4 consists of a mixed group; they are either unhappy couples, couples living in distant places, or boring couples interested in extra-marital relationships or in a physical relationship. All six types are in search of love and companionship which they have been lacking in their lives and relationships.

The technology has advanced and changed the ways of selection, choice, and consent for both brides and grooms. A study conducted by Bellou shows that consumer broadband adaptation "has significantly contributed to increased marriages rates among 21-30 year olds," and the online users search their partners until "a partner is found whose quality equals or

---

14   Lyndsey Wagner, Disharmony and Matchless: Interpersonal Deception Theory in Online Dating. MA Thesis, Lynchburg: School of Communication Studies, Liberty University, 2011.

exceeds an endogenously determined reservation value."[15] These users are also the type of people who prefer to move in a relationship from the virtual to the real world. In this process, they enhance and invest their feelings by a gradual progress of self-disclosure.

Theoretical Foundation

The early research in the study of marriage was initiated by Becker's *A Theory of Marriage* in which he said that "marriage is compelling additional evidence on the unifying power of economic analysis" and "a market in marriages can be presumed to exist."[16] His demand and supply (D & C) model and optimal sorting models make an analogy between marriages and firms. Since then D & C has been applied to the study of dating, extra-marital affairs, and marriages. Bellou compares "the market for romantic partners" with "the labor market", and further claims that both functions in a similar way.[17] Her study shows that broadband diffusion has a measurable impact on the online search process.

Information Systems and Information Technology[18] (IS/IT) have been fused in our day-to-day life and the expectations, promises, myths and consequences birthed from this adopted wave have presented challenges to the people, society and organization.[19] What the professional matrimonial sites are doing today is a transformed version of match searching which was earlier carried out by print media and the 'family pundits' in the towns, villages, and cities of India. However, the effects of new IS/IT are on its usage by the people rather than on the technology itself, and the major challenge is whether to use it or leave it. But the use of new technology depends on the interaction between the technology, the user and the organizational environment. Communication theorists argue that the use of technology is a process of social definition. This, in turn, is related to the concept of reinvention.[20] The new online technology of searching partners has reinvented the themes of marriage, selection, choice, and companionship.

Wagner, in a qualitative study, investigates the communication phenomena of deception as it occurs in the online dating, and concludes that generally online daters are honest and a slight exaggeration and dishonesty is mostly overlooked.[21] Besides this, the websites are affecting more people. It is more popular in cities and metropolises. It has redefined the complex social

---

15 Andriana Bellou, 'The Impact of Internet Diffusion on Marriage Rates: Evidence from the Broadband Market', in Discussion Paper Series (IZA DP No. 7316), Bonn: The Institute for the Study of Labor (IZA), March 2013, pp. 1-6.

16 S. Gary Becker, 'A Theory of Marrage: Part I', Journal of Political Economy 81 (1973): 813-846.

17 Andriana Bellou, 'The Impact of Internet Diffusion on Marriage Rates: Evidence from the Broadband Market'.

18 An information system is a social system which has embedded in it information technology (see Land, 1985: 215).

19 Rodrigo Magalhães, Organizational Knoledge and Technology: An Action-Oriented Perspective on Organization and Information Systems, Cheltenham: Edward Elgar Publishing Limited, 2004.

20 Janet Fulk, 'Social Construction of Communication Technology', Academy of Management Journal 36.5 (1993): 921–950.

21 Lyndsey Wagner, Disharmony and Matchless: Interpersonal Deception Theory in Online Dating.

process of arranged marriages. Whitty emphasizes that social scientists should not develop one grand theory to explain how online users and searchers present themselves in the cyber space, on the contrary, it is rather important to find how cyber space is constructed.[22]

How Matrimonial Sites Work?

The online matrimonial sites generally work on the selective dissemination of the information (SDI). An individual becomes an information seeker and provider in the process of partner search. Seth and Ravi suggest that "the use of matrimonial web sites have implications for family disintermediation, cultural convergence, continuous information flows, and ease of disengagement, virtual dating and reduced stigma in arranged marriages in India."[23]

The focus of the present study is the top-three matrimonial sites in India, namely *Shaadi.com*, *Bharatmatrimony.com*, and *Jeevansahti.com*. All three sites provide free registration, and have common attributes like community specific search, online chat, email and SMS services, horoscope matching, highlighted profile, time-bound subscription, and personalized services.

The difference between a free registration and a paid membership lies in the services and information the website provides. The significant contacts and matches are always in the paid packages, and the customer care executives give care and attention to any paid customer. It is always advised and directed to the users to provide the correct and complete information to attract better matches. The user provides his/her basic information appertaining to age, sex, place and country of birth, marital status, permanent and contact address, landline and mobile phone numbers, email, etc. and the information related to complexion, height, weight, and disorder if any. The user next fills the information about job, education, life-style, and food preferences - vegetarian or non-vegetarian.

Facilities on Matrimonial Sites

The offline ways of searching partners are limited in scopes, while the online matrimonial sites, assisted with the information dissemination technology, facilities the online partner search. It penetrates the complex Indian social structure, and makes the partner search a success. Numerous matrimonial sites are operative in twenty-eight states and seven union territories in India. Pal provides the list of such twenty-two web sites and their global and Indian traffic ranks, sites-linking and when they were founded.[24] The popularity of the top-three matrimonial sites can be observed from the data on Alexa that Shaadi.com's traffic rank is No. 52 and each user spends at least 4.5 minutes on this site. While the traffic rank of Jeevansathi.com is 3,552 but each user spends more than 8 minutes per day. Table 1 indicates the popularity of matrimonial sites in India as a potential partner searcher.

---

22 Monica T. Whitty, "Revealing the 'Real' Me, Searching for the 'Actual' You: Presentations of Self on an Internet Dating Site", Computers in Human Behavior (2007): 1-17.

23 Nainika Seth and Ravi Patnayakuni, 'Online Matrimonial Sites and the Transformation of Arranged Marriage in India', in Celia Romm-Livermore and Kristina Setzekorn (eds) Social Networking Communities and E-Dating Services: Concepts and Implications, London: Information Science Reference, 2009, pp. 329-352.

24 Jiban K. Pal, 'Social Networks Enabling Matrimonial Information Services in India'.

The Peoples Interactive (I) Private Limited Company pioneered Shaadi.com in 1996. This website develops its brand awareness by providing a YouTube link of Indian best- seller *Chetan Bhagat's* Marriage Tips for Anupam Mittal, CEO of the company, and also trends videos showing a superior matchmaking experience on Shaadi.com. It has 1.4 million likes on Facebook and 42.2 thousand followers on Twitter in 2014/2013/1996? It caters the increasing demand for matches by introducing and supplementing Non-Residential Indians (NRI) matrimonial to the traditional community and popular matrimonial. This service seems to promote more security, transparency, and a complete control to customers with a match guarantee challenge in 30 days otherwise they promise to pay the refund of entire fee without question. The customers can also follow the CEO on Twitter and on his blog. The SSL[25] encryption technology secures the payment transactions and makes the customer's buying experience easier and more enjoyable. The plans start from three months for $62 to one year for $170.

BharatMatrimony.com was probably the first to provide community-specific searching experience in regional languages. Established in 1997, *BharatMatrimony* believes to build a better *Bharat* (India) through happy marriages. The company thinks that public relations can be more effective if the native tongue of the online searchers is used.[26] The website displays trendy advertisements in major regional languages, namely Hindi, Bengali, Marathi, Malayalam, Oriya, Tamil, and Telugu. It has 1.1 million likes on Facebook and 16.5 thousand followers on Twitter 2014 again, specify the time here. This is most trusted matrimony brand according to the Brand Trust Report 2014.[27] It has launched two new sections, namely assisted matrimony, a personalized match making service, and elite matrimony, for the rich and affluent, to serve and cover all types of online searchers. There are various paid packages ranging from $62 to $615 with duration from three to nine months. The website directs various payment options, for example, credit card, debit card, net banking, and free door step collection. This matrimonial site provides free SMS alerts and voice messages.

It is a recent venture of a job searching site *Naukari.com,* initiated in September 2004, to serve northern and western Indian communities. Jeevansathi.com provides up to one-year paid packages services starting from US$50 to US$500. The company, along with regular registered account, also advertizes the profiles of HIV positives, Thalassemia Major, physically handicapped, and cancer survivors, for whom searching a life partner is a challenge. This indicates how deeply technology penetrates in the complex social structures.

---

25   Secure Sockets Layer.
26   Bharat Matrimony, 2014.
27   Trust Advisory, 'All India Brand Trust Ranking (Top 1200 Brands)', 2014, http://www.trustadvisory.info/allindia_2014.html.

Matrimony sites	Traffic ranking		Traffic from countries (%)			Daily pages views (per user)	Time on sites (minutes)
	India	Global	India	USA	Others		
Shaadi.com	52	546	90.7	6.0	3.3	5.27	4:30
BharatMatrimony.com	13,261	1,092	92.7	4.0	3.3	1.58	1:47
Jeevansathi.com	3,552	319	91.5	4.5	4.0	12.40	8:19

Table 1 Popularity of Matrimonial Sites in India[28]

Methodology

The data for the study were collected through mixed methods, including telephonic survey, face-to-face interview, analyzing Facebook messages, and feedback and content available on the matrimonial sites. Feedback included the real-life practices and experiences of the searchers which were used to evaluate and analyze the various aspects of events. The content analysis enabled the author to identify and examine themes and trends in information gathered through the matrimonial sites. The objectivity of this study is well-balanced as all the real participants were not able to observe and influence the author.

The telephone survey conducted in Hindi and English in six states, namely Jammu, Punjab, Delhi, Rajasthan, Madhya Pradesh, and Uttar Pradesh, in northern India from 5 January to 5 March 2014, among a random representative sample of 100 respondents 24 years of age and older. However, face-to-face communication[29] was very limited, and it covered only the regions of Jammu and Kashmir with 20 respondents where the author resides. This research also makes use of participant-observation[30] method in the study. The data were collected through 150 feedbacks, mostly testimonies of the users; and content, such as 50 personal profiles, and 50 language samples on matrimonial sites. The participants in the study had income between US$1,500 and US$5,000 per month. The interpretation of data was based on how the use of new technology depends on the interaction between the technology, the user and the organizational environment.

The success stories on websites are testimonials. They not only promote the websites but also provide additional information such as the role of family members, and the context of

---

28   Alexa.com, 3 June 2014, www.alexa.com.

29   I would like to thank Gargi for telephonically contacted people for the data. My special thanks go to Mr. Ganga Swarup and Ms. Uma Rani for interviewing the parents of the partner seekers in the cities of Jammu and Katra.

30   The author opened a free account on the matrimonial sites to observe the trends and patterns of the online users. The identity of the author as a researcher was not disclosed.

their selection of the website. The investigation focused on the formation of profiles, the development of the relationship during the courtship period, and the roles of relatives and parents.

Analysis: Users and Abusers
Users

The changing trend of the Indian men and women in marriages has been reflected from these matrimonial sites. Marriage is now not a closed affair of a family where only a few members are included and aware of the searching process. It has become a business of multinational corporations. However, whether an individual should register an account or not is still a family concern but many individuals open an account without informing their parents. The family members and close friends influence the selection process by providing their views, suggestions, and opinions on looks, age, income, caste, community, complexion, and horoscopes.

As soon as an account is open, it is virtually available to the world unless the user has posed restrictions on the website. It proclaims that an individual has registered himself/herself into the marriage market. Anyone who has opened a paid account can view other users' profile and send messages either by an SMS, mail or in the chat box. However, the elders (60 plus in age) of family still believe that online marriage should be the last option available for men and women. They disapprove it by saying that "only a person who is not getting married goes for it", "how do you know that your prospective partner is a virgin", "company is making a fool of you", "how can you rely on a machine", "how can you make your personal bio-data public", "we are still alive to find a partner for you", "don't become so modern and western if anything goes wrong company won't interfere or solve", alike.[31] Ironically, Indian marriages depend on a "middleman." This person (a relative, friend, family-pundit, etc.) recommends the marriage and he/she is largely responsible for the success of the relationship. If any conflict or dispute occurs it is his/her responsibility to solve it tactfully.

But despite these subjective criticisms the fact remains that the online matrimonial sites are indeed cheaper, faster and more interactive. They provide better conduits to the users for disseminating information. Its updating option never allows the information shared by the users to become obsolete. The searchers can get more detailed information about the prospective partner.

> *I got his request, saw the profile… Our families met and by the end of our third meeting we did* roka[32]… *on 27th feb 2014. Very happy to have found him.*

Another profile says:

---

31 Various comments recorded during face-to-face interviews.
32 Roka is a small but important function which marks the beginning of relationship between the two families. It includes the family members and close relatives of the prospective bride and groom.

> ...*Then the* family interacted to each other* to materialize things and plan for the final day. In less than 2 months we got married.*

And the other says:

> *At the first meeting itself we knew there was no looking around anymore and decided to talk to our parents ... ... even our* kundali's **(horoscope) *matched.*

Even with the online technology the customs and traditions remain intact. Though the online matrimonial sites have transformed the searching process yet arranging a match for oneself is no way a self-arranged marriage. The role of family members or parents has not been marginalized. The online searchers only find a partner for themselves and they convince their parents about their selection. The parents meet each other and they did *'roka'* (a promise) that they will not search further. The interaction between family members has many directions. It finds whether the family of prospective bride and groom is religious, courteous, prosperous, good-looking, and healthy. The *"kundali'* horoscope match is more important than love. It ensures the mutual compatibility, future lifestyle, nature, behavior, preferences, and the longevity of the relationship between the prospective bride and groom.

Who is making a profile is again a socio-cultural decision. It is generally considered indecent for a woman to create her own account. Many times if the account indicates that it is opened by a woman searching for a partner then men do not take that woman seriously and consider her easy-going.[33] Mostly, the women's accounts provide information that they are created by friends, parents, and relatives irrespective of the fact that they have created it. *"How can I indicate that I have opened an account for myself... ... ... men will consider me 'Chaalu' (indecent)"* - replied a woman respondent.

A profile said:

> *I am searching a partner for* my friend* Shruti... ... ...she is charming and well-educated.*

And:

> My daughter Rama is a software Engineer. She is 27, and she works for an MNC.

One woman stated in her desired partner profile:

> *"Govt Job IAS IES IFS IRS PCS ALL India"*[34] and another wanted *"preferably an NRI or from All India Services - IAS/ IPS / Indian Foreign Service. UP MP Rajasthan in India."*

---

33   A connotation in Indian English means 'not virtuous'.

34   Women generally go for economically secure groom while men want a beautiful wife. Women want a groom working in either Indian Administrative Services (IAS), or Indian Engineering Services (IES), or India Forest Services (IFS), or Indian Reserve Services (IRS), or Public Service Commission (PSCS).

Perceptions are changing in the Indian patriarchal society. Earlier annulled, divorced, awaiting divorce, widowed, and single middle-aged women were only taking an initiative to open an account and search for a partner. Now young single women are also going online for a partner of a specific profession, qualification, and location. Inter-state migration and living away from the family have brought changes in their perception. However, men's profiles are largely created and posted by them. They generally prefer beautiful, fair-complexioned and educated wife, but in some cases they want a working wife to support the family.

Abusers
Incidentally online matrimonial sites technology is not free from abuse. Online Matrimonial Abusers (OMA) are of three types: blackmailers, frauds, and maniacs.[35] They register an account for neither love nor for marriage but only for abusing other users.

Blackmailers, Frauds, and Maniacs
There are many fake accounts generated by the OMA on matrimonial sites. The blackmailers and frauds work in a gang where they create many profiles and their targets are emotionally weak, unworldly, inexperienced, gullible people. Since the matrimonial sites are based on the SDI (selective dissemination of information) technology, they trick men and women of different ages, religion and profession by showing keen interest in their profiles, and employing a wide range of false projections.

Blackmailers work in three stages. First, they become the friend of a targeted user. Then, they record a video and conversation with the user (for example, on *Skype,* etc.). Finally, they threaten to expose and make it public if the user does not provide money. Frauds, on the other hand, use different tactics to get money, first, by showing interest and becoming friendly, and then narrating a false story. For example, they met with an accident, and need money, they were robbed in a strange city so transfer money urgently, they have lost their wallet and they need to pay the hotel bills in a new place, etc. The genuine users who have been chatting and talking to these frauds and blackmailers for months generally do not understand their tricks and may easily be trapped and abused.

Maniacs are sexual perverts and nymphomaniacs.[36] They create an account to seduce the genuine online users. They get pleasure by talking, chatting, engaging and involving with someone without any serious engagement. They abuse the technology and person for months and then they shift to a different target.

Conclusion
Online matrimonial sites are influencing the searching practices. The partner seekers are

---

35 The author categorizes the abusers based on the negative feedback provided by few respondents.
36 Two respondents narrated interesting incidences with maniacs. In the first case, the father of the prospective groom was chatting with the girl, only realized it might be … when she persisted in meeting face-to-face. In the second situation, a male acquaintance reported that the already married elder sister of the prospective bride became so friendly that they ended up in telephone-sex.

recognizing it as a potential search engine for a prospective partner. New relationships have been formed and sustained on the basis of selective dissemination of information by the users and service providers. These sites are converting the traditional concept of "love after marriage" into a more rational concept of "first understand each other then marriage."

The so-called "obedience" of sons and daughters to marry a person whom their parents' select is now influenced and directed by the matrimonial sites. These "grown-up" children are expressing their needs of a prospective partner by creating an account on the matrimonial sites. Even before their parents had realized the need of a partner for them, they would have spent a considerable amount of time on deciding, discussing and desiring for a partner.

The rigid societal norms for dating are weakening, and men and women are meeting more frequently with each other without parental permission and supervision. The socializing among opposite sex has increased, and parents are allowing them to spend some time with each other before they tie a knot for life. However, the maintenance of the order of the caste and religion on these sites is possibly the most interesting factor which describes the adaptation and appropriation of technology in a socially complex institution. These sites have brought a change in the searching process only but they have not made a social change in the society. The tradition and cultural values pertaining to Indian marriages in the society remain intact.

In traditional methods of searching a partner, the background of the women and men and their families is cross-checked by the word of mouth mostly accomplished by the parents or the relatives. But in online arranged marriages the users initiate the search by focusing on the background of the prospective partner only. Moreover, this online process leads fast results and it opens many options at the same time. Introduction to new technologies in searching a partner has been working as a medium of pressure release for young adults. The virtually smart communicators who shy away from making any type of physical communication at an early stage of courtship period generally find matrimonial sites beneficial and effective to initiate a search for a partner.

These matrimonial sites are bridging the gap between the traditional offline culture and modern online system of finding a partner. The association of the two practices is complementing each other by providing more varied options and results to their searches. The social construction of technology in the Indian traditional set-up can be well defined and understood by these sites. The interaction between the matrimonial sites and the potential partner seekers is relatively fruitful. This metaphor describes that the matrimonial sites have grown popular among youths, and the partner-seekers have got the prospective partners. There were only 5 cases noted out of 370 mixed samples where the users of the matrimonial sites were not satisfied. Table 2 summarizes the differences between online and offline partner search practices.

Characteristics	Offline Generation	Online Generation
Perception of marriage	Made in heaven	Arranged online/solemnized on earth
Orientation/Beliefs	Love follows marriage	Marriage follows love
Major initiators	Parents and relatives	Self
Objective of marriage for man	To find a house-wife	A loveable partner
Objective of marriage for woman	To gain economic stability	To gain equality
Process of searching	Slow	Fast
Direction	Linear	Multi-directional
Process control (in terms of progress in relationship)	On man's side	Both can control
Options available	Few	Many
Expenditure on searching	More	Less
Decision-making	Parents or elders	Self
Method	Face-to-face	Online
Role of outside consultant	Major	Minor
Ties (Caste and Religion)	Rigid	Flexible
Chances of understanding each other before marriage	Less	More
Participation	Less	More

Table 2 Comparing offline generation to online generation in partner search

Limitations

The research collected data from the states of northern India where people spoke Hindi, or a dialect of Hindi, and understood English. There are other 16 regional languages spoken in the various states of India which were not included due to the limited exposure of the author with the other states and considering the paucity of time for the research.

The spatio-temporal constraint obstructed the author to collect face-to-face data from the other five states, including Delhi, Uttar Pradesh, Rajasthan, Madhya Pradesh, and Punjab.

The data could not include the feedback from the users in term of: how can the matrimonial sites make this overall experience more interactive and beneficial? Similarly, it could not incorporate the feedback and experiences of the respondents who had got a partner offline.

References

Alexa.com. *Alexa.com*. 2014. www.alexa.com.

Becker, S. Gary. "A Theory of Marrage: Part I." *Journal of Political Economy 81*, 1973: 813-846.

Bellou, Andriana. "The Impact of Internet Diffusion on Marriage Rates: Evidence from the Broadband Market." *Discussion Paper Series (IZA DP No. 7316)*. Bonn: The Institute for the Study of Labor (IZA), March 2013.

Bharat Matrimony. *Bharat Matrimony*. 2014. http://www.bharatmatrimony.com/.

Economic and Political Weekly. "Search." Accessed February 25, 2014. http://www.epw.in/search/apachesolr_search/matchmakers%20and%20intermediation.

Fife, Wayne. *Doing Fieldwork: Ethnographic Methods forResearch in Developing Countries and Beyond.* New York: Palgrave Macmillan , 2005.

Fulk, J. " Social construction of communication technology ." *Academy of Management Journal*, 1993: 36(5): 921–950.

Jeevansathi.com. *Jeevansathi.com*. 2014. www.jeevansathi.com.

Magalhães, Rodrigo. *Organizational Knoledge and Technology: An Action-Oriented Perspective on Organization and Information Systems.* Cheltenham: Edward Elgar Publishing Limited, 2004.

McGee, Mary. "Samskåra." In *The Hindu World*, by Sushil Mittal and Gene Thursby, 332-356. New York: Routledge, 2005.

Padfield, Rev. J. E. *The Hindu at Home*. delhi: B. R. Publishing Company, ([1895] 2007).

Pal, Jiban K. "Social networks enabling matrimonial information services in India ." *International Journal of Library and Information Science*, May 2010: 55-64.

Patnayakuni, Nainika Seth & Ravi. "Online Matrimonial Sites and the Transformation of Arranged Marriage in India." In *Social Networking Communities and E-Dating Services:Concepts and Implications*, by Celia Romm-Livermore & Kristina Setzekorn, 329-352. London: Information Science Reference, 2009.

Rinehart, Robin. "Hearing and Remembering: Oral and Written Texts in Hinduism." In *Contemporary Hinduism: Ritual, Culture, and Practice*, by Robin Rinehart, 92. California: ABC-CLIO, Inc., 2004.

Shaadi.com. 2014, www.shaddi.com.

Trust Advisory. 'All India Brand Trust Ranking. (Top 1200 Brands)', 2014, http://www.trustadvisory.info/allindia_2014.html.

Wagner, Lyndsey. *Disharmony and Matchless:Interpersonal Deception Theory in Online Dating*. MA

Thesis, Lynchburg: School of Communication Studies, Liberty University, 2011.

Whitty, Monica T. "Revealing the 'Real' Me, Searching for the 'Actual' You: Presentations of Self on an Internet Dating Site", Computers in Human Behavior, 2007: 1-17.

THE ROLE OF PLACES AND SYMBOLS: A CULTURAL INTERPRETATION OF THE ON-LINE DATING EXPERIENCE IN ISRAEL

DAVID LEVIN

Introduction

This work sets out to address a series of questions concerning online dating in the second decade of the 21st century in the specific case of Israeli users and addresses questions of virtual place: can the cyberspace be seen as a single space? Are there any cultural and local features to the practice of using the Internet to meet new people?

To address these questions, this work employs the terms of place, symbol and culture, in order to describe the unique local nature of 'e-dating' as experienced by Israeli on-line daters. Unlike cyberpsychology literature, which focuses on the individual user, often viewing the whole Internet as a 'signifier of unified and universalizing 'virtual realm',[1] the theoretical starting point of this work is a sociological and cultural one. It helps to (1) conceptualize 'places' and digital 'places' that constitute meeting grounds as distinct from one another and (2) understand the ideological structure of the Israeli-Jewish society, which has the practice of meeting a romantic partner as an integral part thereof.

The analysis was performed using the tools of Dell Hymes' model (SPEAKING), which enable to distinguish between different speech events and by implication, between 'places', refers to a corpus of some 1,500 posts published by users in an Internet forum cluster, falling under the category of 'love and romance' and hosted by a popular Israeli portal of *Tapuz*.[2] Analysis shows a distinction made by users between 'dating websites', 'forums' and *Facebook*. This distinction, elucidated by three symbols emerging from their statements; i.e. 'supermarket/workplace', 'orchard' and 'picture album', creates a mental-distance from dating websites for some users (although some of them use them), who view *Facebook* as an inappropriate place to start a new relationship and prefer the forum – the on-line discussion site they use on a daily basis. As I shall demonstrate, such distinctions have to do not only with structural differences between digital places, but also with local imagination and mythologies.

Literature Review

A Place vs. a Meeting Place

Over the last two decades, starting from the early 1990's, many studies have been published about the Internet's role in establishing intimate relationships[3] (see. The earliest of them

---

1   Jo Barraket, and Millsom S. Henry-Waring. 'Getting it on (line) Sociological Perspectives on E-dating.' *Journal of Sociology* 44. 152.

2   Tapuz. http://www.tapuz.co.il

3   Josef B. Walther, 'Interpersonal effects in computer-mediated interaction: A relational perspective'. Communication Research, 19, 52; Malcolm Parks and Kory Floyd, 'Making friends in cyberspace', Journal of Computer Mediated Communication, 1.4; Leonard Reinecke and Sabine Trepte, 'Authenticity and well-being on social network sites: A two-wave longitudinal study on the effects of online authenticity and the positivity bias in SNS communication.' Computers in Human Behavior, 30, 95.

addressed 'secondary' relationships, confined to the Internet and serving as compensation or complement for the offline reality. In recent years, there have also been sociologic and ethnographic studies[4] into intimate relationships that start online, with the intention of being pursued offline as well. Researchers who opted for this line of study set themselves two objectives: 1) to make a distinction between different digital places, based on differences in the relational dynamics woven within and 2) provide demographic explanations to the choice of the internet as a meeting point. The present work echoes this current literature with all its aspects.

On Places and Places around the Internet

Physical and symbolic places are mutually-distinct entities (like 'home' as opposed to the 'town square') within a given 'space' – the possible range of operation between the place inhabited by one at present and a potential place where one can picture oneself.[5] Internet researchers seem to be divided into those who view the web as a uniform, heterogeneous virtual place-essentially different from non-virtual 'places',[6] and those who perceive it to be a space where different places co-exist.[7]

When meeting other people is concerned, the former argue that some of its inherent features offer a sense of copious opportunities and interaction yet of a poorer kind, which doesn't allow for face-to-face communication, resulting in the objectification of others, as well as shallow, superficial relationships. Others argue that the lack of information and hiding behind masks, i.e. virtual identities, actually allow deeper connections to form; connections that cannot exist offline.[8]

Andrea Baker is one of the researchers who suggested we should ditch the notion of the cyberspace as a single place and focus rather on places around the Internet.[9] It emerged from her study that 'virtual communities' (or forums) and 'dating websites' were perceived by their users as mutually distinct. One of Baker's arguments was that people who met each other in virtual community websites lived relatively further away from each other, met offline later on and their relationships enjoyed greater stability in the long run, thus shifting the focus to the places formed around the virtual social network.

---

4   Jo Barraket,and Millsom S. Henry-Waring. 'Getting it on (line) Sociological

    Perspectives on E-dating.' Journal of Sociology 44. 152.

5   Victor Burgin. In/different Spaces: Place and Memory in Visual Culture.

6   Hubert L Dreyfus, On the Internet. ; Eva Illouz, and Shoshannah Finkelman. 'An Odd and Inseparable Couple: Emotion and Rationality in Partner Selection.' Theory and society 38. 4; Erich Merkle, R., and Rhonda A. Richardson. 'Digital Dating and Virtual Relating: Conceptualizing Computer Mediated Romantic Relationships.' Family Relations. 49. 2.

7   Andrea Baker, 'Two by Two in Cyberspace: Getting Together and Connecting Online.' CyberPsychology and Behavior 3.2.; Andrea Baker, Double click: Romance and Commitment among Online Couples.

8   Aaron Ben-Ze'ev, Love Online: Emotions on the Internet.

9   Andrea Baker, 'Two by Two in Cyberspace: Getting Together and Connecting Online.' CyberPsychology and Behavior 3.2.; Andrea Baker, Double click: Romance and Commitment among Online Couples.

It is my intention to pursue Baker's line of thought; add the *Facebook* social network as a further virtual place and offer some sets of methodological tools to elucidate the distinction between different places. I shall do so by using two models that do not necessarily pertain to online dating per se but help provide a unique perspective: Dell Hymes' model of *SPEAKING*, pertaining to 'speech events', and Ray Oldenburg's 'Third Place or Great Good Place'. Speech events constitute 'activities or aspects thereof that are directly governed by rules or norms for the use of speech'[10] and Dell Hymes suggests they may be analyzed using the *SPEAKING* model.[11] This model consists of eight essentials; two of them have to do with the structural elements of the event analyzed: *setting and scene,* which has to do with place and time, while *participants* pertains to the characterization of those who partake in the event or witness it. Five additional elements have to do with the interactional arrangement that institutionalizes the event: *ends* meant to be accepted by participants, the *act sequence* which participants employ in order to attain the ends, *norms* - which determine the relations between participants and can project on the *key and instrumentalities* associated with the atmosphere in which they partake. *The eighth element* - i.e., the genre that the event is categorized by; encompassing all features of the event with a generalizing definition that attributes the event to a given category.

Studies into e-dating referred to this model. It usually refers to this concept as a 'purposeful form of meeting new people through specifically designed Internet sites'.[12] I shall, of course, explore it further here, as a possible venue for meeting new potential partners, not necessarily in a pre-planned context.

E-dating has been the focus of numerous studies and has been analyzed through sociology, consumer culture and economics.[13, 14, 15] Andrea Baker addressed the features of 'setting and scene', 'ends' and 'act sequence'. Other works analyzed the norms of dating websites - such as the full details disclosure stipulation.[16] Heino et al. in their work-based on a series of interviews with male and female members of a big dating website-learned from their subjects about the 'marketplace metaphor' (or in their terms, the 'marketplace shopping'), which they use in these 'places'. Heino et al argues that these individuals consciously view such websites as places 'where people go to 'shop' for potential romantic partners or 'sell' themselves.' This metaphor affects the conduct around these websites - which sometimes confirmed the metaphor, while at other times served to subvert it.

---

10 Ray Oldenburg, The great good place: Cafés, coffee shops, community centers, beauty parlors, general stores, bars, hangouts, and how they get you through the day, New York: Paragon House, 1989, p. 52.

11 Hymes Dell, Foundations in Sociolinguistics: An Ethnographic Approach.

12 Jo Barraket and Millsom S. Henry-Waring, 'Getting it on (line) Sociological perspectives on edating.' Journal of Sociology 44.2 (2008): p. 149.

13 Jo Barraket and Millsom S. Henry-Waring, 'Getting it on (line) Sociological perspectives on e-dating.' Journal of Sociology 44.2.

14 Celia Romm-Livermore. Social networking communities and e-dating services: Concepts and implications.

15 George M Zinkhan, 'Romance and the Internet: The E-mergence of E-dating.' Advances in Consumer Research, 31.

16 Adam Arvidsson. 'Quality singles': Internet Dating and the Work of Fantasy.' New Media & Society, 8.4.

In order to distinguish, metaphorically, between places, one can also use Ray Oldenburg's work, revolving around the concept of the 'third place' or 'great good place'- utopian places where social encounters take place in a loosened, leveled atmosphere. The conversations developing in places such as the American town's café and barbershop answer the human need for intimacy and affiliation.[17] Oldenburg[18] further elucidated the uniqueness of 'the third place' by pitching it against the home — a place to rest in, retire from the public within the safety of one's family and the workplace, which is built on structured, objective-oriented activity, with constant competition; a setting that doesn't encourage interaction.

It is my intention to address these three sources as symbols; viewing them as a hypothetic tool, which along with Hymes' model, allows me to distinguish between different digital places designed for e-dating.

The distinctions and conceptualizations presented here are portrayed as 'deodorizing'- means, devoid of any cultural scent[19], yet they rely on instances from the American society. Combining the Jewish Israeli historic background lends them, as I shall demonstrate here, a unique cultural undertone.

From the Town Matchmaker to Dating Websites; from Diasporic to American

In the 150 years passed since its inception, the Jewish Israeli society has undergone two major cultural upheavals, pertinent to the following discussions. The first of which occurred with the sharp breaking away from 'diasporic' life-which is how Jewish Israelis refer to the period where most of the nation lived away from the land of Israel; the second one took place roughly forty years ago, with the onset of the massive penetration of American culture to the State of Israel.

In its early days, the Zionist Movement — upholding Jewish settlement in Israel, addressed younger people who resided in conservative, traditional Jewish communities in Eastern Europe, suggesting they realize, body and spirit, ideas of independence: breaking away from their parents and culture and creating instead a new society where they would live with a secular, solidary and supportive peer group — working in agriculture and industries and meeting all their physical and mental needs. This society, so they hoped, would spell the end of their parents' culture.

The way potential romantic engagements came about was an aspect of the necessary change.[20]

---

17   Ray Oldenburg,The Great Good Place: Cafés, Coffee Shops, Community Centers, Beauty Parlors, General Stores, Bars, Hangouts, and How They Get you Through the Day. 63
18   Ray Oldenburg, The Great Good Place: Cafés, Coffee Shops, Community Centers, Ceauty Parlors, General Stores, Bars, Hangouts, and How They Get you Through the Day.
     Ruvik Rosental, Dictionary of Israeli Slang.
19   Iwabuchi Koichi. Recentering Globalization: Popular Culture and Japanese Transnationalism.
20   Almog Oz, Farewell to 'Srulik': Changing Values among the Israeli Elite.

One feature of the diasporic life was the 'familial- community matchmaker': an unsightly, cunning man, trading in 'luftgesheft, Yiddish for 'business of air'; a man who makes incompatible matches, regardless of the subjects' romantic sentiments, with his guiding principles being greed on the one hand and inter-generational continuity on the other.

Most Jewish people living in Israel nowadays have never met this character, yet his mythological implication have naturally infiltrated the collective consciousness through canonical texts, such as the works of Israeli author and Noble laureate, Shmuel Yosef Agnon, or the popular Israeli film, *Two Kuni Lemel*.[21] In this film, a crook matchmaker tries to pair the rich master's daughter with a stammering, lame Yeshiva student, but eventually yields to the intense romantic feelings of the girl and her 'true' sweetheart.

In the new Jewish society created in Israel, the concept of the familial- community matchmaker was converted to unmediated meetings among people in the collective agricultural groups, formed in Israel or otherwise through the introduction by friends. The few familial-community matchmakers left catered for populations who struggled to embrace the Zionist world order: Orthodox Jews or new immigrants arriving at the state as it was founded – Holocaust survivors or immigrants from Arab countries.

Starting from the 1970's, Israel has seen major demographic changes that led to a significant rise in the average marriage age among the secular society. Statistics show that 64% of Jewish men and 46% of Jewish women in Israel aged 25-29 are single (as of 2011), as compared to 54% of Jewish men and 38% of Jewish women back in the beginning of the former decade (2000's). This compromised the option of meeting romantic partners within one's peer group-that is, in high school, during the military service or through higher education. One element introduced into the Israeli society was the professional 'marriage market intermediaries (MMI)'.[22] Forty years after their emergence in the USA, dating offices sprouted around Israel, with the predominant one being Helena Amram's, who branded herself as 'international', by speaking English and espousing the American culture. In addition, Israel witnessed the penetration of a foreign family of words, i.e. Date (dating, dater, date), which stands for casual romantic relationships, devoid of emotional attachment.

Dating websites emerged about twenty years ago. The first of which was a chapter of the international JDate website, followed by a series of similar sites, with some of the key ones adopting American names and appearance: Alpha, Cupid and Loveme. It is interesting to note that some very big dating-based websites, such as eHarmony, who employ scientific tools, never made it to Israel and have failed to generate local imitations. Speed-dating too remains a marginal phenomenon.

One could argue that this duality, i.e. the of legitimacy granted to 'America-like' sites on the one hand and the exclusion of such sites from Hebrew on the other, attests to the general

---

21 Two Kuni Lemel, (eng. The Flying Matchmaker) Dir. Israel Becker, 1970.
22 Aaron Ahuvia, C., and Mara B. Adelman. 'Formal Intermediaries in the Marriage Market: A Typology and Review.' Journal of Marriage and the Family 54. 2

ambivalence of Jews in Israel in their attitudes towards 'America'.[23] Jewish Israelis are in awe of the American technological superiority (the American term Hi-Tech garners a lot of prestige in Israel), but on the other hand, America, especially amongst the middle class and intellectual elite of Israel, is perceived as an over-mechanical kind of culture, intellectually superficial and estranged to any ideal of social relations. Jewish Israelis may refer to a perfect state-of-affairs in terms of 'it's just like in America', followed by 'lest we become America'. The reality of life under security threats and the Jewish tradition, versus the individualism and alienation that have come to signify 'America' for Israelis, still instate a 'collectivism' of sorts, coupled by a sense of 'togetherness'. These do not chime well with a world where everyone, supposedly, is to his own.

Alongside dating websites, Israel shows an avid interest in online forums, open to the public and serving also as places where strangers can meet. These forums are affiliated to online news sites, such as Ynet or Walla, or managed by user-communication designated websites, such as Tapuz (orange fruit), where the data for this work were collected; a site that attracted, according to its own statistics, around 1.5 million users in 2013.

The last five years have seen a high increase in the social networks in Israel, topped by Facebook. A comScore analysis showed that the average Israeli spent 10.7 hours a month on Facebook and Twitter, more than his/her counterparts in any other country. Facebook's rate of penetration in Israel stands at 90%, second only to the Philippines.[24] Over the years, and similarly to the USA, there have been attempts to combine dating websites in Israel with Facebook, in the form of Facebook dating applications, yet there are no proven numerical statistics regarding their success or indeed the success enjoyed by the Israeli e-dating industry as a whole.

Methodology and Procedure
The present study is based on the collection and analysis of posts in several Internet forums activated by the Israeli portal of 'Tapuz' under the 'love and romance' category, which encompasses forums named Him and Her, 30+ Dating and Blind Date, to cite but few.

The corpus was amassed in several steps. First I used the portal's search engine to trace relevant keywords, such as 'Internet', 'dating website', 'forum', "social network' and Facebook. I focused on the years 2011-2014.

The search yielded 1,185 posted messages associated with dating websites. Most users employed this term in its general sense. Only few referred to specific websites (JDate, for example, was cited 82 times). Facebook was cited in 113 posts (with no mention of any other social network). While few posts featured the word 'forum', I traced many instances where the forum groups browsed by subjects were referred to as (citrus) 'orchard' (154 times).

---

23   Azaryahu Maoz, 'The Golden Arches of McDonald's: On the "Americanization" of Israel.' Israel Studies, 5. 1.; Anat First and Eli Avraham. America in Jerusalem: Globalization, National Identity, and Israeli Advertising.

24   http://www.mako.co.il/news-money/tech/Article-5570ef490c27031004.htm

The significance of preferring the 'local' term to the application's universal name shall be discussed later. Once the corpus' limits were defined, posts that pertained to one or more parameter suggested by Hymes were identified: definitions of places, participants' identity and the abiding norms in each place, for example. Much to my surprise and despite my expectations, based on the key role of Facebook in the everyday Israeli reality, I found, during the process, Facebook to be perceived not as a 'place' for dating, but rather as a possible stage.

Observations were conducted in an unobtrusive mode, never interfering with discussions or contacting subjects for their comments and clarifications. Having adopted the premise that when people wrote in open forums-public contexts where entry was not protected by codes, passwords or other access barriers-they were aware their messages could be read and used by anyone, I assumed that forum users had made a rational decision as to which information they wanted to reveal and how to protect their privacy. Nevertheless, I did consider several ethical issues concerning online privacy and possible offence to people's feelings.[25] As recommended by several researchers, I only collected posts from public forums and never looked for further information about their authors[26] other than their age and sex, when they opted to disclose them.

First of all, I coded statements made in posts based on Hymes' analysis parameters, using the ATLAS software. The proximity of features and their common thread (the act sequence and norms, for example, are in close proximity) led me to opt for a presentation in two sections of analysis: structural and interactional features.

Findings

I shall now examine the website users' statements, based on the criteria suggested by Hymes for speech events' analysis. I shall make a distinction between the structural aspects-place, time and type of participants-and the interactional ones: ends, act sequence, norms, key and instrumentalities. The genre component, which actually corresponds with the symbols that come with every place, shall be addressed during discussion, referring to both these aspects.

Structural Aspects

Users, who referred to the 'place' component when alluding to the Cyberspace as a place where new relationships were formed, almost sweepingly did so while distinguishing between three mutually distinct-territorially and symbolically-virtual places of the imagined space: dating websites, rooted in a mythological 'America', the forums they logged on to – associated with Israel's nostalgic past, and the social network of Facebook, as a picture album close to the self of each and every one of them.

Dating websites proved to be places of strangeness and alienation. The latter stemmed from the perception of their activity as instrumental by nature, and they were depicted using

---

25 Gunther Eysenbach and James E. Till. 'Ethical issues in Qualitative Research on Internet Communities',
26 Elizabeth Bassett, H., and Kate O'Riordan, 'Ethics of Internet Research: Contesting the Human Subjects Research Model', Ethics and Information Technology 4. 3.
    Seale Clive et al. 'Interviews and Internet Forums: a Comparison of Two Sources of Qualitative Data.'

expressions and symbols laden with cultural significance:

> Dating websites are just another online shop. The supply on offer is huge and for many people, hanging around in these sites is just part of the shopping culture. When the profile reduces people to mere products with specifications, there are always going to be more attractive products with a more "updated" specification, and the endless browsing of profiles and picture has become for some people the key experience. *Male, 43.*

This sarcastic portrayal of the dating website as a 'place' where mechanic-like activity takes place makes ample use of foreign words, such as *shopping*, alongside 'online shop' and 'virtual shelf'; words whose function here is twofold – at once dwarfing and distancing. The Hebrew language differentiates between 'kniyot', Hebrew for buying, denoting the purchase of a product to be used, from the English 'shopping', which signals the joy derived from the very act of shopping, regardless of the product or its designated use. In other words, the shopping experience or more broadly, the window shopping, refers to the joy from both the very contact with the object, its smell or taste, and to the very visit in the shopping center or hanging put with friends and relative.[27]

To cite the Israeli slang dictionary, 'nothing can beat a shopping spree in drowning your sorrow, the joy of new items'.[28] Nevertheless, when such activity is attributed to dating websites, the joy element described in its definition is very much diminished, devoid of its joy/company-associated significances, leaving the mere narrow, meager aspect of an action with no definite aim, performed at the expense of a human 'object'.

The resemblance between the shallow, superficial image of the act, and one image of the country where the language employed here is spoken, leads one to assume that this kind of shopping is marked by the not-so-flattering image of America, compounded, in this case, by the English-derived terms 'Online' and 'Virtual'.

This image is further stressed, with the word 'supermarket', employed by many users when referring to dating websites.

> Usually loitering around dating websites makes you feel as if you were in a human supermarket, bafflement at the ample choice and the view of people as objects with no feelings. *Female, 29.*

In the late 1950's, year 1958, the emergence of the first supermarket was one of the phenomena that marked the change occurring in the Israeli culture, and in fact the downfall of the solidary agricultural society, as the supermarket was designed to replace the neighborhood grocery shops, which served for meetings and interactions. Originally located at the

---

27 Jennifer Rowley, "Window'shopping and browsing opportunities in cyberspace.' *Journal of Consumer Behaviour* 1.4

28 Ruvik Rosental, Dictionary of Israeli Slang

heart of cities, supermarkets eventually became giant institutes situated just outside them, standing for a galore of products as well as for alienation. It is no wonder then that the word 'supermarket', born as it was in a society fighting for its identity – retained its foreign form and was employed in this context to describe an alienated, 'not from here' kind of place.

In this sense, the forum used by the subjects for sharing their experiences is unlike 'dating websites'. It was referred to at times as a 'community':

> It's a kind of home, a community, something genuine. Warmer, more accepting, more empathic. *Female, 42.*

Or:

> I've been a member of this orchard since 2003... there were forums and communes where I spent years and years... I keep in touch with some of the people there on Facebook as well... This site has been a kind of home for me, ever since I can remember myself online, the orchard is here on the browser every now and then while online. *Female, 29.*

Albeit conduct in this forum, as described here, can be defined as 'devoid of any cultural scent', another instance of Oldenburg's 'great good place', it still showed some traces of the local meaning, in the form of the term 'orchard', frequently employed by users. In the Israeli reality, 'citrus orchard' has come to represent the agricultural period that marked the early Jewish settlement in the Land of Israel, when planting consisted mostly of citrus orchards. Similarly to grocery shops, these too represented interaction and solidarity. Over the last forty years, and coinciding with the emergence of supermarkets that replaced grocery shops, Israelis have witnessed the uprooting of many orchards to make room for urban neighborhoods. These sometimes comprise residential towers, with their typically alienated life style. And thus, this step, by implication, marked the uprooting of the social spirit typical of life at the time.

> While dating websites belonged to another place and the forum to another time, the Facebook social network was the here and now 'place', or as one user put it, 'the least virtual within the virtual world.' *Female, 29.*

The limits of this world, built on friendship confirmations of users, were extensive as far as time and place – they encompassed individuals from the past and present and sometimes included links to former overseas experiences. Yet above all, Facebook constituted a place where users were only meeting people who had already featured in one station or another of their lives; a 'personal picture album' of sorts, a life summary for the time and place they inhabited at present, and as such, for most part – there was no room for strangers there.

The similarity between the three places was sealed by the image of their *users*. When reading their statements, two parameters can be identified: how much human wholeness they possessed and how compatible with reality they proved to be. These bred a tri-prototyped hierarchy of participants that fitted the three places: complete strangers, faceless and nameless friends and everyday acquaintances.

Dating websites users inhabited the bottom of the list. Even after some correspondence, a phone call or even a meeting, they were still perceived as complete strangers and in some cases were seen to have failed both tests. There were also those users who had had some unpleasant experiences and described other users in those sites as 'human trash' or 'mentally-wounded individuals.' Some likened them, figuratively, to robots, in order to describe the personality perversion forced on those partaking in activities on dating websites:

> People should meet each other spontaneously, not mechanically, like the ISCAR factory (Israeli tool-making company). *Male, 34.*

Or:

> You log on to this site or another… the faces are always the same, so are the pick-up lines-and the incredible thing is how they forget they have already written to you and write the same stuff again. *Female, 39.*

Some 'real' robot descriptions were also found – a mechanism activated by the administrators of some websites, dispatching mechanic, fictitious messages from potential candidates. These were designed to deceive users, making them pay subscriptions fees.

> I've come across quite a few sites that boasted of their huge number of users, when in actual fact they numbered significantly less. Think of it in simple terms: the site sends you fictitious messages, you mistake them for real ones and pay up, and they carry on, until at some point you're up to their trick or just fed up. *Male, 29.*

As aforesaid, the robot image, incorporating the lack of tangibility and representation, was often ascribed to individuals as well. It is no wonder then that any interaction with anyone using the dating websites was marred by suspicions.

Forum-using member ranked higher as far as their human wholeness, if not as far as reality was concerned, as presence in said forums was often shrouded in secrets, with users recounting how their families were not aware of their presence there. Nevertheless, users branded their peers as people they could talk to and get helpful advices from, or in some cases even befriend offline, nay, fall in love with and marry.

> Tapuz is a home, it really is, I'm a veteran of forum Blindate and those people there were my rock in many moments, with a lot of consulting, some useless while others more helpful… My first serious boyfriend was from the forum… I started off in the orchard… at 17, and so ten years just went by!!! Wow. *Female, 28.*

In contrast with these two contexts, where it is doubtful whether the actual individual and his/her online image have much in common, it was obvious that users viewed Facebook friends as all-round individuals, both in their online representation and their epistemic meaning.

> Facebook for me is another nice virtual site to see, keep updated and update family and friends... snoop to see what the children are up to, who they are in touch with... to be reminded of friends and family's birthdays, which I would've never remembered otherwise. *Female, 42.*

Facebook therefore ranks higher than the forum. And indeed, in one case, a user found it fit to note that ties with veteran forum members had been tightened by adding them to his Facebook list. Others refused to confirm as Facebook friends, people they had met on dating websites.

> In Facebook there is stuff that's nobody's business, certainly not someone that you don't know at the end of the day. *Female, 39.*

The three 'places' are therefore mutually-distinct, not just in the structural sense, but also through metaphors and metonyms laden with cultural significances. In the symbols broader sense, they constitute a collective imagination map of the world out there. This world holds a place for a set collective nostalgic past, a past not necessarily fulfilled offline (the orchard), as well as for a cruel urban world that is not from here, that is, the 'supermarket', and the personal picture album-where new people are hard to introduce. The users' image completed the general appearance of these places. The dark side of the global cosmos was inhabited by almost non-human residents, while its bright side veered towards the 'us' or 'I', in their various senses.

Interaction Aspects and Process

The five fundamental components in the dynamic and interactional element of the speech event as viewed by Hymes are ends, norms, act sequence and the key and instrumentalities employed in interactions. Perusing users' statements about them elucidates, time and again, the differences between the three digital places presented above. Nevertheless, as users go on to describe the actual conduct, a complexity of sorts emerges.

Unanimous agreement was found among users in regards to the *end* of the dating websites. I.e. finding a serious partner for an offline relationship, yet only partial agreement emerged regarding the *act sequence* required to achieve this end. Some acts were pre-set, practically dictated by the website's structure: defining parameters for search engines, reading the profile text, viewing or requests to view pictures and contacting users. Some had the option of personal decision-the nature of profile texts, timing of correspondence and its nature, opting for a more information-rich channel of communication (chats, telephone, Facebook), the nature of shifting thereto and the logging-off timing.

> Does anything actually come out of dating websites? The answer is definitely yes. It's a matter of how you handle yourself in and off the site. Dating websites are like 'human supermarkets', if you market yourself with attractive pictures, to-the-point, witty and intriguing texts, then you can get to the stage of corresponding with potential dates. From

here on you take it offline, with phone calls, dates and mutual interest generated-it's no longer to do with the site, but rather with what you are in real life. *Male, 34.*

The freedom, though limited, allowed the act to assume a personal key; in choosing a channel for further interaction (some users offered to skip the picture exchange and strive straight for the date) and more often, in the *normative level*. I have found that users of dating websites opted to introduce themselves as 'hard-working'. It is a normative stance adopted with the purpose of overcoming objectification by other people, an objectification implied by the nature of the dating website as a supermarket where you go 'shopping'. Their statements lent new meanings to this notion of 'hard work': going through the necessary steps without looking for shortcuts, giving the text a serious reading, investing in tailoring a unique reply for anyone who contacts you and answering them politely. Some stressed directness and purposeful approach as a moral kind of act, for one's 'self' as well as for others.

> I was registered in a dating website for a relatively short time… First, after a month on the website that led to no more than a single date, I started a year-long relationship. I was very picky along the way. It just saved all of us time and unnecessary dates. I knew exactly what I was looking for and rejected people just like that. *Female, 25.*

'Shallow, rude consumers' served to contrast the 'hard-workers' employed by users to introduce themselves in a 'positive' light; those who indeed were neither interested in having a relationship nor ready for the 'hard work', preferring rather the consumerist shopping. They have no aspirations to excel or even succeed-they do not read deep into the profile. They contact people mechanically and never bother replying; they let connections melt away for no reason and fail to give them a proper closure.

> Yes, I had ten-twenty people a day writing to me, but most of them wouldn't have written to me if they only bothered reading my profile, because then they would've realised there and then it wasn't what I was looking for. *Female, 30.*

The same people absorbed in the 'shopping' experience view others as products. Users recounted how in some cases, following a successful date, they witnessed their companions logging back on to browse the site. Female users complained about users blatantly addressing them, with swearwords hurled in cases of refusal and rejection (one female user explained that this being the case, it was better to ignore inappropriate messages and refrain from replying). One such user recounted in shock how a guy she did not know and had a pleasant online conversation with on a dating website suddenly suggested they carried it in on to bed.

In this vein of 'workers' as opposed to 'consumers', several discussions were held around the legitimacy of the demand to be confirmed as a Facebook friend right at the onset of a relationship:

> (She)… replied: alright, let's confirm friendship on Facebook and take it from there…

I wrote back: listen, let's talk a bit, or even take it to the phone, and then I can approve you. I'm a bit protective of my privacy...

Her answer: no no no, I want to see you

I said: I'm protective of my privacy; if you want to take it further I can send you pictures, no problem, but no friendships.

Over. She never got back to me. I have no picture of myself. *Male, no age mentioned.*

This request had little to do with 'confirming friendship' even in its trifle Facebook sense, and was rather an attempt to obtain a further channel of information, independent of the controlled one offered on the dating website. Nevertheless, it was found to be justified by users who perceived themselves to be the 'hard-working' type, abiding by the dating site norms:

Have a much fuller, more accurate picture of the man... see his friends... the picture. *Female, 27.*

On the other hand, there were those who objected this act, citing the very notions of 'efficient work'; they argued that the digital worlds did not afford purposefulness and that this request was no more than a consumerist act, complete with the joy of purchasing the product, for no particular purpose:

When it gets to the 'add me as Face-Friend', I can tell she's not serious. When it came to girls who asked for that, even when I added them, I moved on, although they looked and sounded high-end. I'm not interested in joining anyone's friends' collection or friends base unless we meet and get to know each other first. *Male, 37.*

Others even perceived the request, aimed at obtaining information behind their backs, as blatant, attesting to a fundamental misreading of the *ends* behind the dating site interactions and the work they entailed:

Sincerity!!! Honesty!!! Reliability!!! These are the key words; these are the cornerstones of romantic partnerships!!! If there's something you want to know about the girl, just ask her!!! Why 'spying' on Facebook... Don't ruin something that's just begun, go it?! *Female, 37.*

The contrasting structural nature of the dating websites on the one hand and the forums on the other was further elucidated in discussions into interactions in these two places. Some users embraced the 'hard work' notion even in regards to forums they surfed, viewing it as potential source of information about the writing subjects, interests or the style, collected vicariously about potential candidates over time. But it wasn't a manifest end and moreover, excessive purposefulness was not well received.

Most users claimed forum discussions were an end in itself, a chance to chat and get to know people; a non-phased act with no definite end, unlike the offline life, described as rife with stages and obstacles.

I witnessed one case when a new member stirred hostility among users, by blatantly declaring he was interested in finding a female or male partner among their ranks. This user was asked to move on to the dating website or follow discussions for several days/weeks, to get a hang on the atmosphere.

> Because I was really late going online, only after the army. I arrived at Tapuz, because everyone was chatting here and it looked interesting. It also suddenly occurs to me that I started writing here following a bad date, went on to have a relationship, then a painful break-up, them on to a long period as a single, followed by a good relationship, and now I'm about to get married. What a piece of life. *Female, 30.*

And thus, the forums, albeit dedicated to dating among singles, could also feature non-singles. The norms entailed anonymity and the use of regular nicknames (with those unwilling to do so posting in their full name); every participant had his/her home zone as well, where they could submit details about themselves. Most provided no details other than age and sex and it was decreed that nobody urged them to. Again, forums also featured married users and a discussion was held on the matter, concluding with the statements that they should not have to expose their identity or be isolated within defined conversation zones, lest the forum became 'just another dating website' and end-oriented.

Studying the 'interactionist' aspects in the two places described here (no such interactions were described on the Facebook social network) reveals clear differences as well. Here too, these differences can be ascribed to the universal dichotomy of 'workplace' versus 'the third place and yet, they may also be viewed in their Jewish-Israeli cultural context. In its Israeli context, the 'hard working' image, designed to compensate for the 'shopping' and 'supermarket' elements, has its two feet firmly set on ideological ground. It tows the protestant ethos and American Capitalism line. Contemporary Israeliness has embraced the American notion of hard work that comes with proper reward, while the media offers a galore of success stories, where senior executives, having worked hard as youngsters, earned their fortune and went on to volunteer, giving back to society. Similarly, the Zionist ideology glorified the modernist idea of hard, productive work; the 'religion of labour' was a key concept in the early decades of the Jewish settlement in the Land of Israel, compounding the negation of the diasporic Jew, who was portrayed as an idler, dealing, as mentioned before, in luftgesheft, 'business of air'. Users who preached 'Dugri Talking'- matter-of-factness were suggestive of the no-beating-around-the-bush language. This kind of language is known and appreciated in the Zionist ethos as a manifestation of the proper degree of sincerity and honesty in interactions with others, for the benefit of all parties.[29]

Interaction in the forums was utterly different, yet could also be seen to echo ideological

---

29   Tamar Katriel,. Milot Mafte'ah: Dfusei Tarbut Vetikshoret Beisrael [Patterns of Culture and Communication in Israel]

cultural aspects. On the one hand, it can be viewed as a manifestation of the mental health discourse penetration to Israel-one instance of the Americanization.[30] But unlike the support groups one arrives at to solve a focused personal problem,[31] hanging around the forum for veteran users was, as I have demonstrated, a way of life. In this sense forums can be seen as a manifestation of the 'heart to heart talks', which is not a mere outcome of Americanization, but rather a steady feature of Jewish people in Israel from as early as the inception of Zionism. It started with the Jewish settlers' custom of holding late night discussions at the end of their work days, talks where they shared all the mental distresses entailed by their breaking away from their parents for a life in the new society. These conversations were marked by sentiment, openness and dialogue.[32] They served as an alternative to the daytime official discussions, with their precise ends and formal key.

Discussion

This study's data decide unequivocally in favor of those who believe Cyberspace to be more than just a 'single place'. The analysis, based on statements of users who were sorted according to Hymes' SPEAKING model parameters, offers a number of differences summarized in the following table:

Facebook	Forum	Dating Websites	
"I"	"Old Israel"	"America"	Place
Friends and acquaintances	Faceless, nameless friends	Unfriendly strangers	Participants
Searching and confirming information	Talks and Discussions - option for a relationship	Meeting potential partners	Ends
A stage in the process of getting to know one another	No clear stage system	Several stages, some dictated by the website, while others by personal choice	Act sequence
A component of the "hard work" of investigating about the potential partner	Anonymity, feelings	"Hard work"	Norms

---

30   Oz Almog. 'Farewell to 'Srulik': Changing Values among the Israeli Elite.'
31   Robert D Putnam. 'Bowling alone: America's declining social capital.'
32   Tamar Katriel. Milot Mafte'ah: Dfusei Tarbut Vetikshoret Beisrael [Patterns of Culture and Communication in Israel]

Facebook	Forum	Dating Websites	
Everyday	Warm, accepting	Purposeful, blatant	Key and instrumentalities
Home, picture album	The great good place "Orchard"	Workplace, Supermarket	Genre (Metaphors and metonyms)

Studying these insights reveals two symbolic systems accompanying and cementing the distinct nature of the places in the eyes of users.

The first one: Has to do with the structural features of the different 'places' and as such, it is cross-cultural. Here I found an analogy between how Israeli online users defined dating websites and forums, and the division offered by Oldenburg, between the 'workplace' and the 'great good place'. The 'market metaphor'[33] proved appropriate for the end definition and worldview of dating websites users as well. The 'efficient' and superficial nature of dating websites, as opposed to forums, can also be found in Andrea Baker's works.

The second one: Bears a cultural nature, elucidating, cementing and compounding the first symbolic system, while the places are also ascribed metaphors and metonyms that are local by nature. Thus, the image of the dating website comprises both work values in their (positive) Israeli and American sense and (negative) cultural associations of consumption (supermarket, shopping).

Despite the fact that America evokes non-positive associations as well, adhering to its partly-positive image allows Jewish Israelis to shake off the horror of the "Jewish matchmaker", an infamous symbol of an infamous world, and view dating websites as a place where one can 'work hard' and successfully find a suitable partner. The urge expressed by users who opted for this path of 'making it on their own' can serve to explain how scientific dating websites (such as the American eHarmony), where professional experts pair subscribers with compatible partners without their active involvement, fail to make it in Israel. Again, atmosphere in forums corresponds well with Oldenburg's great good place notion, but also with the Israeli citrus orchard, a term laden with significances in the local mythology.

Even though the social network (Facebook) proves to be a leisure website, in high demand among many Israeli users, they find it hard, as I have demonstrated, to view it as a site to find a new romantic partner. This can be explained by the emergence of individualistic ideas, which have been surging through Israel over the last forty years, as well as by the nature of the global branding of Facebook, urging as it does to use it in order to 'keep in touch with

---

33 Rebecca D. Heino, Nicole B. Ellison, and Jennifer L. Gibbs. 'Relationshopping: Investigating the market metaphor in online dating.'

the important people in your life', not necessarily with strangers.

This could explain Israel's interest in meeting joints whose features generate intermediate models, particularly the designated Facebook dating groups. These are end-oriented, end-organized groups of people who share an offline relationship fabric, hinted at by titles such as Hot Guys for your Girlfriends, which numbers roughly 15,000 users, or Meet my Friend (male and female) and others. These groups try to enjoy the best of all worlds; the (relatively) end-guided purposefulness of dating websites combined with Facebook's visible faces and the loose nature of the forum, unconstrained by time. It is an emerging phenomenon that received hardly any mention in the forums I reviewed; yet its relative success can attest, among other things, to how uniquely the digital dating issue is received and deciphered in the Israeli context.

Years ago, Murray Melbin[34] discussed the metaphoric link between the conquest of the west and the conquest of the night. In both cases, it meant a slow penetration to territories that had existed for many years alongside cultural civilization and gradually came to resemble it, following this penetration: the prairie and the night have become a multitude of 'places'. In the meantime, the cyberspace also changes from a 'single place' – a separate territory, set apart from anything that is offline-to mutually distinct places, reflecting ideals of people and cultures outside the net.

Thus, while during the Internet's early days it was appropriate to engage mainly with the psychological view of the 'universal individual' who looked for romantic partners online, with the internet viewed as a 'place', nowadays a more local socio-cultural view is required. The present work demonstrated this up-to-date trend of thought.

References

Ahuvia, Aaron C., and Mara B. Adelman. 'Formal Intermediaries in the Marriage Market: A Typology and Review', *Journal of Marriage and the Family* 54. 2 (1992): 452-463.

Almog, Oz. *'Farewell to 'Srulik': Changing Values Among the Israeli Elite*, Haifa: Zmora-Modan, 2004.

Arvidsson, Adam. "Quality Singles": Internet Dating and the Work of Fantasy', *New Media & Society* 8.4 (2006): 671-690.

Azaryahu, Maoz. 'The Golden Arches of McDonald's: On the Americanization of Israel', *Israel Studies* 5.1 (2000): 41-64.

Baker, Andrea. 'Two by Two in Cyberspace: Getting Together and Connecting Online', *CyberPsychology and Behaviour* 3.2. (2000): 237-242.

Baker, Andrea J. *Double Click: Romance and Commitment among Online Couples*, Hampton Press, 2005.

---

34 Murray Melbin. Night as Frontier: Colonizing the World After Dark.

Barraket, Jo, and Henry-Waring, Millsom S. 'Getting it on (line) Sociological Perspectives on E-dating', *Journal of Sociology* 44.2 (2008): 149-165.

Bassett, Elizabeth H., and O'Riordan, Kate. 'Ethics of Internet Research: Contesting the Human Subjects Research Model', *Ethics and Information Technology* 4.3. (2002): 233-247.

Ben-Ze'ev, Aaron. *Love Online: Emotions on the Internet*, Cambridge University Press, 2004.

Burgin, Victor. *In/different Spaces: Place and Memory in Visual Culture*, CA: University of California Press, 1996.

Dreyfus, Hubert L. *On the Internet*, New York: Routledge, 2008.

Eysenbach, Gunther, and Till, James E. 'Ethical Issues in Qualitative Research on Internet Communities.' *Bmj* 323.7321 (2001): 1103-1105.

First, Anat, and Avraham, Eli. *America in Jerusalem: Globalization, National Identity, and Israeli Advertising*, Maryland: Lexington Books, 2009.

Heino, Rebecca D., Nicole B. Ellison, and Jennifer L. Gibbs. 'Relationshopping: Investigating the market metaphor in online dating', *Journal of Social and Personal Relationships* 27.4 (2010): 427-447.

Hymes, Dell. *Foundations in Sociolinguistics: An Ethnographic Approach*, London: Routledge, 2013.

Illouz, Eva, and Finkelman, Shoshannah. 'An Odd and Inseparable Couple: Emotion and Rationality in Partner Selection', *Theory and Society* 38.4 (2009): 401-422.

Iwabuchi, Koichi. *Recentering Globalization: Popular Culture and Japanese Transnationalism*, North Carolina: Duke University Press, 2002.

Katriel, Tamar. *Milot mafte'ah: dfusei tarbut vetikshoret beisrael [Patterns of Culture and Communication in Israel]*. Haifa: University of Haifa Press & Zmora-Bitan 1999.

Melbin, Murray. *Night as Frontier: Colonizing the World After Dark*, New York: Free Press, 1987.

Merkle, Erich R., and Richardson, Rhonda A. 'Digital Dating and Virtual Relating: Conceptualizing Computer Mediated Romantic Relationships', *Family Relations* 49.2 (2000): 187-192.

Parks, Malcolm R., and Kory Floyd. 'Making Friends in Cyberspace', *Journal of Computer-Mediated Communication* 1.4 (1996): 0-0.

Putnam, Robert D. 'Bowling Alone: America's Declining Social Capital.' *Journal of Democracy* 6.1 (1995): 65-78.

Reinecke Leonard and Trepte, Sabine. 'Authenticity and Well-being on Social Network Sites: A Two-wave Longitudinal Study on the Effects of Online Authenticity and the Positivity Bias in SNS Communication', *Computers in Human Behavior* 30 (2014): 95-102.

Romm-Livermore, Celia. *Social Networking Communities and E-dating Services: Concepts and Implications*, New York: Information Science Reference, 2009.

Rosental, Ruvik. *Dictionary of Israeli Slang*, Tel Aviv: Katar, 2005.

Rowley, Jennifer. ''Window'shopping and Browsing Opportunities in Cyberspace', *Journal of Consumer Behaviour* 1.4 (2002): 369-378.

Oldenburg, Ray. *The Great Good Place: Cafés, Coffee Shops, Community Centers, Beauty Parlors, General Stores, Bars, Hangouts, and How They Get You through the Day*, New York: Paragon House, 1989.

Seale, Clive, et al. 'Interviews and Internet Forums: A Comparison of Two Sources of Qualitative Data', *Qualitative Health Research* 20.5. (2010): 595-606.

Walther, Josef B. 'Interpersonal Effects in Computer-mediated Interaction: A Relational Perspective', *Communication Research*, 19 (1992): 52–90.

Zinkhan, George M, 'Romance and the Internet: The E-mergence of E-dating', *Advances in Consumer Research* 31 (2004): 153-58.

STRANGER STRANGER OR LONELY LONELY? YOUNG CHINESE AND DATING APPS BETWEEN THE LOCATIONAL, THE MOBILE AND THE SOCIAL

GABRIELE DE SETA AND GE ZHANG[1]

Introduction: Did You Get Married?

Just around Chinese New Year in early 2014, with most Chinese families gathered around dining tables to celebrate the festivity, local TV stations aired a commercial by a matchmaking company playing on the climax of a grandmother vexing her granddaughter year after year with the nagging half-question, "you got married, right?" (*jie hun le ba*?). Eventually, thanks to the intercession of the sponsored matchmaking company, the granddaughter announces to the old relative lying on a hospital bed, "Granny, I got married!" (*waipo, wo jiehun le*). According to observers of online discussion boards and social networking platforms, the reactions of the younger, marriage-aged audience to this advertising were not the most enthusiastic – "the perception of being held hostage by their families to get married enraged many netizens who viewed this practice as backwards."[2]

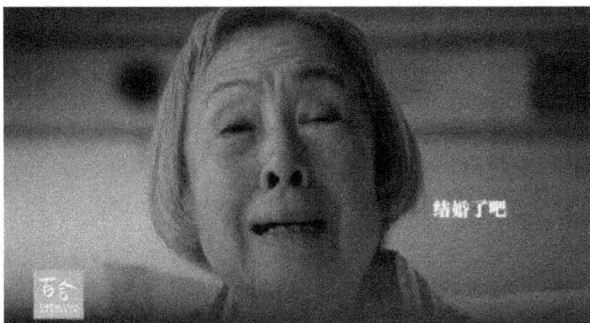

Figure 1 "You got married, right?", screenshot of a Baihe advertisement, 2014.[3]

Around the same time, M.G., a 36 year old single heterosexual male, evidently still troubled about his desire for a stable relationship and a related fraud scheme he was recently victim of, recounts his experience with matchmaking services to one of the authors. His narration, slightly abridged, goes like:

> Zhen Ai[4] is a matchmaking website, and it provides not simply an online service for which you pay to view other people's online profile and contact them [...] but also a matchmaker

---

1   Disclaimer: as a consequence of the double authorship, this chapter is mostly written in the first person plural to help the narrative flow while also reflecting how both authors contributed equally, in terms of content and argumentation, to the essay.

2   Joe, 'Chinese Dating Site TV Ad Promotes Being Forced into Marriage', *ChinaSmack*, http://www.chinasmack.com/2014/videos/chinese-dating-site-tv-ad-promotes-being-forced-into-marriage.html.

3   'Baihewang Guanggao: Yinwei Ai Bu Dengdai', *Youku*, http://v.youku.com/v_show/id_XNjY2NzE2OTA4.html.

4   'Cherished love', translation by the authors.

who is a real person talking directly to you and sending you profiles of selected candidates according to the personal data you provide. I tried their three-month membership plan, priced at 3,000 RMB. According to the plan, the service guaranteed consistent efforts to introduce you to different women during the three months of membership. However, I realized that three months was a short period of time and it was difficult to get to know one woman, let alone many [...] so I told the matchmaker to be more selective. [...] I was introduced to a woman almost immediately, and her appearance immediately captivated me. We started talking on WeChat[5] after the initial exchange through the matchmaker, the conversation went smoothly, and I would call her sometimes at night to talk to her on the phone. But we did not meet during the first month, so our relationship did not develop much. [...] Because I had to leave my hometown for a while and I felt the matchmaker did actually contact me very rarely, I called Zhen Ai and asked them if I could terminate the service and get a refund [...] and eventually I got part of the money back. Anyway, and here is the interesting part, the woman I got introduced to earlier continued to contact me. When our feelings escalated to a degree that I finally asked her to meet, she agreed at first, then suddenly declined claiming that she was currently not living in my hometown. After a few days, she contacted me saying she was at the opening ceremony of her new shop, and asked me if I wanted to congratulate her by sending her a wreath. I agreed, and she told me to call a specific flower shop and transfer the money to their bank account so they could take care of the delivery. I called the number she gave me, and they asked me 1,500 RMB for a wreath. At this point, I had no doubt that the entire thing was a scam. After this episode, I didn't contact her anymore, and she never called me again.

In this chapter, pitched against these two frame-setting snippets about social expectations and pressures around marriage, dating, matchmaking and relationships in general, we would like to present some observations regarding the use of locational social mobile applications in Mainland China. As it is true that China has undergone two decades of accelerated development of its communication infrastructure and IT industries, hosting by now the largest national population of Internet users,[6] it is also the case that the fuzzy concept of "online dating" has diversified into a whole spectrum of services and practices - from traditional matchmaking intermediaries gone online to the flourishing local ecology of social networking platforms, websites and mobile applications, through which Chinese digital media users negotiate their affective needs, desires and social pressures.

These developments often make the news as bits and pieces of 'the latest weird online phenomenon in China'. We argue that there is a rift between the isolated cries of media panics, the claims regarding the revolutionary advent of new online platforms and the actual, everyday life activities of hundreds of millions of Chinese digital media users, who reinvent and deploy these arrangements of software and more or less mobile hardware into the contingencies of their daily existence, with little regard for, and often a cynical angle on, broad

---

5   WeChat (in Chinese *Weixin*), developed by Tencent Holdings Limited, is the instant messaging mobile app most popular in China at the time of writing.

6   CNNIC, *The 32nd Statistical Report on Internet Development in China*, Beijing: China Internet Network Information Center, 2013, p. 7.

sociological interpretations and media crazes. This is especially true in the prurient discursive field of online dating, which often sees commentaries on technology and media practices paired with claims regarding sexual revolutions, degradation of morals or psychological well-being of society at large.

Our intention is to provide a focused, in-depth snapshot of the social practices deployed through a Chinese mobile dating application, presented as embedded in the context of the users' everyday life. This is a small-scale reply to certain grand sweeping statements portraying Asia as one of the main actors of a global communications revolution[7] and Chinese netizen culture as the locus of a generalized sexual rebellion.[8] We start from the assumptions that media in general are "a socially responsive technology"[9] and that their situated deployment in everyday lives is much more revealing than growing percentages and statistics. Our hope is to give evidence, following Stephanie Hemelryk Donald, of how mobile media in particular "allows forms of connection and pathways of communication that are specific and essential to the young",[10] although we would extend this claim beyond generational barriers and show how it is users at large, rather than a specific age group, shape mobile media through the pathways carved by their pragmatic and situated practices.

What we want to illustrate is how users of a popular online dating application shape the pathways of communication of the medium through their courtship practices. The three main sections in which we present our analysis are named after the buzzwords that often describe these apps – *locational, social, mobile* – and seek to question and re-evaluate these terms in light of our findings. These three sections, providing insights into creative usage of locative media, sociality with strangers, and mobile self-presentation, are preceded by a methodological note and a general discussion of our field of inquiry in relationship to our actual site of data collection: contemporary urban China.

Flirting with Methods

The research presented in this chapter belongs to a tradition of ethnographic work on the use of media and technologies, and seeks to suggest a certain kind of situated and participative methodological approach as the most productive way to study courtship practices on digital media. In short, while digital ethnography has been systematized under different names as the bundle of methods useful to collect data about what people do on online platforms,[11] we argue that in the case of mobile media, with its implications of local sociality,

---

7   Jack Linchuan Qiu, 'The Internet in China: Technologies of Freedom in a Statist Society', in Manuel Castells (ed.), *The Network Society: A Cross-cultural Perspective*, Cheltenham: Edward Elgar Publishing Limited, 2004, p. 99.

8   Katrien Jacobs, *People's Pornography: Sex and Surveillance on the Chinese Internet*, Bristol: Intellect, 2012, p. 183.

9   Stephanie Hemelryk Donald, 'Introduction: Why Mobility Matters: Young People and Media Competency in the Asia-Pacific', in Stephanie Hemelryk Donald, Theresa Dirndorfer Anderson and Damien Spry (eds.), *Youth, Society and Mobile Media in Asia*, Abingdon: Routledge, 2010, p. 7.

10 Stephanie Hemelryk Donald, 'Introduction: Why Mobility Matters'.

11 Christine Hine, *The Internet: Understanding Qualitative Research*, New York: Oxford University Press,

networking-in-transit and personal identity, an even higher degree of participation is necessary on part of the researcher: Sheller and Urry define this degree of ethnographic sensitivity to the use of mobile media and social networking in everyday life "mobile ethnography".[12] In addition to the adoption of this sensitivity, given our focus on the affective social practices of courtship and dating, we think it is necessary to integrate a phenomenological component in the process of data collection as a precious addition to participant observation, interviews and other kinds of surveys.

In practice, the authors collected small talk, casual discussions and more or less structured interviews of digital media users online and offline while conducting ethnographic fieldwork in different Chinese cities. This contextual and discursive data is complemented by a more phenomenological, auto-ethnographic component of actual platform experience by the authors, who have used the Momo mobile app for an extended period of time inside Mainland China. Inspired by research such as Jacobs's performative auto-ethnography of AdultFriendFinder users in Hong Kong,[13] the authors got their hands (metaphorically) dirty by actively befriending, chatting and flirting with Momo users, playing on different roles, genders and online personas, and (after the necessary ethical disclosures and clearances[14]) even meeting some of the online contacts in real life for further discussion. To better capture the hues and shades of how research participants shared their everyday life through images, avatars and textual inventions on online platforms, the authors also collected screenshots of other users' personal profiles or image galleries, along the methodological lines of what Choi calls "shared visual ethnography".[15] Some of these visual materials, opportunely anonymized, are presented as supporting evidence throughout the chapter.

Our introduction to the research field has to be completed by a short technical introduction to the mobile application on which we focused our efforts. Momo (陌陌, literally "Stranger Stranger") belongs to the category of social contact mobile applications, a kind of software designed for smartphones and other consumer mobile devices. Features common to this software typology include the linkage between the user account and his/her mobile phone number, an asynchronous multimedia chat capability, friend lists and multiple-user groups, customizable profiles and image galleries. In the case of Momo, these functionalities revolve around a locational search engine through which users can find and befriend each other in function of their actual location, as mapped by the user's mobile device GPS system and network access.

    2013, p. 20.

12   Mimi Sheller & John Urry, 'The New Mobilities Paradigm', *Environment and Planning* A 38.2, 2006, p. 271.

13   Katrien Jacobs, *People's Pornography: Sex and Surveillance on the Chinese Internet*, p. 131.

14   When going beyond occasional online chatting and agreeing to actual meetings with Momo users, we always made a point to disclose our identity as social scientists interested in mobile media usage, and to assure participants regarding the anonymization of the data collected from them.

15   Jaz Hee-jong Choi, 'The City, Self and Connections', in Stephanie Hemelryk Donald, Theresa Dirndorfer Anderson and Damien Spry (eds), *Youth, Society and Mobile Media in Asia*, Abingdon, UK: Routledge, 2010, p. 90.

The choice of Momo as the main focus of our inquiry was mostly based on its popularity in China during the time of fieldwork, both in media coverage[16] and in everyday discussions between our research participants; in fact, the app crossed the milestone of one hundred million registered users[17] right in the middle of our investigation. Creatively hailed as the "one-night stand mystical device"[18] (*yuepao shenqi*), Momo is often described as the best choice to "have fun with girls" (*wan meizi / ba mei*). Yet its use is more often topic for hearsay and speculative stigmatization rather than direct user experiences. While much press presents the application as the "China's sexual revolution"[19] offering Chinese people a "path to the forbidden",[20] the local corporate explanations are more insightful. Tang Yan, the CEO and founder of Beijing Momo Technology Company, describes the app as "a more open platform" for users who have

> a lot of needs that cannot be satisfied by their current social networks [...] Momo provides them with unlimited possibilities and imaginary spaces - for example, the life[styles] that many young users are trying to present in their profiles are not the lives they are living but the lives they dream of[21].

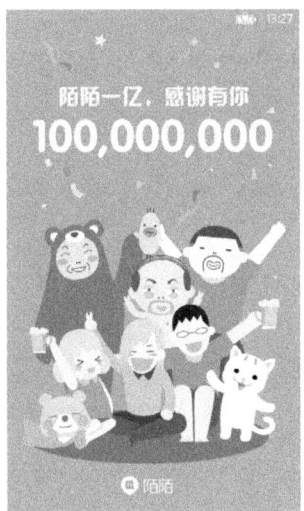

Figure 2. "Momo at one hundred million users, thanks to you for being with us!", smartphone screenshot by the authors, 7 February 2014.

---

16   Katie Nelson, 'Momo App, the "Magical Tool to Get Laid", Reaches 80m Users', *Shanghaiist* (14 November 2013), http://shanghaiist.com/2013/11/14/momo-app-reaches-80-million-users.php

17   See Fig. 2.

18   See Fig. 2.

19   Olivia Rosenman, 'China's Sexual Revolution: "One-Night Stand" App Momo Boasts 80 Million Users', *South China Morning Post* (14 November 2013), http://www.scmp.com/news/china-insider/article/1355124/chinese-instant-messaging-app-momo-boasts-80-million-users

20   Didi Kirsten Tatlow, 'Apps Offer Chinese a Path to the Forbidden', *New York Times* (24 July 2013), http://www.nytimes.com/2013/07/25/world/asia/25iht-letter25.html?_r=1&

21   Tang Yan, 'Momo Yonghu Guo Yi Ruhe Pingjia? Zheme Duo Yonghu Dou Zai Momo Zuo Shenme?', *Zhihu* (February 2014), http://www.zhihu.com/question/22680523

Locating Mobile Sociality: Online Dating and the Chinese City

The story of affective interaction through computer-mediated communication dates back to the early days of the medium, to the little chronicled phenomena of mailing-list flirting, multi-user dungeon (MUD) flings, steamy private chat-room conversations, and discussion board romances.[22] It is only in the late nineties, though, that attention begins to be given to the corporate developments of online affective practices, with commercial platforms designed specifically for the increasing numbers of users looking at the Internet as a new opportunity for desire and romance.[23] As Orr recognizes, online courtship has never been a straightforward issue, its different aspects and individual preferences weaving "a story that was far more complex than I'd imagined. Internet dating [...] had started changing the way in which people socialized in some pretty profound ways".[24] These social shifts involved "multiple dates with different people in a single week" and "searching on your cell phone for someone near the coffee shop you were in", practices that were supposedly "starting to upset traditional notions of courtship".[25]

The efforts to understand why people prefer mediated interaction to actual encounters have been often grounded on the larger theorization of the media in question.[26] It is thus under the looming presence of the concept of cyberspace, portrayed as seductive, seemingly imaginary, egalitarian and risky, that Ben-Ze'ev frames his question, "At any moment, millions of people across the globe are surfing that space, socializing with each other or having romantic affairs. The number is growing by the minute. What is the lure of the Net?"[27] Different approaches have often rested on similar assumptions of a fundamental separation between online and offline lives, and of the defective nature of a mostly asynchronous, anonymous and textual computer-mediated communication. In the case of online affective practices, this has led to inquiries about the relational implications of new media and the ways in which "online relationships substitute for, complement, conflict with, amplify, or innovate new types of relationships".[28]

In reviewing the relevant literature, our impression is that online dating research has yet to catch up, methodologically and theoretically, with leading edge of media studies in general, remaining wedded to early debates "dominated by the image of a Gibsonian cyberspace in which users would lose consciousness of the real world and lose themselves in a universe of

---

22 Jon Pirone, Don Mayo, and Kathy Berkemeyer, *Internet in an Hour: Romance & Relationships*, New York: DDC Publishing, 1999.
23 Andrea Orr, Meeting, Mating, and Cheating: Sex, Love, and the New World of Online Dating, Upper Saddle River: Reuters, 2004, p. xiii; in Jean-Claude Kaufmann, *Love Online*, trans. David Macey, Cambridge: Polity Press, 2012, p. 4.
24 Andrea Orr, *Meeting, Mating, and Cheating: Sex, Love, and the New World of Online Dating*, p. x.
25 Andrea Orr, *Meeting, Mating, and Cheating*, p. xi.
26 Aaron Ben-Ze'ev, *Love Online: Emotions on the Internet*, Cambridge: Cambridge University Press, 2004, p. xi.
27 Aaron Ben-Ze'ev, 'Love Online'.
28 Monica Whitty and Adrian Carr, *Cyberspace Romance: The Psychology of Online Relationships*, Houndmills: Palgrave MacMillan, 2006, p. xii.

abstract forms and disembodied perspectives".[29] It is not surprising, for this kind of research, to espouse portrayals of online dating as inherently positive (revolutionary or liberating) or negative (addictive or vilifying). In opposition to this, by ditching rigid separations between the online and the offline, and by rejecting conceptions of technologically-mediated communication as defective or lacking in significant ways, we postulate the embedding of digital media into everyday life as a move towards "the contemporary debate [which] has shifted onto the terrain of globalizations".[30] Ten years after Terranova's invigorating portrayal of media studies,[31] we would take one step forward and shift our inquiry towards the terrain of *localizations*.

This shift is in keeping with a general "mobility turn" in the social sciences,[32] precious in a historical moment in which "the notion of the city has become wedded to concepts like mobility, networks and mediated interaction," and useful to "capture some of the new complexity characterising contemporary urban everyday life".[33] Our theoretical assumption follows the idea that "the presence of GPSs (global positioning systems), mediated surfaces, RFID (radio frequency identification) and other technologies that all relate to contemporary mobility practices adds a new dimension to the notion of movement and constitutes new arenas and tools for identity-construction and social interaction (as well, of course, for commercial exploitation and state control)".[34] Although we will not focus on the implications of commerce and control, our interpretation of the "mobility turn" links mobile technologies to identity-construction, social interaction and locational practices. Moreover, as Jensen specifies, denouncing accusations of isolationism and asociality, "a fair amount of these technologies not only work as pass-time devices or artifacts that we may 'hide' behind, but they are networked and linked into the many other layers of communication and interaction that make up the contemporary network city".[35]

Aiming at treating the uses of a mobile social contact application as a node in contemporary layered urban networks, embedded in the everyday lives of its users, and enabling individual affective practices, we cultivate "a beginning awareness of the importance of the location, the placement and the situated technologies"[36] and we follow the steps of similar endeavours in the field. For example, in her study of the use of mobile phones use by young rural-to-urban migrant women in China, Wallis shows how the device, integrated into socio-technical practices and norms, provides "immobile mobility", which she defines as "socio-techno means of surpassing spatial, temporal, physical and structural boundaries [...] situated in the every-

---

29   Tiziana Terranova, *Network Culture: Politics for the Information Age*, London: Pluto Press, 2004, p. 42.
30   Tiziana Terranova, *Network Culture*.
31   Tiziana Terranova, *Network Culture*.
32   John Urry, *Mobilities*, Cambridge: Polity Press, 2000.
33   Ole B. Jensen, 'Erving Goffman and Everyday Life Mobility', in Michael Hviid Jacobsen (ed.), *The Contemporary Goffman*, New York: Routledge, 2010, p. 334.
34   Ole B. Jensen, 'Erving Goffman and Everyday Life Mobility', p. 345.
35   Ole B. Jensen, 'Erving Goffman and Everyday Life Mobility', p. 347.
36   Ole B. Jensen, 'Erving Goffman and Everyday Life Mobility', p. 345.

day experience",[37] while also functioning a stabile access point to one's own (existing and potential) social connections. Similarly, Choi propounds the idea of a city understood as a "urban network" criss-crossed by individuals making use of ubiquitous technologies, in which it becomes crucial to study "not only the macro-level design of the city as a network [...] but also its micro-level construction at the intersection of people, place and technology".[38]

Predictably, the theoretical arguments proposed in this section appear familiar to Wang Li, chief operating officer of Momo Technology, illustrates the social context of the success of his app with admirable corporate brevity. He says,

> Over these past two years particularly, social changes have been so incredibly fast as people move to cities and towns [...] Chinese people are fairly introverted [and in a new environment] they tend not to make friends with their neighbours. [Moreover,] Chinese people didn't have choices before and people are getting to middle age and realizing they don't actually get on with their spouse, because they got married for reasons other than love.[39]

The Mobile: Self-presentation on Portable Façades

Since their inception on the Chinese market, online dating platforms had to deal with local social mores and strategies of mediated self-presentation. Ten years ago, Sina's vice-president Jack Hong reportedly explained the difficulties faced by his company's dating service in terms of ethnic and cultural factors: "Ethnic Chinese in general have a tendency to be more passive in terms of selling themselves [...] the result is page after page of single people who are hard to distinguish from one another. They have answered all the questions about their basic characteristics, but offered no additional information. Although some people do, the majority of Chinese on Sina's Club Love provide no photos".[40] With the popularization of mobile communication devices such as smartphones and tablets, often offering personal imaging capabilities, online social platforms have become the stage for a variety of visual self-presentation strategies that easily disproves hypotheses of culturally rooted preferences for passivity and anonymity.

To give some examples of how mobile social apps like Momo as used as a portable façade for platform-specific strategies of self-presentation, we will focus on male-female interaction, and in particular on the role of the face and the body in this process. This choice is part of our general orientation towards the continuity between online and offline lives. "Rather than focusing on a 'body less' self online, new theories must focus on how the body is presented in cyberspace - even if it's not one's 'actual' body".[41] How do Momo users present their

---

37 Cara Wallis, 'The Technological Meets the Traditional: Mobile Navigations of Desire and Intimacy', in Stephanie Hemelryk Donald, Theresa Dirndorfer Anderson and Damien Spry (eds.), *Youth, Society and Mobile Media in Asia*, Abingdon: Routledge, 2010,p. 58.

38 Jaz Hee-jong Choi, 'The City, Self and Connections', p. 90.

39 Quoted from Didi Kirsten Tatlow, 'Apps offer Chinese a path to the forbidden', *New York Times* (24 July 2013), http://www.nytimes.com/2013/07/25/world/asia/25iht-letter25.html?_r=1&

40 Andrea Orr. *Meeting, Mating, and Cheating: Sex, Love, and the New World of Online Dating*, p. 100.

41 Monica Whitty & Adrian Carr, *Cyberspace Romance: The Psychology of Online Relationships*, p. 30.

bodies to other users, and how do they interpret other users' façades? Z.B., one female Momo early user, explained how in her opinion the first principle of interacting with strangers on Momo was "image management". Other female informants, interrogated regarding the principal criteria for selecting among unknown guys' contact requests, emphasized the term *kan lian* ('to look at the face'). Z.B. recounted of receiving ten to fifty friend requests from (presumably nearby) strangers on Momo, and ignoring most of them after a quick glance at their personal pictures.

To better understand this process of selection operating at the first stages of interaction, it is necessary to go back to the workings of Momo's messaging interface. The sender of a message can check its successful delivery it through a colour indicator (yellow if not yet opened, green if opened and thus supposedly read). In our experiences of sending large numbers of friend requests to people in the vicinity, most of our introductory messages remained forever 'unread': we later understood that this was due to the "unappealing" nature of our profiles. As a matter of fact, as Z.B. explained, our messages were received, but the counterpart decided to ignore them without opening them, just by a look at our personal image. "I just have to slide down the notification bar, like this," she shows, "and give a look at the resized profile picture and the preview of the message. Most of the times, I just decide based on this". By lacking this situated knowledge and choosing a profile picture that did not show our face, we doomed our early attempts of initiating conversations on the platform. Moreover, by being judged only according to the message preview, we were completely unaware of the successful transmission of our requests - a strategy that, in fact, functions as a perfect defence against spam and insistent users. Being chosen among scores of other contacts does really depend on one's face as it is encoded in a small 50x50 pixel square, in a radicalization of classical understandings of infatuation and flirting, according to which "face is the principal determinant in the perception of our individual beauty or ugliness".[42] On Momo, 'face' (as a clear, well-framed profile picture or *touxiang* (literally 'head-image') is the first and most important factor determining further interaction.

Besides this initial selection process, how does this *touxiang* work as a façade? Having one is the basic requirement to hope to even get a single, dismissive reply, but the deployment of profile pictures reveals more subtle strategies of self-presentation that are also inextricably linked to geographical contexts. In fact, most of the informants met on Momo were not permanent urban residents but the sort of liminal population floating between urban outskirts and rural areas surrounding the city - a population that, according to Momo's CEO, makes up the largest part of the application user base.[43] Many of the young female users we chatted with recalled features of the country girls moving to the city described by Bourdieu in *The Bachelor's Ball*: "more open to urban ideals, and rendered particularly attentive and sensitive by all their cultural training to gestures and attitudes, clothing and a person's whole demea-

---

42 Anthony Synnott, "Truth and Goodness, Mirrors and Masks: A Sociology of Beauty and the Face", in Ray B. Browne & Pat Browne (eds.), *Digging into Popular Culture: Theories and Methodologies in Archeology, Anthropology, and Other Fields*, Bowling Green: Popular Press, 1991, p. 119.

43 Tang Yan, 'Momo Yonghu Guo Yi Ruhe Pingjia? Zheme Duo Yonghu Dou Zai Momo Zuo Shenme?', *Zhihu* (9 February 2014), http://www.zhihu.com/question/22680523.

nor, readier to deduce deep personality from external appearance".[44]

This impression was reinforced by the personal profiles of our contacts, on which we observed many different examples of bodily techniques including gestures and facial expressions belonging to the tropes of urban fashionable women as portrayed in the media and advertising: pale faces, long and silky hair, red and pouted lips, long lashes, cute poses (Figure 3). These features were often paired to specific objects tied to distinction and taste: handbags, fashionable accessories, trendy food and drinks, items of clothing. Indeed, this does not imply uniformity of banality, as alternative images of femininity were portrayed as well by a segment of our informants: short hair, minimal make-up, rebellious gestures and tomboyish looks tallying to the stereotypes of 'progressive urban woman' or 'boyish girl' (nühanzi). On the whole, and quite expectedly, Momo personal profiles were used as the "imaginary spaces"[45] described by Tang Yan, the company's CEO, on which users inscribed visual experimentations enacting their dream lives rather than just present themselves in the fashion of matchmaking services. When a postage stamp-sized picture functions at the same time as the determinant factor for new interactions and as a site for complicated semiotic strategies, it is not surprising that, following Goffman's classic theatrical framework "facial expressions [...] are generally carefully monitored (and engineered) to preserve the desired mask".[46]

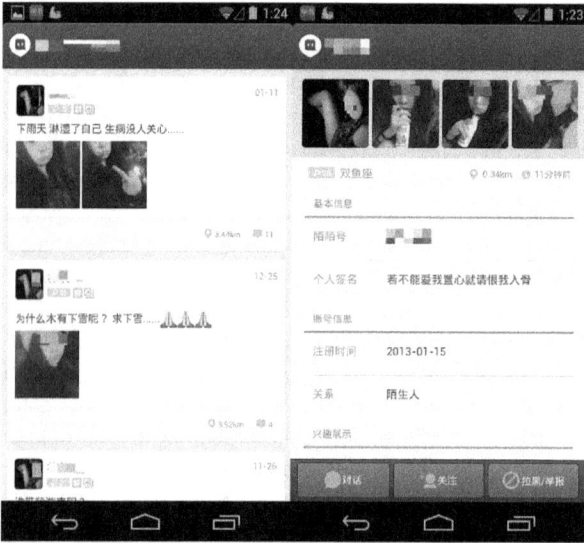

Figure 3: Frowns, bare legs, branded drinks and fashion items linked to situated events. "Why it doesn't snow? Please snow... *praying hands*'" (3.92km away) / "Rainy day, I drenched myself, if I

---

44   Pierre Bourdieu, *The Bachelor's Ball*, Cambridge: Polity Press, 2008, p. 86.
45   Tang Yan, 'Momo Yonghu Guo Yi Ruhe Pingjia? Zheme Duo Yonghu Dou Zai Momo Zuo Shenme?', *Zhihu*, http://www.zhihu.com/question/22680523.
46   Erving Goffman, *The Presentation of Self in Everyday Life*, Carden City: Doubleday Anchor Books, 1959, p. 146.

get sick no one will look after me..." (3.44km away).

Part of these semiotic efforts of constructing a public and social face rely on what Bourdieu calls a "language of urban sentimentality"[47] which juxtaposes selfies with situated comments and referents: the place where one is eating, one's commuting status and the vexations of traffic and weather, all precisely localized by GPS-measured distances. This urban sentimentality, which seems much more related to a nexus of mobility and networked sociality than active flirtation or purposeful romantic searches, does also rely on textual means. Usernames, short biographies and regular status updates become another crucial site of distinction between active members and occasional users. In this context, the practice of posting sentimental quotes from romance novels, rhetorical questions, complaints about boredom or loneliness, in combination with a doctored self-shot of a frowning face or sensual hints of body parts, described scornfully by several informants as *qiu guan'ai* (literally 'begging for love'), appears more as a strategy of attention-management aimed at maintaining a façade of presence and activity for existing and potential contacts.

In conclusion, mobility enables users of social platforms like Momo to construct their own portable façade to be carried around everyday movements and commutes, becoming temporarily visible to other users intersecting paths, as "the many transit spaces of our global network society facilitate meetings of all sorts [...] they are sites of mobile face-to-face interaction".[48] This "mobile face-to-face interaction", as mediated by Momo and similar software, is very different from uploading one's own personal pictures on Internet websites always visible to just about anyone. This difference might explain the success and popularity of this sort of mobile applications offering the lure of an "immobile mobility",[49] a façade that functions as a site-specific point of access for location-based, random encounters. Yet this popularity, especially when paired with gender roles and mores, ends up generating overloads of contact requests and competition for attention. It is for this reason that strategies of self-presentation move away from the obvious goals of romantic searches or flirtatious advances and acquire a platform-specific code: optimizing one's profile picture for attracting replies, managing one's picture gallery to represent lifestyles and dreams, proving one's reliability and involvement in the app through constant updates. As Figure 4 illustrates, the competition in this attention economy stimulates the users to exploit the very structure of the platform to prove their wit, creativity or familiarity with the app.

---

47 Pierre Bourdieu, *The Bachelor's Ball*, p. 88.
48 Ole B. Jensen, 'Erving Goffman and Everyday Life Mobility', p. 336.
49 Cara Wallis, 'The Technological Meets the Traditional: Mobile Navigations of Desire and Intimacy', p. 58.

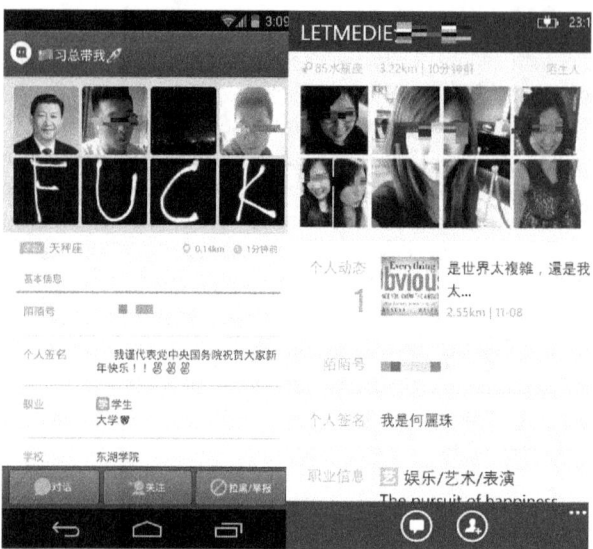

Figure 4: Exploiting the platform. Mixed-media nicknames ('President Xi lead me' with Chinese flag and rocket), and multi-panel pictures split to fit into Momo's predetermined 8-picture profile gallery.

The Social: 'Stranger Stranger' or 'Lonely Lonely'?

We have hinted at how mobility reshapes social networking platforms and the competing self-presentation strategies of their users. Yet, after conversations initiate, what are they actually about? Is most of the sociality between Momo users just about sexual fantasies, one-night stands or romance, as it would seem to be implied by reports on the "mystical tool to get laid" (*yuepao shenqi*)? From our interactions with various informants on Momo, sexually charged conversations appeared to be mostly disdained or deemed uninteresting, likely as another result of gender roles and imbalances, and female users established an array of codes and warnings to discourage straightforward approaches and rude proposals. Besides ignoring contact requests, informants would define these kind of vulgar conversations as boring or *wuliao* (literally 'nothing to talk about'), emphasizing how, more than disturbed by them, they didn't find anything interesting in them, preferring to interact with users who provided smart dialogues, humour and (even flirtatious) wit.

Having shown that, despite the mythology surrounding it, Momo is hardly a 'dating app', we would rather define it as a pastime flirting platform. Ben Ze'ev defines flirting as "a subtle, sexual communication [...] a kind of enjoyable play having the pleasant atmosphere that is typical of the promise of sexual activity" that yet is "not necessarily a prelude to sexual interaction".[50] Despite classical understandings of the term, which define flirting as "in the main, non-verbal behaviour"[51] we would follow Ben Ze'ev and point out how "the crucial element of both flirting and cyberspace" is, in fact, a kind of non-purposive conversation similar

---

50   Aaron Ben-Ze'ev, *Love Online: Emotions on the Internet*, pp. 150-151.
51   Monica Whitty and Adrian Carr, *Cyberspace Romance: The Psychology of Online Relationships*, p.38.

in atmosphere to relaxed gossiping, an "idle, relaxing, and enjoyable talk" which "involves being playful and attaching little importance to the given subject".[52] Informants confirmed this broad understanding. "I once had the congenial company of a girl. For half a month, we chatted every day until 3 a.m. We talked about all kinds of funny things until we were both exhausted and fell asleep laughing", recounts a male user, noting how he never actually met his online night-chat partner. Another male informer analyses his motivation to use Momo quite thoroughly: "On every boring holiday, every sleepless night, I always expect to have someone from the opposite sex feel the same around me. I just want to talk about some bullshit, not for love, not for *yuepao* (getting laid); I just want unadulterated chatting without constraints, under a slightly *aimei* (erotic and ambiguous) atmosphere".

In one of the earliest anthropological analyses of Chinese university students' courtship practices, Moore identifies a peculiar lack of infatuation, and finds superficial flirtatious behaviour not to be "institutionalized in student discourse".[53] It was regarded as a waste of time or just plainly inappropriate. In contrast, we found the recurrence of the terms *aimei* and *wan aimei* ('playing / enjoying ambiguity') among Momo users describing their conversations on the platform to indicate precisely a desire for establishing and maintaining superficial, flirtatious interactions that often remain in the realm of the digital. Moreover, the persistence and recurrence of these conversations ("everyday", "on every boring day", etc.) and the avoidance of *wuliao* interactions (the ones in which there is literally nothing to talk about, because they are just about sex) hints at the fact that the sociality sought by Momo users is an ambiguous one, in constant tension between the possibility of physical contact, as quantified by the distance between the users constantly shown in the conversation, and the pleasure of whiling days and nights away without the pressures of a more demanding relationship. Given the way in which the app seems to be used not so much to find blind dates but mainly to pass time and fight the boring spells of everyday life and transit, Momo might literally mean 'Lonely Lonely' rather than 'Stranger Stranger', as one user comment quips ironically, with a Chinese play on words.[54]

---

52 Aaron Ben-Ze'ev, *Love Online: Emotions on the Internet*, p. 145.
53 Robert L. Moore, 'Love and Limerence with Chinese Characteristics: Student Romance in the PRC', in Victor C. Munck (ed.), *Romantic Love and Sexual Behavior: Perspectives from the Social Sciences*, Westport: Praeger, 1998, p. 262.
54 The play on words relies on the homophony between the two Chinese characters *mo* (陌, 'stranger, unacquainted with') and *mo* (寞 'lonely').

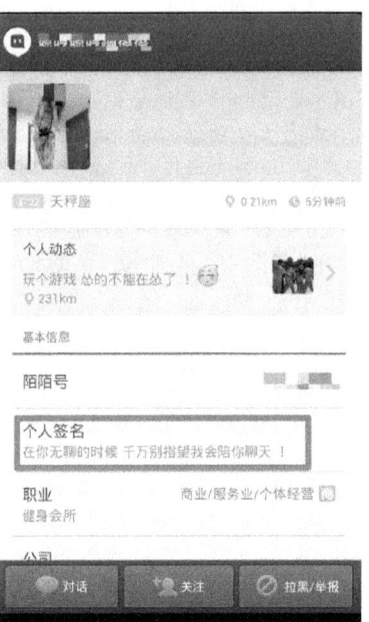

Figure 5: Conversation versus boredom. "Personal signature: When you are bored (*wuliao*) do not hope I will keep you company chatting with you!"

The Locational: Less Than Dating, More Than Doing Nothing

During our fieldwork, one of the authors lived in an old residential area near a night market. He one day got in touch with N.M., a young girl found through browsing local profiles. After ongoing conversations, the girl invited him to join a Momo group with approximately thirty other members, mostly shop-owners, hawkers, and sales personnel working in the vicinity. The group description read: "Absolutely NO *yuepao* [getting laid] (if you want to, please send each other private messages). This group chat is only for everyday pastime chatter". After a while, the author was able to scroll through several pages of the group's chat logs, observing how the recurring topics of conversation were local issues such as: the weather, nearby food joints, and general gossip, often discussed in a carefree and direct way, also by virtue of the fact that group members did not know each other in real life. As N.M. explained, she joined the group because "it is simply too *qileng* ('lonely and cold') to spend the evening sitting there [in the night market], staring at people coming and going". What the members of this group shared is the necessary stasis on their workplace, a cramped, yet not prosperous night market, and the boredom resulting from nights spent sitting among passers-by walking through their stalls in a bitterly cold winter.

In fact, just as illustrated in the previous examples, the mobility of devices makes this kind of sociality possible mostly in conjunction with the locational capabilities of the GPS technology and Internet connectivity. As Hemment explains, "the emergence of locative media signals a convergence of geographical and data space that comes about as soon as computing becomes mobile or ambient, reversing the trend toward the view of digital content as placeless, only encountered in the amorphous and other space of the Internet"[55]. These thirty night market hawkers, bounded by a geographical necessity, work-time and long spells of inactivity, found a way of passing time by using the locational capabilities of Momo to set up a local group and just keep each other's company. Here Wallis' formulation of "immobile mobility"[56] resonates with Goffman's concept of "mobile with":[57] a mobile device connected to the Internet running a locational social platform helps users in escaping their forced immobility into a layer of togetherness that is way more *local*-space than *cyber*-space.

Goffman's further elaboration on the concept of "mobile with" fits with features of the night market Momo group: its components are characterized by a "civil inattention to non-members" (N.M. happened to ignore actual customers while replying to group messages); they maintain a "proximity to members" (sharing both location and activities); they develop "ritual practices for joining and departing" (the Momo group has basic rules of conduct).[58] Yet, quite tellingly, Goffman's original definition of a "mobile with" – that is, "a party whose members are perceived to be 'together'"[59] – does not apply to groups like the one in question. In fact, it is precisely the mediated nature of the night market vendors' sociality that hides their togetherness behind apparently self-concerned interactions with digital devices. When the author eventually took a walk through the night market, the ubiquity of smartphones and tablets in the hands of intent shopkeepers and street vendors suddenly hinted at a kind of sociality very different from the recurring images of the "lonely crowds" of isolated users and alienating technologies portrayed in popular and academic narratives.

In this last example, the locational capability of mobile devices is repurposed a way of passing time with fellow vendors, establish a place of encounter and a loose sense of solidarity in a sometimes boring and unpleasant work environment that requires immobility and constant presence. An implication of this situatedness of networked interactions is a paradigm shift from placeless imaginations of a cyberspace populated by interactions dislocated in place and time to actual digital media practices embedded in everyday lives and proximal sociality. Yet, this does not imply a 'coming back home' from Rheingold's virtual community[60] to the local community of the district or neighborhood. As in the case of flirting, the locational sociality enabled by Momo remains suspended in the ambiguity between a network of emphatic friends sharing hours of chill and boredom in a range of a few hundred meters, and the rarely crossed line between leisurely chatting and getting to meet each other in person. When a group member suggested doing a meet-up in a nearby KTV, only two people showed up, and the organizer himself backed off in hesitation. When, after more than one month of acquaintance, NM agreed to meet the author to get some books he promised to give before

---

55 Drew Hemment, 'Locative Arts', *Leonardo* 39(4), 2006, p. 349.
56 Cara Wallis, 'The Technological Meets the Traditional: Mobile Navigations of Desire and Intimacy'. p. 58.
57 Erving Goffman, *Relations in Public: Micro Studies of the Public Order*, New York: Harper & Row, 1972, p. 19.
58 Jenson Ole B. Jensen, 'Erving Goffman and everyday life mobility', p. 338.
59 Erving Goffman, *Relations in Public: Micro Studies of the Public Order*, p. 19.
60 Howard Rheingold, *The Virtual Community: Homesteading on the Electronic Frontier*, Cambridge: MIT Press, 2000.

her leaving. She was waiting there with her boyfriend, up only for a few minutes of dismissive chit-chat before getting back to work.

Conclusion: If You Are (Not) the One

This book is designed for you... if you're ready to explore the World Wide Web of romance! You'll learn how to get online, and get the search results you want quickly. Whether you're single or already involved, you'll find answers to all your questions about how you can make romance happen every day.[61]

So reads the introduction to *Internet in One Hour: Romance and Relationships*, one of the many guidebooks to the World Wide Web aimed at the growing masses of users approaching the burgeoning consumer Internet of AOL, 14.4kbps connections and Netscape browsing. Twenty years later, in the age of 4G, social networking and locational apps, one has to ask if romance is actually all that users want to happen in their digitally mediated everyday lives. Is Momo really the ultimate *yuepao shenqi*, the 'one-night stand mythical device' portrayed by media narratives, welcomed by sexual revolutionaries and feared by moral panic hustlers, if most of its users do actually use it in different ways?

We answered this question by drawing on a digital, mobile and visually shared ethnography of the actual arrangements of software and more or less portable hardware embedded in the everyday lives of Momo users in China. Following the mobility turn in social sciences, and locating the use of ubiquitous technologies as mobile immobilities and personal façades across layered urban networks, we had several discoveries: that apparently trivial and narcissistic practices of self-presentation play a pivotal semiotic role in the platform environment; that the kind of sociality privileged on Momo is actually more about interesting conversations than speed-dating and sexual encounters; that its locational capabilities are exploited for local solidarities deeply linked to layers of urbanism, work and co-presence.

Given the size of our sample (a few scores of informants), our findings are by no means generalizable to a hundred million users. Yet, we deploy them in order to argue against reductive conceptualizations of 'online dating', 'Internet culture' and similar concepts that rest on dated assumptions of a separation between online and offline lives. In the post-digital, pervasively mediated world of ubiquitous computing, we prefer focusing on the situated practices, platform sociality and vernacular content appearing at the point of encounter between users and technologies.

This theoretical stance is a powerful antidote towards determinist explanations of media use and adoption: if Chinese users went from a cautious preference for passivity and anonymity to an apparently dazzling exhibitionism, this has more to do with the small-scale, everyday media sociality than with ethnicity, culture or communication technology in itself. Similarly, one hundred million users of a pruriently discussed app do not necessarily imply the drastic social changes described by media and academics: "desiring China",[62] "China's hormone

---

61 Jon Pirone, Don Mayo, & Kathy Berkemeyer, *Internet in an Hour: Romance & Relationships*, p. ii.

62 Lisa Rofel, *Desiring China: Experiments in Neoliberalism, Sexuality, and Public Culture*, Durham: Duke

revolution",[63] "people's pornography",[64] "China's sexual revolution"[65] and other slogans have to be carefully verified at the level of localization, since

> major studies of changes in sexual practices [...] lead to much more moderate conclusions. Behaviours are certainly becoming more varied and diversified, and that reveals a growing interest in sexuality, but they are changing relatively slow and have little to do with the explosion of sexualized material in the media.[66]

In other words, actual user practices say more about local contexts than larger theorizations about Chinese society say about the popularity of Momo. As a matter of fact, when embedded in the ensemble of social expectations, peer pressure and family narratives around affects and relationships, the snapshots presented in this chapter outline a larger and more coherent picture. In contemporary China, where the popularity of TV matchmaking reality shows such as *If You Are the One* (*Fei Cheng Wu Rao*) directly reflect most parents' involvement in their offspring's marriage arrangements, their disapproval of dating during school years, and the common resort to matchmaking services. In this context, 'flirting apps' such as Momo provide a much needed safe haven for relational experimentation.

To conclude, without agreeing with her portrayal of social life shifting to "post-familial families" in which people are "alone together, each in their own rooms, each on a networked computer or mobile device [...] spending more time with technology and less with each other",[67] we believe that it is Sherry Turkle who provides one of the best summaries of the kind of pragmatic use of technology we found and described among Momo users in China: "people doing what they have always done: trying to understand themselves and improve their lives by using the materials they have at hand".[68] Momo is mostly not about dating, but also not just about grooming a useless virtual persona or 'doing nothing' in front of a screen. Rather, it enables a kind of *aimei* flirting along the tensions of place, sex and identity with others who are quite not 'the ones' – ephemeral and proximal partners much more interesting than the *wuliao* world of social pressures, prescribed roles, and mediated images.

References
'Baihewang guanggao: Yinwei ai bu dengdai', *Youku*, http://v.youku.com/v_show/id_XNjY2NzE2OTA4.html.

Ben-Ze'ev, Aaron. *Love Online: Emotions on the Internet*, Cambridge: Cambridge University Press, 2004.

University Press, 2007.
63 Evgeny Morozov, *The Net Delusion: The Dark Side of Internet Freedom*, New York: Public Affairs, 2011, p. 70.
64 Katrien Jacobs, *People's Pornography: Sex and Surveillance on the Chinese Internet*, p. 183.
65 Richard Burger, *Behind the red door: Sex in China*, Hong Kong: Earnshaw Books, 2012, p. 4.
66 Jean-Claude Kaufmann, *Love Online*, trans. David Macey, Cambridge: Polity Press, 2012, p. 94.
67 Sherry Turkle. *Alone Together: Why We Expect More from Technology and Less from Each Other*, New York: Basic Books, 2012, pp.280-281.
68 Sherry Turkle. *Alone Together*, p.231.

Bourdieu, Pierre. *The Bachelor's Ball*, Cambridge: Polity Press, 2008.

Burger, Richard. *Behind the Red Door: Sex in China*, Hong Kong: Earnshaw Books, 2012.

Choi, Jaz Hee-jong. 'The City, Self and Connections', in Stephanie Hemelryk Donald, Theresa Dirndorfer Anderson and Damien Spry (eds.), *Youth, Society and Mobile Media in Asia*, Abingdon: Routledge, 2010, p. 88-107.

CNNIC. *The 32nd Statistical Report on Internet Development in China*, Beijing: China Internet Network Information Center, 2013.

Donald, Stephanie Hemelryk. 'Introduction: Why Mobility Matters: Young People and Media Competency in the Asia-Pacific', in Stephanie Hemelryk Donald, Theresa Dirndorfer Anderson and Damien Spry (eds.), *Youth, Society and Mobile Media in Asia*, Abingdon: Routledge, 2010, pp. 3-12.

Goffman, Erving. *The Presentation of Self in Everyday Life*, Carden City: Doubleday Anchor Books, 1959.

_____. *Relations in Public: Micro Studies of the Public Order*, New York: Harper & Row, 1972.

Hemment, Drew. 'Locative Arts', *Leonardo* 39(4), 2006, 349-355.

Hine, Christine. *The Internet: Understanding Qualitative Research*, New York: Oxford University Press, 2013.

Jacobs, Katrien. *People's Pornography: Sex and Surveillance on the Chinese Internet*, Bristol: Intellect, 2012.

Jensen, Ole B. 'Erving Goffman and Everyday Life Mobility', in Michael Hviid Jacobsen (ed.), *The Contemporary Goffman*, New York, NY: Routledge, 2010, p.333-351.

Joe. 'Chinese Dating Site TV Ad Promotes Being Forced into Marriage', *China Smack* (9 February 2014), http://www.chinasmack.com/2014/videos/chinese-dating-site-tv-ad-promotes-being-forced-into-marriage.html.

Katie Nelson. 'Momo App, the "Magical Tool to Get Laid", Reaches 80m Users', *Shanghaiist* (14 November 2013), http://shanghaiist.com/2013/11/14/momo-app-reaches-80-million-users.php.

Kaufmann, Jean-Claude. *Love Online*, trans. David Macey, Cambridge: Polity Press, 2012.

Moore, Robert L. 'Love and Limerence with Chinese Characteristics: Student Romance in the PRC', in Victor C. Munck (ed.), *Romantic Love and Sexual Behavior: Perspectives from the Social Sciences*, Westport: Praeger, 1998, p. 251-284.

Morozov, Evgeny. *The Net Delusion: The Dark Side of Internet Freedom*, New York: Public Affairs, 2011.

Orr, Andrea. *Meeting, Mating, and Cheating: Sex, Love, and the New World of Online Dating*, Upper Saddle River: Reuters, 2004.

Pirone, Jon, Mayo, Don, & Berkemeyer, Kathy. *Internet in an Hour: Romance & Relationships*, New York: DDC Publishing, 1999.

Qiu, Jack Linchuan. 'The Internet in China: Technologies of Freedom in a Statist Society', in Manuel Castells (ed.), *The Network Society: A Cross-Cultural Perspective*, Cheltenham: Edward Elgar Publishing Limited, 2004, p. 99-124.

Rheingold, Howard. *The Virtual Community: Homesteading on the Electronic Frontier*, Cambridge: MIT Press, 2000.

Rofel, Lisa. *Desiring China: Experiments in Neoliberalism, Sexuality, and Public Culture*, Durham: Duke University Press, 2007.

Rosenman, Olivia. 'China's Sexual Revolution: "One-night Stand" app Momo Boasts 80 Million Users', *South China Morning Post* (13 November 2013), http://www.scmp.com/news/china-insider/article/1355124/chinese-instant-messaging-app-momo-boasts-80-million-users.

Sheller, Mimi, & John Urry. 2006, "The New Mobilities Paradigm", *Environment and Planning* A 38(2), 207-226.

Synnott, Anthony. 'Truth and Goodness, Mirrors and Masks: A Sociology of Beauty and the Face', in Ray B. Browne & Pat Browne (eds.), *Digging into Popular Culture: Theories and Methodologies in Archeology, Anthropology, and Other Fields*, Bowling Green: Popular Press, 1991.

Tang, Yan. 'Momo yonghu guo yi ruhe pingjia? Zheme duo yonghu dou zai Mom zuo shenme?', *Zhihu*, http://www.zhihu.com/question/22680523.

Tatlow, Didi Kirsten. 'Apps Offer Chinese a Path to the Forbidden', *New York Times* (24 July 2013), http://www.nytimes.com/2013/07/25/world/asia/25iht-letter25.html?_r=1&.

Terranova, Tiziana. *Network Culture: Politics for the Information Age*, London: Pluto Press, 2004.

Turkle, Sherry. *Alone Together: Why We Expect More From Technology and Less From Each Other*, New York: Basic Books, 2012.

Urry, John. *Mobilities*, Cambridge: Polity Press, 2000.

Wallis, Cara. 'The Technological Meets the Traditional: Mobile Navigations of Desire and Intimacy', in Stephanie Hemelryk Donald, Theresa Dirndorfer Anderson and Damien Spry (eds.), *Youth, Society and Mobile Media in Asia*, Abingdon: Routledge, 2010, pp. 57-69.

Whitty, Monica T. & Carr, Adrian. 'Introduction', in Monica T. Whitty, Andrea J. Baker, James A. Inman (eds.), *Online M@tchmaking*, Houndmills: Palgrave MacMillan, 2007.

WHAT ARE THE *SHENGNV* LOOKING FOR IN ONLINE HETEROSEXUAL DATING AND COURTSHIP? A CONTENT ANALYSIS OF SHANGHAINESE WOMEN'S PERSONAL PROFILES ON JIAYUAN.COM

TAO FU

Introduction

Online dating is the romance-seeking process "in which individuals create profiles and initiate contact with others through an online service."[1] First appearing in the mid-1990s, online dating sites enable users to create personal profiles and find matches according to various criteria[2] with the help of the computer-mediated communication (CMC). Some sites are categorized as the match-making type that help users search for the person with whom they may tie the knot[3] using complicated algorithms for pairing.[4] Some are dating sites where the relationship may not end up in marriage.[5]

The personal profile includes basic demographic information, such as age, gender, physical attributes, hobbies and interests, as well as traits one seeks in a prospective dating partner.[6] Users can decide whether or not to upload photos as part of the profile.

Longer bachelorhood, time constraints due to busy schedules and more geographical mobility contribute to the popularity of finding an online date. With the stigma related to online dating gradually dissipating,[7] online dating has become the second most widely used way for seeking a partner, only after connecting through friends.[8]

China's unmarried population between 18 and 55 accounted for 14.5 percent of the total in

---

1. Jeffrey T. Hancock, Catalina Toma and Nicole Ellison, 'The Truth about Lying in Online Dating Profiles', CHI 2007 Proceedings, *Online Representation of Self*, 28 April - 3 May 2007, San Jose, CA, USA, https://www.msu.edu/\~nellison/hancock_et_al_2007.pdf.
2. Mark Brook, 'How Has Internet Dating Changed Society? An Insider's Look', *IDEA*, January 2011, 1-33.
3. iResearch Consulting Group, '*Zhongguo Wangluo Hunlian Hangye Baogao: 2013-2014* (China Online Personals Industry Report: 2013-2014', http://report.iresearch.cn/2106.html.
4. Eli J. Finkel, Paul W. Eastwick, Benjamin R. Karney, Harry T. Reis, and Susan Sprecher, 'Online Dating: A Critical Analysis from the Perspective of Psychological Science', *Psychological Science in the Public Interest* 13.1 (January, 2012): 3-66, http://psi.sagepub.com/content/13/1/3.full?ijkey=cK9EB6/4zQ0A-M&keytype=ref&siteid=sppsi.
5. iResearch Consulting Group, 'China Online Personals Industry Report: 2013-2014'.
6. Monica T. Whitty and Adrian Carr, *Cyberspace Romance: The Psychology of Online Relationships*, New York, NY: Palgrave Macmillan, 2006.
7. Nicole Ellison, Rebecca Heino and Jennifer Gibbs, 'Managing Impressions Online: Self-Presentation Processes in the Online Dating Environment', *Journal of Computer-Mediated Communication* 11.2 (2006): 415-441. doi:10.1111/j.1083-6101.2006.00020.
8. Finkel, Eastwick, Karney, Reis and Sprecher, 'Online Dating: A Critical Analysis from the Perspective of Psychological Science'.

2011, among whom 85 million were women.[9] With the issue of the new Marriage Law,[10] arranged marriage was banned in 1950,[11] which empowered Chinese women to freely choose their partners. After more than a decade of development since the first online dating site came into being in 1998 in China,[12] 23.8 percent of survey respondents said online dating was a reliable way to get to know a potential date.[13]

The present study focuses on how in Shanghai, China's most populous city, a 'special' social group – *shengnv* – presented themselves on a dating site, Jiayuan.com, in pursuit of a heterosexual relationship. It also explores the social implications of the self-presentation and mate-selection criteria in personal profiles as to how it challenges the stereotypical gender-roles of Chinese women.

Shengnv and Marriage Traditions in China

In the West, well-educated and professionally successful women are considered to be independent and liberated.[14] Their Chinese peers, however, are less fortunate and even stigmatized as leftovers. The word, *shengnv*, sometimes *shengnu*, or 'leftover women', refers to well-educated, economically successful urban single women in their late 20s and older.[15] *Shengnv* became an official word listed by the Ministry of Education of China in 2007.[16] In 2010, All-China Women's Federation, with other organizations, conducted and released a survey on Chinese people's attitude toward love and marriage. The results showed that more than 90 percent of the males thought women should get married before 27.[17] Similar results were found in another survey conducted by Baihe.com,[18] a dating Web site. Some 62.2 percent of male respondents and 64.8 percent females said the ideal age for women to get married was between 25 and 27.[19] Another 28.4 percent of men said 20 to 24 was the ideal marriage age for women, while 22.7 percent of women said the age should be between 28

---

9   iResearch Consulting Group, 'China Online Personals Industry Report: 2013-2014'.

10   Renxin Yang, 'Between Traditionalism and Modernity: Changing Values on Dating Behavior and Mate Selection Criteria', *International Review of Modern Sociology* 37.2 (2011): 265-287.

11   Evan Osnos, 'The Love Business', *The New Yorker*, 14 May 2012, 88.13, http://www.newyorker.com/reporting/2012/05/14/120514fa_fact_osnos.

12   iResearch Consulting Group, 'China Online Personals Industry Report: 2013-2014'.

13   Baihe.com, *2011 Zhongguoren Hunlian Baogao* (A Report on Chinese People's Love and Marriage, 2011), 5 January 2012, http://media.baihe.com/html/71/n-871.html.

14   Sandy To, 'Understanding Sheng Nu ('Leftover Women'): The Phenomenon of Late Marriage among Chinese Professional Women', *Symbolic Interaction* 36.1 (2013): 1-20.

15   Julie Makinen and Don Lee, 'China's *Shengnu*, or 'Leftover Women' Face Intense Pressure to Marry', 13 July 2013, http://articles.latimes.com/2013/jul/13/world/la-fg-china-leftover-women-20130714.

16   Roseann Lake, 'All the Shengnu Ladies', 11 March 2012, http://www.salon.com/2012/03/12/all_the_shengnu_ladies/.

17   Xinhua Net, '*Jiedu 2010 Nian Zhongguoren Hunlian Zhuangkuang Baobao* (Reading and Understanding Chinese People's Love and Marriage Report 2010)', 15 December 2010, http://news.xinhuanet.com/society/2010-12/15/c_13650287_2.htm.

18   Baihe.com, 'A Report on Chinese People's Love and Marriage, 2011'.

19   Baihe.com, 'A Report on Chinese People's Love and Marriage, 2011'.

and 30.[20] Women older than 25 were subdivided into four categories: 25 and above, must fight for a partner; 28 and above, must triumph; 31 to 35, advanced leftovers; and older than 35, ultimate leftovers.[21]

Even though China is known for its skewed male and female ratio estimated to produce a surplus of 24 million men by 2020,[22] except for some less educated males in rural China, it is still *shengnv* who are undergoing more challenges and pressures on the way to the altar. The reasons are complicated. China is a marriage-oriented society. Chinese marriage patterns are characterized by universality of marriage, early marriage, female hypergamy, marriage squeeze and marriage as the precursor to family formation.[23]

As is the case with the older generation of American women, for whom marriage was a core life experience,[24] 98 percent of Chinese women are married in the end.[25] Marriage is considered the final destination for women since taking care of family and children are culturally considered women's duties. Women were found to get more satisfaction than men from marriage.[26] Therefore, if a woman remains single after 25, especially after 30, she is considered incomplete and abnormal.[27]

China has the tradition of hypergamy, or 'marrying up', for a woman to marry a man who is more economically well-off and better educated.[28] Women gain financial security, status, and resources through marrying older men.[29] Chinese men, on the other hand, tend to 'marry down'.[30] They tend to look for younger women as a future partner since males emphasize

---

20 Baihe.com, 'A Report on Chinese People's Love and Marriage, 2011'.
21 Lake, 'All the Shengnu Ladies'.
22 Clarissa Sebag-Montefiore, *Romance with Chinese Characteristics*, 21 August 2012, http://latitude.blogs.nytimes.com/2012/08/21/romance-with-chinese-characteristics/?_php=true&_type=blogs&_r=0.
23 Yan Wei, Quanbao Jiang and Stuart Basten, 'Observing the Transformation of China's First Marriage Pattern through Net Nuptiality Tables: 1982-2010', *Finnish Yearbook of Population Research* XLVIII 2013, 65-75.
24 Antony Giddens, *The Transformation of Intimacy: Sexuality, Love and Eroticism in Modern Societies*, Stanford, CA: Stanford University Press, 1992, p.53.
25 Evan Osnos, 'The Love Business'.
26 Yuan Cheng, Xuehui Han and John K. Dagsvik, 'Marriage Pattern in the City of Shanghai: Behavioral Two-sex Model and Multistage Marriage Life Table Approach', Chinese Sociology and Anthropology 43.4 (Summer 2011): 74-95.
27 Yao Min-G, 'Family Pressure Forces Marriage with *Laowai*', Shanghai Daily, 30 May 2013, http://www.shanghaidaily.com/Opinion/chinese-perspectives/Family-pressure-forces-marriage-with-laowai/shdaily.shtml.
28 Christian Larson, 'China's 'Leftover Ladies' Are Anything But', Bloomberg Businessweek, 23 August 2012, http://www.businessweek.com/articles/2012-08-22/chinas-leftover-ladies-are-anything-but.; Lake, 'All the *Shengnu* Ladies'; Yao, 'Family Pressure Forces Marriage with *Laowai*'.
29 Larry Lance, 'Gender Differences in Heterosexual Dating: A Content Analysis of Personal Ads', *Journal of Men's Studies* 6.3 (Spring 1998): 297-305.
30 Katie Hunt, 'Glut of Women at Shanghai's Marriage Market', 3 November 2013, http://www.cnn.com/2013/11/03/world/asia/shanghai-marriage-market/.

physical attractiveness and youth.³¹ Studies also show richer men get married later in life than do less well-to-do men.³² About 12 million unmarried men will compete with younger men for younger women.³³ In the 2010 survey conducted by All-China Women's Federation, 38.3 percent of the male participants hoped that the ideal occupation of their significant other could be teachers, followed by civil servants, doctors/nurses, and accountants.³⁴ Such jobs usually bring women decent salaries, social status and relatively easy working conditions. More than half of the male participants said they did not care about their significant other's job, which indicated that males hoped that women could spend more time taking care of the family.³⁵

Those well-educated and financially independent women thus are faced with the embarrassment of having few men who want to marry a more capable wife who is no longer 'young', at least in some Chinese sense. The survey conducted by Jiayuan.com, an online dating site, confirmed this paradox – the more education and salaries women have, the more difficult it is for them to find a husband.³⁶ These well-educated urban professional women must downplay their high achievements since they do not want to pressure prospective dates.³⁷

As a result of their cosmopolitan lifestyle, some Chinese women living in big cities, such as Shanghai, date foreign men.³⁸ These women's international love stories become an important construct of their cosmopolitan identity.³⁹ These Shanghainese women choose to marry *laowai*, or foreigners, also because Chinese have the stereotype that *laowai* are superior to Chinese and relatives and friends are less likely to gossip about the past of the foreign partner.⁴⁰

Theoretical Framework
Self-presentation
Self-presentation is "an individual accentuates certain matters and conceals others".⁴¹ It "refers to the process by which individuals attempt to control the impressions others have of

---

31 Lance, 'Gender Differences in Heterosexual Dating: A Content Analysis of Personal Ads'.
32 Cheng, Han and Dagsvik, 'Marriage Pattern in the City of Shanghai: Behavioral Two-sex Model and Multistage Marriage Life Table Approach'.
33 eChinacities.com, 'Love and Marriage in Modern China: Survey Reveals Latest Trend', 30 December 2012, http://www.echinacities.com/china-media/Love-and-Marriage-in-Modern-China-Survey-Reveals-Latest-Trends.
34 Xinhua Net, *Jiedu 2010 Nian Zhongguoren Hunlian Zhuangkuang Baodao* (Reading and Understanding Chinese People's Love and Marriage Report 2010).
35 Xinhua Net, *Jiedu 2010 Nian Zhongguoren Hunlian Zhuangkuang Baodao*.
36 Larson, 'China's 'Leftover Ladies' Are Anything But'.
37 Osnos, 'The Love Business'.
38 James Farrer, 'Good Stories: Chinese Women's International Love Stories as Cosmopolitan Sexual Politics', Sexualities 16.1/2 (2012): 12-29.
39 James Farrer, 'Good Stories'.
40 Yao Min-G, 'Family Pressure Forces Marriage with *Laowai*'.
41 Ervin Goffman, *The Presentation of Self in Everyday Life*, New York: Anchor, 1959, p.67.

them".[42] In this sense, the personal profile on online dating sites is a self-presentation of the dater who posts it. Since prospective dates will use the self-presentation to decide whether or not to initiate a relationship,[43] online personal profiles set the tone for future relationship development.

Earlier studies on personal advertisements in newspapers found gender stereotypes influenced how both women and men described themselves.[44] Females are more likely to show instrumental or male-valued traits.[45] They are more likely to display physical attractiveness such as thinness, and to seek professional status[46] or financially secure older men.[47]

These self-presentation traits women showed in personal advertisements are in accordance with social exchange theory, which posits that each party in a relationship tries to maximize its reward at minimal cost.[48] Social exchange theory, originated from behavioral psychology,[49] has been attested for examining marital and familial relationships.[50] Walther found reduced cues and asynchronicity, two features of CMC, facilitated selective self-presentation.[51] These, plus editability, enable online daters to select and edit what to present to their potential partners[52] and manage their impression and the relationship.[53]

Mate-selection Factors

Various factors affect how people choose prospective partners. Heterosexual women and men have different preferences concerning traits most desirable in prospective partners.

---

42 Joseph R. Dominick, 'Who Do You Think You Are? Personal Home Pages and Self-Presentation on the World Wide Web', *Journalism & Mass Communication Quarterly* 76.4 (1999): 646-658, p. 647.

43 Ellison, Heino and Gibbs, 'Managing Impressions Online: Self-Presentation Processes in the Online Dating Environment'.

44 Marti Hope Gonzales and Sarah A. Meyers, '"Your Mother Would Like Me": Self-Presentation in the Personals Ads of Heterosexual and Homosexual Men and Women', *Personality and Social Psychology Bulletin* 19.2 (April 1993): 131-142.

45 Gonzales and Meyers, '"Your Mother Would Like Me": Self-Presentation in the Personals Ads of Heterosexual and Homosexual Men and Women'; Richard Koestner and Ladd Wheeler, 'Self-Presentation in Personal Advertisements: The Influence of Implicit Notions of Attraction and Role Expectations', *Journal of Social and Personal Relationships* 5 (1998): 149-160.

46 Koestner and Wheeler, 'Self-Presentation in Personal Advertisements: The Influence of Implicit Notions of Attraction and Role Expectations'.

47 Albert A. Harrison and Laila Saeed, 'Let's Make a Deal: An Analysis of Revelations and Stipulations in Lonely Hearts Advertisements', *Journal of Personality and Social Psychology* 35.4 (1997): 257-264.

48 Peter Michael Blau, *Exchange and Power in Social Life*, New York: Wiley, 1964.

49 Richard M. Emerson, 'Social Exchange Theory', *Annual Review of Sociology* 2 (1976): 335-362, http://www.communicationcache.com/uploads/1/0/8/8/10887248/social_exchange_theory_-_1976.pdf.

50 Paul A. Nakonezny and Wayne H. Denton, 'Marital Relationships: A Social Exchange Theory Perspective', *The American Journal of Family Therapy* 36 (2008): 402–412.

51 Joseph B. Walther, 'Computer-Mediated Communication: Impersonal, Interpersonal, and Hyperpersonal Interaction', *Communication Research* 23.1 (February 1996): 3-43.

52 Hancock, Toma and Ellison, 'The Truth about Lying in Online Dating Profiles'.

53 Walther, 'Computer-Mediated Communication: Impersonal, Interpersonal, and Hyperpersonal Interaction'.

Heterosexual women rated social status the most valued while heterosexual men most frequently cited attractiveness.[54]

In studying Malaysian graduate students, Alavi, Alahdad and Shafeqfound found they not only cared about exterior traits, but also interior ones such as religion.[55] Age is another factor in mate-selection. Hill found that among college students, males preferred prospective partner to be younger while females preferred older partners.[56] Out of 18 factors, six were rated most important by both male and female participants: dependable character, emotional stability and maturity, pleasing disposition, mutual attraction, good health, and desire for home life and children.[57] Women also cited ambition and industriousness; education and general intelligence; and good financial prospects, while men said women should take care of the family and be physically attractive.[58] A cross-cultural study showed a similar trend that women tended to value financial capacity, ambition, industriousness and cues to resource acquisition in prospective partners more than did men.[59] Physically attractive women had elevated standards for potential male partner's characteristics, including good genetic indicators, good investment indicators, good parenting indicators, and good partner indicators.[60] Schwarz and Hassebrauck said in their study of heterosexuals aged 18 to 64 that slightly older women were tolerable to men and much younger women were more acceptable.[61] The trends for women are different: as women mature they tend to accept men younger than their own age.[62] Slightly more than one-third of women said they could imagine marrying a man earning much less money than they did.[63] In terms of education, many women said they could not imagine marrying a less-educated partner, and one not regularly employed.[64] Buunk, Dijkstra, Fetchenhauer and Kenrick agreed that men prefer physically more attractive mates, while women prefer mates who are more well-educated, self-confident, intelligent,

---

54 Thao Ha, Judith E. M. van den Berg, Rutger C. M. E. Engels and Anna Lichtwarck-Aschoff, 'Effects of Attractiveness and Status in Dating Desire in Homosexual and Heterosexual Men and Women', Archives of Sexual Behavior 41.3 (June 2012): 673-682; Ischa van Straaten, Rutger C. M. E. Engels, Catrin Finkenauer and Rob W. Holland, 'Sex Differences in Short-term Mate Preferences and Behavioral Mimicry: A Semi-Naturalistic Experiment', Archives of Sexual Behavior 37.6 (2008): 902-911.

55 Masoumeh Alavi, Rezvan Alahdad and Syed Mohamed Shafeq, 'Mate Selection Criteria among Postgraduate Students in Malaysia', Procedia - Social and Behavioral Sciences 116 (2014): 5075 – 5080.

56 Reuben Lorenzo Hill Jr., 'Campus Values in Mate Selection', Journal of Home Economics, 37.9 (1945): 554–558.

57 Reuben Lorenzo Hill Jr., 'Campus Values in Mate Selection'.

58 Reuben Lorenzo Hill Jr., 'Campus Values in Mate Selection'.

59 David M. Buss, 'Sex Differences in Human Mate Preferences: Evolutionary Hypotheses Tested in 37 Cultures', Behavioral and Brain Sciences 12.1 (1989): 1-49.

60 David M. Buss and Todd K. Shackelford, 'Attractive Women Want It All: Good Genes, Economic Investment, Parenting Proclivities, and Emotional Commitment', Evolutionary Psychology 6.1 (2008): 134-146.

61 Sascha Schwarz and Manfred Hassebrauck, 'Sex and Age Differences in Mate-Selection Preferences', Human Nature 23.4 (2012): 447-466.

62 Sascha Schwarz and Manfred Hassebrauck, 'Sex and Age Differences in Mate-Selection Preferences'.

63 Sascha Schwarz and Manfred Hassebrauck, 'Sex and Age Differences in Mate-Selection Preferences'.

64 Sascha Schwarz and Manfred Hassebrauck, 'Sex and Age Differences in Mate-Selection Preferences'.

dominant, well-off and respected.[65] Henry, Helm and Cruz's comparison of 18 desirable traits among college students in mate selection with the studies from 1939 to 2011 also agreed that women preferred of men who were ambitious, industrious and financially well off.[66]

Chinese people's mate selection criteria have been changing and inconsistent as a result of the great social changes. Traditional values, socialist reconstruction, utilitarianism and consumerism have exerted their influence to different generations of Chinese since the founding of the New China in 1949.[67] Li's study of 300 personal advertisements found Chinese men attached more importance to income and household registration,[68] while Chinese women valued personality, height and educational level.[69] Urban residents cared more about educational levels while rural Chinese favored marital status and income.[70] More-educated Chinese emphasized knowledge, moral conduct, shared values and emotions that may help the couple to communicate better spiritually.[71] Based on evolutionary psychological analyses, Tian found 'good genes', 'good provider' and 'good-father' to be factors Chinese female college students and professional women preferred in mate selection.[72] These criteria help ensure male candidate can provide the physical good genes, good socio-economic status, and good personality traits the future generation needs.[73] It is also confirmed that urban-rural differences, educational levels and household incomes, along with some other factors, affected Chinese female college students' preference in mate selection.[74] But, on the whole, Tian's study concluded that modern Chinese female college students valued personal traits more than material criteria.[75]

All of these findings show that to the more educated urban Chinese residents, are un-

---

65 Bram P. Buunk, Pieternel Dijkstra, Detlef Fetchenhauer and Douglas T. Kenrick, 'Age and Gender Differences in Mate Selection Criteria for Various Involvement Levels', *Personal Relationships* 9.3 (2002): 271-278.
66 Jermaine Henry, Herbert W. Helm Jr. and Natasha Cruz, 'Mate Selection: Gender and Generational Differences', *North American Journal of Psychology* 15.1 (2013): 63-70.
67 Yang, 'Between Traditionalism and Modernity: Changing Values on Dating Behavior and Mate Selection Criteria'.
68 A system that classifies all Chinese citizens either as an urban resident or rural. The former enjoys more social welfare.
69 Yinhe Li, Sex and Marriage of the Chinese People (*Zhongguoren De Xing'ai Yu Hunyin*), Zhengzhou: Henan People's Publishing House, 1996, http://v.book.ifeng.com/book/ts/32678/2605023.htm.
70 Yinhe Li, Sex and Marriage of the Chinese People.
71 Shengli Chen and Shikun Zhang, *Dangdai Zeou Yu Shengyu Yiyuan Yanjiu: 2002 Nian Chengxiang Juming Shengyu Yiyuan Diaocha* (Contemporary Expectations on Mate Selection and Child Rearing: An Investigation on Desires and Plans for Marriage and Child Rearing among Urban and Rural Residents in 2002), Beijing: China Population Press, 2002.
72 Qian Tian, 'A study of Chinese Women's Mate Selection Trends: An Interpretation Based on Evolutionary Psychology (*Zhongguo nvxing zeou qingxiang yanjiu: Jiyu jinhua xinlixue de jieshi*)', 2012, Ph.D. dissertation.
73 Qian Tian, 'A study of Chinese Women's Mate Selection Trends'.
74 Qian Tian, 'A study of Chinese Women's Mate Selection Trends'.
75 Qian Tian, 'A study of Chinese Women's Mate Selection Trends'.

concerned whether or not their mate is well-educated. Rather, they care more about good spiritual communication with their partner. Rural residents, however, were more practical.

Shanghainese *shengnv* are on the whole economically successful and no longer young. Accordingly, what personal traits do they highlight in the exchange? Since their need for financial security is comparatively lower, what do they look for in the relationship?

Based on the literature, the following research questions (RQ) were posited:

> RQ1: How do heterosexual never-married *shengnv* present themselves in online dating profiles?

> RQ2: What kind of prospective partners do heterosexual never-married *shengnv* look for?

Method
Dating Site Selection
Baihe, Jianyuan, and Zhenai are the top three dating sites with high brand recognition rate and large number of users.[76] Jiayuan.com, founded in 2003 and listed on the NASDAQ in May, 2011, was chosen for this study because it has more than 100 million registered users – more than that of other competitors.[77] Jiayuan.com offers open access to most information of its users, making data collection and further analysis possible.

The researcher registered to have more access to other users' personal profiles.[78] But in the personal statement part, it was clearly stated that the registration was for academic study, not partner or relation-seeking. Thus the status was set as 'I have found my partner'.

Sample Selection
Shanghai is the largest city in China with a total population of 23 million.[79] Shanghai does not see a skewed female vs. male ratio though it is prevalent nationally in China. It was about 100:106 among Shanghai residents.[80] In the study of two-sex marriage pattern in Shanghai, it was found that people in this city preferred to marry at an older age.[81] Since their male counterparts hold a similar view, the likelihood for Shanghai females to find a good match

---

76 iResearch Consulting Group, 'China Online Personals Industry Report: 2013-2014'.
77 iResearch Consulting Group, 'China Online Personals Industry Report: 2013-2014'.
78 Non-registered guests can have access to limited information of registered Jiayuan users.
79 National Bureau of Statistics of China, 'Communiqué of the National Bureau of Statistics of the People's Republic of China on Major Figures of the 2010 Population Census (No. 2)', 29 April 2011, http://www.stats.gov.cn/tjsj/tjgb/rkpcgb/qgrkpcgb/201104/t20110429_30328.html.
80 National Bureau of Statistics of China, *Communiqué of the National Bureau of Statistics of the People's Republic of China on Shanghai City of the 2010 Population Census*, 28 February 2012, http://www.stats.gov.cn/tjsj/tjgb/rkpcgb/dfrkpcgb/201202/t20120228_30403.html.
81 Cheng, Han, Dagsvik, 'Marriage Pattern in the City of Shanghai: Behavioral Two-sex Model and Multistage Marriage Life Table Approach'.

remains moderate.[82] However, since 1991, more males than females got married in Shanghai, which resulted in women from other areas in China being 'imported' to Shanghai and threatening native Shanghai women's marriage market.[83] Females in Shanghai felt more satisfied with the status of being married than males.[84] Males of 21 to 25 said they greatly preferred not to marry older female partners, although mature males did not find this to be of concern.[85]

Shengnv often designates urban single women 27 and above. Those women "in the age range of 28-33 had more relevant and interesting relationship experience to share".[86]

In this study, 'female', '28-33', 'Shanghai',[87] 'never-married', 'with photos' and 'undergraduate and above', were set as filters for 'gender', 'age', 'location', 'marital status', 'with or without photos' and 'educational level' to generate the samples in April, 2014. According to Jiayuan.com, users posting photos received 11 times more responses than those without photos. Since ethnicity and religion were not Chinese people's top priority in mate selection,[88] they were not included in this study. The fact that the vast majority of Chinese are Han and atheists (or agnostics or pantheists) is accountable for this.[89] On each result page, there were 5x5 candidates. The personal profile of each candidate was searched and content analyzed until a desirable number was reached ($N = 200$). Each user's personal profile was used as the unit of analysis.

Coding Categories

At Jiayuan.com, users register by providing information about their gender, date of birth, marital status, height, educational level, monthly income, email account or phone number for contact and an online nickname. Users can fill in more information about children, blood type, ethnicity, profession, housing, car and self tags. Love Monologue (*wode neixin dubai*) is a self-disclosure section where registered users can write 5 to 500 Chinese characters to show their understanding of love and their expectation of marriage. Each user can upload one face close-up and other photos at My Pics (*wode zhaopian*). Users can substantiate their profiles with physical features, work and study, daily life, and hobbies at Detailed Information (*xiangxi ziliao*). Personality Show (*gexing zhanshi*) describes the user's personal traits, opinions on love, dating, expectation of marriage, life after the wedding and features of ideal partners. My Criteria (*wode zeou yaoqiu*) are specific bars a prospective partner might meet.

---

82 Cheng, Han, Dagsvik, 'Marriage Pattern in the City of Shanghai.
83 Cheng, Han, Dagsvik, 'Marriage Pattern in the City of Shanghai.
84 Cheng, Han, Dagsvik, 'Marriage Pattern in the City of Shanghai.
85 Cheng, Han, Dagsvik, 'Marriage Pattern in the City of Shanghai.
86 To, 'Understanding *Sheng Nu* ('Leftover Women'): The Phenomenon of Late Marriage among Chinese Professional Women', p. 7; Tian, 'A study of Chinese Women's Mate Selection Trends: An Interpretation Based on Evolutionary Psychology'.
87 Household registration was set as "Shanghai" as well to make sure the user was a Shanghainese resident rather than the floating population who were simply working in Shanghai and may settle down in other places.
88 Li, Sex and Marriage of the Chinese People.
89 Li, Sex and Marriage of the Chinese People.

At Jiayuan Self-Tag (*wode jiayuan biaoqian*), users can self-choose some tags that best describe their personality. Physical Features (*waimao tixing*) about height, weight and face shape also are open for fill-in.

In the present study, each user's Jiayuan ID and her Jiayuan nickname were recorded for future retrieval. Demographic information of all participants was collected, including age, height, educational level, income, car ownership, house ownership, professions, types of employers and language proficiency (e.g. Mandarin, English and Spanish).

The following were coded to answer the first research question: self-evaluation (e.g. cute and petite, mature and regal), and self-tags (e.g. beautiful, career-oriented, cute, rational, straightforward).

The Ideal Partner (*lixiang duixiang*) part was coded for answering the second research question. It included personalities of him (e.g. gentleman-like, humorous, romantic or stylish), most valued trait (e.g. responsible, humble, accommodating, honest), and what is most important (e.g. physical features, personality, financial capacity, education). The ideal age and height ranges, geographic location (e.g. in Shanghai, in Shanghai's neighboring areas, abroad), education (e.g. 3-year college, undergraduate, graduate), and marital status (e.g. single, divorced) of the prospective partner in My Criteria were coded as well.

Love Monologue was analyzed to address both research questions. The coding procedures for Love Monologue were adapted from those used by Harrison and Saeed,[90] Deaux and Hanna,[91] Keostner and Wheeler,[92] and Gonzales and Meyers.[93] Three categories: attractiveness, financial security and sincerity, were used to code this subjective description in an offer/seek dichotomous manner. The details of these qualities were:

Attractiveness: petite, cute, slender, attractive, shapely, classy, sophisticated

Financial security: accomplished, well-established, professional, generous, prosperous, successful

Sincerity: committed, faithful, dependable, good morals, honest, trust-worthy, loyal

The researcher did most of the coding since it was objective. A graduate student who is a

---

90 Harrison and Saeed, 'Let's Make a Deal: An Analysis of Revelations and Stipulations in Lonely Hearts Advertisements'.
91 Kay Deaux and Randel Hanna, 'Courtship in the Persona Column: The Influence of Gender and Sexual Orientation', *Sex Roles* 11. 5/6 (1984): 363-375.
92 Richard Koestner and Ladd Wheeler, 'Self-Presentation in Personal Advertisements: The Influence of Implicit Notions of Attraction and Role Expectations', *Journal of Social and Personal Relationships* 5 (1988): 149-160.
93 Gonzales and Meyers, '"Your Mother Would Like Me": Self-Presentation in the Personals Ads of Heterosexual and Homosexual Men and Women'.

Chinese native was trained and then coded the Love Monologue section as a second coder. An acceptable intercoder reliability[94] was reached for seeking attractiveness (Cronbach's α = .93), offering attractiveness (Cronbach's α = .89), seeking financial security (Cronbach's α = .86), offering financial security (Cronbach's α = .95), seeking sincerity (Cronbach's α = .89) and offering sincerity (Cronbach's α = .86). All coding results were entered into Statistical Package for the Social Sciences (SPSS) for analysis.

Findings
Demographic Information
Since the age of the subjects were pre-set, there was no big age difference (M = 30.14, SD = 1.61) among all informants. Their average height was 163.7 cm[95] though individual difference ranged from about 152 cm[96] to 178 cm.[97] Most (94 %) of the subjects posted fewer than six photos. The personal information filled by *shengnv* themselves affirmed the labels attached to them – more educated and more well-to-do. About two thirds had bachelor's or dual degrees. The other one-third held graduate degrees (Table 1). About 81 percent of them had a monthly income of US$800 to US$3,200[98] (see Table 2).The high income made them out-compete women in other areas considering the annual per capita disposable income[99] of urban households in Shanghai was US$7,174[100] in 2013, the highest among all provinces. The high income may be the result of being employed by companies and institutions with good welfare. Most of the informants worked for foreign enterprises (29%), private-owned enterprises (19.5%), public institutions (13%) and *Fortune* 500-enlisted companies (10%). The rest worked for listed companies (7%), state-owned enterprises (5.5%), and the government (2%). There were also a few running their own companies (5.5%) or unknown (8.5%). The subjects' economic competence was also reflected by their car and property ownership and their professional distribution. Some 16.5 percent of the informants had a car and 15.5 percent had bought an apartment of their own. Those who have not bought a car accounted for 52.5 percent with the rest being unknown. As for housing, on a descending scale, these ladies chose 'live with parents' (42.5 %), 'have not purchased yet' (10.0 %), 'rent on my own' (5.5 %), 'will buy as needed' (3.5 %), 'live in employer-offered housing' (2.5 %), 'rent with others' (2 %) or 'unknown' (17.5 %). As professional women, 52 percent of the subjects worked in finance/security/insurance, accounting/auditing, IT/computer, human resources, education/training and academic/research.

---

94 Kimberly A. Neuendorf, The Content Analysis Guidebook, Thousand Oaks, CA: Sage, 2002, p. 145.
95 About 5'4".
96 About 5'.
97 About 5'10".
98 Based on the then exchange rate of US$1 ≈RMB¥ 6.25.
99 Disposable income means real income minus income tax, social insurance, and housing fund.
100 Xu Lin, 'Top 10 Provinces with the Highest Quality in 2013', 13 March 2014, http://www.china.org.cn/top10/2014-03/13/content_31769827_10.htm.

Degrees	Frequency	Percent
Bachelor's	129	64.5
Master's	58	29.0
Ph.D.	11	5.5
Dual Bachelor's	2	1.0

Table 1 Educational Level

Since *shengnv* is a well-educated group, all subjects in this study showed good language competence as a result of Chinese university's curriculum that prescribes a foreign language, usually English, as compulsory. About three fifths of the informants could speak English. Another 19 percent were good at English and another foreign language, such as Japanese or German. About 3 percent showed proficiency in a non-English foreign language. The rest were dismissive to this section and left it uncompleted.

Monthly Income (US$)	Monthly Income (RMB¥)	Counts	Percent
<320	<2,000	1	0.5
320-800	2,000-5,000	19	9.5
800-1,600	5,000-10,000	94	47
1,600-3,200	10,000-20,000	68	34
>3,200	>20,000	16	8
Unknown		2	1

Table 2 Monthly Income

RQ1: How do heterosexual never-married shengnv self-present themselves in online dating profiles?

In the self-tag section, registered Jiayuan users can choose at least one tag that best represents their personalities. Among users who completed this self-tag question ($n = 182$), the most frequently chosen tags were *shanliang*, or kind-hearted; *xiaoshun*, showing great filial piety; and *zhishuang*, or straight-forward (Table 3). Eighteen out of the 200 informants' response to this question was unknown.

Self-tag (in pinyin)	Self-tag (in English)	Number	Percent
shan liang	kind-hearted	107	14.6
xiao shun nv	a woman showing great filial piety	96	13.1
zhi shuang	straight-forward, frank	76	10.4
qi zhi nv	a woman with an aura of elegance	62	8.5
xiu wai hui zhong	elegant and intelligent	61	8.4
ju jia nv	a family-oriented woman	44	6.0
gan xing nv	a sensitive woman	39	5.3
li xing nv	a rational woman	39	5.3
ai yun dong	a fitness freak	36	4.9
ai xiao dong wu	a woman who loves small animals	35	4.8
xiao zi nv	a woman who pursues Western lifestyle, arts, taste and thinking	31	4.2
xiao ke ai	cute	29	4.0
mei shi jia	a gourmet	22	3.0

Self-tag (in pinyin)	Self-tag (in English)	Number	Percent
zhai nv	a woman who always stays at home and seldom goes out	22	3.0
shi ye nv	a career-oriented woman	17	2.3
mei nv	an attractive woman like a siren	12	1.6
ye man nv you	a sassy girlfriend	3	0.4
zi you zhi ye	freelance	1	0.1

Table 3 Self-tags Used by Jiayuan Users

In another self-evaluation, in which users were asked to choose one four-character word to best describe their quality, 52 (26%) informants left it blank. Among the 148 who answered, about half chose to describe themselves as *mei qing mu xiu*, or having delicate facial features (22%); and *xiu wai hui zhong*, or with an elegant look and intelligent mind (16.5%). About 10 percent of the informants did not think they were middle-aged but described themselves as young and energetic, or *qing chun huo li*, as the Chinese would say. The others featured quietness and gracefulness, shortness and sweetness, mature attractiveness, bright eyes and regality and magnificence (Table 4).

Self-evaluation	In English	Number	Percent
mei qing mu xiu	delicate	44	22.0
xiu wai hui zhong	elegant and intelligent	33	16.5
qing chun huo bo	young and robust	18	9.0
dan ya ru ju	quiet but graceful like chrysanthemum	17	8.5

Self-evaluation	In English	Number	Percent
jiao xiao yi ren	petite and cute	16	8.0
cheng shu mei li	maturely attractive	11	5.5
ming mou shan lai	with bright eyes	8	4.0
yong rong hua gui	regal and magnificent	1	0.5
Unknown		52	26.0

Table 4 Self-evaluation

RQ2: What kind of prospective partners do heterosexual never-married *shengnv* look for?

As for their prospective partner's personality, informants valued 'responsible' (32.5%) the most, according to 89 percent who answered. It was followed by 'honest' (18.7%), 'accommodating' (17%) and 'considerate' (13.2%). Other less-cared personalities include 'self-constraint' (5.3%), 'patient' (4.3%), 'full of hope' (3.9%), 'modest' (1.8%), 'satisfied' (1.2%), 'friendly' (1.2%), 'empathetic' (0.4%), 'persevering' (0.2%) and 'sympathetic'(0.2%).

In another similar question, the 175 informants who answered hoped their significant others could have a calm character and take good care of the family (*wen zhong gu jia*) (27.7%), optimistic and positive (*le guan ji ji*) (26.1%), humorous (*feng qu you mo*) (17.5%), wise and brilliant (*jing ming rui zhi*) (11.6%), and gentleman-like (*wen wen er ya*) (10.6%). But the informants did not seem to be in favor of qualities such as extroverted (1.8%), childlike (1.8%), careful and cautious (1.0%), romantic (1.0%), impulsive (0.4%) and stylish (0.4%).

The average minimal ($M = 29.6$, $SD = 2.05$) and maximum ($M = 37.8$, $SD = 3.08$) age of ideal prospective partners spanned eight years. The average minimal ($M = 172.4$[101], $SD = 3.61$) and maximum ($M = 186.5$[102], $SD = 5.26$) height span was 14 cm.

The informants, on the whole, cared about earlier romance of their prospective partner. They preferred to date men who remained single (66%). Only 28.5 percent did not care whether their prospective partner had or not tied the knot before.

Informants sought a similar educational background in their prospective partners. Three-quarters of the informants looked for candidates with at least a college education. About 10.5

---

101 172.4 cm ≈ 5'7"
102 186.5 cm ≈ 6'11"

percent was OK with a three-year college education though another 3 percent of women emphasized that their prospective partner, ideally, should have at least a master's degree. To 11 percent of these women, the educational level of their future significant other seemed unimportant.

Most informants (87.5%) specified that the man should be working and living in Shanghai, followed by Shanghai and abroad (4%). Others chose Shanghai and its neighboring big cities or other cities in China.

Among the four elements most valued, personality (83%) was the most outstanding for the informants. They cared much less about their significant other's financial ability (2.5%), education (2%) and physical features (1%). Another 11.5 percent did not respond.

The analysis of Love Monologue confirmed that financial security did not seem to be what *shengnv* desired. They also offered little financial security. However, physical and personality attractiveness and sincerity were more desirable (Table 5).

	Yes	No
Seek attractiveness	51.5%	48.5%
Offer attractiveness	52.5%	47.5%
Seek financial security	14.5%	85.5%
Offer financial security	15%	85%
Seek sincerity	57%	43%
Offer sincerity	50.5%	49.5%

Table 5 What *Shengnv* Seek and Offer in Love Monologue

Discussion

Shengnv in the present study tended to emphasize their personality and intelligence rather than physical attractiveness when self-presenting at dating websites. Many of them chose '*qi zhi nv*', '*xiu wai hui zhong*', and '*mei qing mu xiu*' as their self-presentation. All of such tags emanate their elegance, brilliance and charm as a result of their education and knowledge. They preferred to choose chrysanthemum as their avatar, blooming in autumn while most other flowers come out in spring. It symbolizes the character of being unwilling to compete with others and persevering in Chinese culture. Therefore, chrysanthemum is different from the flamboyant peony, figuratively, '*yong rong hua gui*', which was chosen by a fraction of informants.

As a group that has been exposed to higher education and working in foreign enterprises and *Fortune* 500-enlisted companies, *shengnv* presented a combination of traditional virtues of Chinese women and Western influence. Confucian virtues emphasized women's compliance, modesty, and caring for the parents.[103] Many informants in this study selected 'kind-heartedness' and 'filial piety' as their self-tags. Vicky, a participant, wrote in About Me: "Elegant enough to show around to guests and diligent enough to make tasty cuisines; demure as a maiden and agile as a rabbit; gentle and kind; caring and elegant". Rachel said, "To better take care of my parents, men living outside of Shanghai will not be considered". By the same token, informants sought filial piety in their prospective partners. Soul Coffee wrote, "I hope he can [...] show filial piety to his parents. Those who are immature and disrespectful to parents, please stay away from me". A Ning mentioned, "I hope he is filial to his parents, virtuous and aspiring". Some *shengnv* in this study also looked forward to Western lifestyle and taste. They referred to themselves as '*xiao zi nv*', translated from 'petit bourgeoisie', who are office workers for foreign companies with good English proficiency and education, consuming foreign products and enjoying Western art.[104] So it is not surprising that four percent of the informants wished their prospective partner could be either in Shanghai or abroad. Xiaoxiong got her undergraduate education abroad and self-claimed as a Christian. Some key words she used to describe herself were Hong Kong-style milk tea/church/American TV dramas/European and American pop music. She said, "I don't care about his location. But it would be better should he live and work in Shanghai/Zhejiang[105]/Hong Kong/abroad." This again confirmed Farrer's observation that dating a foreigner was an outcome of their cosmopolitan lifestyle.[106] The divergent preference of Shanghai *shengnv* shows Chinese values for women maintain persistent bearing on them. However, global mobility has also expanded the spectrum for their mate selection.

Their educational background and decent jobs enlarged *shengnv*'s horizons and empowered them financially. Maggie worked as a consultant, making more than 20,000 yuan[107] a month. Her self-disclosure was representative. She said, "I spend most time on my work. (But my time is flexible.) After all, dedicating to my career gives me the sense of achievement. Before I settle down with a family of my own, I would love to devote myself to things with output. After all, having sufficient and disposable money is one of the cornerstones of the beautiful future [...] I hope I can have some power of influence in my own field. Of course, I want to be financially free as soon as possible. I will never want to retire. Work is part of life".

Therefore, *shengnv* pursued personality and sincerity more than financial security. Xiaoyou said, "I am not that much materialistic. Don't care much about houses or cars. It will be good

---

103 Meng Li, 'Estrangement: A Possible Lens through Which to Understand the Femininity of Contemporary Chinese Intellectual Women', *Front. Lit. Stud. China* 7.1 (2013): 87-116.

104 Xin Wang, 'Desperately Seeking Status: Political, Social and Cultural Attributes of China's Rising Middle Class', *Modern China Studies* 20.1 (2013): 1-44.

105 A province borders Shanghai to the north.

106 James Farrer, 'Good Stories: Chinese Women's International Love Stories as Cosmopolitan Sexual Politics', *Sexualities* 16.1/2 (2012): 12-29.

107 About 3,200 U.S. dollars.

to make these come true with you. But most importantly, you should be a smart and aspiring man". Ling, who studied and worked abroad before, emphasized, "I prefer independence in thoughts and finance. So I don't want my emotional life to be bothered by materialistic standards. I look for a healthy, easy-going, down-to-earth, and accommodating guy who has the same values as me".

Considering the extensive media coverage and presentation of extra-marital affairs, sense of responsibility and honesty were the most-sought disposition. Some personal profiles also showed the social pressure to *shengnv*. They even used this label for self-reference. Xyxy wrote, "Even though I'm already an aging *shengnv*, nothing can prevent me from showing my love to life. I won't make do with a man easily […] If you are sincere to me, I will reward with sincerity, treating you and your family well". Arrogant Dinosaur asked herself, "How come I become leftovers? But I am a leftover woman now". Jiayuan's investigation about *shengnv* showed that more than half of the women aged 28-33 acknowledged the identity as a leftover woman.[108] Sixty-six percent of shengnv thought this word was neutral and their high education and income exacerbated the likelihood of becoming leftovers.[109]

The pressing need to make themselves married urged these women to emphasize sincerity. Jingjing appealed, "I'm hoping my Mr. Right can show up as soon as possible so that I can complete this task before the end of this year". XX emphasized, "The purpose for registering at Jiayuan is to seek my *yinyuan*.[110] Please do not bother me if you are divorced, widowed, younger than 33, older than 40, just for fun, hitting on girls, or not for getting married". Xiaoxiong said, "Hope GG[111] is as sincere as me, dating for marriage". Such attitudes to online courtship reflects a popular saying in China – falsely believed to be said by Mao – Dating that did not lead to the altar is hooliganism. But the soliloquies also disclose *shengnv*'s desperation for love when they no longer have impending professional or financial concerns and their serious attitude to dating and marriage. Chinese parents tend to urge their children to work hard during their school years, especially those high-achieving students. Unlike their American counterparts, who start dating as teenagers, people who study hard in China usually devote too much time to their school work. When they are out of college, their parents then press them to be married. When they reach the 'leftover' age, the need to be married, from parents and society, becomes more intense.

Living and working in China's largest city, these Shanghainese women showed unique preference to Shanghai native men. They either used "I'm a Shanghainese" as the opening remark of their profiles or specified that "Please do not bother if you are not a native of Shang-

---

108 Jiayuan.com, *Zhongguo Nannv Hunlianguan Xilie Diaocha: 2012nian Diyi Jidu Zhi Shengnv De Zibaishu* (Chinese Men and Women's Attitude toward Marriage and Love Serial Investigation: Q1 2012 The Confession of *Shengnv*), 8 March 2012, http://dl.jiayuan.com/doc/marriage/_views/2012Q13SConfession.pdf.
109 Jiayuan.com, *Zhongguo Nannv Hunlianguan Xilie Diaocha: 2012nian Diyi Jidu Zhi Shengnv De Zibaishu.*
110 A Chinese term for love and marriage 姻缘, rhyming with Jiayuan 佳, the name of the dating website.
111 Acronym for *gege*, or elder brother, often used to refer to a young man or as a way to address an elder male lover with endearment by young women in online discourse.

hai". Emily explained that she was hoping her future significant other could speak Shanghai dialect and be immersed into Shanghai culture. Yueming said, "I'm an obedient Shanghai girl [...] For the sake of having the same lifestyle, I prefer guys born and brought up in Shanghai. If not, please do not bother me. Thanks". The survey about love stories in four metropolises showed that 73.2 percent of Shanghainese hoped their significant other could be a native of Shanghai, too.[112] In the present study, the percentage was even higher.

Conclusion

This study about the self-presentation and mate-selection criteria of leftover Shanghainese women shows that traditional Chinese culture still influences modern Chinese women. Shanghai, a global city and China's largest metropolitan area, also affects the mate selection of these women. Good education, decent income and social pressures all encourage Shanghai *shengnv* to pursue sincerity disposition rather than financial security in online courtship.

Future research may explore differences in personal profiles of Chinese women of all ages at online dating sites since they were brought up in different historical eras in which China transformed from a socialist, planned-economy and Confucian society into a consumerism-dominated, economically robust powerhouse. The change of values brought by the social upheaval may affect Chinese women's self-presentation and mate-selection criteria, and warrants more study. *Shengnv* accounts for only a small percentage of all Chinese women. Media coverage, especially by Western press, has drawn more attention to this social group. However, Chinese women who have migrated to urban areas to make a living should be studied as well. Their rigid and long work schedules, limited social capital in cities and less-competent digital literacy make the courtship of migrant women merit further research.

References

Alavi, Masoumeh, Alahdad, Rezvan and Shafeq, Syed Mohamed. 'Mate Selection Criteria among Postgraduate Students in Malaysia', *Procedia - Social and Behavioral Sciences* 116 (2014): 5075 – 5080.

Baihe.com, '*2011 Zhongguoren Hunlian Baogao* (A Report on Chinese People's Love and Marriage, 2011),' 5 January 2012, http://media.baihe.com/html/71/n-871.html

Blau, Peter Michael. *Exchange and Power in Social Life*, New York: Wiley, 1964.

Brook, Mark. 'How Has Internet Dating Changed Society? An Insider's Look', *IDEA*, January 2011, 1-33.

Buss, David M. 'Sex Differences in Human Mate Preferences: Evolutionary Hypotheses Tested in 37 Cultures', *Behavioral and Brain Sciences* 12.1 (1989): 1-49.

Buss, David M. and Shackelford, Todd K. 'Attractive Women Want It All: Good Genes, Economic Investment, Parenting Proclivities, and Emotional Commitment', *Evolutionary Psychology* 6.1 (2008): 134-146.

Buunk, Bram P., Dijkstra, Pieternel, Fetchenhauer, Detlef and Kenrick, Douglas T. 'Age and Gender Differences in Mate Selection Criteria for Various Involvement Levels', *Personal Relationships* 9.3 (2002): 271-278.

Chen, Shengli and Zhang, Shikun. *Dangdai Zeou Yu Shengyu Yiyuan Yanjiu: 2002 Nian Chengxiang*

---

112 Xinwen Chenbao. '*Beishangguangshen De Hunlian Gushi: Waidiren Renwei Lianai Jiu Wei Jiehun* (Marriage and Love Stories in Beijing, Shanghai, Canton and Shenzhen: Immigrants Believe Dating is just for Marriage)', 23 January 2013, http://news.xinhuanet.com/fortune/2013-01/23/c_124269355.htm.

Juming Shengyu Yiyuan Diaocha (Contemporary Expectations on Mate Selection and Child Rearing: An Investigation on Desires and Plans for Marriage and Child Rearing among Urban and Rural Residents in 2002), Beijing: China Population Press, 2002.

Cheng, Yuan, Han, Xuehui and Dagsvik, John K. 'Marriage Pattern in the City of Shanghai: Behavioral Two-sex Model and Multistage Marriage Life Table Approach', *Chinese Sociology and Anthropology* 43.4 (Summer 2011): 74-95.

Deaux, Kay and Hanna, Randel. 'Courtship in the Persona Column: The Influence of Gender and Sexual Orientation', *Sex Roles* 11. 5/6 (1984): 363-375.

Dominick, Joseph R. 'Who Do You Think You Are? Personal Home Pages and Self-Presentation on the World Wide Web', *Journalism & Mass Communication Quarterly* 76.4 (1999): 646-658, p. 647.

eChinacities.com, 'Love and Marriage in Modern China: Survey Reveals Latest Trend', 30 December 2012, http://www.echinacities.com/china-media/Love-and-Marriage-in-Modern-China-Survey-Reveals-Latest-Trends.

Ellison, Nicole, Heino, Rebecca and Gibbs, Jennifer. 'Managing Impressions Online: Self-Presentation Processes in the Online Dating Environment', *Journal of Computer-Mediated Communication* 11.2 (2006): 415-441. doi:10.1111/j.1083-6101.2006.00020.x

Emerson, Richard M. 'Social Exchange Theory', Annual Review of Sociology 2 (1976): 335-362, http://www.communicationcache.com/uploads/1/0/8/8/10887248/social_exchange_theory_-_1976.pdf.

Farrer, James. 'Good Stories: Chinese Women's International Love Stories as Cosmopolitan Sexual Politics', *Sexualities* 16.1/2 (2012): 12-29.

Finkel, Eli J., Eastwick, Paul W., Karney, Benjamin R., Reis, Harry T. and Sprecher, Susan. 'Online Dating: A Critical Analysis from the Perspective of Psychological Science', Psychological Science in the Public Interest 13.1 (January, 2012): 3-66, http://psi.sagepub.com/content/13/1/3.full?ijkey=cK9EB6/4zQ0AM&keytype=ref&siteid=sppsi.

Giddens, Antony. *The Transformation of Intimacy: Sexuality, Love and Eroticism in Modern Societies*, Stanford, CA: Stanford University Press, 1992, p.53.

Goffman, Ervin. *The Presentation of Self in Everyday Life*, New York: Anchor, 1959, p.67.

Gonzales, Marti Hope and Meyers, Sarah A. '"Your Mother Would Like Me": Self-Presentation in the Personals Ads of Heterosexual and Homosexual Men and Women', *Personality and Social Psychology Bulletin* 19.2 (April 1993): 131-142.

Ha, Thao, van den Berg, Judith E. M., Engels, Rutger C. M. E. and Lichtwarck-Aschoff, Anna. 'Effects of Attractiveness and Status in Dating Desire in Homosexual and Heterosexual Men and Women', *Archives of Sexual Behavior* 41.3 (June 2012): 673-682.

Hancock, Jeffrey T., Toma, Catalina and Ellison, Nicole. 'The Truth about Lying in Online Dating Profiles', CHI 2007 Proceedings • Online Representation of Self 28 April - 3 May 2007, San Jose, CA, USA, https://www.msu.edu/\~nellison/hancock_et_al_2007.pdf.

Harrison, Albert A. and Saeed, Laila. 'Let's Make a Deal: An Analysis of Revelations and Stipulations in Lonely Hearts Advertisements', *Journal of Personality and Social Psychology* 35.4 (1997): 257-264.

Henry, Jermaine, Helm Jr., Herbert W. and Cruz, Natasha. 'Mate Selection: Gender and Generational Differences', *North American Journal of Psychology* 15.1 (2013): 63-70.

Hill Jr., Reuben Lorenzo. 'Campus Values in Mate Selection', *Journal of Home Economics*, 37.9 (1945): 554–558.

Hunt, Katie. 'Glut of Women at Shanghai's Marriage Market', 3 November 2013, http://www.cnn.com/2013/11/03/world/asia/shanghai-marriage-market/.

iResearch Consulting Group. '*Zhongguo Wangluo Hunlian Hangye Baogao: 2013-2014* (China Online

Personals Industry Report: 2013-2014', http://report.iresearch.cn/2106.html.

Jiayuan.com, '*Zhongguo Nannv Hunlianguan Xilie Diaocha: 2012nian Diyi Jidu Zhi Shengnv De Zibaishu* (Chinese Men and Women's Attitude toward Marriage and Love Serial Investigation: Q1 2012 The Confession of *Shengnv*)', 8 March 2012, http://dl.jiayuan.com/doc/marriage_views/2012Q13SConfession.pdf.

Koestner, Richard and Wheeler, Ladd. 'Self-Presentation in Personal Advertisements: The Influence of Implicit Notions of Attraction and Role Expectations', *Journal of Social and Personal Relationships* 5 (1998): 149-160.

Lake, Roseann. 'All the Shengnu Ladies', 11 March 2012, http://www.salon.com/2012/03/12/all_the_shengnu_ladies/.

Lance, Larry. 'Gender Differences in Heterosexual Dating: A Content Analysis of Personal Ads', *Journal of Men's Studies* 6.3 (Spring 1998): 297-305.

Larson, Christian 'China's 'Leftover Ladies' Are Anything But', Bloomberg Businessweek, 23 August 2012, http://www.businessweek.com/articles/2012-08-22/chinas-leftover-ladies-are-anything-but.

Li, Meng. 'Estrangement: A Possible Lens through Which to Understand the Femininity of Contemporary Chinese Intellectual Women', *Front. Lit. Stud. China* 7.1 (2013): 87-116.

Li, Yinhe. Sex and Marriage of the Chinese People (*Zhongguoren De Xing'ai Yu Hunyin*), Zhengzhou: Henan People's Publishing House, 1996, http://v.book.ifeng.com/book/ts/32678/2605023.htm.

Lin, Xu. 'Top 10 Provinces with the Highest Quality in 2013', 13 March 2014, http://www.china.org.cn/top10/2014-03/13/content_31769827_10.htm.

Makinen, Julie and Lee, Don. 'China's *Shengnu*, or 'Leftover Women,' Face Intense Pressure to Marry', 13 July 2013, http://articles.latimes.com/2013/jul/13/world/la-fg-china-leftover-women-20130714.

Min-G, Yao. 'Family Pressure Forces Marriage with *Laowai*', Shanghai Daily, 30 May 2013, http://www.shanghaidaily.com/Opinion/chinese-perspectives/Family-pressure-forces-marriage-with-laowai/shdaily.shtml.

Nakonezny, Paul A. and Denton, Wayne H. 'Marital Relationships: A Social Exchange Theory Perspective', *The American Journal of Family Therapy* 36 (2008): 402–412.

National Bureau of Statistics of China. 'Communiqué of the National Bureau of Statistics of the People's Republic of China on Major Figures of the 2010 Population Census (No. 2)', 29 April 2011, http://www.stats.gov.cn/tjsj/tjgb/rkpcgb/qgrkpcgb/201104/t20110429_30328.html

_____. 'Communiqué of the National Bureau of Statistics of the People's Republic of China on Shanghai City of the 2010 Population Census', 28 February 2012, http://www.stats.gov.cn/tjsj/tjgb/rkpcgb/dfrkpcgb/201202/t20120228_30403.html.

Neuendorf, Kimberly A. *The Content Analysis Guidebook*, Thousand Oaks, CA: Sage, 2002.

Osnos, Evan. 'The Love Business', The New Yorker, 14 May 2012, 88.13, http://www.newyorker.com/reporting/2012/05/14/120514fa_fact_osnos.

Schwarz, Sascha and Hassebrauck, Manfred. 'Sex and Age Differences in Mate-Selection Preferences', *Human Nature* 23.4 (2012): 447-466.

Sebag-Montefiore, Clarissa. 'Romance with Chinese Characteristics', 21 August 2012, http://latitude.blogs.nytimes.com/2012/08/21/romance-with-chinese-characteristics/?_php=true&_type=blogs&_r=0.

Tian, Qian. *A study of Chinese Women's Mate Selection Trends: An Interpretation Based on Evolutionary Psychology (Zhongguo nvxing zeou qingxiang yanjiu: jiyu jinhua xinlixue de jieshi)*,Ph.D. diss., 2012.

To, Sandy. 'Understanding Sheng Nu ("Leftover Women"): The Phenomenon of Late Marriage among Chinese Professional Women', *Symbolic Interaction* 36.1 (2013): 1-20.

Van Straaten, Ischa, Engels, Rutger C. M. E., Finkenauer, Catrin and Holland, Rob W. 'Sex Differences in Short-term Mate Preferences and Behavioral Mimicry: A Semi-Naturalistic Experiment', *Archives of Sexual Behavior* 37.6 (2008): 902-911.

Walther, Joseph B. 'Computer-Mediated Communication: Impersonal, Interpersonal, and Hyperpersonal Interaction', *Communication Research* 23.1 (February 1996): 3-43.

Wang, Xin. 'Desperately Seeking Status: Political, Social and Cultural Attributes of China's Rising Middle Class', *Modern China Studies* 20.1 (2013): 1-44.

Wei, Yan; Jiang, Quanbao and Basten, Stuart. 'Observing the Transformation of China's First Marriage Pattern through Net Nuptiality Tables: 1982-2010', *Finnish Yearbook of Population Research* XLVIII 2013, 65-75.

Whitty, Monica T. and Carr, Adrian. *Cyberspace Romance: The Psychology of Online Relationships*, New York, NY: Palgrave Macmillan, 2006.

Xinhua Net, '*Jiedu 2010 Nian Zhongguoren Hunlian Zhuangkuang Baodao* (Reading and Understanding Chinese People's Love and Marriage Report 2010)', 15 December 2010, http://news.xinhuanet.com/society/2010-12/15/c_13650287_2.htm.

Xinwen Chenbao. '*Beishangguangshen De Hunlian Gushi: Waidiren Renwei Lianai Jiu Wei Jiehun* (Marriage and Love Stories in Beijing, Shanghai, Canton and Shenzhen: Immigrants Believe Dating is just for Marriage)', 23 January 2013, http://news.xinhuanet.com/fortune/2013-01/23/c_124269355.htm.

Yang, Renxin. 'Between Traditionalism and Modernity: Changing Values on Dating Behavior and Mate Selection Criteria', *International Review of Modern Sociology* 37.2 (2011): 265-287.

KEEPING IT UNREAL:
ONLINE DATING WITH CHINESE CHARACTERISTICS

YANN-LING CHIN

The success of *The First Intimate Contact*, a novel written by Taiwanese student Cai Zhiheng in 1998, created a frenzy about online romance in China. Many envisaged the romantic experience of meeting a loved one online just as depicted in the novel. Though the hype surrounding online romance may have dissipated, the practice has certainly not gone out of fashion. As the country with the largest Internet population in the world, dating somebody online has become a mainstream mode of courtship for many Chinese, similar to Internet users in the West. In fact, existing studies suggest that Chinese Internet users embrace social media more extensively than their Western counterparts. For example, according to business consultant group, BCG's press release dated 12 April 2012, 79 percent of Chinese used instant messages (IM) compared with 21 percent of U.S. Internet users.[1] *Sina Weibo*, the most popular microblogging service provider boasted 300 million registered users by the end of 2011 in less than three years of operation,[2] compared with Twitter which has operated since 2006 and is reported to have 100 million users as of September 2011.[3] The results of an online survey involving Chinese and American youths showed that the Internet was much more appreciated in China than in America.[4] For instance, 77 percent of the 1,104 Chinese participants agreed with the statement "the Internet helps me make friends", compared to only 30 percent of the 1,079 American participants. The study also showed that 66 percent of the Chinese surveyed thought that online interactions had broadened their sense of identity only 26 percent of American respondents reported to have this benefit.

Yet despite China's exponential growth of its Internet population and enthusiastic embrace of social media, our understandings of online relationships are mostly limited to studies based in the Western context. The development of the information and communication (ICT) industry in China is even more astounding if we take into the consideration of stringent state control, monitoring and information censorship. My research into China's online dating scene has revealed culturally unique understandings and practices of online romance, reflecting the impact of the country's on-going socio-cultural transformations.

Since the economic reforms in the late 1970s, the state loosened it controls on labor, capital and commodities markets to stimulate growth. Individuals were liberated not only to pursue their own economic activities, but also to reclaim their private life from the control of the

---

1 Boston Consulting Group (BCG), Online Retail Sales in China will Triple to More than $360 Million by 2015, as the Internet Adds Nearly 200 Million Users, 12 April 2012, http://www.bcg.com/media/PressReleaseDetails.aspx?id=tcm:12-103641.

2 Xinhua, *Xinlang Weibo Zhuce Yonghu Tupo Sanyi, Meiri Faboliang Chaoguo Yiyitiao* (Sina Weibo has More 300 Million Registered Users, More than 100 Million Weibo are Posted Everyday), 29 February 2012, http://news.xinhuanet.com/tech/2012-02/29/c_122769084.htm.

3 Twitter Blog, One Hundred Million Voices, 8 September 2011, http://blog.twitter.com/2011/09/one-hundred-million-voices.html.

4 IAC and JWT, China Leads the US in Digital Self-expression, 22 November 2007, http://iac.com/media-room/press-releases/china-leads-us-digital-self-expression.

party-state and parental authority. The new culture of courtship and marriage that emerged as a result of state sponsored structural changes emphasizing freedom of love and material comfort is at odds with the old ideal of romantic love founded on feelings and emotional satisfaction.[5] The relentless pursuit of materialism and economic growth has rendered many feeling bewildered and with a strong sense of emotional emptiness. My study shows that many Chinese are increasingly turning to relationships online to satisfy their unfulfilled emotional needs.

The following discussion is based on the findings of my online participant observations in *Love Apartment*, a relationship site, *Renren*, China's equivalent of Facebook, and the *Tianya* bulletin board system. The online participant observations took place for 10 months beginning from May 2009. Love Apartment was chosen because of its unique game-like appeal.[6] *Renren* is the ideal site to observe the online interactions of Chinese Internet users, especially among students. Tianya has several discussion forums dedicated to relationships, including online romance. This is where personal stories of online romance, concerns, problems encountered, and others' opinions towards online romance can be heard and shared. For ethical reasons, my identity as a researcher was made explicit in my profile on these sites and was stated upfront to all users with whom I came into contact. The analysis of participants' views on online romance suggested that there were three ways in which Chinese Internet users conceptualized online romance. I referred to the three categories as 'pragmatic fantasists', 'romantic realists' and 'sceptics', each holding different attitudes towards online romance. Participants' quotes in my discussion are credited to the authors' user names on the site. I also relied on my participants' narratives of their online romance to elucidate these categories and how their different experiences demonstrated the diverse social potentials of online romance.

All data collected were originally in Chinese. My role as both researcher and translator may have ensured greater transparency and consistency, but translation is more than a technical issue of transferring meanings from one language to another. Translation decisions have epistemological and ontological implications.[7] My translation added another layer of meanings, despite my desire to feature participants' own voices more prominently and allow readers an active role in interpreting the original messages. Following Birbili's advice, to best represent participants' words, in my translation, the structure, tone and style of participants are preserved as closely as possible, but not to the extent where word-by-word translation would seriously invalidate English grammar and risk distorting the meanings and undermin-

---

5   James Farrer, Opening Up: Youth Sex Culture and Market Reform in Shanghai, Chicago: University Chicago Press, 2002.

6   *Love Apartment* allows members to play the game of online cohabitation. The homepage of each member is presented as a virtual room with his/her avatar residing in the room. Members can furnish and decorate their virtual room, dress up their avatar with fashion items using virtual currency that can be bought with real money. Members can invite either a same-sex or cross-sex member for 'cohabitation'. Should the invitation be accepted, the two avatars would appear in the same room, usually standing next to one another.

7   Bogusia Temple and Alys Young, 'Qualitative Research and Translation Dilemmas', Qualitative Research 4.2 (2004): 161-178.

ing readability.[8] In other words, minor grammatical error is tolerated and since I prioritize semantic equivalence over structure, I occasionally rearrange sentence sequence if it helps to better convey participants' meanings in English.

In this chapter, I will also introduce 'Platonic emotional love' and 'play', the two keywords in Chinese discourse of online romance. I will examine the theoretical underpinnings of these two words and how they relate to the three categories. This chapter begins by exploring the meanings of online romance in China. My study shows that there is a conceptual ambiguity associated with the term 'online romance' and this has resulted in confusion among Chinese Internet users.

Meanings of *Wanglian* (Online Romance)

Although the term *wanglian* is frequently used, its precise meaning varies and contains ambiguity to all Chinese. Some of my participants referred it to romantic relationships initiated online and gradually expanded into the offline world, maybe even cumulating into long-term relationships or marriage. But substantial numbers of Chinese Internet users also understand online romance as the act of romancing online, or referring to exclusively Internet-based relationships. By definition, *wang* means net and *lian* refers to love. Online romance would, indeed, imply romantic relationships happening and confined within cyberspace. Some users were confused. For instance, Zhang Caiyuan wrote on the forum at *Renren*,

> I think I have a misconception of online romance. Online romance is a romantic relationship taking place online without any offline interactions. I met her online, but our relationship developed in the offline world, I think strictly speaking, it cannot be categorized as online romance. This is a very ambiguous concept.

Similarly, when discussing if online romance could become an offline reality at *Tianya* forum, Jipingliuer replied that "I think online romance is not the same as turning an online acquaintance into a courtship partner." The answer suggests that the user thinks the two are different romantic experiences that should not be conflated. Other nuanced differences that cause confusion include whether online romance applies to romantic relationships that developed only after face-to-face meetings, and amorous affiliations developed online between partners who were first introduced by an offline friend. For example,

> I met my current partner through a colleague's recommendation. We first contacted each other online and because of the distance, we rely on the Internet to keep in touch. I am not sure whether this counts as online romance or not (Nakai).

In short, *wanglian* does not denote a single homogeneous type of computer-mediated relationship. Its contestable meanings have led to different implications depending on the way the term is used.

---

8   Maria Birbili, 'Translating from One Language to Another', Social Research Update 31 (2000), http://sru.soc.surrey.ac.uk/SRU31.html.

For the purpose of this study, I will focus on the two main types of online romance as defined by a Chinese scholar in his theoretical discussion of online romance.[9] The first is romantic relationships that exist exclusively online in which couples refrain from having any offline contacts with each other. The second is relationships that rely on the Internet merely as a tool for communication in which couples first meet online but gradually expand their relationship into the offline world. These relationships are ultimately not very much different from conventional courtship. A similar definition was also used in research of online romance involving 4,811 students across nine provinces in China.[10] In the report, online romance is defined as Internet initiated relationships that flourish into romantic bonds, remaining either exclusively online or materializing into the offline world. The definition provided in Chinese literature nevertheless seems to emphasize the presence of romantic sentiment prior to any offline interactions. In other words, in the Chinese definition, couples that meet online but only become romantically involved after meeting in person and spending time together offline would not be considered as online romance.

The definition of online romance in China intrigues me because Western literature on online romantic relationships is concerned mostly with only the second type. For instance, Merkle and Richardson highlighted how online relationships develop through an inverted sequence that eventually leads to face-to-face meetings;[11] McKenna, Green and Gleason conducted a path analysis to explore the sequence of moving online relationships offline;[12] Baker defined successful online relationships as those that cumulate into long-term courtship, cohabitation or marriage in the actual world.[13] I once came across a personal advertisement in a *Tianya* online romance forum, dated 15 September 2009, from a male aged 22, specifying that he was looking for a strictly online romantic relationship, precluding any face-to-face interactions. This may seem almost inconceivable in the West, but is rather common among Chinese Internet users. An online survey involving Chinese and American youths showed that 61 percent of the former said they had a parallel life online, compared to only 13 percent of the latter. In fact, 63 percent of Chinese participants agreed with the statement that "it is perfectly possible to have real relationships purely online with no face-to-face contact" compared to only 21 percent of Americans.[14] Chinese Internet users' tendency to demarcate the online and the offline world, and their motivations for doing so, appeared to me as a culturally

---

9   Jianpeng Zeng, *Xuni Yu Xianshi: Dui 'Wanglian' Xianxiang de Lilun Fenxi* (Virtuality and Reality: A Theoretical Analysis of Online Romance), Chinese Academy of Social Science, 23 December 2004, http://www.sociology.cass.net.cn/shxw/qsnyj/t20041223_4103.htm.

10 Xiaohong Wei, Caili Li, Min Lu, and Bing Peng, *Diaocha Cheng: 87% de Shoufang Daxuesheng Renwei Wanglian Shi Manzu Qinggan Xuyao de Yizhong Fangshi* (Survey showed that 87% of the university students interviewed think online romance is a means to satisfy emotional needs). China Youth Online, 27 December 2007, http://zqb.cyol.com/content/2007-12/27/content_2011436.htm.

11 Erich R. Merkle and Rhonda A. Richardson, 'Digital Dating and Virtual Relating: Conceptualizing Computer Mediated Romantic Relationships', Journal of Family Relations 49.2 (2000): 187-192.

12 Katelyn Y.A. McKenna, Amie S. Green and Marci E.J. Gleason, 'Relationship Formation on the Internet: What's the Big Attraction?', Journal of Social Issues 58 (2002): 9-31.

13 Andrea Baker, 'What Makes an Online Relationship Successful? Clues from Couples Who Met in Cyberspace', CyberPsychology & Behavior 5.4 (2002): 363-375.

14 IAC and JWT, China Leads the US in Digital Self-expression, 22 November 2007, http://iac.com/media-room/press-releases/china-leads-us-digital-self-expression .

distinct phenomenon.

This is not to say that exclusively Internet-based relationships do not exist in the West, or all Western online daters desire to move their relationship offline, it does, however, show that this type of relationship is not on top of Western scholars' agenda, presumably because it is perceived, rightly or wrongly, to be insignificant or impossible. For example, Ben-Ze'ev argues that 'profound online only romantic relationships' are transitional and unsustainable because without embodied interactions offline, these relationships are incomplete.[15] His underlying assumption is that people typically want to expand the relationship offline, but this does not apply to all Chinese Internet users as some of them make their choice to confine their romantic liaisons online. The 'incompleteness' is actually desirable for them, because by confining it within cyberspace, the effectiveness of the relationship to fulfil couples' emotional needs is enhanced, yet without creating many complications in their everyday life. This group of individuals is what I referred to as 'pragmatist fantasists', who tend to understand online romance as a kind of 'Platonic emotional love'. To fully understand the motivations of pragmatist fantasists, we need to first examine the notion of Platonic emotional love as used in the context of Chinese online discourse.

Platonic Emotional Love

'Platonic love' is often used interchangeably, or sometimes together, with 'emotional love' to refer to exclusively Internet-based romantic relationships with a strong emphasis on emotional gratification. During my participant observations, I regularly came across participants talking about how online romance could provide emotional solace (*jingshen weiji*) to lovers that would help to rejuvenate their worn-out self.

> Online romance, even if you can't be together, you can, at least, enjoy the illusionary quality, the purest emotional love. Even if heartbreaking, it is still a wonderful and unforgettable [experience] (Luohuarumeng).

> Most people's everyday life is full of regrets and adversities, and the dull daily routine makes everyone crave for excitement. In the real world, too many worries and inhibitions make it difficult to relieve tension. The Internet can satisfy these needs and stir people's imagination. Albeit just virtually, it is a way to relieve tension. People can then get on with their study or work when back to the real world. Online romance is the emotional supplement [that invigorates] the everyday life (Jimogaoshou).

> Life is full of frustrations. Unable to find what you wish for in real life, then the Internet is the best you can count on... Nothing wrong with going online to unwind and readjust your emotion. So moderate online romance is actually good [for the individuals] (Xueshangfeier).

The last two arguments are underpinned by a utilitarian attitude to strategically make use of online romance to promote lovers' psychological wellbeing. It reflects the pervasive ther-

---

15   Aaron Ben-Ze'ev, Love Online: Emotions on the Internet, Cambridge: Cambridge University Press, 2004, p.131.

apeutic ethos of contemporary society, in which emotional life, as pointed out by Illouz, is "in need of management and control and on regulating it under the incessantly expanding ideal of health."[16] Achieving emotional competence, "namely self-awareness, the ability to identify their feelings, talk about them, empathize with each other's position and find solutions to a problem", becomes imperative to success in both public and private lives.[17] Online relationships are particularly good at helping participants to develop their emotional competence as the performance of intimacy online relies on constant verbalization and exchange of private inner feelings. Nevertheless, not all online daters are content with mere emotional interactions, yet their physical separation makes regular corporeal interactions difficult.

> The warmest of online love you can hope for is in the form of text, at best the voice of the lover. When in trouble or feeling upset, emotional support is what you can get … there isn't a shoulder for you to lean on … no open arms to comfort you. When you needed him/her the most, you might not be able to get hold of him/her, like a loose kite flying on the sky… (Fanfan).

Describing online romance as largely an emotional affair excluding actual bodily interaction coincides with the way some Chinese Internet users understand online romance as romancing exclusively online. Although the relationship can be extended to the offline world, ideally, it should be confined within cyberspace for safety, moral and practical reasons.

> Online romance should only be online. It cannot be extended to real life. The Internet is a virtual world, people you meet online are not the same person offline. You can't be sure of his/her character, life or family circumstances. Therefore, it is alright to have online romance, but you can't transfer the relationship offline (Hongsexianrenqiu).

> In cyberspace, emotions become even more crucial. Social interactions seem much purer. Romancing online, everything turns illusory yet wonderful, like a fairy, untouched by worldly concerns… If everything stopped here, it would be fabulous (Stefanie).

> Online romance is largely about emotional solace; it brings emotional support and happiness but when the relationship grows deeper and becomes an offline reality, everything will not be the same (Fanfan).

> Online romance literally means romantic relationship online. So what can you rely on to maintain the relationship? Occasionally seeing each other using webcam? Getting intimate through the keyboard? Sometimes online romance indeed provides us a unique feeling, a sense of emotional comfort, but… (Ermodang).

'Platonic emotional love' is frequently used to refer to these exclusively Internet-based romantic relationships because of the absence of actual bodily interactions between the dyads. For example, Internet user Maio Chenlin wrote, "Platonic love ~ ~ very much the theory of online romance ~ ~ ~ ~", while Zhe said, "online romance is the legendary Platonic love. If you

---

16   Eva Illouz, Cold Intimacies: The Making of Emotional Capitalism, Cambridge: Polity, 2007, p.63.
17   Ibid, p.69.

wish for true love ... arrange a meeting with the loved one in the real world." Similarly, another Internet user, Keerhu argued against using the Internet to pursue 'Platonic-style emotion love' as he considered it wrong to exclude corporeal interactions in a relationship.

Some online daters choose to partake in 'Platonic love', by which I mean they have no intention or desire to expand the relationship offline and are content with the relationship's mere online existence. Others reluctantly become Platonic online daters as they are either unable to overcome the physical distance that separates them or to defy the social norms that discourage their amorous liaison. Despite their longing for corporeal intimacy, this latter group of online daters unwillingly accept that their relationship cannot goes offline. As they call themselves Platonic lovers, they unintentionally broaden the meaning of Platonic love to include also relationships with erotic impulses which regrettably cannot be consumed. In other words, *Platonic*[18] love used in Chinese discourses of online romance refers to emotional love without physical interactions, but might not necessary preclude sexual desire.

Those pursuing *Platonic* online romance by choice seem to approach their relationship strategically for self-gratification. They rely on this relationship for the excitement or distractions needed to spice up their banal everyday life, satisfy their unfulfilled emotional needs, and provide solace in the face of life's adversities. They carefully demarcate the online and offline world to limit the negative impacts their online activities may have on their offline life and show no sign of confusing the two. There is a clear priority put on the offline reality and they utilize their online relationship to improve the quality of their daily life. They are, therefore, content with the disembodied presence of their lover in the virtual world, motivated not by physical intimacy. Calling their online romance *Platonic* love not only conveys a sense of lofty spiritual love unsullied by carnal lust, it also softens the image of a cheating partner as a mere online emotional liaison is allegedly innocuous. Although there are also *Platonic* online daters who genuinely appreciate the coming together of the two minds, and treasure the deep emotional bonds that developed as a result of their regular mutual self-disclosure, most express a rather practical attitude towards online romance. For instance,

> Life pressure in contemporary society is enormous. There is nothing wrong with using online romance to rejuvenate one's life. Many people's family life is not perfect anyway. Chatting with several boyfriends and girlfriends online doesn't make it worse. It can perhaps even improve the family relations (Wodeaizaoyibuzai).

> Family life is tedious and boring, but most people refuse to be content with the prosaic life. Everyone is longing to re-experience passion and romantic love, and inject new exciting elements into life, but there is a heavy price to pay for infidelity... Online romance easily fulfils this emotional void... (Baobeibuku)

In the post-Mao China, Marxist ideologies and class struggle no longer dominate the political discourse and are replaced by pragmatism, which also becoming the guiding philosophy of the society.[19] Deng once said that "it doesn't matter whether a cat is white or black, as long

---

18   In the rest of the chapter, I will use italic to emphasize this ironic use of the word 'Platonic'.
19   Elaine Jeffreys and Gary Sigley, 'Governmentality, Governance and China', in Elaine Jeffreys (ed.) China's

as it catches mice" to make the argument that socialism is not strictly defined by a planned economy, and a market economy can also serve the socialist state to promote growth and improve the living standards of the people.[20] As the nation embraced the late Deng's exhortation that "to get rich is glorious", this has had profound implications on the society as most people adopted an instrumental approach in their everyday life. Compounded with the party-state's ideological commitment to atheism, many in the society experienced a sense of moral vacuum, emotional emptiness and spiritual bankruptcy.[21] Furthermore, since the market reforms, individuals have been told to take greater personal responsibilities in life as the state withdraws the social supports that once catered for each individual from the cradle to the grave.[22] Yet the development of individualization in China is curtailed by the absence of a democratic culture and welfare system to protect and support individuals.[23] The lack of constitutional protection and social support render life in contemporary post-socialist Chinese society highly competitive and stressful for many ordinary people. This explains the motivation of pragmatist fantasists who strategically make use of online relationships to romanticize their everyday life and as a means to seek emotional comfort. In the following section, I will elucidate the practice of pragmatist fantasist through the story of one of my participants.

The Pragmatist Fantasist

Online romance presents pragmatic fantasists the opportunity to re-experience the stereotypical romantic love, or at least the fantasy of it. This can be seen in the way many online daters describe the experience of being engulfed by the flame of passionate love beyond their rational control. The outpouring heightened emotions have a mysterious self-transforming and transcendental quality. It allows lovers to put aside all worldly concerns, such as money, status, background differences, social norms, and concentrate only on their innermost feelings with the ideal lover. These feelings of stereotypical romantic love also provide pragmatic fantasists with the therapeutic function of distraction away from the miseries felt in everyday life and through the constant practice of 'disclosing intimacy' online,[24] they also come closer to being a self-reflexive subject. Therefore, they treat online romance as an effective means to the end of self-help and improvement.

Despite the romantic undertone, couples engaging in this type of online relationship may not necessarily consider their relationship a serious romance. Often, they are regarded as flexible, contingent and open forms of emotional relationship, not always motivated by sexual desire. Although some participants may have longing for physical intimacy with their partner, this desire is usually not acted upon. The decision not to have anything to do with each other offline is made for several reasons. Firstly, to limit the online relationship's potentially

---

    Governmentalities: Governing Change, Changing Government, New York: Routledge, 2009, pp. 1-23.
20   Ibid, p.8.
21   Yuezhi Zhao, 'After Mobile Phones, What? Re-embedding the Social in China's "Digital Revolution"', International Journal of Communication 1 (2007): 92-120.
22   Yunxiang Yan, The Individualization of Chinese Society, Oxford; New York: Berg, 2009.
23   Ulrich Beck and Elisabeth Beck-Gernsheim, 'Foreword: Varieties of Individualization', in Mette H. Hansen and Rune Svarverud (eds) iChina: The Rise of the Individual in Modern Chinese Society, Copenhagen: NIAS Press, 2010, pp. xiii-xx.
24   Lynn Jamieson, Intimacy: Personal Relationships in Modern Societies, Oxford: Polity, 1998.

negative impact on the primary relationship or family life offline; secondly, to help sustain its magical quality that is crucial to invigorate their tedious everyday life and make them feel rejuvenated. The kind of relationship they desire, in fact, thrives in the virtual enclosure because its distance from reality is crucial for the relationship to fulfil its therapeutic function of self-discovery and romanticizing everyday life. In other words, pragmatic fantasists pursue largely *Platonic* emotional love. The nature of relationships of this kind is akin to Giddens' notion of pure relationship, the self-gratifying relationship.[25] The relationship is 'pure' because it is no longer organized by the network of kinship and community, but driven by the reflexive self, and it is continued so long as it is fulfilling to the individuals involved.

Giddens' pure relationship is in practice difficult to achieve or possible only among the privileged. In China, despite the emergence of a nouveau riche and growing middle class, making ends meet is still the daily preoccupation of the majority. The high cost of marriage, the social anxiety of being single, family responsibilities and reputation give many no liberty to walk out regardless of how dissatisfied they are with their relationship. It is only within cyberspace that many have the opportunity to experience the therapeutic self-satisfying pure relationship based on equality of emotional exchanges. Acting as a release valve, online romance provides feelings of being understood, happiness, gratification, hope and intimacy, hence hard-pressed Chinese feel invigorated when they go back to the reality of everyday life. Some of them may occasionally be tempted to cross the online and offline boundaries. However, such boundary crossing does not serve their purposes of seeking emotional sustenance and distraction, and thus, reaffirm the distinction between the two realms.

AZ (not real name) is one of my participants who, like so many other pragmatist fantasists, turned to online romance for solace, emotional support and self-experimentation. He is a married school teacher I met on *Love Apartment*. He disguised his actual occupation and used somebody else's photograph in his profile because he was worried that his activities on the site would compromise his role model image for his students and raise suspicion of extramarital affairs. He told me that so far he had had about 10 experiences of online cohabitation with different female members, mostly initiated by him, lasting from six months to just a few days. With just one exception, he mostly refrained from having any offline contact beyond the site with his female partners. "I don't know and don't want to know their real names, addresses or telephone numbers." He took none of these relationships seriously, nor did he perceive them as romantic. "What I am looking for is fun, nothing significant or meaningful, which means I am not going to expand these relationships into the real world. They are merely emotional." His statement suggests that 'emotional' is secondary to his life in the physical world in which he has established social roles to play and maintain. "To be honest, I enjoy the freedom and excitement online. I am lacking in these in my life. I have no opportunity to pursue these needs due to work, family, finance, norms and other social strictures." He perceived the site as a place where he can relax and unwind himself. "When I am feeling tired from work and prosaic daily routine, I come here for relaxation. Perhaps here helps me to adjust to my everyday life." The easy availability of distant intimacy from the site is liberating and entertaining to AZ. He light-heartedly enjoyed the therapeutic functions of

---

25 Anthony Giddens, Modernity and Self-identity: Self and Society in the Late Modern Age, Cambridge: Polity Press, 1991.

his online relationships. These included a boosted sense of self and feelings of invigoration, but at the same time a dismissiveness of the significance of these relationships.

Pursuing *Platonic* emotional love that is devoid of physical embodied interactions should, however, not be mistaken as embracing the Cartesian view of the superiority of the mind over the body. All the Chinese Internet users I encountered during the course of my study had no doubt on the importance of the body in romantic relationships. Neither were they enthusiastic about cyberspace's disembodiment in general. They are taking advantage of the Internet for what it does best, in this case, connecting people, extending human communication capacities which, in the process, fulfils their emotional needs and promotes their psychological wellbeing.

In addition to *Platonic* emotional love, 'play' is another important conceptual term that Chinese Internet users draw on heavily in their discussion of online romance. Cyberspace provides a perfect playground for self-immersion and exploration, reflecting the view of the 'sceptic', the second category of Chinese online daters which will be discussed after examining the notion of 'play' in the Chinese discourse of online romance.

Play

It is perhaps not a surprise that many associate online romance with game as most users I observed online, indeed, met their lover while playing games online. They often expressed doubt in the seriousness of their relationships. Relationships originating from the play domain have often been the target of online romance critics. These critics are suspicious of online daters' levels of commitment and the authenticity of the relationships. My study showed that critics' scepticism often also turns into cynicism as they urge online daters to adopt a playful approach to the relationship to avoid getting hurt. Not surprising that this creates a self-fulfilling prophecy for 'players' as they fall in and out of love more quickly than those who take the relationship seriously.

> Online romance can be described as a type of adult game. It is illusory and cannot be materialized (Wodeaizaoyibuzai).

> ...online romance is only a play, a dream (Guoguo).

> Online romance is love play, whoever becomes serious, he/she will be the loser (Taxiangyu).

> Games are governed by rules. Online romance also has its rules. The rule is never to take it too seriously. If not, it would turn prosaic. Frustrations would also ensue. Plagued with too many miseries, it would no longer be online romance (Baobeibuku).

The commentator of the last quote suggests that online romance's enchantment would vanish when it stops being a game. She continues to argue that there are advantages in deliberately treating online romance as play. Online romance is fascinating because

> it has no responsibilities. Love without responsibilities is relaxing, but at the same time

illusionary ... just by talking everyone can enjoy being in love, no monetary investment required, not much obligation and is mutually entertaining. Such a good deal should indeed be encouraged!

The playfulness of online romance renders it unreliable, but a low-investment, low- risk romantic pursuit, in turn, encourages Internet users to explore and experiment with love online. Players have low expectations on what they can hope for because commitments are rare and they are therefore unburdened by the weight associated with serious love affairs. Turning online relationships into play also implies that the relationship ought to be enjoyed as an intrinsic activity in itself, not as a means to find an offline date or a long-term partner. Play by nature is short lived and the only purpose is to have fun, enjoying the excitement and amusement play brings. Huizinga defined play as

> a free activity standing quite consciously outside 'ordinary' life as being 'not serious', but at the same time absorbing the player intensely and utterly. It is an activity connected with no material interest, and no profit can be gained by it. It proceeds within its own proper boundaries of time and space according to fixed rules and in an orderly manner.[26]

This definition's emphasis on the separation between play and reality is especially germane to the discussion here. According to Huizinga, to play means stepping out of real life into a temporary sphere of activity with its own governing rules. Play is captivating and satisfying in itself, complementing life in general. Without such separation, playing make-believe of a second reality would be difficult and it is the rules that create and sustain the frame of play within certain limits of time and place.[27] Playing at love online could be liberating, stimulating and transforming, if not at least entertaining and relaxing. The engrossment provides a form of escape or distraction from the mundane and often disappointing everyday realities.

Whitty also theorized online relationships as a form of play, external to everyday reality, fragile and ephemeral as it can only be sustained if players play by the rules and thereby keep its own frame alive.[28] In the psychodynamic view, play can promote the development of self and facilitate psychological growth and general health. The Internet provides a safe place for users not only to play with the relationships, but also their identities that could lead to increased self-awareness and acceptance with improved self-esteem.[29] This indeed reflects the motivation of some *Platonic* daters who pragmatically turn to the Internet to promote their emotional wellbeing. But for sceptics of online romance, when using the term 'play or game', they tend to downplay its psychological benefits, but focus instead, on its spirit of non-instrumentality and inconsequentiality, which, according to Simmel, in his article about sociability,

---

26 Johan Huizinga, Homo Lundens: A Study of the Play Element in Culture, Boston: The Beacon Press, 1955, p.13.
27 Roger Caillois, Man, Play, and Games, trans. Meyer Barash, Urbana: University of Illinois Press, 2001.
28 Monica T. Whitty, 'Cyber-flirting: Playing at Love on the Internet', Theory & Psychology 13.3 (2003): 339-357.
29 Monica T. Whitty and Adrian Carr, Cyberspace Romance: The Psychology of Online Relationships, New York: Palgrave Macmillan, 2006.

are the gaming principles that also govern most social events.[30]

The 'ludus' way of loving, a casual and noncommittal game playing romantic relationship, is nothing new as suggested in Lee's typology of styles of loving,[31] but the Internet provides a context particularly suitable for this style of love. Participants of 'ludic(rous)' Internet relationships often show "an utter lack of concern for depth, solemnity, seriousness, civility, and respect."[32] Getting sexually or emotionally closer to someone met online, yet calling it mere play has the effect of trivializing the relationship and making it innocuous because play is not real. The 'only pretending' consciousness of play makes everyday moral ethics, virtues, manners, social norms and strictures less readily applicable to play.[33] This explains why transgressive love affairs are likely to be condoned if confined within cyberspace. A transgressive online relationship that expands into the offline world would stop being play, hence needing to be regulated.

Through play, players can exercise their agency, try to take control, defy and oppose the status quo. Henricks summarized Huizinga's work on play as

> to play is to take on the world, to take it apart, and frequently to build it anew. So understood, play for Huizinga is a protest against determinism, a claim that humans need not merely endure existential conditions but can reform these according to their own desires and insights.[34]

Although players are unable to directly challenge and immediately undermine the dominant ideologies, play, nevertheless, is a way for them to express themselves, to tell their stories, and form a community of support. As argued by Scott, symbolic resistance and defiance by society's underdogs should not be dismissed lightly.[35] Furthermore, play may seem opposed to everyday reality, but it is also simultaneously part of it. The relationship between a society and the games it likes to play is reciprocal and mutually reflective of one another.[36] In other words, games affect the culture of the society as much as being affected by it.

Other advantages of a playful approach to online romance include allowing incongruous

---

30 Georg Simmel, 'Sociability', in Donald N. Levine (ed.) Georg Simmel on Individuality and Social Forms, Chicago: University of Chicago Press, 1971, pp. 127-140.

31 Johan A. Lee, 'A Typology of Styles of Loving', Personality and Social Psychology Bulletin 3 (1977): 173-182.

32 Dennis D. Waskul and Phillip Vannini, p.243, 'Ludic and Ludic(rous) Relationships: Sex, Play, and the Internet', in Samantha Holland (ed.) Remote Relationships: In a Small World, New York: Peter Lang, 2008, pp.241-261.

33 Johan Huizinga, Homo Lundens: A Study of the Play Element in Culture, Boston: The Beacon Press, 1955, p.13.

34 Thomas S. Henricks, Play Reconsidered: Sociological Perspectives on Human Expression, Urbana; Chicago: University of Illinois Press, 2006, p.185.

35 James C. Scott, Domination and the Arts of Resistance: Hidden Transcripts, New Haven; London: Yale University Press, 1990.

36 Roger Caillois, Man, Play, and Games, trans. Meyer Barash, Urbana: University of Illinois Press, 2001.

motives or conflicting interests to co-exist and minimizing the risk of failure, lightening the pain of rejection, and making exploration or experimentation possible. "Online romance is not real romance, so even if split up, it would not result in too much pain", pointed by participant Jitenglian. Becoming a playboy or playgirl online and feeling desirable is also a boost to one's self-esteem.

Online daters' playfulness may appear superficial to sceptical outsiders, but it requires digital competency and emotional rhetoric to successfully manoeuvre between play and reality. Just as the boundaries between the offline life and the online world are permeable, the border of play and ordinary life is not always clear-cut. When and where reality stops being reality, and play stops being play is not always obvious or undisputable, therefore each can have considerable influence on the other. For example, excessive playing of flirtatious relationships online can have negative effects on the primary relationship despite the idea that play would normally imply not having real and serious consequences in the wider world. In his study of games as social encounters, Goffman argued that what makes the encounters fun is a selective connection to the world beyond. Too much separation may render the play trivial and boring, too little separation may discourage players' engrossment in the play.[37] In summary, successful play is one where players themselves control the level of separation to achieve the right balance, simultaneously maintaining the sense of both connection and disconnection. However, ideal it may seem, only seasoned players would have the competency to negotiate between the two for maximum joy. Most would risk turning initial pleasure into compulsion, enjoyment into obsession, a casual and responsibility-free relationship into a serious love affair.

The Sceptic

Those users not in favor of online romance are mostly sceptical about its feasibility and authenticity. Their apprehension is based not only on the problematic tendency to contrast the virtual with the real, but also the conviction that online romance is a free play of make-believe, an imagined fairytale that is fun but transient, therefore should only be consumed incorporeally within cyberspace.

> Online romance has enchanted beauty. Online romance makes some people obsessive. Online romance makes love even more romantic. Online romance embellishes life with the beauty of confusion. But no matter what, regardless of how much more beautiful is online romance, it is just too virtual (Ermodang).

The virtual nature of online romance that frees participants from social norms and moral obligations is the main worry of online romance sceptics. Those who desire to move the romantic relationship offline would be regarded by the sceptics as confusing play with reality and representing a futile attempt because transcendental romantic affairs are always short-lived. They argue that the excitements and enchantments of online romance lie precisely in its virtual nature with a distance away from reality. It allows misrepresentations and sustains the illusion of a fairytale with heightened and volatile emotions.

---

37   Erving Goffman, Encounters: Two Studies in the Sociology of Interaction, Harmondsworth: Penguin, 1961.

I think online romance is only suitable in cyberspace. When it goes offline, its quality deteriorates (83gzhuazi).

Reality is never as good as the virtual world. It is romantic, because the Internet hides its ugly side. Only when keeping the online romance within cyberspace, does it remain perfect (Heizi).

Sceptics of online romance subscribe to the realist model of prosaic love. They are critically aware of the incompatibilities between idealistic online romance and the semantic and phenomenological properties of everyday life which is tedious and occupied with earthly petty concerns and chores.[38] Therefore, they are critical of the fantasy online romance creates but encourage recreational consumption of this fantasy by playing along and enjoying the feel-good effects it brings. In other words, play has become the rhetorical answer for the sceptics of online romance. It resolves the significance of their concerns and allows them to conveniently enjoy the online romantic's romantic ideals while at the same time cynically laughing at its triviality.

As opposed to the sceptics, the romantic realists have the aspiration to turn online romance into a social reality. They perceive online romance as not essentially different from romantic relationships initiated in the face-to-face world. In fact, relationships online built upon a foundation of constant emotional exchange and deeper mutual understandings are considered to be more meaningful by this category of online Internet users which will be discussed next.

The Romantic Realist

Romantic realists argue against the idea of 'romancing online' and understand online romance as initiated online but gradually expand offline and potentially cumulate long-term courtship, cohabitation or marriage. This perception of online romance is consistent with the dominant understanding of online romance. As romantic realists harbor the intention to move online romance offline, sustaining the heightened emotion and turning it into offline reality is the challenge. Embracing realistic expectations and not deliberately misrepresenting oneself online are advice given to couples to help overcome the challenge of transition from online to offline. *Jian guang si*, or perish upon exposing to the reality offline, is the most commonly discussed problem facing the romantic realists. It refers to the inevitable end of an online relationship when the dyad crosses the boundary by expanding their relationship offline. It is not the only worry that puts many online daters off from meeting in person. Physical distance between the two can also be a practical problem. Until either one relocates to be with the other, regular bodily interactions are impossible. Having to endure romantic love devoid of embodied presence is one of the serious drawbacks of online romance for romantic realists. Many online daters in this category lament the pain of being deprived of corporeal intimacy.

Romantic realists' concerns are closely related to their realization that technologies do not liberate human beings from the constraints of physical distance and embodiment which are paramount to the maintenance of romantic relationships. Advice given to online daters often

---

38   Eva Illouz, 'The Lost Innocence of Love: Romance as a Postmodern Condition', Theory, Culture & Society 15.3 (1998): 161-186.

includes regularly spending time together offline to truly understand each other and to make sure both get along well. If the relationship survives *jian guang si* and is successfully transferred offline, it will then be subjected to the same influence of social conventions, cultural practices, familial norms and values that affect people's dating behaviors, for example, "we dated online for two years and went offline. It went well, but was eventually destroyed by family members...", a personal experience of Wujunnan.

Of course in reality, the three categories (pragmatist fantasists, sceptics and romantic realists) identified in this study are not mutually exclusive. An individual may pragmatically choose to pursue *Platonic* emotional love online, but in the process get carried away by the intense romantic affection that leaves him/her contemplating the possibility of expanding the relationship offline. Meanwhile, he/she remains sceptical because of the conviction that the reality of everyday life is simply incompatible with the idealistic online romance. In the next section, I will discuss the similarities and differences of the three categories.

The Dynamic of the Three Categories

One thing in common between sceptics and pragmatic fantasists is they see online romance as a fairytale, too good to be true in the offline world and it is the virtuality of the Internet that sustains the wonderful illusion. The difference between sceptics' playful approach and pragmatic fantasists' utilitarian approach to online romance lies in the former's ruling spirit of non-instrumentality and inconsequentiality. According to Simmel, non-instrumentality means that socializing and playing is engaged in for its own sake, not as a means for attaining certain goals; while inconsequentiality insists on the importance of not being in earnest and just having fun.[39] Pragmatic fantasists, on the other hand, are motivated to use the relationships to help meet those emotional needs unfulfilled in everyday life. The relationships could turn serious and meaningful for some couples.

Chinese romantic realists desire to gradually expand their mode of communication, often from the initial textual interaction online to face-to-face meetings in due course. While the Internet may eventually become obsolete in their relationship as they shift flexibly between the online and the offline, this is however the opposite of how sceptical online daters and pragmatic fantasists experience their online romance. Romantic realists see the intertwining between the online and offline world as natural and inevitable, but the other two groups on the contrary, attempt to re-enact the boundaries between the online and offline world by repeatedly emphasizing on the benefits of keeping two realms apart from one another. In their discussion of online romance, the Internet is constantly being contrasted with the real life, the reality of offline world, the physical, the tangible, and the actual. Many of them opposed the idea of expanding online romance to the offline world, either because of their belief that the idealistic relationship can only live within cyberspace or it is morally wrong or irresponsible to let online activities affect the primary relationships or family life.

Residing in a northern province of China, Nakai (not real name) aged 24 in 2010, worked as an administrator at a careers service center. She shared her personal experience of online

---

39   Georg Simmel, 'Sociability', in Donald N. Levine (ed.) Georg Simmel on Individuality and Social Forms, Chicago: University of Chicago Press, 1971, pp. 127-140.

romance with me. Her narrative showed how she flexibly shifted between the three attitudes and how the Internet empowered her to pursue a homosexual relationship.

The Self-empowerment Story of Online Romance

At the time of my study in 2010, Nakai was in a relationship with someone met online. She revealed to me that "my current partner is a woman. My previous partners were all men." The relationship began after her colleague passed her contact number for QQ, a Chinese online instant messaging service, to Mei (not real name). Mei contacted her online and their relationship developed as they chatted regularly. Mei came to visit her after three months of online liaison and their first face-to-face meeting functioned to affirm and consolidate their romantic relationship. Mei later relocated to be with Nakai, but moved back after four months because the job she had there was not suitable. However, Mei planned to come again the following year.

Mei had been Nakai's colleague's offline friend of two years. Since they became romantically involved, her colleague was apologetic as she did not know that Nakai had a homoerotic impulse and regretted making the introduction which was initially intended to be merely a social relationship. This homosexual relationship has been hidden from Nakai's parents because she anticipated their strong reaction and prohibition. However, she became determined that when Mei returned in 2011, she would move out of her parents' home to live with Mei, without confessing the nature of their relationship to her parents. Mei is a year younger than Nakai. And according to Nakai, she was "born a lesbian. She always loved women and has dated several women in the past." When asked if she had deliberately suppressed her true sexual orientation in the past, Nakai replied that she only realized that she also loved women after she met Mei. However, it was not Mei who transformed Nakai from a heterosexual to homosexual. Nakai told me that

> When I was in high school and university, I admired two female fellow classmates. But I was not sure whether this feeling was friendship or romantic love. Furthermore, at that time, I was not convinced that it is possible for two females to be together. I thought this only happened in TV drama. Unrealistic. So I did not do anything. After I started to work, I began to contemplate the idea of dating a women. I knew a lesbian, who confided to me that she liked to be with me, but I had no feelings towards her. So I refused... Previously, I was not clear whether or not I really like women, because I had not tried. So I was uncertain about my true feelings.

After being in relationship with Mei, Nakai realized that a homosexual relationship suited her better than a relationship with the opposite sex. "I love her very much, much more than any of my ex-lovers. I want to be with her regardless of family's disapproval." Most of her friends knew that she was dating a woman and they were mostly supportive. The main challenge she encounters, like so many other homosexuals in China, is to ask for her family's acceptance. Her initial doubt on the feasibility of same-sex relationships is understandable in a society that exercises compulsory heterosexuality.[40] Although she previously did not act upon her

---

40   Tze-lan D. Sang, The Emerging Lesbian: Female Same-sex Desire in Modern China, Chicago: University of Chicago Press, 2003.

homoerotic impulse, her interest in same-sex love remained and it later facilitated the acceptance of her own sexuality. When asked if she felt confused and struggled to come to terms with her own sexuality, Nakai replied, "No struggle at all. I felt as natural as loving a man." When talking about the role of the Internet in her self-identification with a marginal sexual identity, she replied that

> I have been researching online to learn more about lesbianism, especially since I met Mei. It enhanced my understanding of the community, clarified my doubts, knowing that it is possible for females to develop romantic relationships and live together gave me lots of courage.

The exposure to a homosexual community online convinced Nakai that there was nothing wrong or abnormal about same-sex love. Interacting with other female same-sex couples gave her assurance and encouraged her to live the life she desired. Narrative is one of the resources we turn to for self-understanding and construction of the self.[41] Through narrative, individuals reconfigure the present and reinterpret the past in order to present a coherent and integrated sense of self. When Nakai narrates her current relationship with Mei, she relates it with her past experience of sexual curiosities with women. By so doing, the same-sex relationship does not constitute a break in her sexual identity. Her continuous sense of self could have led to the smooth transition from cross-sex love to same-sex love.

Talking about her first online romance, Nakai said it was her first love, the most memorable experience of all, but also the most hurtful. They met in an online forum in 2006 when she was 20, and had just started at university. They met in person once. Despite living far apart she looked forward to visiting him during holidays and was prepared to relocate to the south of China to be with him after graduation. He was also a student, but soon to graduate from university. Sadly, Nakai later found out that he already had a girlfriend offline and was not serious in their relationship. After the relationship was over she continued to develop several other cross-sex online romances. The longest relationship lasted for a year, while the shortest was only a month. She came to know almost all of her lovers at online forums. When I asked if she was serious in these relationships, she replied,

> Hard to say. I was once serious in all these relationships, but how long my seriousness lasted varied. I was serious throughout some of the relationships, but there were also others in which I was serious to begin with but after I became aware that the relationships had no prospects, I treated them as play.

This flexibly adjustable level of seriousness indicates Nakai's pragmatic approach towards online romance. When the relationship is not likely to deliver the ideal outcome, she turns it into play. By doing so, she can enjoy the distractions brought by the relationships while minimizing the risk of getting hurt.

Nakai enjoys developing relationships with others online because as an introvert, face-to-

---

41   Jane Elliott, Using Narrative in Social Research: Qualitative and Quantitative Approaches, London: Sage, 2005.

face communication with people she does not know is not easy. The Internet not only increases her opportunity to meet new friends and engage in communication on a deeper emotional level, but also allows greater control of her self-presentation. Her second motivation for developing online relationships is they are good "when feeling bored. They can be used for recreation." These relationships although not profound love, can still temporarily "satisfy the need of being loved and cared for." What is most important is not to be too serious and let oneself delve too deep into the relationship, otherwise, one risks breaking one's own heart." Not surprisingly, she did not seem to be disappointed by short-lived online love affairs. She also argued that over reliance on the Internet for solace can be debilitating. "Long-term indulgence in cyberspace will result in loss of confidence in real life, having difficulties to communicate with others face-to-face." Nakai's attitude reflects the quintessential element of the pragmatic fantasist who prioritizes the quotidian existence in the offline world, and the sceptic's playful approach to relationships online.

Nakai admitted that she once dated two or three different men online at once. But these relationships were short-lived and she was exhausted from trying to maintain all these relationships. When asked if she considered herself cheating, she replied that these relationships were just play, so faithfulness was not relevant. Nakai contended that only online romance that stood the test of offline reality can be called genuine love and deserves commitment. Online romance in itself is just a temporary outlet for emotional stimulation and for one to indulge in casual love affairs. This statement demonstrates that she is not rejecting the romantic realist's aspiration. Her own experience with Mei is, in fact, a vivid example of online romance going offline and becoming a social reality.

Nakai's overall experiences of the Internet, and online romance in particular, were beneficial to her self-experimentation and acceptance. She was not only able to explore and affirm the other side of her sexuality, but also improved her social skills online. Nakai's self-confidence may not be particularly high, but she has a strong sense of self-efficacy in overcoming challenges and life adversities. Her determination to live with Mei, to pursue her own choice of life is perhaps the most vivid example of the exercise of agency. The way she describes her transitions and identification with the marginalized sexual identity is surprisingly smooth, unlike many reported accounts of internal struggle and self-rejection. Familial traditions and social norms might be a constraining force for Nakai, but she is not afraid of the obstacles. As a self-determining person, she is adept at looking for resources and support online, therefore has the means to empower herself in living her choice of same-sex love.

Conclusion

'Platonic emotional love' and 'play' are two key conceptual terms in Chinese discourse of online romance. Both are made possible by a deliberate and careful demarcation of the online and offline world into two separate terrains. Instead of simply dismissing Chinese Internet users' online and offline dichotomy as regressive or naive, I focused instead on what it can achieve for them. Chinese are acutely aware that the online and offline worlds are inextricably linked but when it comes to interpersonal relationships, they choose to reinstate the online and offline boundary because it serves their purposes of looking for distraction and emotional solace. What they aim for is not a replacement for their often less satisfied everyday life in the offline world, but to use online relationships as a means to help them to improve the quality of their daily existence.

The 'pragmatic fantasist' is the key character in exclusively Internet-based *Platonic* emotional love. They approach online relationships instrumentally, aiming to find sustenance in these relationships of distant intimacy, making them the source of emotional stimulation and solace. Some of these relationships grow in intensity over time and become meaningful to the couples. Others remain shallow but are nevertheless appreciated for the good fantasies and reinvigoration provided that ease participants' tense and mundane everyday lives, while being weightless and risk free. I argue that the desire for pure affection, anything 'emotional' as opposed to embodied, materialist or mercenary by pragmatic fantasists is a reaction to the highly commodified and stressful quotidian existence in contemporary Chinese society.

The word 'play' is frequently used by the 'sceptic' to describe online romance. Their sceptical attitude towards online romance often also turns into cynicism when they call for a playful approach to online romance and argue that it is unwise to take online romance too seriously as it is just an inconsequential game. Treating online relationships as social gaming has the dual functions of warning online daters not to commit too easily to the relationship, or expect too much from it, and providing a license for experimentation in carefree online intimacies. A playful approach also helps some to cope with the inherent conflicts between reality and virtuality. Through play, the real is rendered virtual and players have the opportunity to work out their problems and test out options available.[42]

I use the term 'romantic realists' to label those who consider online romance as not essentially different from romantic relationships initiated face-to-face. They follow the Western trajectory of online romance in defining successful online romance as cumulating in marriage and long long-term relationships in the offline world. Once the relationship goes offline, the couple is subjected to the same cultural practices, traditions, social norms and conventions governing familial life and love affairs. Keeping a relationship online and calling it a play is a way to shield it from the influence of prevailing normative forces.

In therapeutic culture, online relationships could be empowering as they help couples to deal with their emotional emptiness and pain, preparing them to cope with the tensions and uncertainties resulting from the volatile and chaotic nature of selfhood and social relationships in late modernity.[43] The therapeutic model of relationship also helps individuals to discover their true-selves and become autonomous persons leading an authentic life.[44]

Finally, the experience of online romance and its social implications depend on the participants' attitudes towards online romance, whether they are being pragmatic, sceptical or realistic in their pursuit of the relationships online. As pointed out by Hine, the Internet's functions and meanings do indeed vary from individual to individual because its risks and opportunities are perceived differently in relation to each individual's concerns and needs.[45]

---

42 Pat Kane, The Play Ethic: A Manifesto for a Different Way of Living, London: Pan, 2005.
43 Eva Illouz, Cold Intimacies: The Making of Emotional Capitalism, Cambridge: Polity, 2007.
44 Ann Swidler, Talk of Love: How Culture Matters, Chicago: University of Chicago Press, 2001.
45 Christine Hine, 'Virtual Methods and the Sociology of Cyber-social-scientific Knowledge', in Christine Hine

References

Baker, Andrea. 'What Makes an Online Relationship Successful? Clues from Couples Who Met in Cyberspace', *CyberPsychology & Behavior* 5.4 (2002): 363-375.

Beck, Ulrich and Beck-Gernsheim, Elisabeth. 'Foreword: Varieties of Individualization', in Mette H. Hansen and Rune Svarverud (eds) *iChina: The Rise of the Individual in Modern Chinese Society*, Copenhagen: NIAS Press, 2010, pp. xiii-xx.

Ben-Ze'ev, Aaron. *Love Online: Emotions on the Internet*, Cambridge: Cambridge University Press, 2004, p.131.

Birbili, Maria. 'Translating from One Language to Another', Social Research Update 31 (2000), http://sru.soc.surrey.ac.uk/SRU31.html.

Boston Consulting Group (BCG), Online Retail Sales in China will Triple to More than $360 Million by 2015, as the Internet Adds Nearly 200 Million Users, 12 April 2012, http://www.bcg.com/media/PressReleaseDetails.aspx?id=tcm:12-103641.

Caillois, Roger. *Man, Play, and Games*, trans. Meyer Barash, Urbana: University of Illinois Press, 2001.

Elliott, Jane. *Using Narrative in Social Research: Qualitative and Quantitative Approaches*, London: Sage, 2005.

Farrer, James. *Opening Up: Youth Sex Culture and Market Reform in Shanghai*, Chicago: University Chicago Press, 2002.

Giddens, Anthony. *Modernity and Self-identity: Self and Society in the Late Modern Age*, Cambridge: Polity Press, 1991.

Goffman, Erving. *Encounters: Two Studies in the Sociology of Interaction*, Harmondsworth: Penguin, 1961.

Henricks, Thomas S. *Play Reconsidered: Sociological Perspectives on Human Expression*, Urbana; Chicago: University of Illinois Press, 2006, p.185.

Hine, Christine. 'Virtual Methods and the Sociology of Cyber-social-scientific Knowledge', in Christine Hine (ed.) *Virtual Methods: Issues in Social Research on the Internet*, Oxford: Berg, 2005, pp.1-13.

Huizinga, Johan. *Homo Lundens: A Study of the Play Element in Culture*, Boston: The Beacon Press, 1955, p.13.

IAC and JWT, China Leads the US in Digital Self-expression, 22 November 2007, http://iac.com/media-room/press-releases/china-leads-us-digital-self-expression.

Illouz, Eva. 'The Lost Innocence of Love: Romance as a Postmodern Condition', *Theory, Culture & Society* 15.3 (1998): 161-186.

Illouz, Eva. *Cold Intimacies: The Making of Emotional Capitalism*, Cambridge: Polity, 2007.

Jamieson, Lynn. *Intimacy: Personal Relationships in Modern Societies*, Oxford: Polity, 1998.

Jeffreys, Elaine and Sigley, Gary. 'Governmentality, Governance and China', in Elaine Jeffreys (ed.) *China's Governmentalities: Governing Change, Changing Government*, New York: Routledge, 2009, pp. 1-23.

Kane, Pat. *The Play Ethic: A Manifesto for a Different Way of Living*, London: Pan, 2005.

Lee, Johan A. 'A Typology of Styles of Loving', *Personality and Social Psychology Bulletin* 3 (1977): 173-182.

McKenna, Katelyn Y.A., Green, Amie S. and Gleason, Marci E.J. 'Relationship Formation on the Internet: What's the Big Attraction?', *Journal of Social Issues* 58 (2002): 9-31.

(ed.) Virtual Methods: Issues in Social Research on the Internet, Oxford: Berg, 2005, pp.1-13.

Merkle, Erich R. and Richardson, Rhonda A. 'Digital Dating and Virtual Relating: Conceptualizing Computer Mediated Romantic Relationships', *Journal of Family Relations* 49.2 (2000): 187-192.

Sang, Tze-lan D. *The Emerging Lesbian: Female Same-sex Desire in Modern China*, Chicago: University of Chicago Press, 2003.

Scott, James C. *Domination and the Arts of Resistance: Hidden Transcripts*, New Haven; London: Yale University Press, 1990.

Simmel, Georg. 'Sociability', in Donald N. Levine (ed.) Georg Simmel *On Individuality and Social Forms*, Chicago: University of Chicago Press, 1971, pp. 127-140.

Swidler, Ann. *Talk of Love: How Culture Matters*, Chicago: University of Chicago Press, 2001.

Temple, Bogusia and Young, Alys. 'Qualitative Research and Translation Dilemmas', *Qualitative Research* 4.2 (2004): 161-178.

Twitter Blog, One Hundred Million Voices, 8 September 2011, http://blog.twitter.com/2011/09/one-hundred-million-voices.html.

Waskul, Dennis D. and Vannini, Phillip, p.243, 'Ludic and Ludic(rous) Relationships: Sex, Play, and the Internet', in: Samantha Holland (ed.) *Remote Relationships: In a Small World*, New York: Peter Lang, 2008, pp.241-261.

Wei, Xiaohong., Li, Caili., Lu, Min., and Peng, Bing. *Diaocha Cheng: 87% de Shoufang Daxuesheng Renwei Wanglian Shi Manzu Qinggan Xuyao de Yizhong Fangshi* (Survey showed that 87% of the university students interviewed think online romance is a means to satisfy emotional needs). China Youth Online, 27 December 2007, http://zqb.cyol.com/content/2007-12/27/content_2011436.htm.

Whitty, Monica T. 'Cyber-flirting: Playing at Love on the Internet', *Theory & Psychology* 13.3 (2003): 339-357.

Whitty Monica T. and Carr, Adrian. *Cyberspace Romance: The Psychology of Online Relationships*, New York: Palgrave Macmillan, 2006.

Xinhua, *Xinlang Weibo Zhuce Yonghu Tupo Sanyi, Meiri Faboliang Chaoguo Yiyitiao* (Sina Weibo have more 300 million registered users, more than 100 million weibo are posted everyday), 29 February 2012, http://news.xinhuanet.com/tech/2012-02/29/c_122769084.htm.

Yan, Yunxiang. *The Individualization of Chinese Society*, Oxford; New York: Berg, 2009.

Zeng, Jianpeng. *Xuni yu Xianshi: Dui 'Wanglian' Xianxiang de Lilun Fenxi* (Virtual and reality: Theoretical analysis of online romance), Chinese Academy of Social Science, 23 December 2004, http://www.sociology.cass.net.cn/shxw/qsnyj/t20041223_4103.htm.

Zhao, Yuezhi. 'After Mobile Phones, What? Re-embedding the Social in China's "Digital Revolution"', *International Journal of Communication* 1 (2007): 92-120.

TALKING TO STRANGERS: TEMPORALITY, IDENTITY AND POLITICS IN LIVE WEBCAM SEX CHANNELS

ARAS OZGUN

Immediacy has been a constitutive characteristic of electronic and online communications from the very beginning. E-mail, instant messaging, bulletin boards and user forums, and later RSS technologies[1] and social media networks have relied on the immediacy of information exchange, and have gradually replaced traditional forms of interpersonal written communications. The emergence of electronic text —writing on the screen— has radically altered the ontology of text as had existed before in the print cultures, by depriving it of its authoritative permanence, destabilizing it and making it dynamic, ever-changing, and temporal. Up until recently, because of a variety of technological limitations, this 'instantaneousness' remained confined to the exchange of this new kind of (electronic) 'text'. Although digital media platforms and networks had the potential to connect distant people, locations and events, not only textually but audio-visually as well, this potential has been limited by availability of access to the networks, bandwidth, and technical equipment. Over the past few years, with the increasing popularity of camera-equipped smart phones, laptops, and wireless and mobile data networks, these limitations have been largely surpassed.

This development has an obvious practical impact primarily on face-to-face communications: Skyping, using Facetime, and video chatting increasingly substitute or supplement face-to-face communications in general. However, the potential of webcam for one-to-many communications, as a 'broadcasting' device, is still neglected or unfulfilled, and this is largely due to the economic logic of media industries rather than technological limitations. 'Televisuality'— that is, the immediate and live transmission of events, which has been the definitive power of TV - still remains under the monopoly of television networks. The emergence of the webcam as a technological form only marginally challenges the monopoly of television in defining social time and collective temporality. 'Real-time,' as a term that refers to a computer's capacity to render image streams continuously while they are being displayed on the monitor (or, any other process in which the tangible results/effects of the process is simultaneously displayed), emerged with the introduction of digital media technologies to distinguish this new form of temporal immediacy from the latency of print cultures. Yet, the 'real-time' of social life in general ironically remained associated with television. Television networks sustained their monopoly over the information regarding what is happening at that very moment. So far, except substituting face-to-face communications, the Internet has provided a vast archive of past 'moments' of collectively experienced 'real-time,' in the form of digital video recordings, shared and made available online on YouTube, Vimeo or other social media networks. The instant availability of such a wide video archive had been a fascination in new media studies during the second decade of online communications. Before us now is another potential; a new, truly decentralized technological form of television (that does not require the massive organizational structure of corporate television networks) available to individuals. This creates new temporal depths apart from the hegemonic time regimes constructed and

---

[1] RSS stands for 'Rich Site Summary', and refers to the automatic syndication of data between publishers, which also enables the users receive timely updates.

sustained by television networks. What I am going to discuss in this article, live webcam sex channels, is one of these marginal instances in which online video challenges television in its own realm, and claims the rights over 'live-ness.' I will argue that the 'live-ness' of the webcam constitutes a new type of reality effect, which I will provisionally call 'realness.' In the last part of the article, I will analyze a particular interaction that occurs in Turkish live webcam sex channels as a result of such realness, in which feminine desire falls into confrontation with patriarchal moralism, which leads to a productive crisis that makes enjoyment impossible.

'I See, Therefore I Am': The Ontology of Televisuality

The ontology of the webcam is that of television on a minor scale; it possesses the same 'live-ness' and 'immediacy.' 'Live-ness' of the televisual image, as pointed out by many media theorists from Raymond Williams to Mary Ann Doane, provides television with a unique potential for relating to the event it presents. In this respect, the televisual image has an 'ontic' condition, in Heidegger's terms. Martin Heidegger used 'ontic' in reference to the undeniable existential quality of being, of things and events, which surpass any ontological inquiry.[2] We can inquire into how we perceive the outside world, how we gather our knowledge of things and events, but we cannot deny the existence of things and events— that was the ontic condition of being, according to Heidegger.

The tense of the image, its perpetual reference to the present, distinguishes the iconic signifier of television from that of cinema and photograph. The 'live-ness' of the televisual image transfers the ontic quality of the things and events it depicts to the screen they appear on; the televisual image thus possesses undeniable presence of the outside world it shows. We can always question how things and events are represented to us on the television screen; we can always associate particular instances of such representation with ideological constructions beyond epistemological questions; we can always remain doubtful about the 'truth value' of these representations and question what is really happening there; but we can never deny that what television shows us does exist somewhere at that very moment. The 'truth' of the televisual representation is primarily the event itself; that something happens at that very moment. "What happened, really?" is a posterior concern.

The webcam image claims the same ontic quality in a similar way; the existence of what it shows us on the other end of the line at that very moment is undeniable, beyond any questions regarding its identity and its truthfulness. The early incarnations of webcams were online cameras placed in various remote locations from Antarctica to Times Square. These webcams did not attempt to impress the Internet-savvy voyeurs with the photographic quality of their low-resolution pictures, which were only updated in every few seconds, but indeed fascinated them with a different type of realism—with their temporal reference. They quietly, without any commentary, showed us what was going on at a remote part of the world, somewhere that exists beyond our sight at that very moment. Against the hyper-realism of larger-than-life LCD billboards, multi-monitor TV walls, high-precision satellite imagery and HD projections on every facade, the tiny pixelated webcam image offered the realism of a

---

2 Martin Heidegger, Being and Time, trans. John Macquarrie and Edward Robinson, Harper and Row Publishers, 1962.

'trace' rather than a map, of a silhouette rather than a portrait. The uncanny truth of the jerky video stream recalled a Vertovian dream amid the spectacle of high-tech visual media: 'life as it is,' at that very moment. What becomes clearly expressed in the intensified eroticism of live webcam sex channels, in their seductive power, as I will try to explain below, is this temporal reference—the extended sight that simply registers what exists there at that moment, beyond any question regarding its 'representation.'

After the proliferation of bandwidth and camera equipped computers, a 17-year-old Russian high school student, Andrey Ternovsky, cultivated the true nature of the webcam by combining it with two other constitutive characteristics of online communications: anonymity and interactivity. The algorithm Ternovsky deployed on the site he founded, Chatroulette, allowed the users to randomly connect to other users through their webcams. In complete anonymity, users could video chat with others, perform acts for complete strangers, just look at each other, or try to catch another's attention before he or she clicked on the 'next' button - or if all failed, to just hit the 'next' button and jump to another random user's webcam. Without any advertisement, the users of Ternovsky's Chatroulette exponentially grew; when the site launched in November 2009, it initially drew 500 visitors per day. Within a month, there were fifty thousand daily users, and Chatroulette is still one of the top five video chat sites in the world. [3]

The popularity of Chatroulette revealed the erotic potential of the medium. According to an informal study published in 2010, hitting the 'next' button on Chatroulette yielded a 1 in 8 chance of seeing someone apparently naked, exposing themselves or engaging in a sexual act, a considerable chance of seeing a 'show your tits' sign, and a considerably lesser chance of seeing actual female flashers.[4] The amount of users seeking erotic pleasure and anonymously exhibiting themselves on the site eventually generated a series of public controversies, to the degree that Ternovsky finally had to modify the website's program to detect skin tone and block nudity, and employ users with 'moderator' privileges to filter out obscenity.

Webcam sex sites that appeared in the recent years were built on the idea of providing an open space for what has been excluded from Chatroulette and other video chat sites: nudity, obscenity, exhibitionist thrill, voyeuristic orgy, purely and intensely erotic communication.

Although the content of most popular live webcam sex sites are open to all adult Internet users, they are economically sustained through paid membership as well as advertisement revenues.[5] Any adult Internet user (or, in fact, any Internet user who confirms that she or he

---

3 Robert J. Moore, (2010-03-16). "Chatroulette Is 89 Percent Male, 47 Percent American, And 13 Percent Perverts." TechCrunch. Retrieved http://techcrunch.com/2010/03/16/chatroulette-stats-male-perverts/ 14-05-2010.

4 Robert J. Moore, (2010-03-16).

5 In fact, there are also sites that offer commercial "live webcam sex shows," not unlike online peep-shows, which are performed by sex workers to an adult audience for a fee. The dynamics that I want to draw attention in this article are found on "open" sites such as cam4.com, chaturbate.com, myfreecams.com etc., in which everybody who connects to the sites with a webcam can broadcast themselves and there is not a clear distinction between performer and audience, nor between sex work and erotic pleasure.

is over 18 years old) can access the sites and follow the broadcasts. The members whose webcams are open, who are visible to other viewers, are marked as 'broadcasting.' The use of the term 'broadcasting,' a term borrowed from television in this context, once again reminds us the closeness between TV and the webcam as a technological form. The broadcasting members are listed according to their self-declared sexual preferences, under the sections: female, male, transsexual and couples (not necessarily heterosexual). Different sites offer different extra categories, such as the 'party' category on cam4.com (in which a group of people gather in front of the webcam), or 'featured broadcasts' (which include the performers selected by the sites administrators). The listings of members performing/broadcasting at that moment in each section of the sites are displayed in order of popularity—meaning that the performers with more viewers are displayed on the top of list. On cam4.com and chaturbate.com, top-ranking performers can draw an audience of a few thousand members depending on the time of day. Membership, although free, is a requirement for broadcasting. Members can also purchase 'tokens,' which can be offered and transferred to other members. Members who receive tokens from other members can convert these tokens to cash, and the site operators cut a commission from this exchange. Token exchange sustains the economy of the sites as well as facilitating the sex work they provide.

My interest is not in the economic aspects of the sex work on these channels. The income derived from performing sex work on webcam must differ hugely from performer to performer, and it is difficult to estimate it without an in-depth analysis of overall exchange. As I'll try to explain later, the fact that not all performers seek sex work, plus the fact that sex work and erotic pleasure become almost indistinguishable on these sites, makes it difficult to analyze the volume and intensity of the sex work without referring to the site operators' records. While pointing to the erosion of the perceivable difference between sex work and erotic play, I also acknowledge the fact that these are already fluid and problematic categories, and I don't intend to espouse a clear-cut, hierarchical distinction based on moral standards between these. My interest is in the psychodynamics and sociodynamics of this particular form of communication, in which further indiscernibility of these loose categories becomes an important feature. This indiscernibility, as I will argue, while intensifying the erotic thrill, also generates a crisis in the patriarchal language. This is crystallized in the interactions between Turkish female performers and male audience.

Among these dynamics, what becomes immediately recognizable is a heightened sense of anonymity. At the basic level, the anonymity of the webcam offers certain conveniences, such as providing a safe space for the expression of uncommon forms of desire in respect to erotic imagination, and in respect to sex work. Additionally, one does not have to leave home to watch a strip show, nor does a performer need to drive to a different city's strip club to avoid being recognized by their neighbors.

Anonymity is not only something convenient for circumventing the moral norms and taboos surrounding sexuality, but it is also a vehicle for constructing virtual identities. Combined with the intensity and interactivity of communication that is involved, anonymity creates the grounds for a few different layers of indiscernibility, which I consider to be the constitutive element of the medium that provides its distinct seductive power.

The first layer of indiscernibility is between the performers and the audience: audience members turn on their cameras and perform too while watching each other performing; performers sometimes participate in each other's sessions; and performers can turn on the viewers' cam and make them a part of the performance as such. In this respect, webcam channels resemble the form of a 'carnival' in the Bakhtinian sense. Russian Formalist literary theorist and philosopher Mikhail Bakhtin was pointing to the carnival form in his analysis of polyphony and dialogism in narratives: As a non-scripted event that is constituted by its participants, a carnival can only be experienced through participation as such, and does not leave any space for passive 'spectatorship.' [6]

Another layer of indiscernibility, which I find to be even more important for constructing the seductive power of the medium, appears between the professional sex workers, who perform regularly (sometimes every day, sometimes even all day, every day) as a means of subsistence, the amateur sex workers, who casually perform to earn extra money, and the common exhibitionists and voyeurs who just seek erotic pleasure. It is this layer of indiscernibility that blurs the distinction between sex work and erotic thrill and provides the perfect ground for fantasy, giving the webcam its seductive power.

We can see this at work when we look at the most popular performers' channels. Contrary to the common wisdom, the rankings that are apparent in the listings show that the popularity of the performers does not directly correlate with their physical attractiveness or attributes (in other words, the conformity of their physical appearance with the hegemonic conventions of 'beauty'), or how much nudity they display, or how explicit their broadcast is and to what distances they go to satisfy their audience.

'Realness' of the Webcam Image: Benefit of the Doubt

Oftentimes the popularity of performers is related to their ability to construct 'verisimilitude' - an effect that I will provisionally call 'realness.' 'Realness' is an immediate effect of a direct, unprocessed, unscripted and unedited visual reference - something with which we are now becoming familiar, by the multitude of cell phone and amateur video images we are being exposed to in our everyday communication environment. What I call 'realness' here is, on one hand, a certain kind of 'reality effect' that is somehow different from and opposed to what we find in Hollywood narratives, and, on the other hand, a strategy that is born out of such layers of indiscernibility that is inherent to this particular form of communication.

'Realness,' as such, is embedded in the 'live-ness' of the webcam. 'Live-ness' appears to be an integral part of the erotic pleasure, to the degree that, although the streaming of a 'pre-recorded' video feed to the site (instead of the live video image from the webcam) is technically and practically possible, this is considered 'cheating' and it is highly undesirable among webcam users. The sites are therefore designed with a particular administrative attention to sustain 'live-ness'; the audience is given the chance to mark the performers' feeds that they determine to be 'recorded' and these channels appear marked as such on the listing page. 'Live-ness' is an essential element for the 'realness' of the webcam, to the effect that

---

6   Mikhail Bakhtin, *Rabelais and His World*, Bloomington, IN: Indiana University Press, 1984.

'recorded' is a synonym for 'fake.'

The 'live-ness' of the performance includes (or, it is constructed through) the performer's interaction with the audience. This interaction does not merely consist of passively responding to the demands of the audience to perform sexual acts, but largely, and more profoundly, and sometimes counterintuitively, sustained by talking with them, engaging with them communicatively. At various intensities, interaction ranges from pathic communication (such as "hey joe, you are here again?") to in-depth, intimate personal conversations that do not necessarily revolve around sexual topics.

Such conversations construct the 'realness' of the performer as an individual, as a social subject, as a desiring subject, and not as a sex worker who submits herself to her customers' desires. At the moment that such 'realness' is constructed by the performer, the difference between erotic play and sex work becomes indiscernible, and the flow of desire, the erotic exchange, appears to be authentic.

It is possible to see female performers in these sites in heavy makeup, lying down naked in bed in front of Manhattan-skyline wallpaper, lit with pink and purple lamps, masturbating all day and just asking for tokens with a big forced smile on their face all the time. This is obviously sex work, and in fact, what is displayed bare here is the reality of the sex work. But no matter how good-looking these women are and what sort of challenges they undertake, what often draws more audience are the female performers who appear at home, on a laptop computer in their bed, or at work, in rather casual situations, interacting with their audience 'as they are.'

A cam4.com member, Shygirl652, regularly broadcasts from a library. Without showing her face, she places the camera between her legs and plays with herself under her skirt, or places it on the desk and unbuttons her shirt, and from time to time turns the camera around to show other people working on the desks behind her. Stella, another cam4.com member, typically broadcasts from her jewelry shop, exposes herself in the store when there are no customers, or even in front of the shop when the street is empty. A few performers regularly broadcast discreetly from their workplaces while doing their day jobs, and their discretion while exposing themselves to the webcam becomes a part of the thrill for the audience as well. Yet, all these performers accept tokens, and the 'realness' of the 'coworker exposing herself' shatters only if the audience is presented with a 'workspace' composed of a desk in an empty room and the performer does not do any work other than exposing herself and asking for tokens.

Exchange of tokens, and the performers demand for tokens for continuing the show can be considered as a marker of sex work. But even this is not a clear marker, since it is possible to see the sex workers appearing on their channel declaring they are not 'working,' they are just there to 'talk,' and socialize with their audience. In some cases, the performers who don't accept tokens - and therefore appear as they are only interested in erotic pleasure - draw their audience to other sources of commercial exchange. For example, *BusinessLady* describes herself as a sexually active financially secure professional businesswoman who is seeking erotic thrill on chaturbate.com.[7] She writes on her profile page; "I work hard and have way too much stress in my life... I do this for fun. I don't get to read much of the screen because I am busy pleasuring myself... If you join my room and I do not seem to be putting on a show, it is because I am resting. I may work on cam, and have even read articles aloud to viewers. It may be boring, so change the channel." She explains the fact that she accepts token as: "Any tokens / tips are donated to a respected 501(c)(3) animal rescue charity. I wish I could prove this, but it really is the truth." But her profile page directs her more than 6,500 followers to her personal blog on Blogspot, where she shares her experiences and fantasies in writing, and also offers a paid membership for her fan club that gives free "phone sex in every other month" and privileged treatment for "free private 1 on 1 camera time."

Vnmses, who is one of the most popular performers on that same site, whenever she is online, gives us one of the best examples of 'realness' as such.[8] Her performances are almost intimate live-broadcasts of the everyday life of a dissatisfied suburban American teenager. In contrast with the heavy makeup and forced welcoming smile of the third-world sex workers on the site, whenever she turns it on, *Vnmses* looks through her webcam with curious big eyes, and a serious face that searches for a smile. She talks to her audience/friends before she goes to sleep and when she wakes up, while she hangs out naked around her suburban house, while she steals her mother's wine from the fridge, when she lounges in the yard. She keeps broadcasting when she occasionally goes out to shopping with her girlfriends, and introduces the boys she occasionally picked up before they had sex in front of the webcam. The parallel scars on her arms and legs, she explains, were because she likes to cut herself when she feels down. She talks with her audience members on punk music, movies and anything that can be a subject of mundane conversation. She also shares her intimate stories: Her first boyfriend was black, and because she was being raised by her conservative grandparents, and because she and her boyfriend were stupid enough to try, they started with having only anal sex —"God, that was so painful!". And then, when they got caught by Grandpa together in the shower, things became obvious. Her masturbation sessions in front of the webcam seem more to be curious experiments to overcome the profound boredom that she shares with her audience, than a service to them. Excess and mundane, boredom and orgasm, friends and audience mix into each other in *Vnmses*' broadcasts. She does not appear as a sex worker trying to satisfy an audience, but as a twenty-something punk seeking satisfaction in her life with them. She never asks for tokens, but takes them as they come, plentifully.

In the case of *Xaida*, a chaturbate.com member, who often broadcasted in highly professional, Hollywood-grade zombie makeup and outfit during 2012, her makeup and outfit did not appear to jeopardize her 'realness,' but on the contrary, offered proof of authenticity: Sex workers don't look like zombies, and aren't assumed to know much about the zombie literature either, therefore sophisticated makeup and costuming establishes the fact that the performer is a female artist seeking erotic thrill rather than a sex worker seeking customers.

---

7   See http://chaturbate.com/businesslady/ (1.15.2014)
8   See http://chaturbate.com/vnmses/ (4.7.2012)

This is what I refer to 'realness as a strategy' as well as an effect. As much as the female performer on the webcam can really be a 'housewife,' a 'coworker,' or a 'bored teenager' seeking erotic thrill, she could be a sex worker presenting a carefully and meticulously constructed fantasy. So, any fantasy as such that is presented with sufficient believability, lacking any other reference, receives the power of 'real' by having the effect of 'real.' I choose to use the term 'realness' in order to distinguish this form from other kinds of reality effects. What we register as 'real' often appears to us as a whole, verifiable and perpetual discursive construction, whereas the verisimilitude of the webcam is a temporal effect sustained by its partial and unverifiable image. Its irrefutable partiality also distinguishes the webcam image from the 'illusion of reality' that is aimed at achieving cinematic realism. 'Illusion of reality' in cinema is an effect of 'realistic fiction,' whereas a webcam bears no script and it is decidedly not fiction. Rather than an 'illusion of reality,' a webcam, like an illusionist, inspires us to accept what it presents: it is impossible not to believe what happens before your eyes, although your logic tells you that a rabbit wouldn't fit into that hat.

'Realness' in this sense also differs from what Baudrillard calls simulation: simulation, in his terminology, refers to an artificially constructed event that assumes the authority of the real, and substitutes the real without having any reference to it. By contrast, 'realness' asserts an ambiguity by being partial, its verisimilitude stems from its lack, its vagueness, in contrast with the overarching narrative of the simulation; it doesn't project the whole that envelopes the present in the way Baudrillard problematizes.

'Realness' in this sense, resonates more with what Gilles Deleuze describes as 'virtual' at various points of his philosophical inquiries (from his early work in Difference and Repetition, to his late works on Cinema).[9] Virtual, in his terminology, is not something 'unreal,' or 'opposite of real,' but a 'potential,' a 'nebulous state' of the real that constantly becomes 'actualized.' For Deleuze, 'reality' is the outcome of the dynamic passages between the 'virtual' and 'actual' state of events and things. The 'actual' here, what becomes 'actualized' in the context of webcam sex, is the erotic desire. Therefore 'realness' is the 'virtual' constitution of the desiring subject on/through the webcam. With no reference to the past or the future, with no other identifiers or discursive elements apart from (or use: beyond) the image itself, a webcam virtually constructs and affirms the 'desiring subject', purely within the temporality of that moment. 'Realness', the power of the webcam to virtually construct a 'desiring subject' as such, is therefore the constitutive element of the medium, and it is directly related with 'live-ness.'

'Live-ness,' the temporality of the webcam, then, brings about a double transgression. On the one hand, it imposes the transgression of the sex work by blurring the markers between 'desire' and 'work', and amplifies the core erotic fantasy by unhinging it from its subordination to 'sex work'. The female performer, as non-sex-worker, ordinary woman - a desiring subject - becomes more desirable as she fulfills the fantasy perfectly with her 'realness'. By appearing as a 'desiring subject', the female performer fulfills the underlying fantasy, and calls for

---

9   Gilles Deleuze, Difference and Repetition, Columbia University Press, 1995. Gilles Deleuze, Cinema 2: The Time-Image, University Of Minnesota Press, 1989.

active participation from the other party, who has to respond in kind and join the game by generating his own desires, just like the erotic play in physical intimacy. On the other hand, the escapist erotic fantasy itself transgresses the banality of mundane, uneventful everyday life - as in the case of *Vnmses*, the proper suburban girl breaking moral restraints through immediately shared affective intensities. The seductive power of the webcam is closely related with this two-fold transgression that stems from indiscernibility, which becomes the definitive characteristic of the webcam image.

Fear and Loathing on Live Webcam Sex: The "Turkish" Case

The suspension of physical distances leads to a truly international audience in live webcam sex channels. Yet this international audience is divided into linguistic spheres because of the nature of communication—which once again shows the importance of verbal interaction in these channels: the performances are not merely displays of flesh, nor is the audience just a crowd of passive voyeurs; the verbal interaction is an essential erotic component. The flag symbol chosen by a performer for his or her profile indicates the language s/he is comfortable speaking. Major linguistic spheres are the usual internationally spoken languages; English, Spanish, German, Italian, etc.

Among these international linguistic spheres, we find an unusual one, a Turkish sphere. The presence of Turkish-speaking performers and audiences on these channels is not surprising when we consider the size of Turkish-speaking public worldwide.[10] Although there is a large Turkish-speaking immigrant population living outside of Turkey, considering the fact that Turkish immigrants are not limited to speaking only Turkish but have access to other, more popular linguistic spheres (such as English or German), it is safe to presume that the Turkish-speaking audience mainly consists of people logging in from Turkey. The conversations within the audience also clearly confirm that they are overwhelmingly from Turkey. But considering the circumstances surrounding these channels, not only conservative social norms and but also Internet regulations in Turkey, the presence of such a community may be seen as highly unusual. Unlike in other countries that compose other linguistic spheres, live webcam sex sites are entirely banned in Turkey together with other pornographic and 'harmful' sites. Since 2007, the Telecommunication and Transmission Authority in Turkey has been able to impose bans on Internet sites without prior judicial approval, through an IP filtering system. This IP filtering system is installed on the domain name servers and blocks access to the banned sites by displaying a generic error page that informs the user that the website is blocked. The nature of such Internet censorship and the controversies surrounding the

---

10   Now, I will refer to this particular audience as the "Turkish-speaking audience", since, contrary to the assumptions of the nationalist fantasy I will discuss later, speaking Turkish language is not necessarily an indicator of "Turkish" national identity. Ethnic and cultural minorities in Anatolia (such as Kurdish people, or various non-Muslim minorities) also speak Turkish along with their native language, and a considerable number of people, such as myself, refuse to associate themselves with a national identity, as "Turks," for ideological reasons. The problematic occurrence of the nationalist fantasy I will discuss later also confirms that speaking Turkish is not an indicator of national identity. Therefore, in this article, I will refer to this audience as "Turkish-speaking" with reference to language, rather than "Turks" or "Turkish people," which denotes national identity. As the case I will discuss eventually confirms, it is a "linguistic sphere" rather than a "national identity."

regulations are also somehow related with the nationalist political culture that becomes crystalized in the Turkish-speaking male audience's interaction with female performers.

The sites that are banned by the Turkish Telecommunication and Transmission Authority include some of the highly popular social media sites such as YouTube, because of a particular statement in Turkish criminal law that prohibits 'insulting Turkishness'. The vagueness of the legal term, the extra-judiciary power of the censorship authority, and the technicalities of the IP filtering system (which does not only censor the particular prohibited content on the sites, but blocks access to the IP address—to the server/site—entirely) opened up arbitrary censorship practices over the past years. In the face of the huge controversy resulting from the censoring of some of the most popular sites, Turkish Prime Minister, still not willing to ease the censorship regulations formally, yet still trying to uphold his populist image, famously declared: "My people know how to circumvent the censorship if they want to, and to access to the sites they want". So, while a huge number of Internet sites (including the webcam sex sites) are still banned in Turkey, various types of easily available technological devices (such as proxy servers, IP tunneling applications or DNS scripts) to bypass the censorship are legitimate, and are widely deployed by Internet users on their personal computers in Turkey.

Therefore, assuming the majority of the Turkish-speaking audience on webcam sex sites connects from within Turkey, these individuals are not only overriding social norms regarding sexuality, but circumventing the legal regulations related with Internet usage.

In addition, the size of this audience is unexpectedly large, considering the circumstances. One can often see audience members with Turkish nicknames watching performers from other linguistic spheres, quietly enjoying the performances. There are few Turkish performers present under the 'male' category at any time of the day. But the real size and dynamics of the Turkish audience become apparent as soon as a Turkish-speaking female performer starts broadcasting. The Turkish-speaking male audience immediately crowds the performer's channel, and the number of attendees becomes large enough to push the ranking of the performer quickly to among the top viewed. The popularity of any Turkish-speaking performer is so readily guaranteed that it is possible to find female sex workers from other countries who choose to appear under Turkish flag in order to lure the Turkish-speaking male audience to their broadcast (which becomes a futile effort, of course, because as soon as the audience realizes they cannot communicate with the performer, they leave her channel).

The interaction between the Turkish-speaking performers and audience is distinctly interesting, since it displays a quite productive paradox between the national identity (which is a product of nationalist fantasy) and erotic fantasy—the essential seductive power of the medium.

Quite often we find Turkish-speaking transexual sex workers performing under the 'female' category in these live webcam sex sites—although, as I mentioned, the sites are organized according to sexual preferences and there is a separate section for 'transexual' performers. These performers do not hide their transsexuality or sex work, although they do not tend to directly disclose or forefront these either—these become apparent very soon in the course of their performance, and go unquestioned. The appearance of transexual performers under female category as such does not seem to be an issue for the Turkish-speaking male audience; on the contrary, they participate in the performance as aware of the performers' transsexuality and sex work, and their interaction with the performers shows that some of the audience members are regulars, followers, and even fans of the performers.

A similar negotiation applies to Turkish female performers. The overwhelming majority of Turkish female performers we find on live sex channels don't show their faces, or choose to wear a mask. A male partner often accompanies them (who also doesn't show his face). They do interact with their audience, and while they play out the fantasy —of the bored housewife, or the sexually adventurous couple—the female performer openly demands tokens/rewards for acting out the acts her audience demands - which sometimes include her male partner. These performers appear to be quite familiar with sexual slang and the jargon of sex work. The settings of the webcam show are always in a domestic space, seldom revealing identifying markers. The interaction with the audience almost never involves personal details or depth, and often remains at the level of seduction-oriented small talk, or trivial coquetry. Any details revealing hints of identity (such as a performer's location, her 'job' etc.) appear blatantly fake - oftentimes such details echo very common clichés of the Turkish erotic imagination: if she is a bored housewife or secretary, she is always from Izmir, which is an Aegean town famous in the rest of the country for its good-looking libertine women; if she is a student, she is always from Ankara, the capital city, which is also the home of some famous universities; if it's a couple looking for sexual adventure, or a transsexual sex worker, they are always from famously decadent Istanbul. All these clichés, and the performers' insistent demand for tokens/rewards to continue with the show or in performing the acts her audience asks for, clearly reveal the fact that the performance is a part of sex work. The interaction and exchange is not intended to build up a 'realistic fantasy' (or 'realness'), but function as a 'protocol,' a mutually agreed convention through which the parties declare their positions and agree on the nature of the exchange; the common clichés presented by the performers about themselves do not reveal anything other than reifying their identity and their presence before the audience as sex workers. Unlike in other linguistic spheres, the inept visibility, or direct disclosure of sex work in Turkish linguistic sphere is not a turn-off. On the contrary, in fact, it is almost a requirement.

Occasionally, a Turkish-speaking female performer who doesn't observe this mutually agreed-upon convention will appear on these channels. Her broadcasts immediately receive the same attention as for the performers that 'play the game'. But, at the moment the Turkish-speaking male audience members gather the clues that the performer may indeed be a 'real' housewife or a student, a 'real' woman just seeking erotic thrill by playing out a sexual fantasy or by exposing herself, or just 'talking to strangers' of the opposite sex, they respond with a particular reaction. If the performer is not asking for 'tokens', if she seems to be hesitant to respond to their insistent demands for showing more flesh, or performing the acts they desire, the doubts of the audience grow. They resist buying the idea that they are actually interacting with a woman who is not doing sex work but just seeking erotic thrill. The audience first starts to question the authenticity (the 'realness') of the performer, often claiming that the performance is fake or recorded. If the performer proves that the performance is a 'live broadcast' (by spontaneously responding to her audience's comments), and she confirms that she is really there talking to them, the reaction of the audience becomes more aggressive. Their demands to see more flesh in exchange for tokens become more insistent. If the performer continues to ignore their demands and imposes her own will, which proves that she is not interested in rewards, she is not a sex worker, she is just a woman looking for erotic thrill, the tension turns into a crisis. The 'realness' of the performer in other linguistic spheres, which serves to amplify her seductive power in this medium, is enhanced by her disambiguating herself from sex workers; in the Turkish sphere, however, this would function in the opposite way, with such 'realness' creating a sober repulsion in Turkish-speaking male audience members. Confronted with proof of such 'realness,' the only response left for the audience is the denial of enjoyment through a moral reaffirmation that is attached to the nationalist fantasy. 'This woman can't be Turkish...!' the audience cries, 'She is either Armenian, or Kurdish, or Greek perhaps?' And before the frustrated woman finally decides to end her show, we often see remarks about how bad this webcam is for Turkish culture, how it corrupts the social values. "These things are not good for us!" the Turkish speaking male audience concludes.

This pattern repeats itself almost every time a Turkish-speaking female performer who does not seem to be a sex worker appears on live webcam sex channels and stays long enough to build such tension among her audience. Occasionally, some audience members may choose to voice their opinion towards not caring about moral virtues and enjoying the performance, but then they also receive their share of aggression, and this time by fighting among themselves the audience makes it impossible for them to enjoy the show.

How should we interpret this crisis, then? This pattern shows a few things at once: First of all, it displays a patriarchal fantasy that intends to confine female sexuality into the service of male desire; sex work is negotiated and accepted, but feminine sexual desire that seeks and imposes its own satisfaction is not. Then, when this patriarchal fantasy is shattered by an insistent 'realness' of the feminine desire, the Turkish male audience responds by escaping to a larger fantasy - the fantasy of nationalism, and reestablishes the moral ground on that front: "She can be a real woman, but in that case she can't be a Turkish woman." National identity, as imagined as it is - as a purely modern fantasy in the case of Turkish identity - offers a last refuge for patriarchy that female desire cannot enter and cannot lay claim to.

Because of the nature of communication and the medium, we can consider that live webcam sex channels are open to various manifestations of misogyny in all linguistic spheres - to the degree that other linguistic spheres are structured through patriarchal cultural forms as well. But the particular appearance of misogyny within the Turkish speaking audience, that it paradoxically leads to the denial of erotic pleasure itself, must be associated with the strength of a particular cultural ingredient: nationalism. In the final stage of the confrontation between misogyny and feminine desire, what glues back the shattered male ego and opens the gates for a proud, hateful exit is a greater fantasy of nationalism.

In any linguistic sphere, male or female, people are born with desire, not with national identities. In the Turkish case, the nationalism that expresses itself so schizophrenically at this moment has been cultivated for decades in popular culture. Turkish national identity was a fiction that enabled the foundation of modern Turkish Republic, and became an ideal model (rather than an existing 'type') for molding its modern social subjects. Militarism, authoritarianism, and patriarchy became interrelated components of the political culture of 'modern' Turkey, as the previously non-existing 'Turkish identity' was built by embodiment of these notions. After 1980's military coup, a 'national culture industry' emerged, emphasizing the same notions that are now seen in a liberal market environment. This national and nationalist culture industry started to dominate the local cultural markets particularly with the emergence of private TV channels by the 1990s. Since the early 2000s, only one or two foreign films per year have broken the top 10 box-office list (from the lower ranks) in Turkey, and hybrid pop forms produced by the Turkish music industry dominate most genres in the local music market.

Under these circumstances, the crisis in these seedy, dimly lit internet rendezvous houses can be seen as offering a productive tension: not only productive for exposing and understanding the Turkish patriarchal culture, but further offering a fertile confrontation with it.

References

Bakhtin, Mikhail. Rabelais and His World, Bloomington, IN: Indiana University Press, 1984.

Deleuze, Gilles. Difference and Repetition, Columbia University Press, 1995.

___. Cinema 2: The Time-Image, University Of Minnesota Press, 1989.

Heidegger, Martin. Being and Time, trans. John Macquarrie and Edward Robinson, Harper and Row Publishers, 1962.

Moore, Robert J. (2010-03-16). "Chatroulette Is 89 Percent Male, 47 Percent American, And 13 Percent Perverts". TechCrunch, *http://techcrunch.com/2010/03/16/chatroulette-stats-male-perverts/*

PERFORMATIVE ACTS OF GENDER IN ONLINE DATING: AN AUTO-ETHNOGRAPHY COMPARING SITES

MEGAN LINDSAY

Introduction

Last year, one in ten Americans reported using online dating; I am one of these many users.[1] Dating websites are intended to mediate a space for meeting new people and provide access to a dating market.[2] The site's culture and design offer suggestions about how to find a partner through optimal dating presentation. In turn the site subtly suggest ways to construct a personal identity, including gender presentation. When I participated in online dating, I struggled with how to present my identity authentically to another person through online interactions. Specifically, how could I shape my dating profile to represent a virtual extension of myself? I hypothesize, describe, and reflect on how a woman can present herself as a feminist in a manner that avoids the stigma associated with the term, through autoethnographic methods. In fact, many women do not associate with the term "feminist," and I ultimately conclude that creating an authentic personality using online dating websites is difficult and dehumanizing for men and women based on restrictive traditional gender performances. When asking Internet users what they think of online dating the approval rate steadily continues to improve.[3] In the future, we can expect the number of online daters to continue to increase.

Dating courtships have been complicated both by the changing roles of women and men and by the new approaches afforded by technology.[4,5,6] It should be the responsibility of both men and women to negotiate the new possibilities (specifically new norms and expectations around courtship) afforded in dating relationships, "but the media would certainly have us think that . . . women must figure it out before we end up desperate and alone".[7] To add to the complication, online dating sites, despite their potentially alternative media form, further perpetuate a traditional view of love and romance. The websites present narrow examples of user narratives that fit what finding love should be and how people should act, rhetoric being used would have daters believe they should present themselves as well-behaved characters in a romantic comedy. This paper is intended to be an informative recounting of my experience trying to present an authentic identity while using online dating for the first time. This paper theorizes about the role of corporate dating site owners and the existing platform constraints/affordances that are shaping identity for heterosexual dating experiences. In

---

1   Smith, Aaron, and Maeve Duggan.Online Dating & Relationships. Pew Internet & American Life Project. 21 October 2013, http://www.pewinternet.org/Reports/2013/Online-Dating.aspx.

2   Michael Hardey, 'Mediated relationships', Information, Communication & Society, 11, 2004.

3   Smith, Aaron, and Maeve Duggan.Online Dating & Relationships. Pew Internet & American Life Project. 21 October 2013, http://www.pewinternet.org/Reports/2013/Online-Dating.aspx.

4   Nicole B Ellison et al. 'Profile as Promise: A Framework for Conceptualizing Veracity in Online Dating Self Presentations', New Media & Society. 2012.

5   Nicole B Ellison et al. 'Managing impressions online: Self-presentation processes in the online dating environment', Journal of Computer Mediated Communication, 2006.

6   Angela McRobbie 'Post-feminism and popular culture.' Feminist Media Studies, 2004.

7   Angela McRobbie 'Post-feminism and popular culture.' Feminist Media Studies, 2004.

applying the work of Judith Butler[8], the performative acts of gender will be considered both in my personal process and choices and in the way that online dating sites encouraged me to behave. What began as a study of "objective" observations of the pedagogical aspects of dating websites, particularly Match.com and Okcupid.com, evolved into a weaving of my own personal story about the informal learning that happens in these spaces. While autoethnography is a less traditional method, using my own experiences and observations from participating in several online dating sites was selected as an ethical approach for respecting others' online dating experiences and provided a great deal of information.[9,10,11] I will use reflexive practices to examine how popular commercial dating sites play a pivotal role in shaping and re-shaping my online identity choices.

Previously research has shown that heteronormative culture and traditional gender roles are pervasive in the online dating experience. A content analysis of a Canadian dating site showed men and women have overlapping interests regarding a potential partners character qualities, such as morality and passion, were frequently mentioned by both men and women.[12] Some male profiles emphasized certain masculine qualities that were less traditional; presenting a new more polished modern man who was in touch with certain aspects of his own femininity.[13] Yet, the men's profiles did not abandon all tradition and certain qualities, especially work and the ability to provide, were highlighted in the virtual self. Women's profiles that were analyzed also performed gender scripts to a degree; certain profiles mentioned sexuality but in an illusive way, in contrast the male profiles more explicitly talked about sex. Women online who were older than 40, and looking for a partner, emphasized romance and waiting for the right person to be physically intimate with.[14] Several studies demonstrate that while individuals may show nuance, more often than not, familiar gender performances are used for constructing virtual selves.[15,16,17,18]

---

8   Judith Butler, 'Performative Acts and Gender Constitution: An Essay in Phenomenology and Feminist Theory', Theatre Journal (1988): 519-531.

9   Annette Markham, 'Ethic as Method, Method as Ethic: A Case for Reflexivity in Qualitative ICT Research', Journal of Information Ethics. 2006.

10 Annette Markham. "Fabrication as ethical practice: Qualitative inquiry in ambiguous Internet contexts." *Information, Communication & Society* 15.3 (2012): 334-353.

11 Tom Boellstorff,, Nardi, B., Pearce, C., & Taylor, T. L. (2012). *Ethnography and virtual worlds: A handbook of method*. Princeton University Press.

12 Melonie Fullick, "'Gendering' the Self in Online Dating Discourse,' Canadian Journal of Communication, 2013.

13 Melonie Fullick, "'Gendering' the Self in Online Dating Discourse,' Canadian Journal of Communication, 2013.

14 Susan Frohlick, and Paula Migliardi 'Heterosexual Profiling: Online Dating and 'Becoming' Heterosexualities for Women Aged 30 and Older in the Digital Era' Australian Feminist Studies, 2010.

15 Nicole B Ellison et al. 'Profile as Promise: A Framework for Conceptualizing Veracity in Online Dating Self Presentations', New Media & Society. 2012.

16 Nicole B Ellison et al. 'Managing impressions online: Self-presentation processes in the online dating environment', Journal of Computer Mediated Communication, 2006.

17 Melonie Fullick, "'Gendering' the Self in Online Dating Discourse,' Canadian Journal of Communication, 2013.

18 Susan Frohlick, and Paula Migliardi 'Heterosexual Profiling: Online Dating and 'Becoming' Heterosexual-

Contemporary dating relationships provide individuals' an opportunity to personally define relationship needs and seek partners according to these needs.[19] Previous research documents that the combination of casual and loosely defined relationships, with the onset of online dating and personal advertisements in print newspapers, lead to a dating industry. [20] The dating industry helps people become objects or products within the dating space, "Science and commerce are entwined in the relationship-scientific endeavors of these [online dating] organizations."[21] Before online dating began men and women would use print advertisements to market themselves in order to entice other singles.[22] In Jagger's content analysis of dating newspaper advertisements she concludes this is consumerism at work, and to be marketable as a dater one many daters relied on mentioning their physical attractiveness and likability.[23] In the conclusion Jagger describes how gender performances remain present, but are being redefined based on new masculinities and femininities.[24] Daters must present themselves as attractive products, and identify a target market.[25] In an experiment by Yang and Chiou, adolescents' were asked to select dating preferences off a checklist; then the participants were given an opportunity to scroll through potential dates online. The results demonstrated that the more options available, the more young people would become distracted and abandon their original preferences.[26] The medium of online advertisements could potentially influence daters' rational dating process, making it increasingly difficult to stand out among other daters. Based on previous online dating literature many individuals' perform heterosexual gendered scripts, potentially to attract a target audience. Using autoethnography to describe the online dating experience from the perspective of the dater I will discuss at length how I navigated these spaces[27, 28, 29, 30, 21]

---

ities for Women Aged 30 and Older in the Digital Era' Australian Feminist Studies, 2010.

19   Wendy Manning et al., 'The Changing Institution of Marriage: Adolescents' Expectations to Cohabit and to Marry', Journal of Marriage and Family, 2007.

20   Phillip Roscoe and Shiona Chillas, 'The State of Affairs: Critical Performativity and the Online Dating Industry', Organization, 2013. http://org.sagepub.com/content/early/2013/05/01/1350508413485497.

21   Phillip Roscoe and Shiona Chillas, 'The State of Affairs: Critical Performativity and the Online Dating Industry', Organization, 2013. http://org.sagepub.com/content/early/2013/05/01/1350508413485497.

22   Elizabeth Jagger, 'Marketing the Self, Buying an Other: Dating in a Post Modern, Consumer Society', Sociology, 1998.

23   Elizabeth Jagger, 'Marketing the Self, Buying an Other: Dating in a Post Modern, Consumer Society', Sociology, 1998.

24   Elizabeth Jagger, 'Marketing the Self, Buying an Other: Dating in a Post Modern, Consumer Society', Sociology, 1998.

25   Elizabeth Jagger, 'Marketing the Self, Buying an Other: Dating in a Post Modern, Consumer Society', Sociology, 1998.

26   Mu-Li Yang and When-Bin Chiou, 'Looking Online for the Best Romantic Partner Reduces Decision Quality: The Moderating Role of Choice-making Strategies', Cyberpsychology, Behavior, and Social Networking, 2010.

Methodology

The analyses and information offered in this auto-ethnography are based on my experiences as an online dater as interpreted using Foucault's discourse analysis theory. [32] Foucault describes how large institutions create predefined roles, and members of the institution select a role they associate with while a member of the institution. Thus, the "institution" defines the roles in order to maintain a position of power over individuals, yet those individuals believe they are creating a unique and individual representation of themselves.[33] Applying Foucault's theory, I will attempt to determine if users can create an individual and complex identity within the sponsoring site's structure. I will focus particularly on whether a site's pedagogy inhibits individuals' from establishing a nuanced gender identity by limiting their responses to an abstract assortment of predetermined roles.

During the first phase of the discourse analysis, I will analyze the content of the websites based on the "site of the image" as well as the "textual materials, both visual and written." [34] Although it may seem that using one technique or methodology may offer a clearer understanding, the complexity of the sites requires using both methods. When setting up a dating profile, there are specific templates provided for users to create a unique dating profile. I will examine these templates to determine what the site defines as necessary dating information. This examination will be useful in identifying how the website shapes a user's dating experience and how gender roles are integrated into the site's structure. The visual context and culture of the Internet is different than traditional media; "users of the Internet collaboratively produce digital images of the body – very particular things for very particular uses – in the context of racial and gender identity formation".[35] This analysis will demonstrate how my individual experience was a constant interplay between the institution of commercial dating

---

27 Nicole B Ellison et al. 'Profile as Promise: A Framework for Conceptualizing Veracity in Online Dating Self Presentations', New Media & Society. 2012.

28 Nicole B Ellison et al. 'Managing impressions online: Self-presentation processes in the online dating environment', Journal of Computer Mediated Communication, 2006.

29 Tom Boellstorff,, Nardi, B., Pearce, C., & Taylor, T. L. (2012). *Ethnography and virtual worlds: A handbook of method*. Princeton University Press.

30 Melonie Fullick, "Gendering' the Self in Online Dating Discourse,' Canadian Journal of Communication, 2013.

31 Susan Frohlick, and Paula Migliardi 'Heterosexual Profiling: Online Dating and 'Becoming' Heterosexualities for Women Aged 30 and Older in the Digital Era' Australian Feminist Studies, 2010.

32 For more on this theory, see Gillian Rose, Visual Methodologies: An Introduction to Researching with Visual Materials, Sage Publications Limited, 2011.

33 Scott Yates and David Hiles, 'Towards a "Critical Ontology of Ourselves"? Foucault, Subjectivity and Discourse Analysis', *Theory & Psychology*, 2010.

34 For more on this theory, see Gillian Rose, Visual Methodologies: An Introduction to Researching with Visual Materials, Sage Publications Limited, 2011.

35 Lisa Nakumara, Digitizing Race: Visual Cultures of the Internet, Minneapolis: University of Minnesota Press, 2008.

sites and user-created material.[36] It will detail how web designers create the choices that its users may select to individualize their online personality. This process of interactivity between user and creator sets Internet studies apart from traditional media studies.[37]

The second portion of the discourse analysis will seek to explain how "the institution[s] put[s] images to work," and the dating site users hold up the websites expectations.[38] Images are a powerful way to promote a message. An institution can promote certain types of images to present an idea to its members. In this way, the site is used to promote an idea. A site, however, may also reinforce to its users ways to conform to an idea (e.g., attractive bodies). This can be seen where dating sites allow user to select only predetermined body types. Fuchs calls this a socio-technological space where institutions recreate the societal norms where its online members exist.[39] I will analyze the choices commercial dating sites offer users to find whether the site has greater power when creating the experience, or, conversely, whether users create their own experience within the site. I will use reflexivity to discuss my experiences dating online and demonstrate how gender matters and corporate institutions now facilitating dating markets shape identity possibilities. Further, the shaping of this process can influence the ways individuals interact during first encounters with potential partners.

Lastly, throughout this paper I plan to use reflexivity. In discussion of the relevance of previous research findings, I will analyze my experiences participating in online dating. Previous research describes what reflexivity is and why we may use it: "The ability of humans to reflect (on the past and the future) has a long intellectual history and heritage growing out of Enlightenment belief in the ability of (wo)man to reason in a reasonable manner about his(her) fate, impact the future, and transcend the present"[40] In order to demonstrate how the sites interact with the users, I will discuss my dating experience using both Okcupid, and Match.com. The use of ethnographic methods in virtual worlds is useful because it can "explore beliefs and practices within and between cultures, linking together materials…"[41]

I did receive approval from my institution's IRB before creating a faux profile to make observations about how Match.com and Okcupid operates and communicates with members. My "research profile" informed users I was observing the site and encouraged users to contact me if they had questions or concerns. No users contacted my research profile. I then de-

---

36 Nicole B Ellison et al. 'Managing impressions online: Self-presentation processes in the online dating environment', Journal of Computer Mediated Communication, 2006.
37 Lisa Nakumara, Digitizing Race: Visual Cultures of the Internet, Minneapolis: University of Minnesota Press, 2008.
38 For more on this theory, see Gillian Rose, Visual Methodologies: An Introduction to Researching with Visual Materials, Sage Publications Limited, 2011.
39 Christian Fuchs, 'The Internet as Self-organizing Aocio-technological Systems', Cybernetics and Human Knowing, 2004.
40 Wanada Pillow, 'Confession, Catharsis, or Cure? Rethinking the Uses of Reflexivity as Methodological Power in Qualitative Research', International Journal of Qualitative Studies in Education, 2003.
41 Tom Boellstorff,, Nardi, B., Pearce, C., & Taylor, T. L. (2012). *Ethnography and virtual worlds: A handbook of method*. Princeton University Press.

cided to research the site as a consumer of its product instead of making inferences about other individuals' experiences. The examples given are based on my experiences. Ethnography methods commonly present "key critical cases, incidents, stories, or events to illustrate patterns"[42]. The description is intended to resonate the cultural experience of online dating rather than give a factual accounting of individual behaviors.[43],[44] "We must take into consideration possible harm or embarrassment that can be brought about through romantic, sexual, and intimate activities." [45] While I considered doing interviews and providing information from others' profiles as part of the data within the paper, this practice seemed deceptive since I knew during the early phases of my research that I was on both sites as a researcher and as a dater. For this reason, specific examples are fictionalized to protect the privacy of other daters with whom I had interactions. This protection is two fold; first, I intend to reshape certain phrases and words so that in an era of search engines no other daters' information could be directly linked back to them. Secondly, I believe most interactions unfolded as a sincere and honest attempt to reach out to me as a dater and not as a researcher. To unveil these potentially intimate moments word-for-word felt like a breach of ethics as a researcher.

Attracting an Audience

Standard features found on dating sites include an original profile where individuals can display content including pictures, and a short text description about themselves. On both Match.com and Okcupid, daters have multiple ways for interacting through the site. These include less direct methods meant to seem more like gestures, such as the wink on Match, or adding someone to a list of favorite users on Okcupid. Additionally, users can email and direct message one another when logged onto the site. After a short period of using Match.com, I quickly noticed several fields on my profile providing a numbers report. Emphasis on these statistics showed the site had a vested interest in attracting users and site traffic over helping individuals finding a life partner. The website consistently encouraged my participation, by reminding me to check, update, and attend to my profile. The faux research profile I had created received several notifications; between March 27th and May 9th, the site generated 68 emails, an average of two per day, encouraging my participation even though I rarely logged in and no other daters had contacted me. The emails suggested "potential matches" and encouraged me to contact them. Love, it seemed, was available only for the most active users. But the constant suggestion to look more, click more, and send more messages is dangerous. Men may feel justified in unwanted pursuit, and women, who are traditionally encouraged to be submissive, may have a difficult time stopping unwanted communications.[46]

---

42 Tom Boellstorff,, Nardi, B., Pearce, C., & Taylor, T. L. (2012). *Ethnography and virtual worlds: A handbook of method.* Princeton University Press.

43 Annette Markham, 'Ethic as Method, Method as Ethic: A Case for Reflexivity in Qualitative ICT Research', Journal of Information Ethics. 2006.

44 Annette Markham. "Fabrication as ethical practice: Qualitative inquiry in ambiguous Internet contexts." *Information, Communication & Society* 15.3 (2012): 334-353.

45 Tom Boellstorff,, Nardi, B., Pearce, C., & Taylor, T. L. (2012). *Ethnography and virtual worlds: A handbook of method.* Princeton University Press.

46 Judith Butler, 'Performative Acts and Gender Constitution: An Essay in Phenomenology and Feminist Theory', Theatre Journal (1988): 519-531.

Further, the activity of flipping through profiles became exciting and fun, but I was unsure if it was helping me narrow down my dating pool. If anything the longer I was spending collecting potential profiles, the broader the range on my spectrum of dates.[47]

To the websites credit, knowing I was female, I was encouraged to reach out and contact potential dates. I hesitated to do this, believing that men still have an expectation of making first contact. When engaging in a site specifically designed to (re)create dating opportunities, I felt it necessary to craft an image that was at least moderately compliant with gender norms. Match.com, knowing prevailing cultural dating practices, was "offering available norms for the act of recognition." [48] Match.com never stated explicitly on the website when a wink should be used, but a mediating flirt option seems to be a convenient way for women to indicate interest without seeming aggressive. People would take this interaction as the first step towards flirtation. Viewing profiles became the catalyst for more user interaction, and even though I did not send a wink first, some men communicated with me simply because I had viewed their profile. After viewing a profile, I would often receive a wink from the user. Then I would wink back, and a conversation would ensue. This reincarnation of traditional dating pursuits affirms that in the online world, many men still felt comfortable in their role as initiators.

Similar to Match.com, OKcupid.com reported the number of viewers I had on my page each day, which told me the number of people interested enough in my picture to click to my page. Every time I logged into these sites, it was difficult not to view these numbers as a report of my success. During my youth, I can recount numerous occasions where young men described how they ranked women. The woman became an object in this rating game, an exercise in who deserves a man's attention. The higher the number, the more desirable she was considered. In the 11th grade, Shane told me that on a scale of one to ten, I was a "six" because I wore my hair short, and my chest was too small. My anxiety about "low numbers" was fostered from an awareness that my ability to find a partner was hinging on my ability to compete with other women, and again, here was my score right in front of me. According to the site, this is how the world of dating goes for everybody. As stated upfront in one Okcupid.com blog, "we all know that beautiful people are more successful daters"[49] However, different from men, women at a much earlier age internalize the messages that their inherent value to other people comes first from their attractiveness and their ability to secure a partner.[50] Men do have to compete based on looks; yet just based on the use of women's modeling photo's or professional pictures as their dating profile icon, my impression was their pressure did not come with the same intensity.

The numbers game elicited different emotional responses. Some days, I had many views,

---

47   Mu-Li Yang and When-Bin Chiou, 'Looking Online for the Best Romantic Partner Reduces Decision Quality: The Moderating Role of Choice-making Strategies', Cyberpsychology, Behavior, and Social Networking, 2010.
48   Judith Butler, Giving an Account of Oneself, Fordham University Press, 2005. p. 22.
49   Okcupid, http://blog.okcupid.com/index.php/your-looks-and-online-dating/.
50   James Mahalik, et al. 'Development of the Conformity to Feminine Norms Inventory', Sex Roles, 2005.

and I felt validated and attractive. Other days, I felt insecure and uncertain about my attractiveness, because I had received no messages. To win at the numbers game, I found myself spending more time on both sites, frequently checking my winks, watching for new messages, and viewing more profiles. I became easily distracted by the prospect of being datable or likeable for an audience rather than a partner. Nowhere on either site does it suggest that less is more or that narrowing down your potential daters will benefit you. Rather than emphasize certain attributes that make me stand out as an individual, generating high volumes of traffic meant presenting a commodified pleasurable package of myself. My online self became a product, not a person.

Marketing Tools

Both Match.com and Okcupid.com provided information that instructed daters on different ways to present themselves. Match.com has an "advice center" that gives direction on how to write the perfect first email, pick out the perfect outfit, be sensual on the first date, and win anyone over. To illustrate, according to Match.com, to write the perfect email: 1) keep it simple, 2) be honest, 3) mention something specific from the person's profile, 4) let your voice come through, 5) have fun with the format, and 6) check your spelling. However, daters should not: 1) focus on your match's looks, 2) go on and on via email, 3) ask too many questions, 4) use edgy humor, 5) send multiple users the same message, or 6) rely on sexual innuendo. Essentially the site attempts to teach people to be polite and avoid taking risks. According to online dating presenting risks, such as edgy humor, may mean no dates. Based on the sites advice I assumed the objective was not to help other daters rule you out based on differences, or a clear mismatch, but to subdue off-putting characteristics so that potentially more users could relate to you.

Match.com also promotes certain dating behaviors with its online magazine, "Happen." [51] Just as it is stated in the slogan, "because love doesn't come with instructions," is telling, The magazine includes articles such as:

- "8 things that make women crave sex"
- "Dating when you are a parent"
- "6 bad traits that make him a good partner"
- "7 text messages that scare men off"
- "Women's 5 biggest dating lies"

The magazine reinforced the notion that there were limitless opportunities for a social connection, and if I failed at love, I must have done something wrong. As another example, in the article "Women's 5 biggest dating lies," women are berated for having low self-esteem. "Sure, it's normal to have a few negative thoughts (which Ahlers[life couch] refers to as "Big Fat Lies") while you're dating, but what's not OK is allowing that mindset to prevent you from finding real, true love. According to the online life coach, women should simply stop any neg-

---

51   Happen Magazine, http://www.match.com/magazine/.

ative self-talk because it prevents us from dating.[52] The article never mentions where self-doubt comes from, or how consumerism and gendered scripts being reiterated through the site may contribute to feelings of inadequacy. The article asks women to question their inner critic (e.g., "too fat compared to whom?"). Additionally, the article never addresses the website's role of mediating the dating space. Instead, all responsibility for success or failure was squarely placed on my shoulders. It seems Match.com perpetuated an overarching message: love is for all people, and if you market your online profile just right, you too can find love.

Okcupid.com matches potential daters according to test results. The site informs users that it will "do the math" as you look for a partner. Additionally, Okcupid.com offers many blog entries where general trends are presented as info-graphics, charts, and quantified information. At the bottom of the homepage, the OkTrends section reports on a number of topics, similar to Match.com's online magazine.[53] The content is comparable; "Don't be ugly by accident," and "Exactly what to say in a first message" instruct users on what tone to use when writing and how to pick the best image for their profile picture. Okcupid.com attempts to use a casual, humorous tone, which suggests their willingness to help a user find whatever they are looking for at the moment. For example, one blog discusses the sexual trends of site users while creating the impression the writer is a friend, and the two of you are having a conversation.[54]

Okcupid.com emphasizes being matched based on the quantified and tested attributes of our personality. The site offers several tests, some of which are traditional psychological metrics meant to capture personality while others are more playful. This is not a unique feature of Okcupid.com; other dating sites promote their ability to help you make the right match using algorithms.[55] The claimed magic of the site is it can match you based on science, which implies love is based on a formula or algorithm. If the users have a successful relationship, it supports the rhetoric; love is logic. Historically, relying on math, abstract logic, and traditional sciences has been categorized as male in nature and superior to female ways of knowing.[56] Okcupid.com's discourse has a subtle but powerful implication; don't rely on your intuition or heart. Use logic, science, and authority for best results during online dating.

An interesting feature found only on Okcupid.com is the use of crowdsourcing. As previously mentioned, site members can upload their own tests to the website, giving other daters an opportunity to measure features not covered by the tests offered on the site. Users can also submit photos to "My Best Face," a program that allows daters to rate the attractiveness of other users' photographs. Crowdsourcing acts, such as My Best Face, are a perfect exam-

---

52 Chelsea Kaplan, http://www.match.com/magazine/article/13157/Womens-5-Biggest-Dating-Lies/.
53 Okcupid trends: http://blog.okcupid.com/.
54 Okcupid trends: http://blog.okcupid.com/.
55 Phillip Roscoe and Shiona Chillas, 'The State of Affairs: Critical Performativity and the Online Dating Industry', Organization, 2013. http://org.sagepub.com/content/early/2013/05/01/1350508413485497.
56 Noretta Koertge, Critical Perspectives on Feminist Epistemology. Handbook of Feminist Research: Theory and Practice, Thousand Oaks, CA. Sage Publications, 2006.

ple of how online dating can construct online spaces in conjunction with the designers. [57] Previously, researchers have demonstrated how commercial images are so common place in our day-to-day lives, that often times individuals' mimic or recreate the images on their one. [58]Despite the opportunity for freedom of expression, users' ranking patterns matched those images which are typically considered commercially attractive.[59] Recently, WIRED magazine was given permission by Okcupid.com and Match.com to use their data and determine, on average, what attracts daters. For heterosexual daters, both men and women prioritized a flat stomach above all else. [60] Eventually I came to understand that if I wanted to attract a dater, my physique was the most important thing.

Online dating culture is influenced by the coproduction of knowledge through the site as well as broader society; each individual profile actively shapes and conforms to the culture.[61] Men and women seem to rely on the social context of the site to define gender roles and self-presentation. This includes the visual culture, and that culture still promotes the idea that a woman's ultimate value is in her looks.[62] Match.com and Okcupid.com subtly promote bodies as advertisements. A reoccurring advertisement on my page was for Weight Watchers. The ad featured a petite blonde and, given my recent understanding that my looks mattered most, suggested to me the idea that "thin" is a desirable attribute. The message seemed clear. Consumer culture emphasizes thin, small, docile bodies as a representation of true femininity.[63] Many men and women wanted a model like date, and in order to find love, I should look like one, or so I was told.

Commercial dating sites promote the idea that it is not only convenient to meet potential partners online; it is also common. Below are a list of Match.com slogans and marketing, found on the website and through television commercials. The first slogan reiterates that the relationships start online, not during the in-person phase. Love is guaranteed for any user. The promise of love for any user may not be logical, but individuals are sold the idea that their existence, or at least their happiness, it contingent on finding a partner. Form women they may have received even stronger messages about how their self-worth depends on that love, especially the love from a successful hetero-man.[64] Lastly, the slogans reinforce that online

---

57 Christian Fuchs, 'The Internet as Self-organizing Aocio-technological Systems', Cybernetics and Human Knowing, 2004.
58 Susan Bordo, Unbearable Weight: Feminism, Western Culture, and the Body, Berkley: University of California Press, 1993.
59 Susan Bordo, Unbearable Weight: Feminism, Western Culture, and the Body, Berkley: University of California Press, 1993.
60 Caitlin Roper, http://www.wired.com/design/2014/02/how-to-create-good-online-dating-profile/.
61 Christian Fuchs, 'The Internet as Self-organizing Aocio-technological Systems', Cybernetics and Human Knowing, 2004.
62 Susan Bordo, Unbearable Weight: Feminism, Western Culture, and the Body, Berkley: University of California Press, 1993.
63 Susan Bordo, Unbearable Weight: Feminism, Western Culture, and the Body, Berkley: University of California Press, 1993.
64 Judith Butler, 'Performative Acts and Gender Constitution: An Essay in Phenomenology and Feminist

presentation trump other factors involved in love. Finding a mate is about keeping a fresh marketing approach, and even though the environment has changed, your appearance is still a strong (perhaps the strongest) indicator of your chances for love.

- "1 in 5 relationships start online. And more of them start at Match than any other site."
- "Find Love. Guaranteed."
- "Your interests change, so should your profile."
- "Attract 15x more attention. Add a photo."

Regarding performativity, the act of gender is not a role, it is a series of acts. [65] Thus, if the site or its users' minimizes the importance of a woman's career, other users may begin to minimize their career to remain an acceptable woman based on the standards of the site.[66] Since the site, and users who maintain the culture within the site, strongly emphasize physical attractiveness, than the users are best to invest their time in presenting a physically attractive self. The culture and profile space provided limits individual expression and reduces bodies to online advertisements. After spending my time immersed in online dating sites I learned that the responsibility of creating and maintaining a sense of self that is authentic is up to me, the user, and the majority of getting to know other daters would happen in the real world.

Personal Marketing Strategy

When first creating my dating profile I looked to other users, and not just the advice and features of the site, to better understand the culture. I was unsure how I wanted to present myself to other daters. Early on people speculated the Internet would allow individuals to create a neutral space removed from the body and void of cultural identities such as gender, race, and class.[67] Yet, the internet has evolved into a socio-technological extension of society where individual identities are important. [68,69] My initial expectations of the sites were changes my observation of other users and the suggestions of the dating sites. At first, it seemed best to present myself as authentically as possible if I wanted to make an authentic connection. I wanted to present a nuanced gender identity but worried that my message would be misinterpreted. It was difficult to know if my choice to mute certain aspects of my identity was a sell out of my personal values. [70] Before I even began to build my profile I already had certain advantages, being young and white are both highly competitive in online

---

Theory', Theatre Journal (1988): 519-531.

65   Judith Butler, 'Performative Acts and Gender Constitution: An Essay in Phenomenology and Feminist Theory', Theatre Journal (1988): 519-531.

66   Judith Butler, 'Performative Acts and Gender Constitution: An Essay in Phenomenology and Feminist Theory', Theatre Journal (1988): 519-531.

67   Lisa Nakumara, Digitizing Race: Visual Cultures of the Internet, Minneapolis: University of Minnesota Press, 2008.

68   Lisa Nakumara, Digitizing Race: Visual Cultures of the Internet, Minneapolis: University of Minnesota Press, 2008.

69   Amber McRobbie, 'Post-feminism and Popular Culture', Feminist Media Studies, 2004.

70   Judith Butler, 'Performative Acts and Gender Constitution: An Essay in Phenomenology and Feminist Theory', Theatre Journal (1988): 519-531.

dating space.[71] Would taking advantage of certain selling points, attract the type of person I would really want to be with?

I reviewed other females' profile to decide how I wanted to portray myself. Just like real or offline dating, to some degree I would be competing with other women, or at the very least our online presentations would be compared.[72] Some of the content I saw was worth mimicking; such as offering a practical reason using the site i.e. moving to a new city. Other portrayals seemed so cliché that they failed to provide any sense of the person outside of their ability to perform gender. Usernames like "ms.cherrypie" or "bubbleycutie" made me wonder if these women chose youthful personas intentionally, or were these women just doing what was needed in order to compete for attention in the dating market? Other usernames hyper-sexualized a woman's persona such as "pullmyhair" or "bombasticblondie" or "vampirehottie". There was a wide range of usernames, but culture is influenced by these extreme presentations of womanhood. I was having a hard time feelings like an individual when some of the women seemed to be presenting identities that positively reinforced the acting out of gendered scripts.[73],[74] I chose an androgynous username, mlindsa3, because neutrality felt safer than having every email message start with the line, 'Hello naughty4you' or 'Hi sweety14'.

Another interest I had was related to the way in which women presented careers, ambitions and goals.Match.com has an online dating community where individuals presented traditional gender scripts such as traditional pursuit or heteronormative family roles. Arguments made for the "naturalness" of gendered identities are based in the perceived need for society to create a proper family unit.[75] Women in their childbearing years are expected to publicly display and justify their choices for reproduction.[76],[77] While not scientific, I tallied the education preferences of fifty men and fifty women and noticed a telling pattern. Men and women tended to emphasize traditional gender roles within the structure of the family. For example, men commonly listed their education but had no preference for their partner's education.[78] Yet, women commonly preferred a partner with a higher education.[79] I began to wonder if

---

71   Oktrends, http://blog.okcupid.com/index.php/your-race-affects-whether-people-write-you-back/.

72   Sara Hill et al., 'Courtship, Competition, and the Pursuit of Attractiveness: Mating Goals Facilitate Health-related Risk Taking and Strategic Risk Suppression in Women', *Personality and Social Psychology Bulletin*, 2011.

73   Judith Butler, 'Performative Acts and Gender Constitution: An Essay in Phenomenology and Feminist Theory', Theatre Journal (1988): 519-531.

74   Susan Frohlick, and Paula Migliardi 'Heterosexual Profiling: Online Dating and 'Becoming' Heterosexualities for Women Aged 30 and Older in the Digital Era' Australian Feminist Studies, 2010.

75   Judith Butler, 'Performative Acts and Gender Constitution: An Essay in Phenomenology and Feminist Theory', Theatre Journal (1988): 519-531.

76   Judith Butler, 'Performative Acts and Gender Constitution: An Essay in Phenomenology and Feminist Theory', Theatre Journal (1988): 519-531.

77   Susan Frohlick, and Paula Migliardi 'Heterosexual Profiling: Online Dating and 'Becoming' Heterosexualities for Women Aged 30 and Older in the Digital Era' Australian Feminist Studies, 2010.

78   Melonie Fullick, "Gendering' the Self in Online Dating Discourse,' Canadian Journal of Communication, 2013.

79   Melonie Fullick, "Gendering' the Self in Online Dating Discourse,' Canadian Journal of Communication,

my commitment to higher education was a disposable quality to men, or at least something I should be clear would not prevent me from prioritizing a family. Perhaps because the site forces users to prioritize their preferences, my value was still measured according to traditional roles for women, and I should strive to present myself as a good wife and mother. Even online, it seemed men chose to present themselves as the breadwinner, and women emphasized their qualities as a homemaker. [80],[81],[82]

My opening paragraph needed to be interesting and authentic but somehow stand out among many profiles. "Reciprocity takes the form of self-promotion. Culture is to become precisely nothing but advertising." [83] I wondered if it was better to be cute or smart. Was there room in the online dating world to be both? I consider my stubbornness, independence, out-spoken nature, logic, and sarcastic sense of humor my more masculine traits, and my more feminine traits are my kindness, passion, and my nurturing nature. I am comfortable with these traits, and I hope my partner has similar qualities. However, I felt certain if I emphasized my masculine qualities too strongly, I would drive people away. Deciding which side of me to present raised interesting questions not just about female stereotypes, but feminist stereotypes. If I wanted a partner was I daring enough to dismiss all men who may not relate to feminist ideas presented in my profile? How important should I consider these feminist values in relation to my future partner? I felt pressured to be vague about some things such as my career plans and my love of politics. Acting cute appeared the best way to get noticed. Here is what I posted:

"I just moved to Phoenix this year. I am doing grad school here and I really love it so far. I am pretty ambitious about career goals and decided in the new year I should be more social. I have some old fashion values about family, but overall I would say I am a pretty modern woman. The most uncomfortable part of this whole profile stuff is picking your body type- I think I have a "great body" but that wasn't an option. Humor is really important for me, and I can't picture spending a lot of time around someone unless they make me laugh and laugh at my jokes too. I can be very sarcastic and argue at times, but I am very much a people person and I enjoy socializing. If you are looking for a girl who will follow, that isn't me- eek sorry. I am very interested in making friends, and don't mind a more casual get together. I only date people who really stand out to me."

The problem of presenting a feminist self is not a unique problem:

"To count as a girl today appears to require this kind of ritualistic denunciation, which in

---

2013.

80   Smith, Aaron, and Maeve Duggan. Online Dating & Relationships. Pew Internet & American Life Project. 21 October 2013, http://www.pewinternet.org/Reports/2013/Online-Dating.aspx.

81   Melonie Fullick, "Gendering' the Self in Online Dating Discourse,' Canadian Journal of Communication, 2013.

82   Susan Frohlick, and Paula Migliardi 'Heterosexual Profiling: Online Dating and 'Becoming' Heterosexualities for Women Aged 30 and Older in the Digital Era' Australian Feminist Studies, 2010.

83   Jaron Lanier, *You are not a Gadget: A Manifesto*, Vintage Press, New York: 2010.

turn suggests that one strategy in the disempowering of feminism includes it being historicised and generationalised and thus easily rendered out of date."[17_Lindsay_5]

An online persona has the potential for self-expression, at the time I felt it was necessary to qualify my own behavior and minimize certain characteristics. When retrospectively analyzing my own content I felt some shock and embarrassment. In my attempt to follow the "norms", I found myself apologizing for my strengths. I wanted to present a strong feminist identity but feared the stereotypes that would be unnecessarily placed on me. Personality traits, which may be authentic, can be off-putting if they do not conform to gender performanc.[84] So I opted to reduce my complicated essence to something simpler, an advertisement...a potential date.

I had other opportunities to present my persona to potential dates. I could check off interests from the site's predetermined checklist. I had numerous options, such as reading, hiking, working out, travel, "hot" spots, and other options for first date topics. I quickly learned that the topics were broad enough to match me with almost anyone. Certain leisure activities and consumer behaviors nearly all members were included.[85] For example, I can assume nearly all men are interested in weight lifting because that always came up as a common interest. This simplification of people is dangerous because, "...that reduction of life is what gets broadcasted between friends [daters] all the time. What is communicated between people eventually becomes their truth. Relationships take on the trouble of software engineering".[86] Reducing ones self means that other daters viewing your profile are relying on limited information, largely based on consumer behaviors, and have no way of knowing how important a person's interest is based on a checkmark.[87] The checklist is left open for interpretation, and if a woman selects an activity, her identity is decided for her by that checkmark.

For example, a user might "like" dancing. I chose this category because I was a dance instructor and still enjoy attending classes occasionally. However, this could easily be construed as dancing in nightclubs, which I also enjoy, but does not accurately represent what I meant when I selected "dancing." Further, dancing and nightclubs and are typically associated with "bad girl behavior." Thus, reduction to a category brings with it the performativity of other woman's behaviors and choices, now on the dating site, and throughout history.[88] The selection of "dancing" or any other behavior becomes redefined by the male reader and conformed to his assumptions about women who enjoy dancing. Interestingly, after my experience on Match.com I decided that for Okcupid I would I only post a picture. I did not include

---

84 Judith Butler, 'Performative Acts and Gender Constitution: An Essay in Phenomenology and Feminist Theory', Theatre Journal (1988): 519-531.
85 Elizabeth Jagger, 'Marketing the Self, Buying an Other: Dating in a Post Modern, Consumer Society', Sociology, 1998.
86 Jaron Lanier, *You are not a Gadget: A Manifesto*, Vintage Press, New York: 2010.
87 Elizabeth Jagger, 'Marketing the Self, Buying an Other: Dating in a Post Modern, Consumer Society', Sociology, 1998.
88 Judith Butler, 'Performative Acts and Gender Constitution: An Essay in Phenomenology and Feminist Theory', Theatre Journal (1988): 519-531.

a bio or answer questions about my personality, but I received a similar level of interest from potential suitors as I received on Match.com. Although I had struggled with how to present my identity as a modern, feminist woman to daters, apparently my most important attribute was my appearance. All that mattered was the picture. Despite my personal hopes of tweaking, and altering my profile in order to indicate the type of person I am to other daters, I remained an advertisement in the space.

Consumer Satisfaction

To conclude the story of my experience in online dating culture I will describe interactions with the other users. After investigating the online spaces of commercial dating sites, I would like to offer the following examples as key incidents that influenced the interactions.[89] I believe that many of these incidents were part of a larger set of socio-cultural norms found in all dating situations that allow daters to treat one another as objects. My virtual presentation (advertisement) led to interactions where I was treated as a product, more so than as a person. Often my silence was mistaken for intentional mysteriousness and an invitation for a follow-up. However, Match.com and Okcupid do not offer a mechanism to signal disinterest. With face-to-face interactions, men are more likely to take safe bets and wait for a perceived signal or appropriate body language. At the very least, I can offer a signal of disinterest by walking away or turning my back to continue a conversation with friends. Online, the cues are filtered, and hopeful emotions may prompt a user to be even more courageous.[90] Men may have genuine hopes based in a false reality. Yet, when a real person rejects someone, the feelings are real. The intensity of the emotion may not be experienced any differently at all, even thought the interaction took place online. Some men have lashed out, and others tried to change my mind through repeated offers, other men did not pursue beyond the first message. All of these problematic dating rituals began offline, but continue in this space. However, just as in the offline world, women are supposed to be flattered and intrigued by all offers. [91]

The first example is a fabricated account based on a real email exchange between myself and a potential suitor: "You know, you look better as a brunette." At first I could not figure out why would a complete stranger felt compelled to critique me without ever having spoken any other words to me? My initial thought was, "Who does he think he is?!" I replied, "I don't ask or take advice from complete strangers." Within minutes I got another reply. "Wow. I was just trying to be helpful. No wonder you are single— you cunt." The majority of the I met online did not make such bold moves. However, I couldn't help but wonder if the rejection he felt was enhanced because in an online space people are supposed to treat one another as products. And especially, myself as a female dater should have been grateful and receptive to his feedback as a consumer.

---

89   Tom Boellstorff,,, Nardi, B., Pearce, C., & Taylor, T. L. (2012). *Ethnography and virtual worlds: A handbook of method*. Princeton University Press.
90   Jaron Lanier, *You are not a Gadget: A Manifesto*, Vintage Press, New York: 2010.
91   Judith Butler, 'Performative Acts and Gender Constitution: An Essay in Phenomenology and Feminist Theory', Theatre Journal (1988): 519-531.

By emphasizing traffic, the site clouds users' judgments about the purpose of online dating. The site teaches users to value consumption by measuring success as the number of views your profile receives, and in the age of hook-up culture I wonder if people don't see this endless pool of daters as a means of shuffling different partners in and out with efficiency. The second example I offer is a fabricated version of a very common text conversation I had with many daters.

> Suitor: "Hey, whats up?"
>
> Me: "Hi, not much, how are you? This is Mike, right?"
>
> Suitor: "Yeah, it's Mike. I'm good."
>
> Me: "Sweet. So what are you up to?"
>
> Suitor: "Nothing really, just watching TV relaxing a little bit."
>
> Me: "Nice."
>
> Suitor: "Wanna send me a pic?"
>
> Me: "No thanks, I don't really do that."
>
> Suitor: "You don't have to take your clothes off! Lol."
>
> Me: "Oh I know, I just don't really like send pics to people I have never met. Lol. I know it might seem strange, but I just don't do that."
>
> Suitor: "Oh common, why not? You must be trying to hide something."
>
> Me: "Lol, nope. I just feel weird sending an image or picture of myself to a complete stranger. Its always been my policy. Don't worry!"
>
> Suitor: "So you really won't send one at all?"
>
> Me: "No, nothing personal."
>
> Suitor: "K. I'm not sure if I want to meet up then, unless you will send the picture."

As previously discussed there is great emphasis on attractiveness. The more you are viewed, the better your chances, and the more gender conforming the profile, the more views you will attract.[92] My private conversations with men lead me to believe that they were invested and

---

92 Judith Butler, 'Performative Acts and Gender Constitution: An Essay in Phenomenology and Feminist Theory', Theatre Journal (1988): 519-531.

interested in making sure the attraction level translated into real life. That is understandable, the question I was always left with, is how the potential for deception left men feeling they had a right to access my image on command. After giving very rational and what I believed, justified reasons for not sharing cell phone pictures; I was often dismissed. I believe this dismissal was based on two reasons, one the idea that I was a replaceable product in a flooding market. The second, reason was that as a woman setting clear and firm boundaries around the ownership of my body was seen as unattractive and difficult, no matter how politely I state it. [93] Not all users behaved this way, but the site potentially facilitates these experiences. [94]

The last incident, or example I will use presents more questions than answers. However, I think if we are to dismiss the experience of sexual aggression from the online dating experience, it will not offer a holistic picture. To be clear I have had these types of conversations in bars, at schools, at night clubs, over text message, and through online chat after I got to know someone. Yet in real life, when a man would approach me in a public place, for the first time, the conversation rarely evolved so quickly. This is not a condemnation of casual sex, or an attempt to explain or hypothesize about when sex should be introduced into relationships. It is important to note, that in my experience men would often discuss quickly, even before actually meeting me, topics of sexuality and physical intimacy. Here is an example of a fabricated conversation with a man met online, but not in person.

> Suitor: "Hi there beautiful. How have you been?"
>
> Me: "Good, how are you doing?"
>
> Suitor: "I'm great, just kinda lonely."
>
> Me: "Lol, oh yeah? You are lonely?"
>
> Suitor: "Ok, well I'm actually horny. Ha. Wanna hang out?"

Research is still developing theories and hypotheses around intimacy the perceived meaning, influences, and changes brought on through new technologies.[95] Walther believes that mediated spaces enhance the opportunity for hyperpersonal communication. Research about college students communication patterns shows that there is a progression or pattern for mediated exchanges; participants described meeting people in person and then finding one another through social media, followed by private direct message conversations, and lastly giving out cell phone numbers for text messages and phone calls. The spaces where privacy

---

93 Judith Butler, 'Performative Acts and Gender Constitution: An Essay in Phenomenology and Feminist Theory', Theatre Journal (1988): 519-531.
94 Joseph Walther, 'Computer-mediated Communication Impersonal, Interpersonal, and Hyperpersonal Interaction', Communication Research 23.1 (1996): 3-43.
95 Sherry Turkle, Alone Together: Why We Expect More from Technology and Less from Each Other, Yew York: Basic Books, 2011.

is perceived, especially text messaging and direct messaging through chat, could evoke feelings of intimacy that lead to conversation about sex more quickly. The topic is certainly a part of contemporary dating experiences, and sexual practices within relationships could be influenced by online dating culture. "In online life, the pace of relationships speeds up. One quickly moves from infatuation to disillusionment and back. And the moment one grows even slightly bored, there is easy access to someone new"[96] People already use online space to find casual sex, but in the near future I wonder how as users we will keep casual sexual networks separate from dating relationship networks. In my own experience the boundaries between these two spaces is already becoming blurred, and perhaps all dating networks will blend together in the future.

Conclusion

Essentially online dating sites transform people into advertisements whose worth is determined by the amount of traffic they can generate. Many commercial dating sites follow a similar format setting a precedent for online dating culture. In this regard, a dating profile is not much different than a personal ad in the local newspaper, yet the pace of online dating is much faster, more resourceful, and growing in popularity. For the sake of keeping profiles in a pleasing and enticing state, the sites promote traditional gender roles that inhibit users from creating a more nuanced identity. To compete, women and men are forced to market themselves like products. This ritual can dehumanize and in turn encourage daters to objectify one another. However, I believe these sites provide a valuable service to their users, so long as the users realize the profiles on the sites are limited and the information portrayed is restricted by the space. It takes time and effort to develop a personal relationship with a potential partner, and dating sites can only provide a forum; the real work is still up to the individual.

Acknowledgments

I would like to thank people who have spent time discussing, reading, and fleshing out major themes and ideas included in this paper: Charles W. Brown, Jake Burdick, Jennifer Sandlin, Heidi Adams, Jonel Thaller & Judy Krysik.

References

Boellstorff, Tom, (ed.) Ethnography and Virtual worlds: A Handbook of Method, Princeton: Princeton University Press, 2012.

Bordo, Susan. Unbearable Weight: Feminism, Western culture, and the Body, Berkley: University of California Press, 1993.

Butler, Judith. 'Performative Acts and Gender Constitution: An Essay in Phenomenology and Feminist Theory', Theatre Journal, Washington, D.C., 40, (1988): 519-531.

_____. Giving an Account of Oneself, Fordham University Press, 2005.

Ellison, Nicole B., Jeffrey T. Hancock, and Catalina L. Toma. 'Profile as Promise: A Framework for Conceptualizing Veracity in Online Dating Self-Presentations', New Media & Society 14 (2012): 45-62.

Ellison, Nicole, Rebecca Heino, and Jennifer Gibbs. 'Managing Impressions Online: Self- Presenta-

---

96 Sherry Turkle, Alone Together: Why We Expect More from Technology and Less from Each Other, Yew York: Basic Books, 2011.

tion Processes in the Online Dating Environment', Journal of Computer Mediated Communication, 11 (2006): 415-441.

Frohlick, Susan, and Paula Migliardi. 'Heterosexual Profiling: Online Dating and 'Becoming' Heterosexualities for Women Aged 30 and Older in the Digital Era', Australian Feminist Studies 26.67 (2010): 73-88.

Fuchs, Christian. 'The Internet as Self-organizing Socio-technological Systems', Cybernetics and Human Knowing 3 (2004): 57-88.

Fullick, Melonie. ' "Gendering" the Self in Online Dating Discourse', Canadian Journal of Communication 38.4 (2013): 545-562.

Hardey, Michael. 'Mediated Relationships', Information, Communication & Society, 7 (2004): 207-222.

Happen Magazine, http://www.match.com/magazine/.

Hill, Sarah E., and Kristina M. Durante. 'Courtship, Competition, and the Pursuit of Attractiveness: Mating Goals Facilitate Health-related Risk Taking and Strategic Risk Suppression in Women', Personality and Social Psychology Bulletin 37.3 (2011): 383-394.

Jagger, Elizabeth. 'Marketing the Self, Buying an Other: Dating in a Post Modern, Consumer Society', Sociology 32.4 (1998): 795-814.

Kaplan, Chelsea. http://www.match.com/magazine/article/13157/Womens-5-Biggest-Dating-Lies/.

Lanier, Jaron. You are not a Gadget: A Manifesto, Vintage Press, New York: 2010.

Mahalik, James R., Elisabeth B. Morray, Aimée Coonerty-Femiano, Larry H. Ludlow, Suzanne M. Slattery, and Andrew Smiler. 'Development of the conformity to feminine norms inventory', Sex Roles 52 (2005): 417-435.

Manning, Wendy. D., Longmore, M. A., and Giordano, P. C. 'The Changing Institution of Marriage: Adolescents' Expectations to Cohabit and to Marry', Journal of Marriage and Family 69.3 (2007): 559-575.

Mario Tronti, ⊠The Strategy of Refusal⊠, trans. Red Notes, in Sylvère Lotringer and Christian Marazzi (eds) Italy: Autonomia, PostPolitical Politics, New York: Semiotext(e), 1980, pp. 2835.

Markham, Annette. 'Ethic as Method, Method as Ethic: A Case for Reflexivity in Qualitative ICT Research', Journal of Information Ethics 15 (2006): 37-54.

_____. 'Fabrication as Ethical Practice', Information, Communication & Society 15 (2012): 334-353.

McRobbie, Angela. 'Post-feminism and Popular Culture', Feminist Media Studies 4 (2004): 255-264.

Nakamura, Lisa. Digitizing Race: Visual Cultures of the Internet, Minneapolis: University of Minnesota Press, 2008.

Okcupid, http://blog.okcupid.com/index.php/your-looks-and-online-dating/.

Okcupid trends: http://blog.okcupid.com/.

Oktrends, http://blog.okcupid.com/index.php/your-race-affects-whether-people-write-you-back/.

Pillow, Wanda. 'Confession, Catharsis, or Cure? Rethinking the Uses of Reflexivity as Methodological Power in Qualitative Research', International Journal of Qualitative Studies in Education 16.2 (2003): 175-196.

Roper, Caitlin. http://www.wired.com/design/2014/02/how-to-create-good-online-dating-profile/.

Roscoe, Philip, and Shiona Chillas. 'The State of Affairs: Critical Performativity and the Online Dating Industry,' Organization (2013): 1-24. http://org.sagepub.com/content/early/2013/05/01/1350508413485497.

Rose, Gillian. Visual Methodologies: An Introduction to Researching with Visual Materials, Sage Publications Limited, 2011.

Smith, Aaron, and Maeve Duggan. Online Dating & Relationships. Pew Internet & American Life Project. 21 October 2013, http://www.pewinternet.org/Reports/2013/Online-Dating.aspx.

Turkle, Sherry. Alone Together: Why We Expect More from Technology and Less from Each Other, Yew York: Basic Books, 2011.

Walther, Joseph. B. 'Computer-mediated Communication Impersonal, Interpersonal, and Hyperpersonal Interaction', Communication Research 23.1 (1996): 3-43.

Yang, Mu-Li, and Wen-Bin Chiou. 'Looking Online for the Best Romantic Partner Reduces Decision Quality: The Moderating Role of Choice-making Strategies', Cyberpsychology, Behavior, and Social Networking 3.2 (2010): 207-210.

MEDIA'S EFFECT ON ONLINE DATING PRACTICES: TURKISH TV MARRIAGE PROGRAMS AND ONLINE DATING AS A MEDIUM

ENVER OZUSTUN

Introduction

For the last 10 years, major private television networks have been broadcasting series of highly criticized reality shows with good ratings. As these shows continued to be screened, their large advertisement revenue is generating controversies. These shows with their ratings and controversial advertisement revenues are still invading precious broadcast time to this date. The practices of the TV shows forged the basis for the online dating community in Turkey. The language that is used online as well as its increasing popularity is in parallel with these TV shows. This study analyzes the TV show within the cultural context and tying it to online dating practices.

One of the primary criticism for the TV shows was the occupation of the valuable broadcast time that could be utilized for current issues in Turkish society. Despite all the criticism these shows got, another analogue to Reality TV, marriage shows currently occupy and continue to occupy valuable broadcast time.

Just because a topic is being discussed a lot in daily life, it does not always have a big impact on the society. Despite this, we still talk, discuss and criticize these shows in media and other outlets that are being broadcasted on a variety of channels. These shows are far from being a reference to a similar occurrence in daily life, yet they still find a way to be relevant. Online dating practices also are an important issue of daily experience; alternative dating sites such as Solcuolsun.com (users are primarily left leaning) or religious marriage sites are among the biggest networks. The niche group that the sites addresses, categorize and define the users life styles and social status.

Understanding the TV Marriage Shows

There are a number of reasons why these TV shows have been taking up so much space in our agenda. Firstly, the mass media (newspapers, magazines, radio channels and internet broadcasting) are being controlled by a handful of broadcasting companies. Thus, a single subject can be repeatedly published in a variety of different media owned by a single company. As the same type of shows are being repeatedly broadcasted on different channels of the same network, the strength of the shows agenda increase, pushing them into our everyday life by repetition. Television networks have also been blocking other types of shows by filling up their daytime schedule with marriage shows that have long screen time. Leading audience to complain about the omnipresence of the marriage shows in every channel they watch.

While this is the strategic point in the high ratings of marriage shows, we should not skip the audience's interest. Values that form the traditional structure of Turkish society are still largely a taboo and have an untouchable status. Everything related with marriage is a curious subject in Turkish society. To put it short, these shows contain interesting elements worthy of audiences' attention.

In conclusion, networks are being managed in a way that keep their audience interested to a delicate subject by utilizing their affiliated networks' advertisement power and it's capabilities.

While the power of media can be debated, let's open a parenthesis; it is power originates from its ability to present "things" to its audience. This "power" shapes around 2 aspects. First one is "choosing" and the second is "presenting as you like". Roles of the television and other mass communication methods are being increasingly questioned as society begins to examine the ethics of how this power is being wielded.

Ratings of programs being broadcasted on television have an important aspect in the public relations with the media, investment in its infrastructures and its perceived cultural value. As the government monopoly of the mass media declined after Turkey's moved towards free market economy, the notion that a public service is being performed by television broadcasters declined, while they began to be solely perceived as a commercial entity. These changes shaped the contents of broadcasts. Higher ratings results in increased advertisement of the shows; popular shows get more screen time for higher ratings, leading to a positive feedback loop. As Korkmaz Alemdar and İrfan Erdoğan puts it, "Popular culture is not a consumption. It is the active building and distribution of meanings and pleasures in the social system". [1]

On top of the dubious economic relationship between political powers and media bosses, controversy have arisen on the heavy influence of the political establishment on the contents of the media. We can claim with ease that the deciding factor for the broadcasting of individual programs and networks editorial policy as a whole is to be consistent with the dominant agenda of the sector. The primary reason for the preservation of this consistency is because of other commercial interests of media tycoons.

Various theories have been created since the initial widespread use of mass communication devices on a global scale. Each of these theories have their merits, however the impact media has on its audience is still debatable. Judging this impact without taking other variables and social dynamics into account will only oversimplify the problem.

In this context, before we discuss whether marriage shows have any effect on society or not and how successful they are, we should ponder about impact of televisions.

Rather than assessing the direct impact marriage shows broadcasted on Turkish television has on it's audience or it's indirect impact on society, this study aims to figure out the purpose of these shows. In order to do this, a wider perspective is needed.

Society underwent a change as mixed economy, a foundation principle of Turkish Republic, moved towards liberal economy. Researching a society without taking thousands of years of culture into account would make the microstructure/macrostructure models to rigid for

---

1   Alemdar, Korkmaz-Erdoğan, İrfan, 'Popüler Kültür ve İletişim', Ankara, Ümit Yayıncılık, 1994, p. 149.

practical use. Therefore, it is vital to keep the bond between the two in mind, as this will be of great help in the understanding the subject.

We need to investigate the aim of this process and the conditions that it was prepared under for these heavily criticized shows on the headlines listed below.
- Neo-Liberal Order and Social Engineering
- Marriage in the Structure of Turkish Society
- Mass Communication Devices, Media and Its Effects

ABOUT MICROSTRUCTURE/MACROSTRUCTURE
Neo-Liberal Order and Social Engineering

People in Anatolia, usually dubbed as Turks, are traditional and sentimental. Neo-liberal policies imposed after the military coup in September 12th 1981 caused a change in this society, which provides an interesting case study for sociologists.

The magnitude of changes, which had occurred were large enough to spark off conspiracy theories. A change that traditional Turkish-Islamic structure and Anatolia's multi-cultural nature left marks on its culture. It was a period where spiritual values got replaced with material values.

Foundations of this change had been set with a strikingly hasty manner with pro-liberal Anavatan Partisi (ANAP) coming to power shortly after 1982. Following governments didn't see any hindrances building up their policies upon this understanding. The most important aspect of the era was the social construct, subjected to change by the force of the newly created free market economy. Closed and financially self-sustained construct left its place to a relatively pro-liberty and a market where capitals roam freely.

While liberal policies created the middle class and designed to continue it's existence, middle class was trying to make easy profit. Through privatization of public properties, mining rights, civil construction industry and projects; a socio-economic imbalance was created. No longer was social status to be measured with education or ethics, it was now measured with money. Popular culture has successfully changed the main goal of the individual and the society, which is the task of earning more money indefinitely.

In 2014, 32 years since the military coup, we can feel the resulting policies more sharply. It is suffice to look at the current socio-economic and political state, if we were to discuss how much of these were natural and how much of these were results of those policies with the data we have.

It wouldn't be unrealistic to say all this strategic undertaking was for the reconstruction of the country's political environment and social construct. Without a shadow of a doubt, there was a big effort to create a country that was prepared for the new socio-economic and political landscape. Here, we have the chance to observe and study a large-scale usage of social engineering, a term that we hear often.

Social engineering is described as a job that can manipulate the identity of the society, it's social texture and control it's reactions, desires, passions and hatred.

Social engineering can be done by other professions with the help of financial support, communication and various other assistances. Also local supporters are produced. Like Tunç Sipahi emphasized on, cultural codes being inherited from family and learned from social circles doesn't change the fact that they are produced. 'Consent' is produced and masses are established in order to achieve transition of 'power' to them.

In this context, neo-liberal system could not ignore a tool such as the mass media considering it used all its resources towards that goal. In the first half of 1990's, private stations started broadcasting without any government license; in fact, the governments of that period had preferred to turned a blind eye and at times, even supported the illegal broadcasts, meant the missing part of social engineering was starting to participate.

It would not be erroneous to state Turkish television networks were formed with this mindset. In order to compete in free market, a new kind of relationship between the broadcasters and political figures were formed, these became the two most important components that define the media.

It would be easier to understand the unqualified contents of television shows, if we think about how much social support is needed for an understanding that supports conservatism in social life and free market in economy.

"Marriage Shows" are another product of this lower quality circle. However, before we move on to the contents of these shows, we should take a look at the institution of marriage in the typical Turkish family structure.

Marriage in the Structure of Turkish Society

Anatolia, home to a mixture of cultural values, has a dominant Turkish identity in its geopolitical structure.

In his book, *Türkçülüğün Esasları*, Ziya Gökalp, named the Turkish nation as "Not as a union of race, tribe, geography, politics or volition but as a community of people that received the same teachings of language, religion, ethics and sense of aesthetics". Yusuf Akçura, did not use the word "race" as in the biological definition but as a sense of culture, custom and a partnership of history.[2]

Historian Karal [3], voiced his opinion in the foreword of Yusuf Akçura's essay "Üç Tarz-ı Siyaset" with: "With the proposal of creating a middle class, Yusuf Akçura had more influence on Turkish Revolutionary movement than Ziya Gökalp".

---

2   Yusuf Akçura, A. Kemal and A. Ferit. 'Üç tarz-ı siyaset' (Vol. 73). Türk Tarih Kurumu Basımevi. 1976.
3   Yusuf Akçura, A. Kemal and A. Ferit. 'Üç tarz-ı siyaset'.

Turkish Revolution, under the leadership of Mustafa Kemal Atatürk was founded on these principles; this gave people from different cultures in Anatolia with an official identity.

Even with it's many local properties, institution of marriage that has been built around this common understanding continues to this day. Although Turkish Revolution ensured many rights for women, the institution of marriage remained patriarchal.

Another aspect of institution of marriage in Turkish family values is that everything stays in the household. Home and marriage are viewed as private, with the rules of law being seen as inapplicable or at the very least, a tendency to not to put it into practice.

The third aspect of marriage is the necessity to procreate. The continuation of lineage is not only important for the parents but for the family of parents and even for relatives and friends. Therefore, biological parents are not the only one entitled, it is everyone who has a sentimental bond with it. In this case, it forces the parents to produce children within a set timeframe, a slight preference for male offspring has been observed.

In every society, there are different meanings associated with the institution of marriage. While conflicting with individualism, this institution founded on heterosexual values, transfers the conservative values to the next generation. This is the reason why political authorities support and defend the institution of marriage. If we evaluate marriage over Gramsci's [4] hegemony concept, it would be clear why the authorities are putting so much importance to this institution.

So far, we have come up with a framework for generations we define as the middle age. With the parents' power of influence over their children, we can safely assume that the framework we mentioned will have an effect on the next generation.

In order to analyze young generations thoughts on life and marriage better, Nazmi Avcı's "Toplumsal Değerler ve Gençlik"[5] study has much to offer.

This study has been made on young people receiving education in Süleyman Demirel University's faculties and two-year programs in Isparta during the years 2005 and 2006. Accordingly;

> Most important sense of value according to subjects' native region:
> East-Southeast Anatolia: 48.4% a beautiful world, 46.6 percent having a place in heaven
> West Anatolia: 40% a comfortable life
> Central Anatolia: 54% a beautiful world
> Mediteranean : 39.8% a beautiful world, 35.7% a comfortable life
> Subjects' biggest desires
> Financial Independence : 44.9%

---

4   Gramsci, Antonio. Prison Notebooks. Vol. 2. Columbia University Press, 1996.
5   Avcı, Nazmi. Toplumsal değerler ve Gençlik. Siyasal Kitabevi, 2007.

To Have a Nice Family : 26.9%
Note: 81% of female students differ from males' by concentrating on expectations other than (house, car; being the first in every field; financial independence) having a nice family.
Devotion to religious values
Yes, I am devoted : 51.7%
No, I am not devoted but I have faith: 32.9%
Meaning of marriage with devotion to religious values
Yes, I am devoted and I think family is a sacred institution : 53%
It is essential for the continuation of society : 42.4%
I am not devoted in any way but I have faith and I think family is sacred : 48%
It is unnecessary : 21.4%
It is necessary : 30.2%

It is clear as the results of this study show that new generation has conflicted views on marriage. Youth's biggest concern being uncertainty in their future, they tend to steer for financial independence. With the current world order and liberal economy, building up a traditional family with what little money they earn seems impossible even without the struggle of their everyday life.

In this current situation, with the views on traditional marriage and the reality that we live in, there will be inevitable conflict. On one hand: comfortable lifestyles, that young people dream of, and a happy marriage; exploitation of labor on the other. Since the two are contradictory, what kind of world can we promise to our younger generations?

The best course of action for the new free market system is to avoid creating more contradictions, which will upset and enrage the masses, increasing the amount of populist elements.

As the mass media is one of these areas, looking at its attitude on this matter, will without a doubt give us a new perspective to comprehend the subject.

Mass Communication Devices, Media and Its Effects

Debates about mass communication devices started in the 1920s, during the rise of popular press along with the cinema and radio. Many empirical studies were conducted in the 1930s followed by other studies over the years.

Lazarsfeld and Merton with their publications in 1948, Horkheimer and Adorno[6] with " Dialectic of Enlightenment" in 1947, Marshall McLuhan from Canada with "Understanding Media" in 1964, F.R. Leavis often remembered from Leavivism from 1960's United Kingdom, Stuart Hall after Raymond Williams with his published work "Communications" and French philosopher Jean Baudrillard on the other hand are the first names come to mind.

These studies, containing quite different approaches to the media's power and effect on an

---

6   Horkheimer, Max, and Theodor W. Adorno. Dialectic of enlightenment: Philosophical fragments. Stanford University Press, 2002.

era's social structure, tried to solve the relation between media and society like today.

Neil Postman summarized the influence of television on its audience in his book[7] (Amusing Ourselves to Death, Public Discourse in the Age of Show Business) in these words; "Because there are better ways to learn the truth, they would have a healthier influence on cultures that adopt them. My actual aim is to convince you that the decline of an epistemology based on printed words with connection to the rise of an epistemology based on television causes serious results for public life, stupefying us more every passing minute."

Communication between individuals and industrial society changes the status of social-political structure profoundly, and because of this it seems like the communication field will continue to be a debated topic in the future, as it has been subject to many studies in the past. Television, arguably still the most important communication device, is in the middle of these debates. It boldly comes inside our homes, inviting itself with its content. Content creators and producers favor television for this reason.

Producers who work in television aim to make the best of this invitation. To stay long in a place you have been invited, requiring knowledge of what the homeowner wants. We call this the 'production approach'.

Production approach contains two elements: determining the content of program and its technique. These can be named as 'Content Approach' and 'Effect to Purpose Approach'.

'Content Approach' is unique to public broadcasting and ignores the demand of audience. Producer turns the information received from experts to television shows, abiding television production principles. Purpose of this approach is to raise awareness among people about their basic rights and freedoms, therefore providing a better understanding of the world.

'Effect to Purpose Approach' is unique to commercial broadcasting. It dwells on how viewers will experience the message and what their reactions are going to be more than content. Producer creates the program while keeping the message in mind.

What is being done by this approach is to merge the program with elements people can relate to therefore increasing ratings. Viewers tend to accept information on television as long as their needs are satisfied. So there has to be a pre-satisfaction. There is a need for distinctive traits that will provide pre-satisfaction on television. This will make the program appealing at least for some viewer groups. These traits are such as; thriller, action, sexuality, comedy, information, importance, values, reality, curiosity, innovation. Television programs are increasing their ratings through these codes, making them popular thus sustaining their visibility.

Whether a television program's has an economic, political, or ideological agenda, increasing its ratings will always be one of the primary objectives. Higher the program's ratings, the

---

7   Postman, Neil, 'Televizyon: Öldüren Eğlence, Gösteri Çağında Kamusal Söylem', Osman Akınhay (trans.), İstanbul: Ayrıntı Yayınları, 1985, p. 34

higher percentage of the population it reaches, this will enable its agenda to permeate into others people in the society, affecting much wider social and political areas. The goal is to create an area of effect, not to give information.

According to an article Jay G. Blumler and Elihu Katz published in 1974,[8] the viewers choose according to three expectations from the content of television programs.

These are:
1. Cognitive demand: Viewers demand to receive information about the society they live in and around the world.
2. Looking for an escape: The desire of the people to look for an escape from the stress of their daily lives and to have a pleasant time.
3. Identification Function: Viewers emphasizing on something from their lives or status.

This study is insufficient in the separation of the audience's demands for present day. For what is information and what is entertainment isn't so clear anymore as lines are blurred. Even worse, concepts switched places. Of course no concept is pure; and have practical transitive properties. However if these transitive properties start to keep experiences from being analyzed, then it would mean serious troubles would emerge. After this point we start to participate willingly to the demands of ruling structure, even moving together with them. In order to do this, the bourgeois tend to use every mechanism they have to something other than its intended use.

Based on the last sentence; let's look at how marriage shows manage to invade so much broadcast time and our agenda even though they don't have high ratings and an important presence in the advertisement revenues.

MARRIAGE SHOWS ON TURKISH TELEVISION

Instead of democratization of producing information and its spread, with the commercialization of media, we see that it has become easier to direct information for the powerful owners of the media.

Only certain groups collecting the main revenue of media, advertisements, means power is also collected in these groups. Advertisement pie in Turkey is shared between a couple big media groups. As an example, only five television channels in Turkey hold the 68% of total revenues from advertisements since 2010. These are:

-Doğan Medya Grubu- Kanal D (24%) -Turkuvaz Medya-ATV (20%) -Doğan Medya Grubu-Star TV (9%) -Çukurova Grubu-Show TV(9%) -FOX (7%)

The most sought out advertisement period in television is 'prime-time' when the viewer count

---

8 Katz, Elihu, Jay G. Blumler, and Michael Gurevitch. 'Uses and gratifications research.' Public opinion quarterly (1973): 509-523.

is at it's highest. Advertisement competition mostly occurs during this time period. According to this, we can assume shows broadcast during this period are the most preferred types by the viewers.

Media Monitoring Center's research in 2008 indicated domestic soap operas have an eye-catching dominance in genres that get the most advertisements.

According to the research by Istanbul Chamber of Certified Public Accountants (İSMMMO) when we look at prime time and outside prime-time data, soap operas have 40 percent; news programs have 29 percent and women's programs have 6 percent viewing rates. Revenues of soap operas broadcast on prime time and women's programs broadcast outside prime time differ greatly. For example, 70 percent of advertising revenues of ATV in Turkey come from soap operas, while women's shows are the closest contender with only 16 percent.

Most important viewers of these shows are women. Purposes of women's television usage shows proportional differences compared to males.

	Female	Male
Education	3.3%	3.4%
Entertainment	23.7%	17.8%
News-Information	29.4%	50.8%
All	43.6%	27.9%
Total	100.0%	100.0%

Why Do You Watch Television? (Distribution by Gender)

As we can see in the statistics above, television is a source of entertainment for women, in addition to benefit the flow of news-information and education processes. So the line between information, processes-education and entertainment starts to disappear. This leads us to this conclusion; women accept things popular culture presents as information.

While Turkish people got introduced to reality shows quite late, it is quite early for private television networks. Shortly after private networks started broadcasting, reality shows like "Biri Bizi Gözetliyor"(Big Brother), "Evcilik Oyunu"(Playing House), "Gelin-Kaynana"(Bride vs. Mother-in-law) launched and marriage shows of today followed.

First marriage show on private networks was a production presented by Ebru Akel named …Successors followed such as "Evlen Benimle" (Marry Me) in ATV, "Ne Çıkarsa Bahtına" in

Flash TV, "Su Gibi" in Fox TV, "Desti İzdivaç" in Star TV.

In conclusion, contrary to popular opinion, although marriage shows invade a wide period of time, they have low advertising revenues and ratings.

At this point we should ask the first question again: what can we take from these programs staying on air all week against all objections?

Before we try to find an answer, we should take a look at which elements marriage shows are prepared with and what considerations they have.

Sociological Analysis of the Shows

For most of us marriage shows are "a waste of time"; however, it is a great research opportunity for sociologists with its subject, participants and affairs around the marriage concept. Can these shows give us an idea about Turkish society's approach to marriage?

Because of their participants, diversity and an open attendance, we have an important sample group. Still, would these data be enough for us to make correct observations? In the end we are talking about a television show. So, let's write down the subjects below in order to make healthy observations and analysis.

1. Representative properties of the participants of the show, meaning their ability to represent their society.
2. Participants' sincerity to show their true characters and identities.

Let's not forget that every television show has a design and every design has a team working behind it. The purpose of this team is to introduce projects suited to network broadcasting policies with the goal of staying on air as long as possible with high ratings.

While these shows create their own target audience, they receive more criticism than their ratings, taking up space in our agenda. These shows achieve their real success through this conflict.

Before we touch on what this design is built upon and what it contains, we should mention a few points about the contents and the structure of shows.

1. These shows have nothing to do with the arranged marriage practice in our custom. Arranged marriage requires certain rituals. In this marriage type, families come together before their children. Sociologist Süheyb Öğüt explains this situation: it is possible to claim that the matchmaking shows, recently appearing on screen, are to a certain extent, a modern version of the arranged marriage practice. However we should stress that it only corresponds to an arranged marriage to a certain degree. The main reason behind arranged marriage is because families know each other on first hand or indirectly.
2. It contains an important part of characteristics of the women in its society. We can list these as; women seeing marriage as a salvation, having no financial freedom as the employment of women is inadequate, feeling the need to go under someone else's

authority instead of being an individual, to have a chance to start a new life or even changing their social status.

3. In these shows, family establishment is encouraged with conservatism instead of 'sexual revolution' that signals a new social order. Prof. Dr. İsmail Hakki Ünal, member of Board of Religious Affairs, comments are supporting this claim by saying, that it is a good thing marriage shows are encouraging people to marry and create families but while this is being done they should be careful not to hurt the values and morals of society.

4. All the instruments of capitalism support institution of marriage. Because marriage contains all the elements needed to be captured by the wheels of capitalism.

5. It is an indicator of government failure, the inability and unwillingness to provide social security for women. Women see their husbands as a social security, not their jobs, skills or government. Women are encouraged to be employed by their husband by not working, thus leaving them to their husband's mercy.

6. Other than government, it is an important result that shows us how inadequate these non-governmental organizations are about woman's rights. Apparently civil organizations have failed their duties, if we look at these shows.

7. It is interesting that there are so many participants over 50 years old. Thinking about marriage at this age, shows us that our elders are asking for a nest of their own. Elder population of Turkey which is around 5 million people who is over 65 years old, are looking for peace in marriage not in nursing homes.

8. It is where man and women who wants to get married are defined with certain lines, thus standardizing family. While women search for a man that can take care of her and her kids, who will be good with her family and a husband that has to have a job and a house, while the men's look for a woman who is well manicured, tame and who can look after his kids and housework even if she has a job. In short, television shows, display marriage as a shelter.

9. Both sides show an attitude complying with values like monogamy, neo-local (staying in a separate house from family) and official wedding in these shows…

As you can see, marriage shows have been designed to defend the marriage institute and generally accepted version of the family structure, to ensure its continuation. Television turns this into the accepted culture for masses, therefore creating a reference for the public to reproduce their own popular culture.

On the other hand, show doesn't ignore social changes while bringing the traditional values to the screen. These shows have women approaching men, asking questions and declining them. So, while they still hold traditional values, they also have more current values. While they increase their viewer base, they can take advantage of the conflict of romantic and reality and be the center of discussions.

Now, let's look at how marriage shows are adapted to television under the guidelines above. This adaptation contains the properties that make the show watched and debated in various parts of society.

Components of the Show and Keeping Audience Interested

There are two main components needed to make a show. One of these is the subject of the show, idea-product and the other is the suitors, meaning the audience.

Products of the show is the participants who wanted to marry someone, suitors is the audience watching curiously what is happening.

Subject of the show is open to manipulation in every way. This accordance is a system that doesn't require coercion. This is a system formed because of the desire people have, finding a suitable partner. Conflicts generated by this desire, carries an invaluable television material. If we add the fact that this process is much more conflicting in conservative societies, we can say that social interest to this will be much more higher.

On the other hand, even though finding a partner is a private matter, it doesn't only concern you. There are always other relevant individuals. Like a stone dropped in water, ripples it generates will get bigger as you move forward; meaning, curiosity, excitement, interest, faith, desire, disappointment. Everyone who adds a feeling to this event will witness this excitement, live it.

Finding a partner stays as a topic until after getting married and having kids. So, that troubles in family, events and developments are followed with interest. If the relationship didn't end in marriage, rumors will spread, until finding a new candidate.

In short, source material itself is so powerful, variable and from life itself, only thing left to do is to make it suitable for television format.

Second element is the suitors, which is the audience. Audience isn't only the witness to what they watch, they are also the intelligent participant of it. Situations, comments about people who are exposed to it, highly anticipated decisions, results of these decisions everything is followed with interest. Whether it is conscious or not, conservative system is supported and social problems get disrupted, this is how unemployment, bribery, corruption of politics, anti-democratic practices, etc. leaves their place to stories like abandoned women, a widow with 5 kids, a man having been cheated on.

Audience not only cares for the problems on screen, they make suggestions to find solutions. That is how they participate actively as a volunteer in the designed system.

This two elements of marriage shows taken from real life, feeds the real life with other figures. Instead of family, relatives, friends there is a lodge. People on this lodge make comments and direct the couple, while they are on the spotlight as well. For this reason they have to attract the audience and couples by making right comments and giving good directions.

Process is very simple and clear; a presenter represents authority and directs the whole thing. Participants are under presenter's full control and they bow down to it. This presenter-director represents the fair order.

Show also has lawyers, psychologists and sociologists. Instead of using their knowledge and information, these people prefer to hide behind their titles and talk big words. So, knowledge get sacrificed for ignorance once again. Here intuition is used instead of mind. While keeping in mind it's target audience presenter tones simple words by fluctuating them, grabbing you; it's like a friend came to visit you, a neighbor or even a close relative. There is also a hidden authority behind the presenter's warm approach like; do me a wrong and you will pay for it. Presenter's authority on the candidates and thoughts on them is a reason itself to watch the show.

Orchestra plays appropriate music for the show and its audience, cheering them up. Everything is now ready for the couple to see each other. We see a writing below the screen telling us a surprise is waiting for us. At the same time couple move behind the opposite sides of the screen, asking each other questions. Presenter tells us the information they forgot to mention there. A short music break after they ask questions to each other; then comes the comments from the other participants on the lodge. Each comment from them gives audience a new perspective. Participants turn comes after the comments of lodge; audience holds their breath as the long awaited time comes. Excitement peaks as the curtain between them opens. This is the moment we have all been waiting for, what will the invited person say about the person he sees for the first time? Yes or no. If the answer is yes, candidates go to their corner where they have tea. This is the first step before they make any more decisions. However if the answer is no, candidates withdraw for a later time. Meanwhile viewers call and express their interest to candidates from the lodge. If they get a positive reply back, a date is set. During this time presenter gives examples from the weeks before, orchestra starts playing music, songs are sung, hands are clapped afterwards we get a new couple behind the curtain. While this process goes on, we see a couple from weeks before getting married.

For 4 hours, same scenario repeated with different actors, audience never gets a chance to question what they watch. They are now a part of this game. They may have to experience the past, present and future all at the same with intertwined messages making, while events go before their eyes like a film. Live music, lodge, candidate couples, presenter, subtitles, past couples decisions, surprises set for the couples who decide to get married, viewer calls, poems, dramas told, shedding tears and laughter. In short, those never ending marriage rituals, family gossip, all the running around, cheerful and sad moments are reproduced in various ways and presented to the audience. Every program is like a condensed version of the premarital period and after.

In contrast to all its fuss, show, oversees the conservative side of the society, presenting and reproducing the same subject to us over and over again for hours. Many elements making show attractive for the audience are put together precariously; however the main aspect is the marriage process filled with questions. In this process select couples are placed in front/back of the curtain with different demands. Viewer starts to worry for them. Will this two person be a couple or not? Are they fitting for each other? They got along and left together, what if they are not right for each other? This man will only use this women or that women is just a gold-digger...

When the base material is so rich and ready to put mental processes in motion, this game looks like it will stay on television for years to come. Television using its own narrative to recreate this process, reveals a colossal drama when its' combined with the obligatory nature of marriage. For those who accept it... We are living in a reality, where an old social event shaped by traditional values is presented with its design on television.

So much so, life of what is real, switch places with what should be and stands before us as the true real. To put it briefly, our sense of reality gets re-established. If we push a bit harder, we are going to be able to believe a frog can turn into a prince when it's kissed.

But the story doesn't end here - it is just starting. How so?

CLAIMS

Readings made about television ratings, shows that women programs are watched around 6% mark. Whereas it has very striking figures on occupying society's agenda. It becomes a topic in daily life conversations, gets written and argued about because of its participants or because of something they did on the show. Even commented by politicians.

Broadcasted marriage shows in Turkey get criticism especially for:

- For hurting the values of the marriage institution,
- Causing insecurity with participants,
- Taking up long screen times during daytime.

Against all criticism, another matter we should stand on, Esra Erol presenting a show on Fox TV with her name on it, having two million followers on her Facebook page.

What this format appeals to, what it affects and exploits is rather obvious.

The television producers' job is to make money. Producing a show that is watched for 4 hours with little cost is a big achievement, even a victory, from a commercial perspective.

However the real achievement is television successfully maintaining its hegemonic structure. These shows occupying all of television against all criticism, exaggerated ratings and low advertising revenue is the most important point. To maintain their permanence, new characters and scenarios must be created. Whatever necessary must be done in order to achieve it. Claims are often made about some participants of these shows being hired from casting agencies.

There are many examples of these with concrete evidence. Like some of the participants rumored to be seen as extras in soap operas quite often.

Likewise, officials of Turkey's first and only marriage agency said they declined an offer from the producers requesting access to their portfolio.

Even though every TV show is a design, it shouldn't contradict with its claim. Marriage shows claim they set out from the attendance of real people planning their futures', however there are rumors going around contradicting that. There is a fiction here with every aspect of it. This fiction is aimed to keep these shows on air as long as possible.

Serap Öztürk's article has this to say about "Evlilik Programları/Show'ları" (Marriage Programs/Shows) "This staged show receiving disapproval from the individuals of the society continues to be a point of interest. Comments from the audience and the experts of the fiction and nonfiction concept, adds life to the show. Life is the experience of past things. It is possible to determine this clash of personal differences concept on screen is more damaging than any good. Is it impossible to understand the participants extra time to free time? To think staged scenes reflect the reality of life is the real inexperience."[9]

As this is the situation, we can say effort to maintain these program are not in line with their ratings and advertising revenues.

Parallels Between the TV Show and Online Dating Sites in Turkey

CONCLUSION

In the beginning of the article we proposed that it is difficult to understand the subject of marriage shows without examining the topics, institution of marriage in Turkish society, media influence and the restructuring of society.

We will continue to have different results as long as new data, on the effect of media on society, is gathered. As 'New Media' enters the lives of younger people as a more decisive and an effective communication model this is especially true. However, it is an irrefutable fact that society's mutual cultural values have a much higher priority to set its own level of consciousness.

As the understanding, thought, belief, tradition, cultural remains of old way of producing loses their dominance, they don't go away and they haven't.[10]

Sovereign powers have many practical strategies for their own management, to gain the consent of people under their dominance. We call this hegemony for short. What the sovereign power wants to do, is to make the other part of society to accept their values. They tend to do this by their consent. Military coup in September 12 1981 and aftermath of it is the most apparent indication of this. Media is one of the most important instruments for this and becomes successful often in short-term operations.

Young population showed their discomfort of the oppressive structure in Gezi Park Protests, which started in İstanbul in June 2013 and quickly spread to all of Turkey in a short amount of time.

---

9   Oncevatan, http://www.oncevatan.com.tr/.
10 Alemdar, Korkmaz-Erdoğan, İrfan, 'Popüler Kültür ve İletişim', Ankara, Ümit Yayıncılık, 1994, p. 263

In a survey done by Foundation for Political, Economic and Social Research (SETA) in 2007 on 2727 subjects, some questions have been asked about the preservation of cultural values that constitute the identity of Turkish society.

Results of the survey are very striking and contradictory to what is being claimed on television.

	Number	Percentage
Cultural values that constitute the mutual identity of society in Turkey should be preserved.	2489	%91,3
There is no need to preserve the cultural values that constitute the mutual identity of society in Turkey.	80	%2,9
No opinion.	158	%5,8
Total	2727	%100

Opinions About the Preservation of Cultural Values that Constitute the Mutual Identity of Turkish Society in Turkey (Which of the Two Options are Closer to Your Opinions Below?) Source : Seta, October 2011

- While 91,3 percentage of the total subjects think cultural values that constitute the mutual identity of society in Turkey should be preserved, 2,9 percentage think there is no need for it.

	Low Level (%)	Medium Level (%)	High Level (%)
Cultural values that constitute the mutual identity of society in Turkey should be preserved.	90,6	92,3	94,2
There is no need to preserve the cultural values that constitute the mutual identity of society in Turkey.	2,8	3,7	2,7

No opinion.	6,6	4,3	3,1
Total	100	100	100

Opinions About the Preservation of Cultural Values that Constitute the Mutual Identity of Turkish Society in Turkey (Distribution by Level of Education) Source : Seta, October 2011

- While 90,6% of the participants who have low level education, think that cultural values that constitute the mutual identity of society in Turkey should be preserved, 2,8% of them said there is no need for it.
- While 92,3% of the participants who have medium level education, think that cultural values that constitute the mutual identity of society in Turkey should be preserved, 3,4% of them said there is no need for it.
- While 94,2% of the participants who have high level education, think that cultural values that constitute the mutual identity of society in Turkey should be preserved, 2,7% of them said there is no need for it.
- A homogeneous spread is seen in all categories.

As we can understand from the survey, Turkish society defends their cultural values with an overwhelming majority, furthermore this opinion gets more popular as the level of education increases.

Again, from the same survey, it becomes clear that the Turkish people have a negative opinion about marriage shows.

	Number	Percentage
I think, marriage shows on TV has a negative effect on Turkish family structure and marital relationships.	2156	79,1
I don't think, marriage shows on TV has a negative effect on Turkish family structure and marital relationships.	395	14,5
No opinion.	177	6,5
Total.	2727	100

Opinions About the Effects of Marriage Shows on Family Structure and Marital Relationships (Which of the Two Options are Closer to Your Opinions Below?) Source : Seta, October 2011

	Female	Male
I think, marriage shows on TV has a negative effect on Turkish family structure and marital relationships.	76,7	81,5
I don't think, marriage shows on TV has a negative effect on Turkish family structure and marital relationships.	15	12,9
No opinion.	7,3	5,6
Total.	2727	100,0

Opinions About the Effects of Marriage Shows on Family Structure and Marital Relationships (Distribution by Gender) Source : Seta, October 2011

	Low Level (%)	Medium Level (%)	High Level (%)
I think, marriage shows on TV has a negative effect on Turkish family structure and marital relationships.	77,5	80,1	88,8
I don't think, marriage shows on TV has a negative effect on Turkish family structure and marital relationships.	15,5	13,2	9,3
No opinion.	7,0	6,7	1,9
Total.	100	100	100

Opinions About the Effects of Marriage Shows on Family Structure and Marital Relationships (Distribution by Level of Education) Source : Seta, October 2011

- 77,5% of low level educated, 80,1% of medium level educated and 88,8% of high level educated, said that they think marriage shows on TV has a negative effect on Turkish family structure and marital relationships.
- 15,5% of low level educated, 13,2% of medium level educated and 9,3% of high level educated, said that they think marriage shows on TV has a negative effect on Turkish family structure and marital relationships.
- As the education level increases, rate of people who think marriage shows on TV having

a negative effect on Turkish family structure and marital relationships steadily increases.
- As the level of education increases, people who have no opinion about the subject steadily decreases. It is thought to be because of the correlation between higher education and awareness, that this percentage is very low.

Expert Psychologist Çiğdem Demirsoy, gave a statement in Yeni Şafak newspaper about marriage shows claiming, "Perception and expectations about marriage are shaped by family and close social circles. That is why I don't believe these shows have a direct impact on the institution of marriage and the establishment of family". Therefore stating, marriage shows have no interest in claiming or presenting anything different about couples meeting and getting married.

Fears and concerns about marriage shows are focused on the argument of them breaking the structure of society. It seems no one intends to change the definitive structure and the traditional rules of marriage, against these fears. Any sexual revolution that hints at a new form of social structure looks to be far away for now. Besides, softened corners of marriage with accordance to today's conditions are far from the level of fiction in marriage shows.

Participants of these shows are thought to be uneducated, desperate, have nothing better to do and doing it for the money or for being famous. They are accepted as a part of a television show for most of the viewers.

> If we rewind and take a look;
> A society bound to its tradition but open to change by the present
> Debatable effect of media,
> Are put to one side,

Then, if we combine these together with the effort to put these shows on air, even with low advertisement revenues and ratings, same question emerges. What could be the reason for this effort?

Answer of this question, should be given with the shows that couldn't be broadcasted. How so? The real impact these shows have on society is to generate distrust. Real trust issue here, lies with the media imposing shows with questionable content to people instead of informing people to create a democratic and free society. Distrust would be focused on the media, which uses its resources to steal your time and ask for your money in return.

Media, wants us to accept the featureless content by broadcasting shows that people wouldn't request back and fade away from memory if they get cancelled. However the no matter the age, gender and level of education, audience is well aware of everything; to not to trust "what should be trusted" is what is being tried to be created. In short, media wants us to become "things".

As Terry Eagleton said, "Reification fragments and dislocates our social experience, so that under its influence we forget that society is a collective process and come see it instead merely as this or that isolated object or institution". [11]

While Turkish televisions reserve an important part of their broadcast hours to these hollow shows even though there is no demand, news programs are spreading disinformation, doing their part of the society engineering so to speak. In June's great resistance, "Revolution will not be televised" slogan people wrote on walls shows the current state of Turkish television. Public couldn't watch a big uprising from their television, CNN Türk showed a penguin documentary instead of broadcasting this big event. In the long run, marriage shows are doing what that penguin documentary did. What this policy has under it is the reaction against dominant power, once the natural progression of society is restored.

The media tycoons know doing their responsibilities would make it difficult for the capitalist system to continue, so they put sensationalist shows on air, keeping people busy thus putting what shouldn't be to the place of what should be. These shows are not the only option. Numbers indicate that these shows are not bringing revenues or ratings as they make it out to be.

Social construct of Turkish society is evident. Building its future while progressing its own traditional structure with education, science and under the light of modernity. Every part of society actually knows the media and not their minds are stealing their time. Media is stubborn and determined to steal this time. The breaking point starts here; this point is the distrust, media causes by abusing their authority, demanding your time and money. Others will replace today's marriage shows. It is a fully intentional policy of media to ignore the political, social and economic conflicts and follow a straight path.

It is clear as day that people who watch these shows won't set their future accordingly and take what is happening there as a reference and the media tycoons are aware of that. Yet the sociological implication the TV shows set for the type of atmosphere has also seeped into the online dating and marriage websites. The marriage websites are designed exactly like the programs; http://www.evlilikmerkezi.com states on its welcome page: "… our biggest advantage is that all our users are here to get married". This statement was also uttered in the opening of almost all the TV shows.

Another similarity of the TV shows with the marriage websites is the economical emphasis. During the shows, the candidate would be asked about their income several times to ensure that the person to marry him or her would benefit from the marriage. Online marriage sites such as memurevlilik.net is based upon the fact that all its users are working for a government institution.

These factors in the TV shows clearly have set the stage for online marriage and dating sites. The expectations of the users are categorized according to the standards set by the marriage TV shows.

---

11 Eagleton, Terry, İdeoloji (Ideology; An Introduction) (Trans .Muttalip Özcan), Ayrıntı Yayınları, 1991, p. 140

REFERENCES

Alemdar, Korkmaz-Erdoğan, İrfan, 'Popüler Kültür ve İletişim', Ankara, Ümit Yayıncılık, 1994.

Avcı, Nazmi. Toplumsal değerler ve Gençlik. Siyasal Kitabevi, 2007.

Eagleton, Terry, İdeoloji (Ideology;An Introduction) (Trans .Muttalip Özcan), Ayrıntı Yayınları, 1991, p. 140.

Gramsci, Antonio. *Prison Notebooks. Vol. 2*. Columbia: Columbia University Press, 1996.

Horkheimer, Max, and Theodor W. Adorno. *Dialectic of enlightenment: Philosophical fragments.* Stanford: Stanford University Press, 2002.

Katz, Elihu, Jay G. Blumler, and Michael Gurevitch. 'Uses and gratifications research.' *Public Opinion Quarterly* (1973): 509-523.

Postman, Neil, '*Televizyon: Öldüren Eğlence, Gösteri Çağında Kamusal Söylem*', Osman Akınhay (trans.), İstanbul: Ayrıntı Yayınları, 1985, p. 34.

Yusuf Akçura, A. Kemal and A. Ferit. 'Üç tarz-ı siyaset' (Vol. 73). Türk Tarih Kurumu Basımevi. 1976.

Oncevatan. http://www.oncevatan.com.tr/.